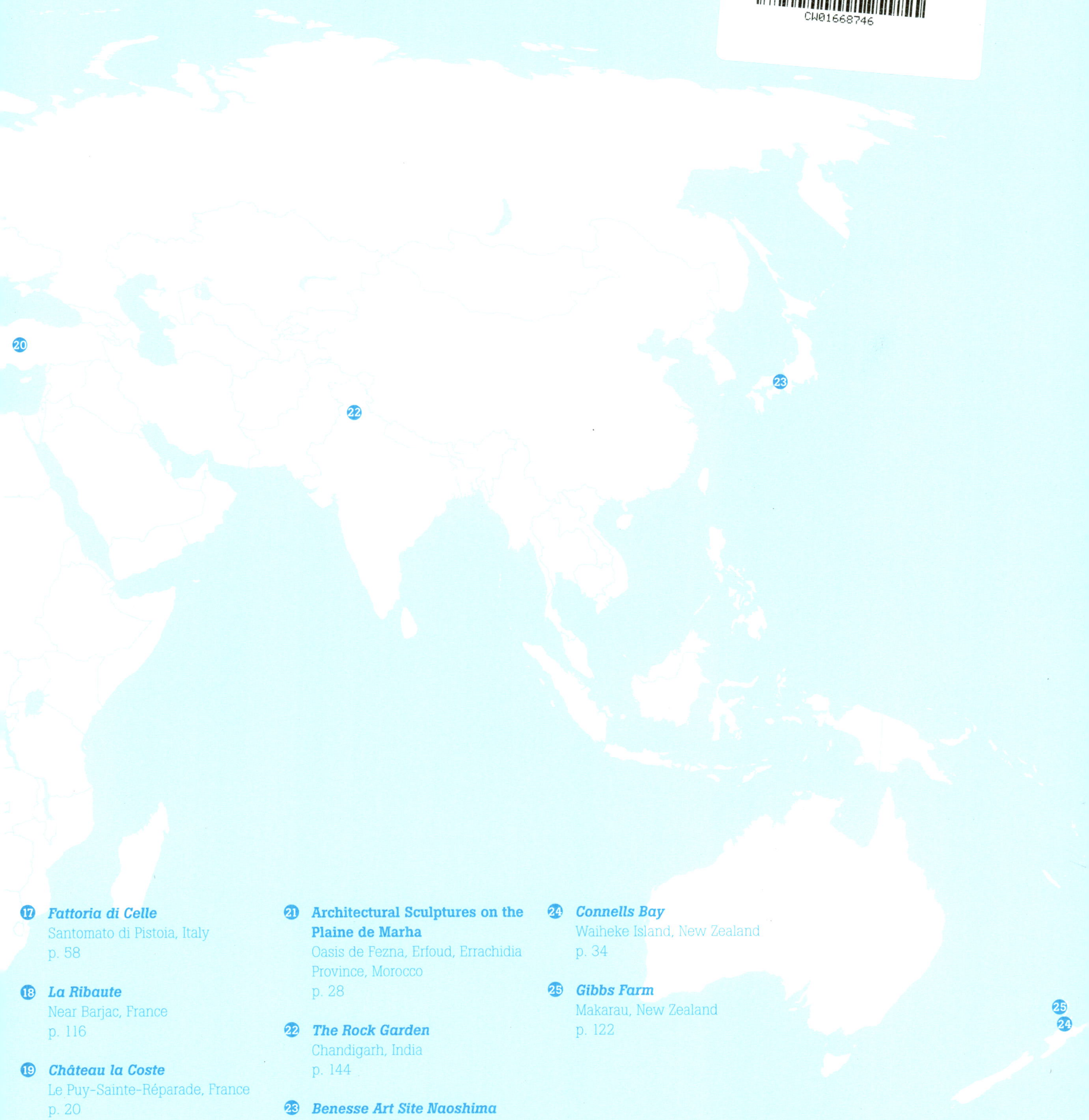

17 ***Fattoria di Celle***
Santomato di Pistoia, Italy
p. 58

18 ***La Ribaute***
Near Barjac, France
p. 116

19 ***Château la Coste***
Le Puy-Sainte-Réparade, France
p. 20

20 ***Time and Space***
Between Avanos and Nevşehir, near Göreme, Turkey
p. 130

21 **Architectural Sculptures on the Plaine de Marha**
Oasis de Fezna, Erfoud, Errachidia Province, Morocco
p. 28

22 ***The Rock Garden***
Chandigarh, India
p. 144

23 ***Benesse Art Site Naoshima***
On the islands of Naoshima, Teshima and Inujima, Japan
p. 86

24 ***Connells Bay***
Waiheke Island, New Zealand
p. 34

25 ***Gibbs Farm***
Makarau, New Zealand
p. 122

OUTDOOR ART

OUTDOOR ART

EXTRAORDINARY SCULPTURE PARKS AND ART IN NATURE

Silvia Langen

PRESTEL
Munich • London • New York

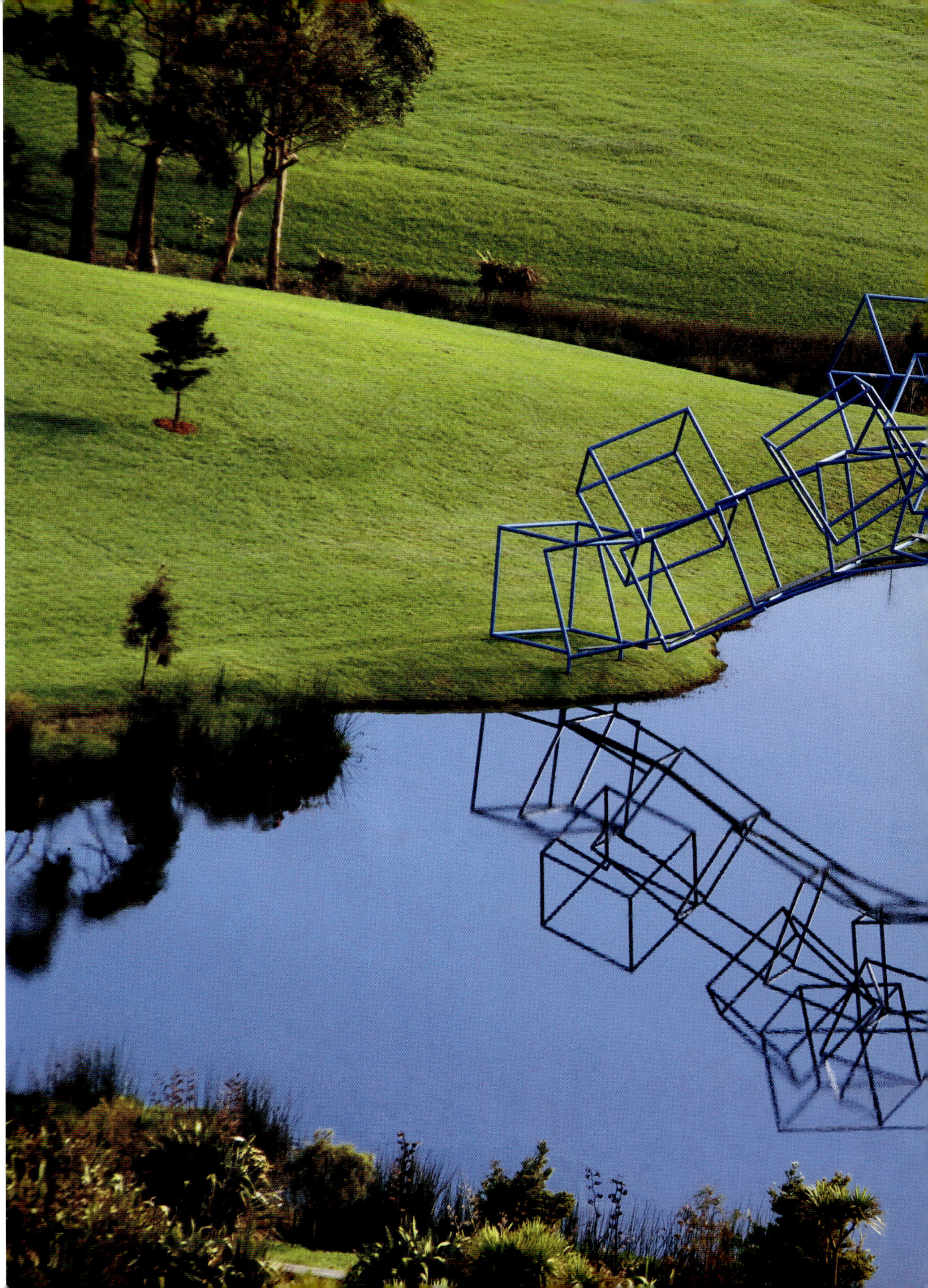

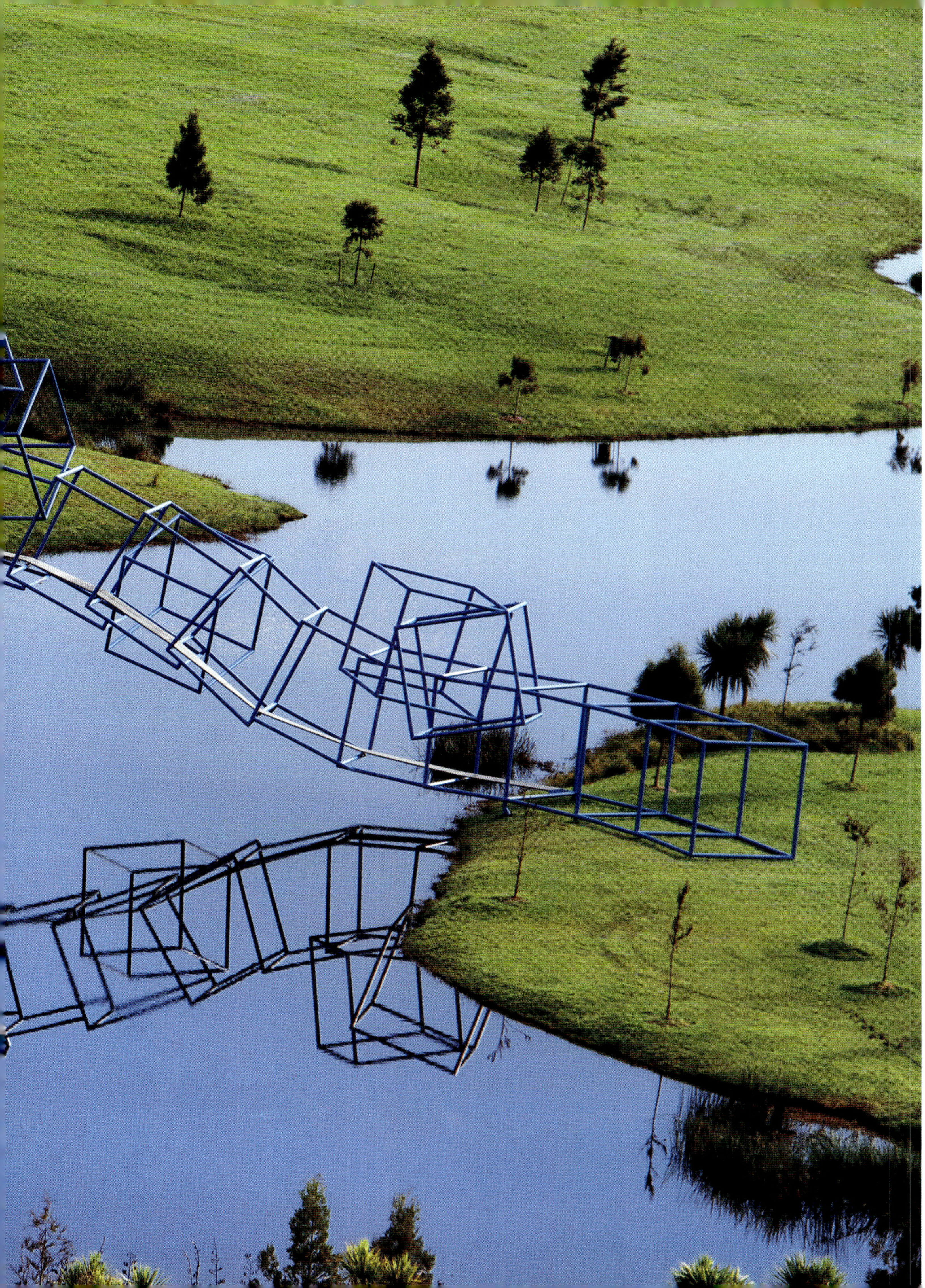

CONTENTS

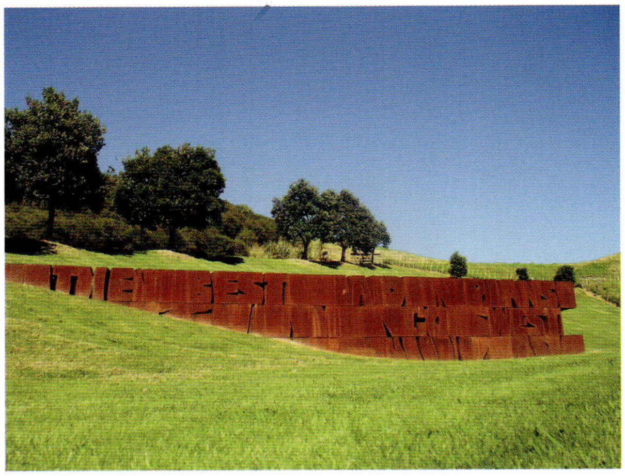

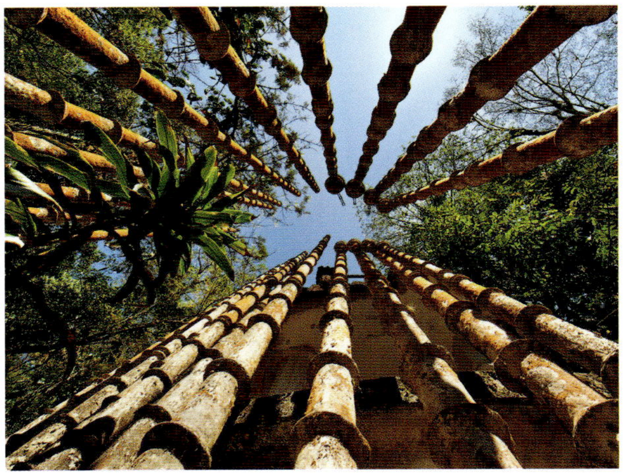

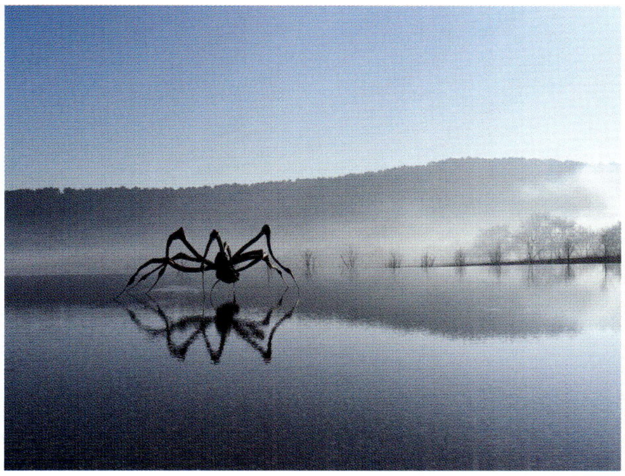

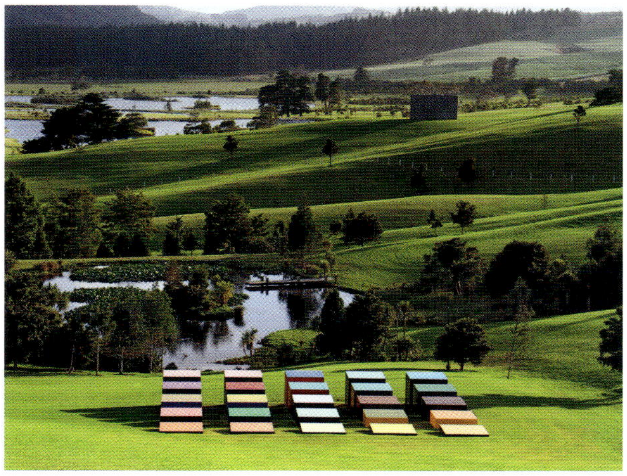

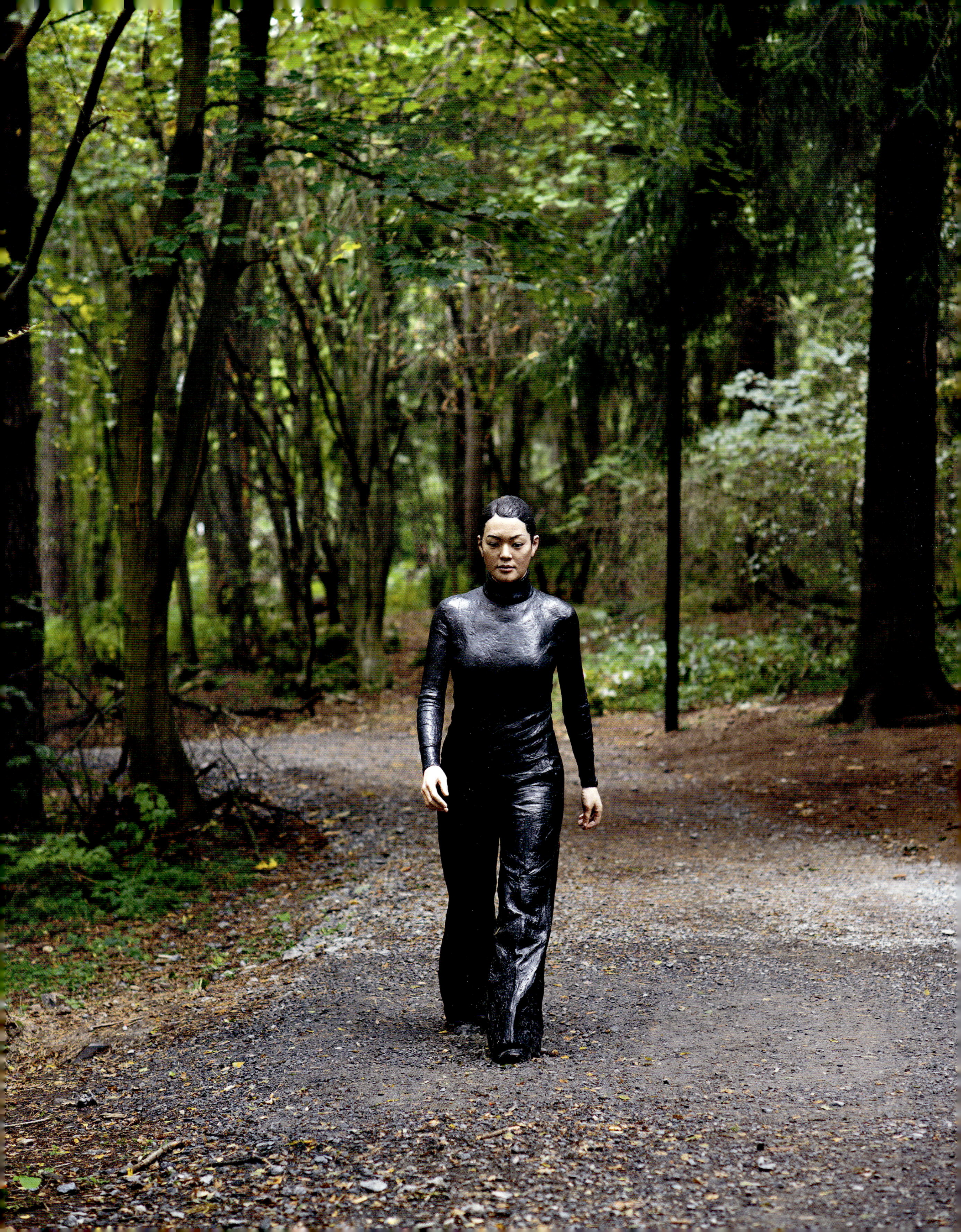

ART IN NATURE

Art and womanhood: Sean Henry's ***Walking Woman*** **(2010) in Ekebergparken, Oslo.**

What makes art in nature so pleasing? Why are the most interesting sculpture parks mainly created by private individuals, that is to say, art collectors and artists? What is their aim? And lastly: What makes a sculpture park special today? During my research for this book I constantly came back to these questions. For two years my husband and I travelled the world visiting remarkable sculpture parks in remarkable landscapes and asking their makers these same questions. At times those trips were quite demanding, because these parks and gardens are almost always situated in faraway places – huge sculptures in the desert, installations anchored in the Caribbean, a surreal Garden of Eden deep in a tropical rainforest.

A striking number of new sculpture parks have been created since the 1980s, not only in Europe and the United States but also in Asia, South America, Africa and Australia. 'Green maze' instead of 'white cube', in other words, art in nature rather than in traditional exhibition spaces: this is the latest trend in the art world. At biennials and major exhibitions, at art fairs and in private collections there are more and more outdoor sculptures and installations. International conferences have been organised and new exhibition formats devised, all focussed on art in the open air and attracting throngs of visitors. The fact is that outdoor sculptures have conquered the art market and there is a huge demand for them. The major auction houses and galleries even print their own catalogues and hire splendid parklands in order to display works to potential buyers who might be thinking of creating their own private sculpture parks. Because art – and sculpture in particular – is seen in ever-larger formats. Sculpture, in the form of installations, often occupies entire rooms, to the extent that some can only be shown outside. This is a challenge that publicly run museums and institutions, with their chronic lack of space and funds, can scarcely rise to. With so many museums occupying expensive city-centre sites it is rarely possible to build extensions and any outside space is generally strictly limited. And that is where the collectors – sometimes even the artists – step in, many of whom are fascinated by the potential of art in landscape settings that provide the scope for large-scale spatial experimentation, free interaction between the viewer and the work of art, a dialogue with different landscapes, changing seasons and weather conditions, close contact between the client and the artist. And above all the possibility of creating art for a particular place – as part of a *Gesamtkunstwerk*. Works of art are permanently installed in these outdoor locations – immovable and, as such, not for sale. At last the true art collector and philanthropist can make a stand against the art market with its increasingly speculative tendencies. This has already triggered discussions as to whether displaying art in nature could be a model for new museums, notably the many private museums that will be founded in the twenty-first century. Attention is now turning to such illustrious precedents as the sculpture park at the Kröller-Müller Museum in Otterlo, the Storm King Art Center in upstate New York, the Yorkshire Sculpture Park in England and the Louisiana Museum near Copenhagen. As examples of sites with first-class art in particularly beautiful landscapes these are all much to be admired and are rightly regarded as some of the best museums in the world. And they have been a source of inspiration to many of the founders of the parks described in this book. But with the large numbers of 'outdoor galleries' of this kind currently being founded, the notion of a sculpture park as an exhibition concept is in danger of becoming increasingly diffuse. Many parks are without distinguishing features.

For many collectors and artists it is (and was) no longer enough to *merely* position first-rate art in a particularly appealing landscape. Instead they prefer to develop their own independent concepts with a theme that connects individual works of art with each other and/or mediates a particular message: an image of the universe, art on the largest possible scale, a utopian vision of a better life, a sculpture park as an ecological enterprise. The themes are many and varied, as are the works of art. Of course the quality still has to be high and the relationship with nature is a given. My aim was therefore specifically to seek out extraordinary sculpture parks and even whole landscapes given over to art. This book provides an insight into twenty-five selected examples.

Since the theme of a sculpture park is generally closely connected with the personality of its initiator, I soon decided to concentrate on sculpture parks that were founded by individuals: art collectors who also have a love of nature, philanthropists, entrepreneurs and garden designers with a passion for art, and of course artists, too. All are visionaries; some may even be described as eccentric. Their goal in their life's work is to realise certain ideas through the medium of an art project in natural surroundings and, in so doing, to make their own, enduring mark – sometimes with a light touch, sometimes with deadly seriousness, sometimes with supreme intellectualism. Visitors should ponder what they have seen, whatever the theme – from social responsibility, ecological concerns, the mediation of cultural identity, patterns of visual perception, natural phenomena in the world around us, to autonomous cultural spaces where new ways of living can be tested out – or just fun. The parks' initiators all have their own stories to tell, which often cast light on their own personal vision. This book is therefore not only the first publication exclusively devoted to themed sculpture parks, it is also a collection of portraits of outstanding individuals with exceptional ideas.

With their often unusual themes, these sculpture parks are frequently in spectacular topographies, which the works of art respond to, thereby creating a singular *Gesamtkunstwerk* – from an archipelago to a desert, from the ocean to the rainforest or a sublime mountain landscape. John Gow and his wife Jo even went so far as to ensure that not only is the vegetation in their park exclusively indigenous but that all the works of art also originate in New Zealand. In other cases a whole landscape has become a work of art – as in James Turrell's *Roden Crater* or Charles Jencks's cosmological garden. After all, gardens and landscape parks first arose from human beings' innate yearning for paradise. Early garden designers in eighteenth-century England already actively sought to create a lost paradise in their poets' gardens. They constructed classical 'ruins' – as symbols of Arcadia – in landscapes that viewers perceived as perfect nature, although in fact it was the result of the supreme skills and finesse of contemporary garden design. Similarly, the exponents of Land Art in the United States in the 1970s were longing for unspoilt nature when they used their site-specific installations to highlight nature and the damage done to it.

In an era such as our own, which has been coloured by urbanisation, industrialisation and environmental pollution, the unprecedented, enduringly high level of interest in all things horticultural, in nature and ecology is readily understandable. And so it makes perfect sense to place art in natural settings, particularly since nature is itself the original, perfect, multifaceted work of art. Above all, when works made by human hand are presented in a natural setting, it is essential that there is a balanced relationship between art and nature. Ultimately this balance is seen in all the sculpture parks that feature in this book.

As a passionate art collector and garden lover, I would like to introduce my readers to a selection of particularly pleasing combinations of art, nature and a unique theme, and provide a source of inspiration in the very individual histories of these widely varied projects.

Silvia Langen, Munich, February 2015

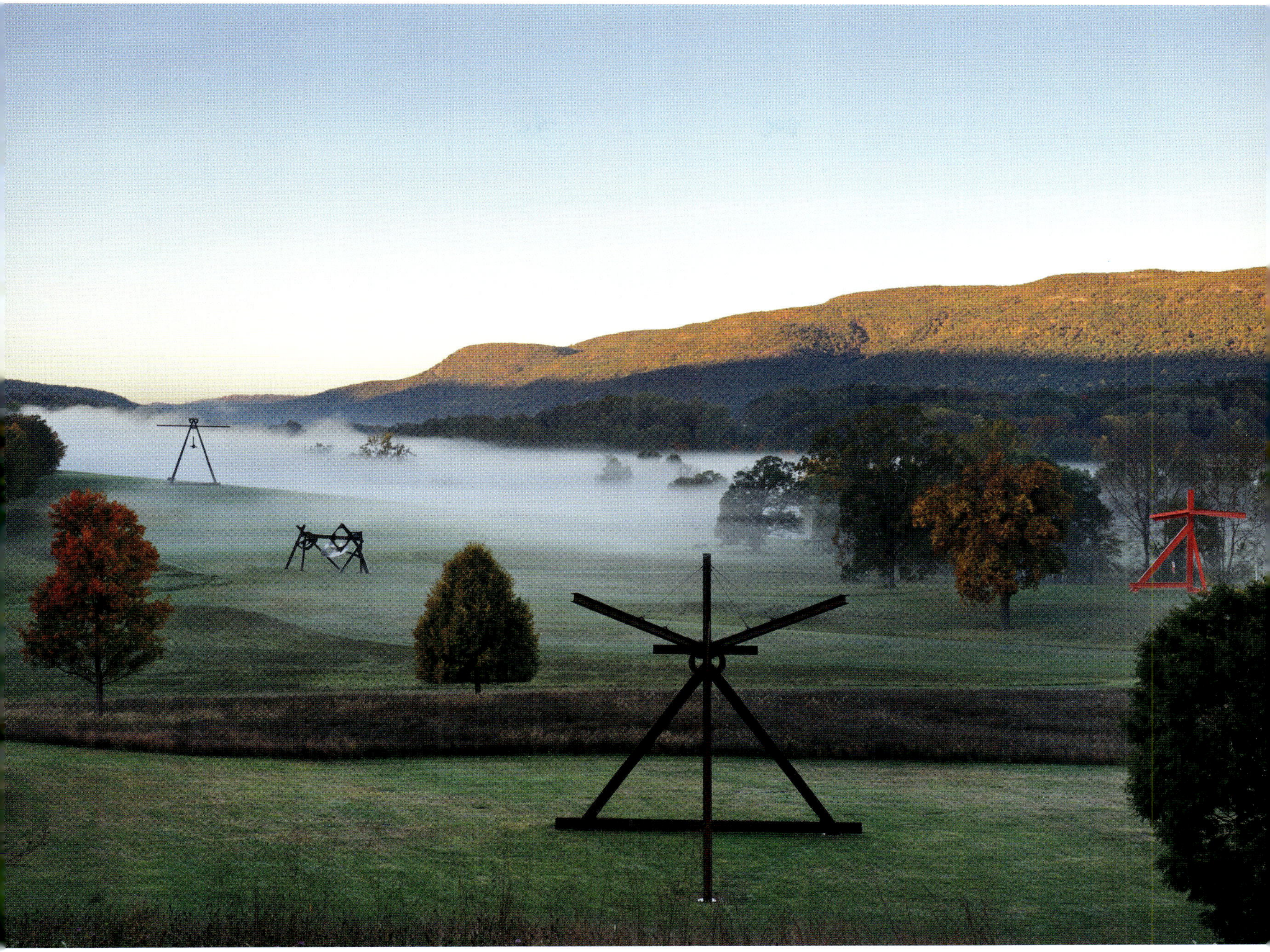

Important pioneers in the USA: Ralph Ogden and Peter Stern founded the Storm King Art Center with a collection of sculptures by Mark di Suvero, amongst others.

A REFLECTION OF A NEW WORLD

CENTRO DE ARTE CONTEMPORÂNEA INHOTIM, BRUMADINHO, BRAZIL

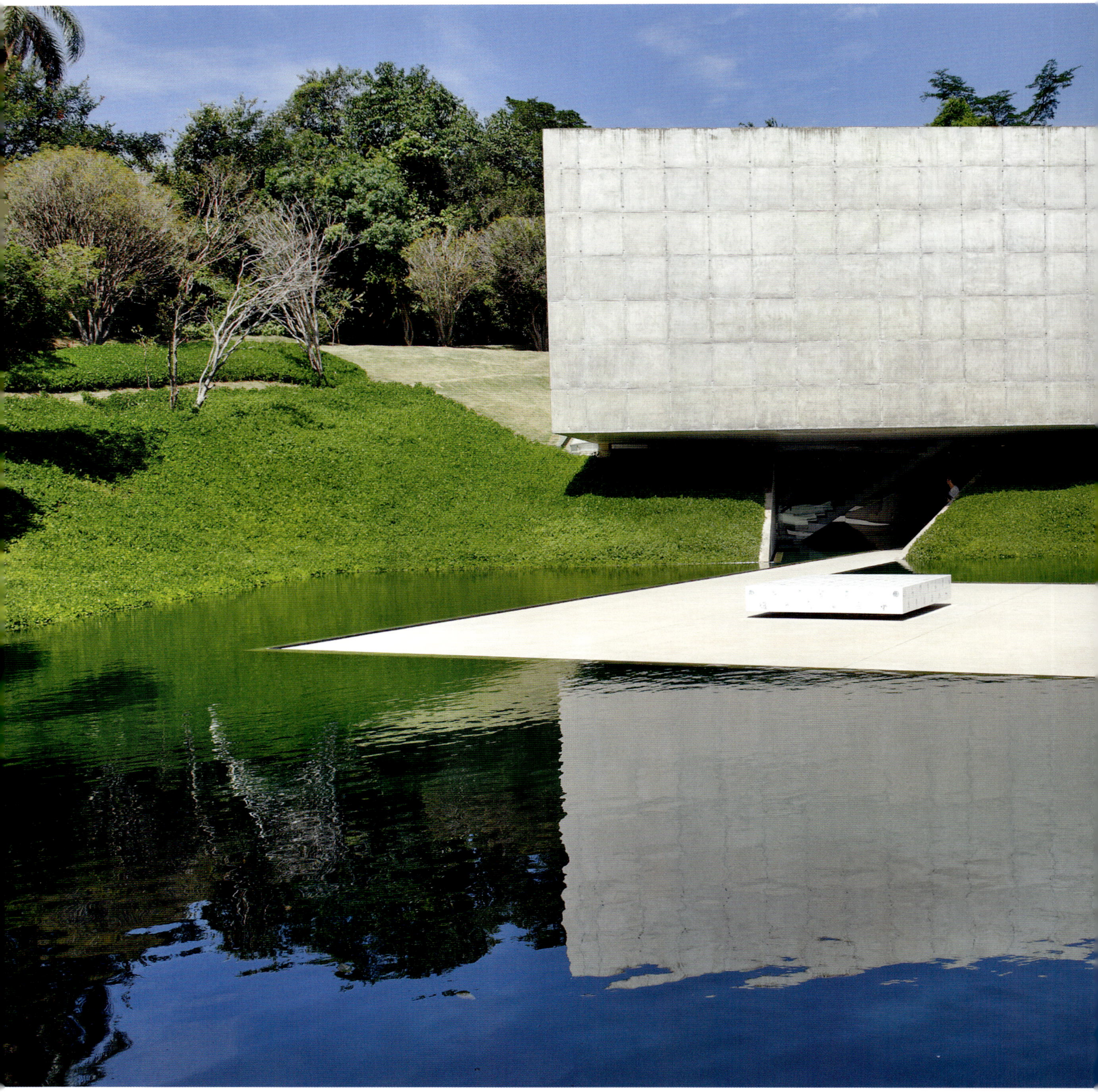

A rarity: artists' pavilions at Inhotim. Adriana Varejão can display works of art here that are too large for any other museum.

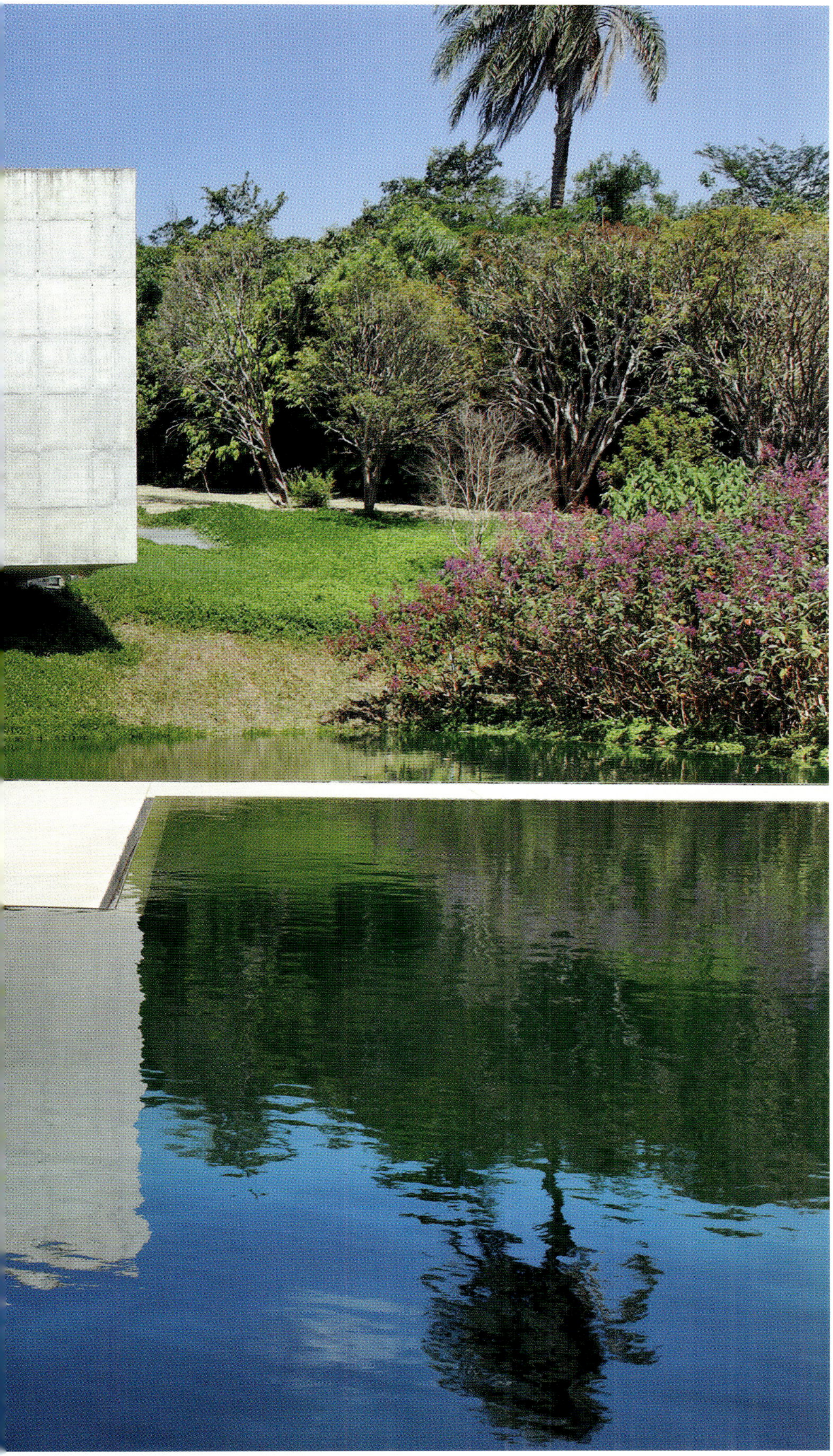

It is a long journey. Even the drive from Belo Horizonte in south-eastern Brazil along the dirt road to the mining town of Brumadinho takes a good two hours. Iron ore is mined in this area on the grand scale, above all for the booming Chinese market. In 2004, just a few kilometres away, the mining magnate Bernardo Paz (b. 1951) started to create his unique art empire, Inhotim, a mixture of sculpture park, botanic garden, social project and spiritual retreat. His aim is to use it to change society. "It should be like a magic path, a magic walk," as the philanthropist, with his mane of silver hair and full beard, says of Inhotim. "People come here and leave again. They will probably only understand much later what they saw and experienced here – because it is about beauty. It should affect one's spirit, it should do people's eyes and hearts good. It is the beginning of a new world." Anyone who may initially think Bernardo Paz is exaggerating or even boasting soon realises that this is not the case when they see Inhotim. The site itself is immense. By now this hilly domain with its artificial lakes and exuberant tropical vegetation extends across an area of over 5,000 acres. Bernardo Paz already started to systematically acquire forests, farmland and fields in the 1980s in order to save these areas from being swallowed up by the iron-ore mining business. Even though no more than a tenth of it is given over to art, as yet, and visitors are chauffeured by friendly young people in golf carts, it is barely possible to see it all in one day – around 130 works by artists from thirty nations, including leading artists such as Matthew Barney, Steve McQueen, Olafur Eliasson, Janet Cardiff and George Bures Miller, as well as ground-breaking Brazilian artists such as Cildo Meireles and Hélio Oiticica. In addition there are works by a further 500 artists in the permanent, private collection. All these works of art – some are outdoor pieces while others are on show in exhibition spaces – are distributed across the vast area of Inhotim. Many were made in situ. And many of the installations are so large and elaborate that they can only be displayed here at Inhotim. Even major museums would not have sufficient space for them. Allan Schwartzman, one of the curators at Inhotim, explains its particular situation: "Art museums are almost all located in the most expensive districts of cities and all are plagued by a chronic lack of space. They have little scope for showing large-format works. This has led to important key figures in the contemporary art world, such as Chris Burden, not yet receiving the recognition that is their due." However, this is now changing. Bernardo Paz recently bought three major installations by Burden, namely *Samson* (1985), *Beam Drop Inhotim* (2008) and *Beehive Bunker* (2006). Each now has a home in the midst of nature – forever. At Inhotim artists can do what they have always dreamed of doing. "There are no limits," promises Paz.

This sculpture park is also distinguished by its twenty-two pavilions dedicated to individual artists spread throughout the site. Many of these pavilions have been designed in collaboration with architects and botanists. Each is a *Gesamtkunstwerk* that connects with nature. This is perfectly exemplified in the pavilion dedicated to the work of the renowned Brazilian conceptual artist Adriana Varejão, which was designed in collaboration with the architect Rodrigo Cerviño Lopez and takes the form of a monolithic concrete block that appears to hover above a deep blue, artificial pond. On the roof terrace all the bird species found in Inhotim, 280 in total, are illustrated on the pale tiles of the visitors' benches. Inside the block, on the ground floor, there are large canvases – painted to look like tiles – depicting a churning wave, divided into 184 single sections. The lower ground floor contains Adriana Varejão's large-format sculpture *Linda do Rosário* (2004), a partially broken ceramic wall that appears to be built from pieces of meat, which are in fact also painted. This work recalls the brothel of the same name in Rio de Janeiro, which collapsed in 2002, killing a couple in one of the rooms. The interplay of perfect beauty and violent destruction features in many of the works at Inhotim. For *Beam Drop Inhotim*, Chris Burden used two cranes to drop seventy-two solid steel beams from a height of forty-five metres into a pit of wet cement. These then turned into a ghostly forest of rusty steles. Over the space of four years, in a clearing in a eucalyptus forest, Matthew Barney created a mirrored, geodetic dome over a mud-spattered monster tractor, which is in the process of uprooting a polyethylene-coated tree trunk. Moulded branches reach up like oversized candles. The heavy tractor seems to have mounted some concrete blocks and is on the point of toppling over.

Many of these works of art are unwieldy and unsettling, but they match views the visitor has of the surrounding area from some of the higher points in the park. Outside the park, ravaged, naked hillsides stand as symbols of a damaged and exploited natural world; inside it we find verdant Arcadia. Works such as Olafur Eliasson's *Viewing machine* (2001–08) challenge the visitor to observe the different facets of nature. Devised as a kaleidoscope, this work splinters the subtropical rainforest into countless hexagons. Thoughts of childhood come to mind. And that is precisely what pleases Bernardo Paz, who feels that "we've lost the ability to be surprised by life.

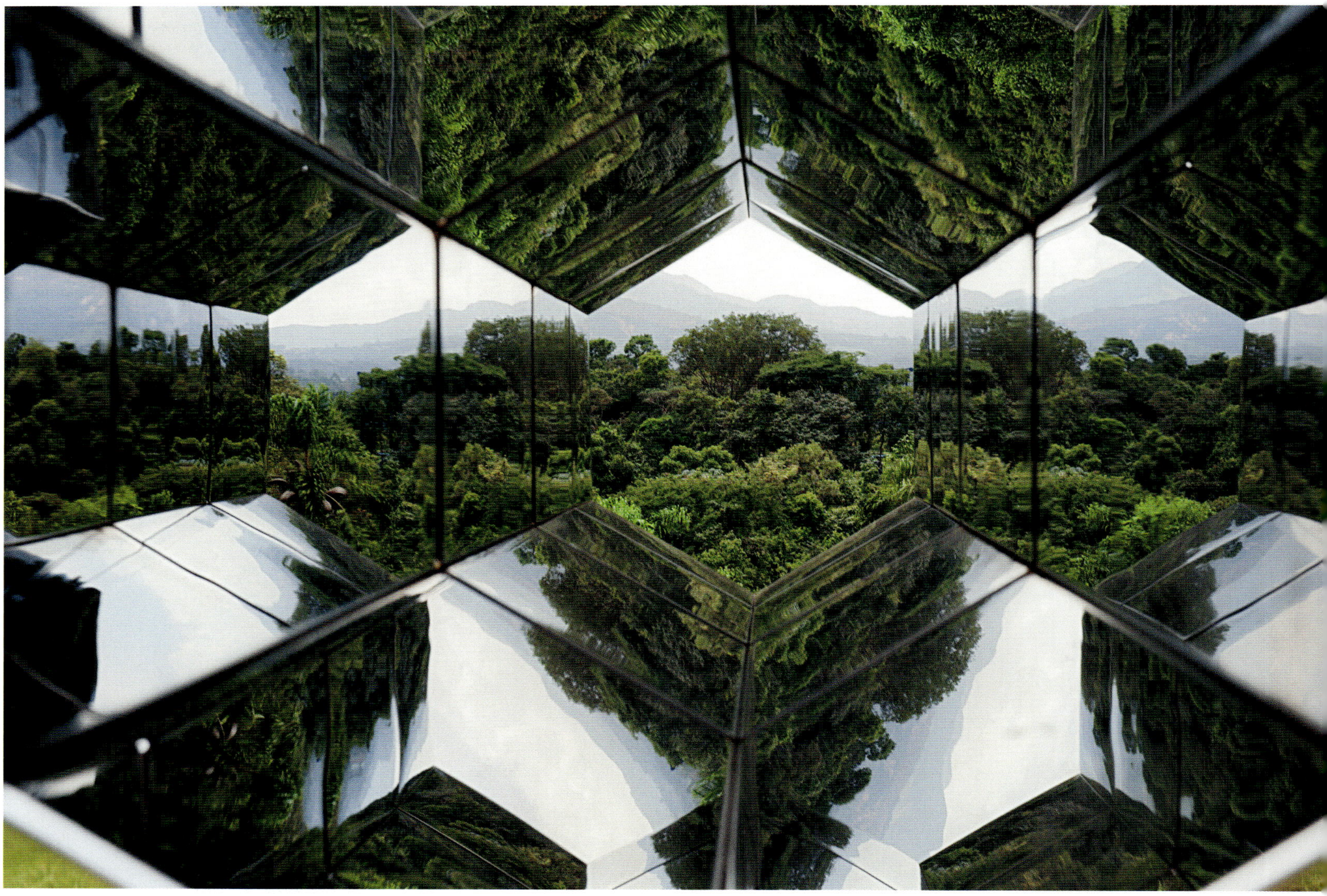

We have to regain the sense of being a child again."

Paz's radical decision to concentrate his attention on art and nature followed a heart attack brought on by overwork. And having previously profited so remarkably from mining iron ore, he now does everything in his power to alert others to the exploitation of our natural resources. In the 1980s Bernardo Paz became one of the first entrepreneurs to travel to China, where he won a contract to build steel plants. At the time, China's need for raw materials was positively exploding due to the massive growth of its economy. This led Paz to concentrate on mining and trading in iron ore, which in turn made him into one of the wealthiest men in South America. His heart attack made him completely change his life. "All I had ever done was amass money, but I hadn't lived out any dreams." So he moved to his farmhouse, called Inhotim. The locals had named it after its original owner, a British engineer known as "Mister Tim" (or "Nho Tim" in the local dialect). Paz now started to collect Brazilian art from the 1920s to the 1950s, although, in his own words, "it was an intuitive thing, not because I understood it." However, the artists Tunga and Cildo Meireles persuaded him to turn his attention to contemporary art instead. Paz sold his entire collection and started afresh – this time he purchased works by younger artists, such as Ernesto Neto, Albert Oehlen, Janet Cardiff, George Bures Miller and Olafur Eliasson, and built pavilions to house their work. Above all through his friendship with the painter and internationally renowned landscape architect Roberto Burle Marx (1919–1994), Paz became increasingly interested in connecting art with nature by creating an art landscape – partly because Burle Marx had inspired Paz with his passion for botany and plants. He showed Paz that Inhotim – located between the edge of the Brazilian savannah and the Atlantic – is in one of the regions in the world with the greatest biodiversity.

In 2011 scientists started to compile an inventory of its 4,500 plant species, including 1,300 types of palm. Paz has set up a research station specifically for this purpose. With the help of Burle Marx, Bernardo Paz laid out the site as a botanic garden, so that visitors who come to see the art can also experience and learn more about the diversity of this tropical landscape. For artists and architects this multifaceted natural setting poses a particular challenge that requires a response: art in dense palm groves, between shrubs with brightly coloured blooms and bizarrely shaped flowering plants. For the visitor the gardens provide a retreat that plays an important part before and after engaging with the works of art. Along the paths that lead from one work of art to the next, visitors see huge butterflies; they hear exotic bird calls and animals scurrying through the undergrowth. Nature provides time for reflection, allowing visitors to switch off their minds before the next encounter with the unknown. Accordingly there is no distinct starting point for visitors. There is no centre, either in terms of the design of

Left: Olafur Eliasson's *Viewing machine* creates a kaleidoscopic, multifaceted image of the tropical landscape.

Metals beams were dropped into wet cement from a height of 45 metres. *Beam Drop Inhotim* points to the brutal destruction of the environment in that region.

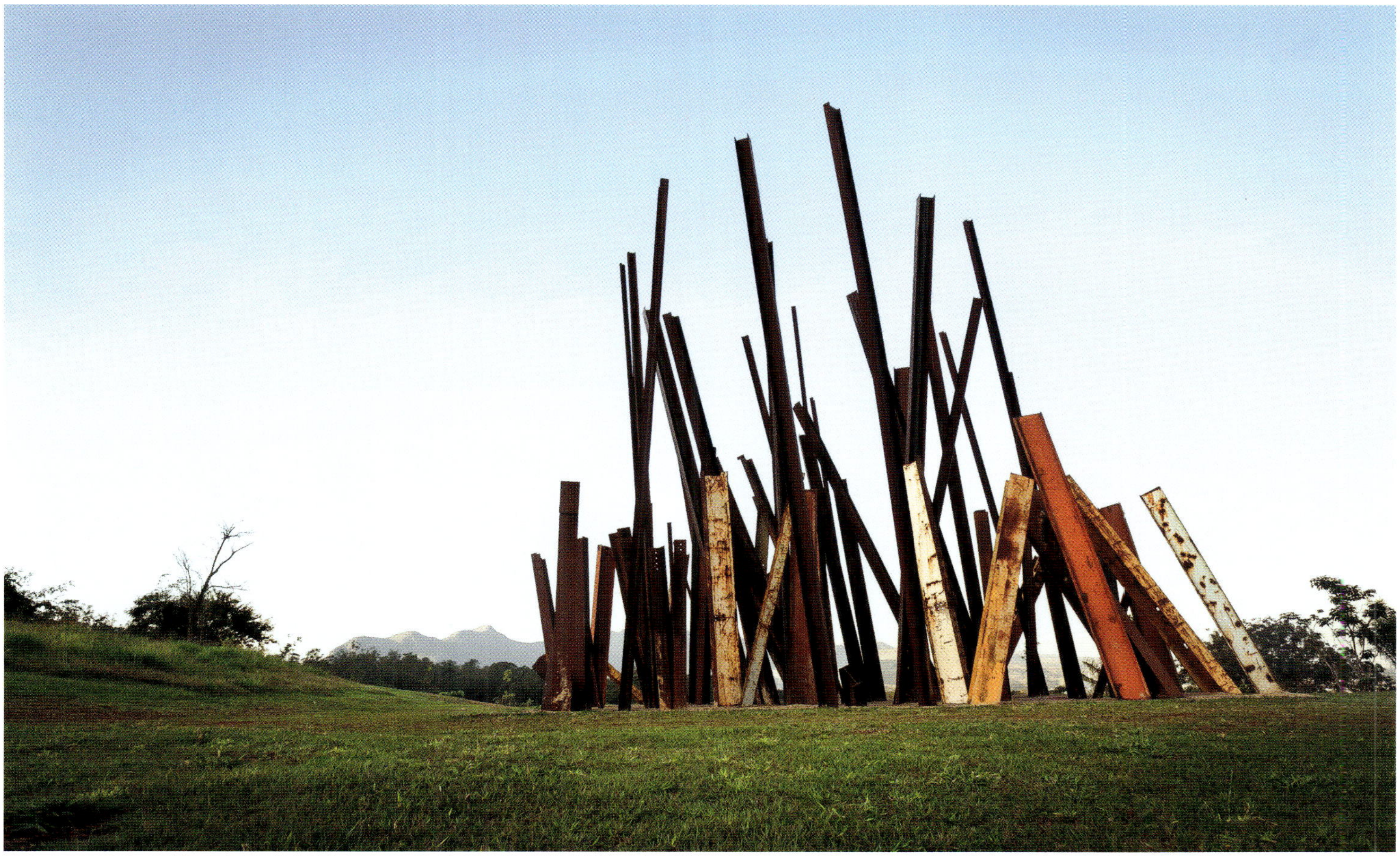

Centro de Arte Contemporânea Inhotim, Brazil

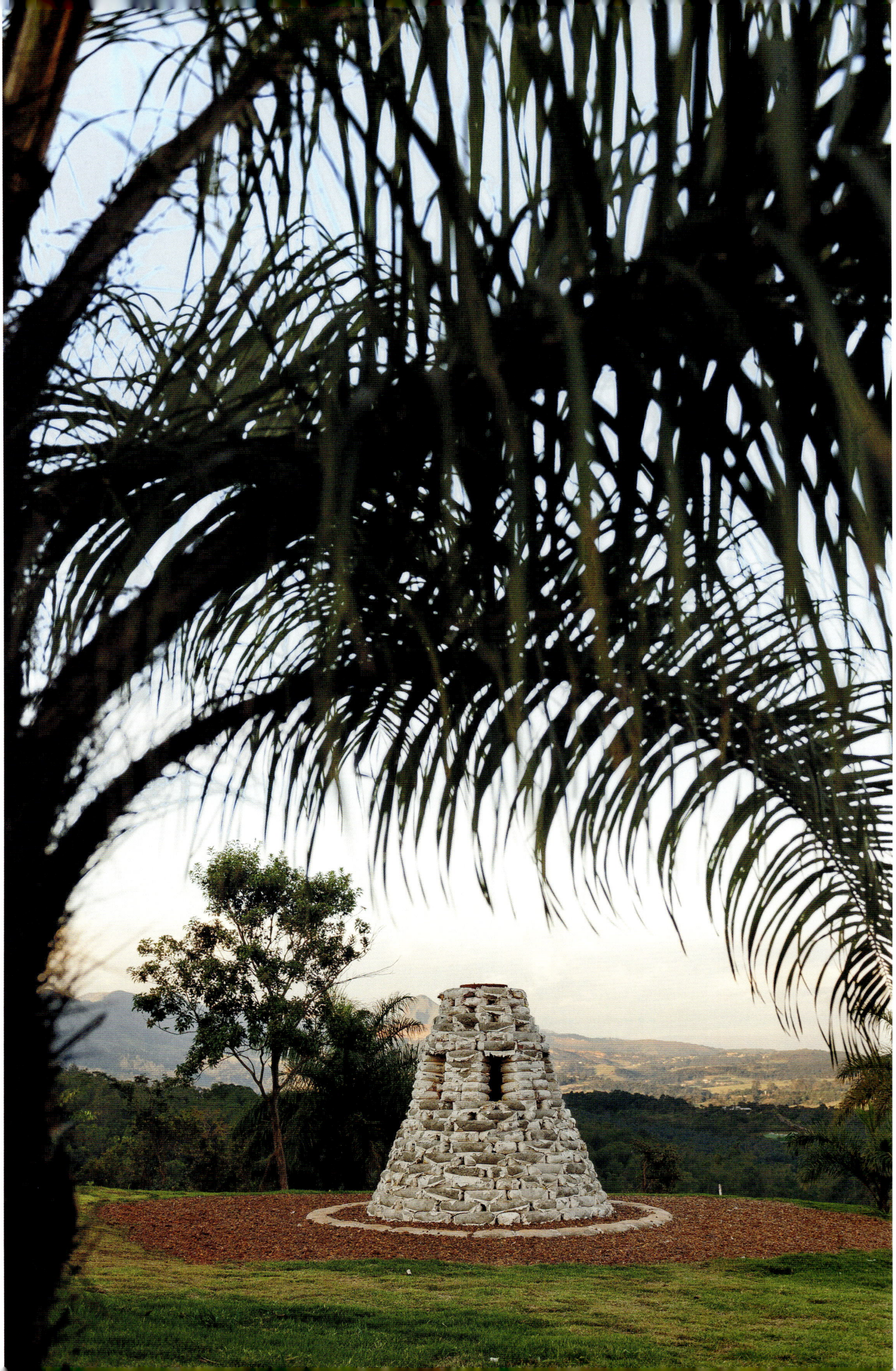

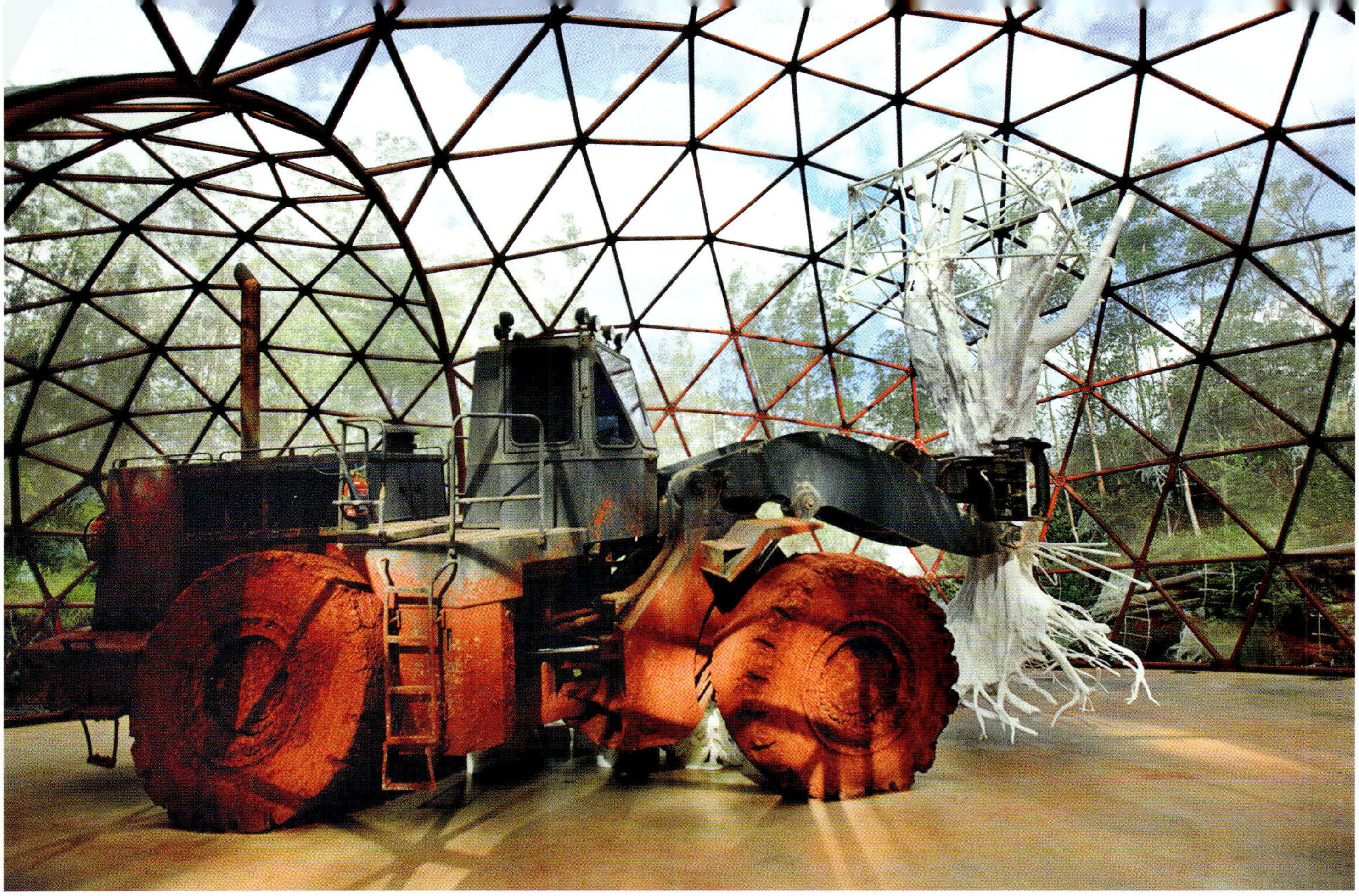

Left: For ***Beehive Bunker*** **Chris Burden used cement sacks to transform a beehive into a bunker, which now ominously tops a hill in the midst of palm groves.**

Matthew Barney's monster truck uproots a eucalyptus tree – the same species that is planted when rainforests have been cleared.

the grounds or of the works exhibited there. Visitors are free to make their own way through Inhotim at their own speed and to experience this dialogue with art and nature from ever-new perspectives. In one spot it may be the perfectly designed grounds, in another it may be the issues raised by the artists that prompt us to consider the meaning of time and space or our own role with regard to the natural world.

Bernardo Paz feels that particularly in a Western society increasingly shaped by ongoing technological revolutions our perceptions and emotions are of crucial importance. His aim is to achieve a new kind of dialogue with nature – through art: "Art wakes people up, it gives them the motivation to pursue their visions. So that they become active! So that they learn!" Inhotim is thus an avowedly unfinished project. The international team of curators – Rodrigo Moura (Brazil), Júlia Rebouças (Brazil), Allan Schwartzman (US) and Jochen Volz (Germany) and their assistant Inês Grosso (Portugal) – is constantly introducing new ideas into this park with new art from all five continents.

In 2006 Inhotim, as the Centro de Arte Contemporânea Inhotim, opened its doors to the public, in fulfilment of Paz's vision of a completely new museum as the antithesis of urban temples to art and as a seed for a better, multicultural society, where thoughts connect through art. Bernardo Paz has always been a bold thinker, especially since he sold all his company shares to the Chinese. His institution also serves as a cultural agent and, as such, works specifically with primary schools and universities throughout the region. Wide-ranging education courses and social programmes bring new hope to the population of the underdeveloped state of Minas Gerais. With a staff of 1,400 Inhotim is the second-largest employer in the region. Instead of having to work as miners or lorry drivers, locals can find employment in a cultural context, setting up exhibitions, working in art conservation or as tour guides. Thanks to a programme run jointly with Tate Modern in London, recently a group of interns from Inhotim even travelled to London. The locals learn from Inhotim how natural resources can be preserved, how to farm ecologically and how houses can be maintained using only basic materials. As a consequence of all that is done at Inhotim, the government now takes a greater interest in the town of Brumadinho; recently, for instance, Brumadinho has been designated a 'music city', which means that all its schoolchildren receive art and music lessons free of charge.

But even that is not enough for Bernardo Paz. He wants not only much more art but also new film festivals and dance festivals. And above all he wants an infrastructure that can accommodate even more visitors. Plans are already being drawn up for a new complex of hotels with a conference centre and an amphitheatre. As Paz says himself: "Inhotim is a place, not a museum. I am building Inhotim for people who have never come into contact with art and culture. We are opening their minds. And that is the way forwards."

The deep sound that fills Doug Aitken's *Sonic Pavilion* (2009) comes from the innermost realms of the Earth. Meditative listening can change the visitor's view of the world.

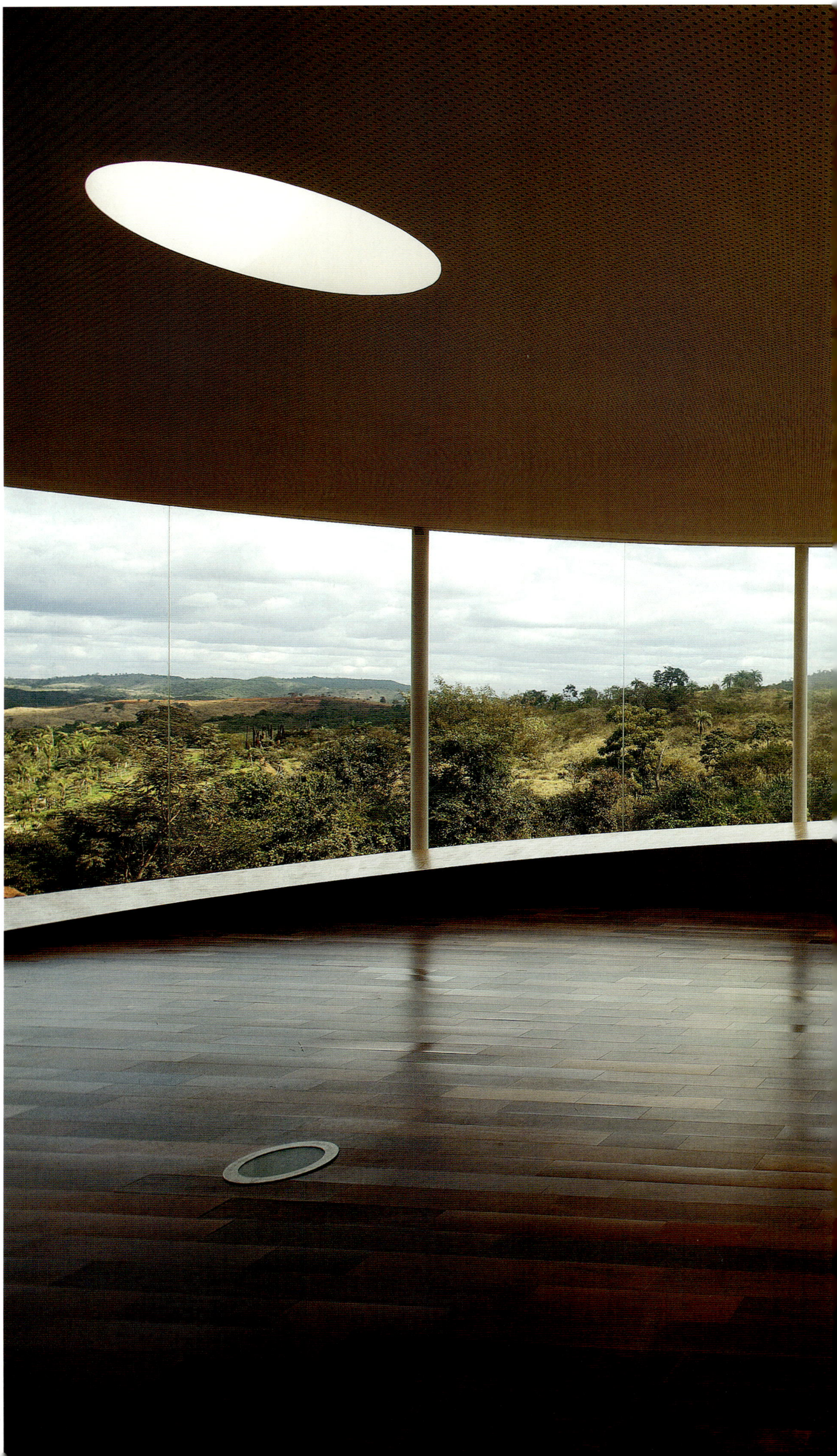

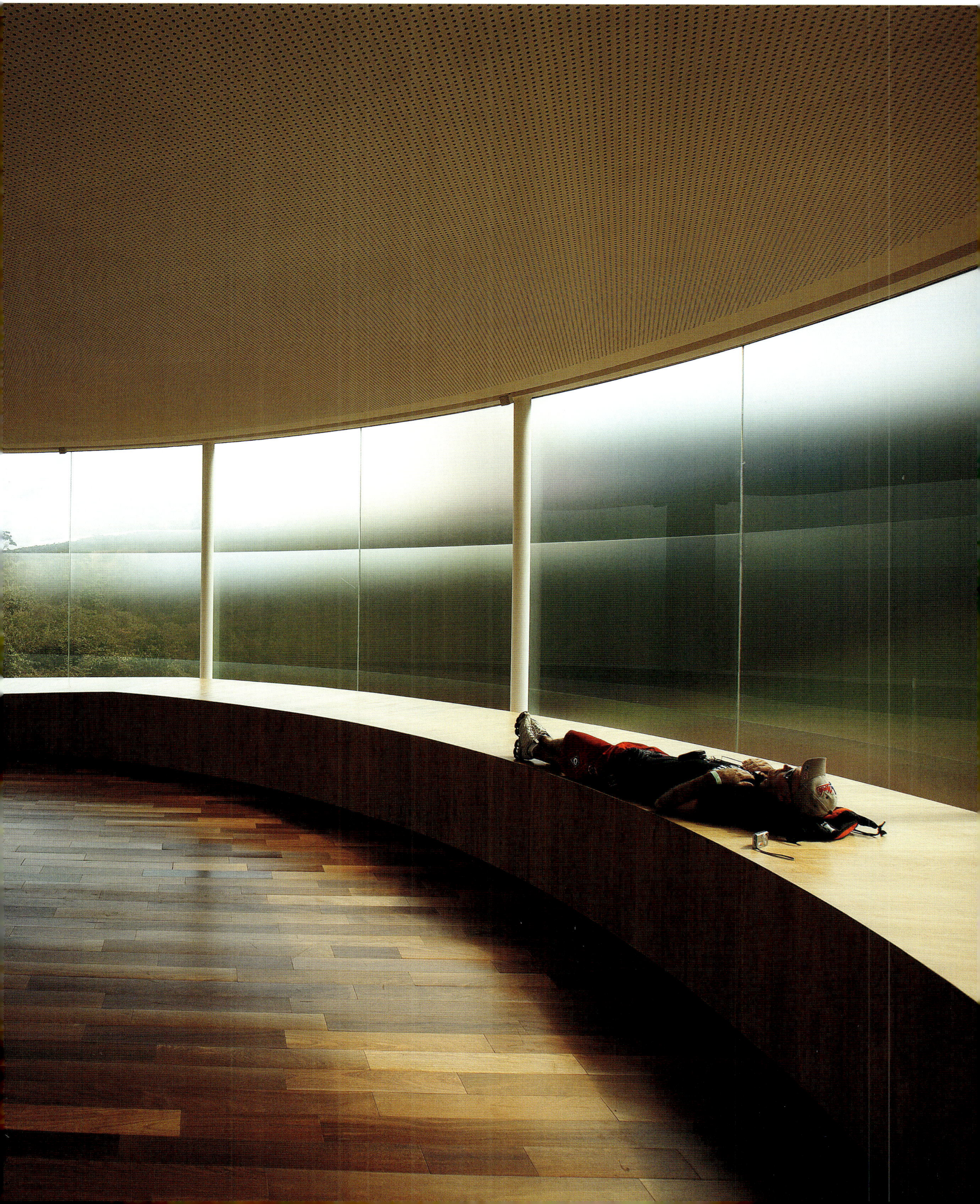

ARCHITECTURE AND ART IN A PROVENÇAL VINEYARD
CHÂTEAU LA COSTE, LE PUY-SAINTE-RÉPARADE, FRANCE

Fields of lavender, vineyards – a Mediterranean lifestyle. Any mention of winemaking estates in Provence will generally call to mind historic villas – particularly if the winery is named after a castle, as in the case of Château la Coste. This renowned vineyard is located north of Aix-en-Provence near the small town of Le Puy-Sainte-Réparade; at the heart of the estate is a fine mansion, a *bastide*, as it is called in this part of France. That is where Patrick McKillen (b. 1956) retreats to when he comes to visit his estate. McKillen, a property investor and impassioned art collector from Ireland, avoids any form of publicity. He barely gives any interviews and is reluctant to be photographed. His dreamy, old estate is thus deliberately hidden behind an elegant new glass-and-steel Art Centre that already catches one's eye from a distance. McKillen prefers the architecture to be in the limelight. In this case it is the work of the Japanese star architect Tadao Ando, who designed this building, with two narrow arms that seem to hover above a vast infinity pool. On both sides of the building a colonnade leads out into the vineyards. Nature and architecture merge harmoniously into a single entity. In the middle of the pool stands one of the huge spiders by Louise Bourgeois, *Crouching Spider 6695* (2003). In the two rear sections the sun catches Hiroshi Sugimoto's metallic cone, *Infinity* (2010), while Alexander Calder's mobile *Small Crinkly* (1976) dances on the water – fragile works of art that celebrate the dissolution of matter, like Ando's minimalist architecture surrounded by water with reflections of the landscape. It is not for nothing that this building is called the "Art Centre". For although one can also drink wine and eat here, everything is about art – and about a sculpture park that is in fact also an architectural park and covers the whole of this vast estate.

Wine and architecture – McKillen is not the only person to be passionate about both. In recent years the owners of vineyards have increasingly employed star architects to design eye-catching buildings, above all in the United States. But McKillen has gone a lot further than that. Not only has his particularly spectacular Art Centre raised the bar for contemporary vineyard architecture, he has created an entire architecture park on his 600-acre estate. No less than five recipients of the Pritzker Architecture Prize have created masterpieces for McKillen: Tadao Ando, Frank Gehry, Jean

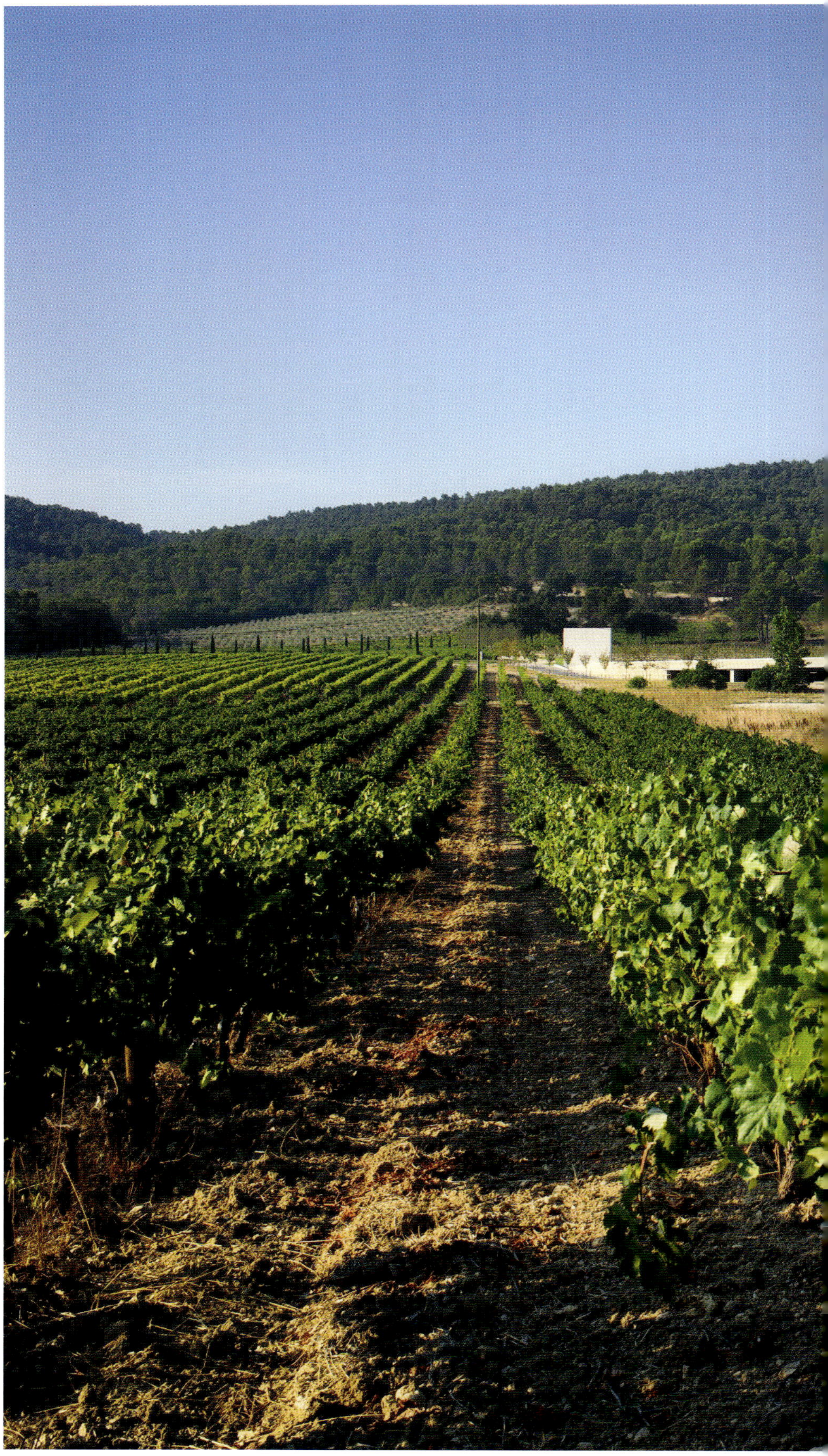

An architectural jewel in a vineyard: Jean Nouvel's *chai* (cellar) – where grapes are pressed and wine is bottled.

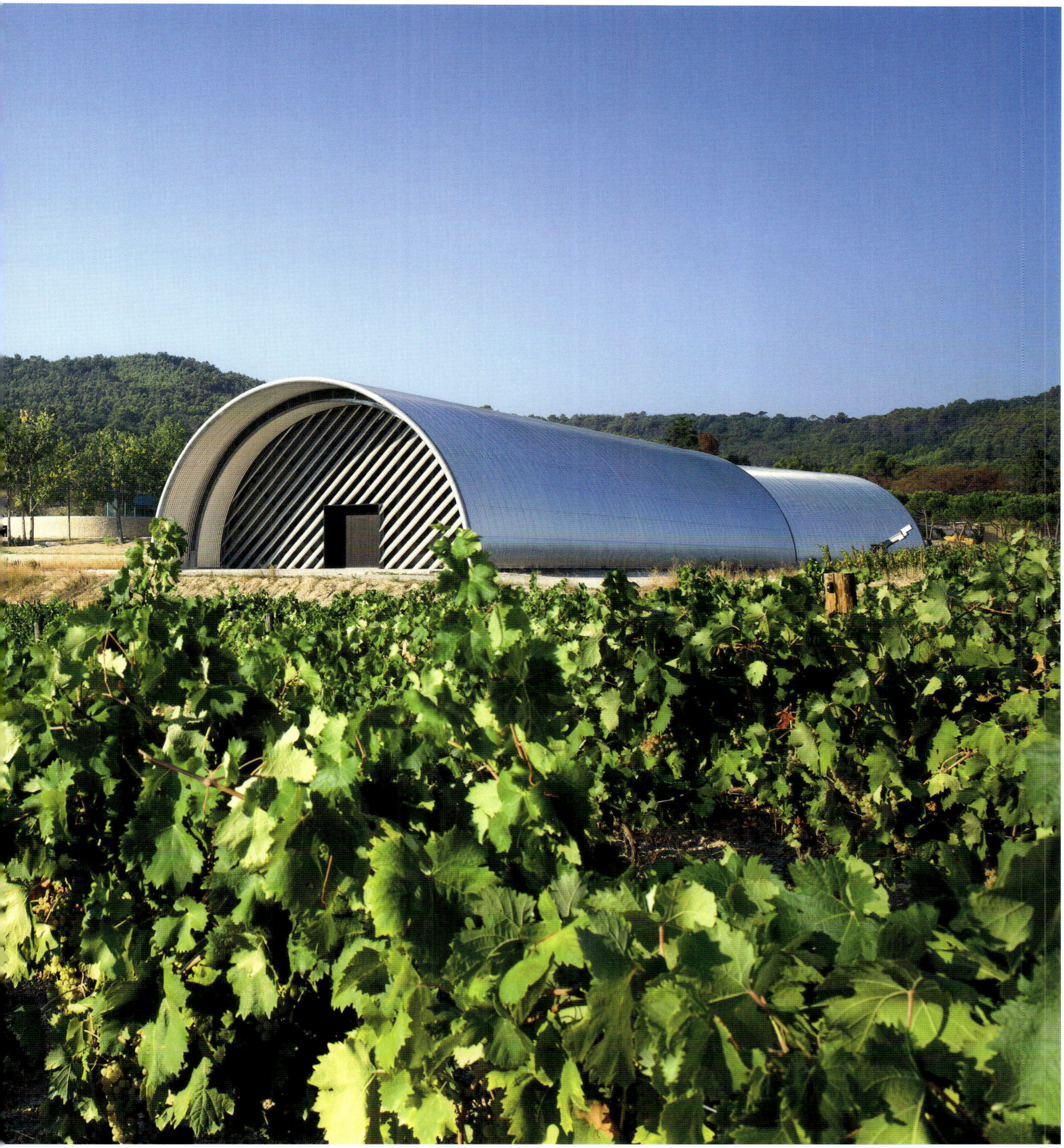

Château la Coste, France

Right: **Unusually for Andy Goldsworthy, his *Earth Room* is a permanent installation: a sophisticated mesh of branches and twigs.**

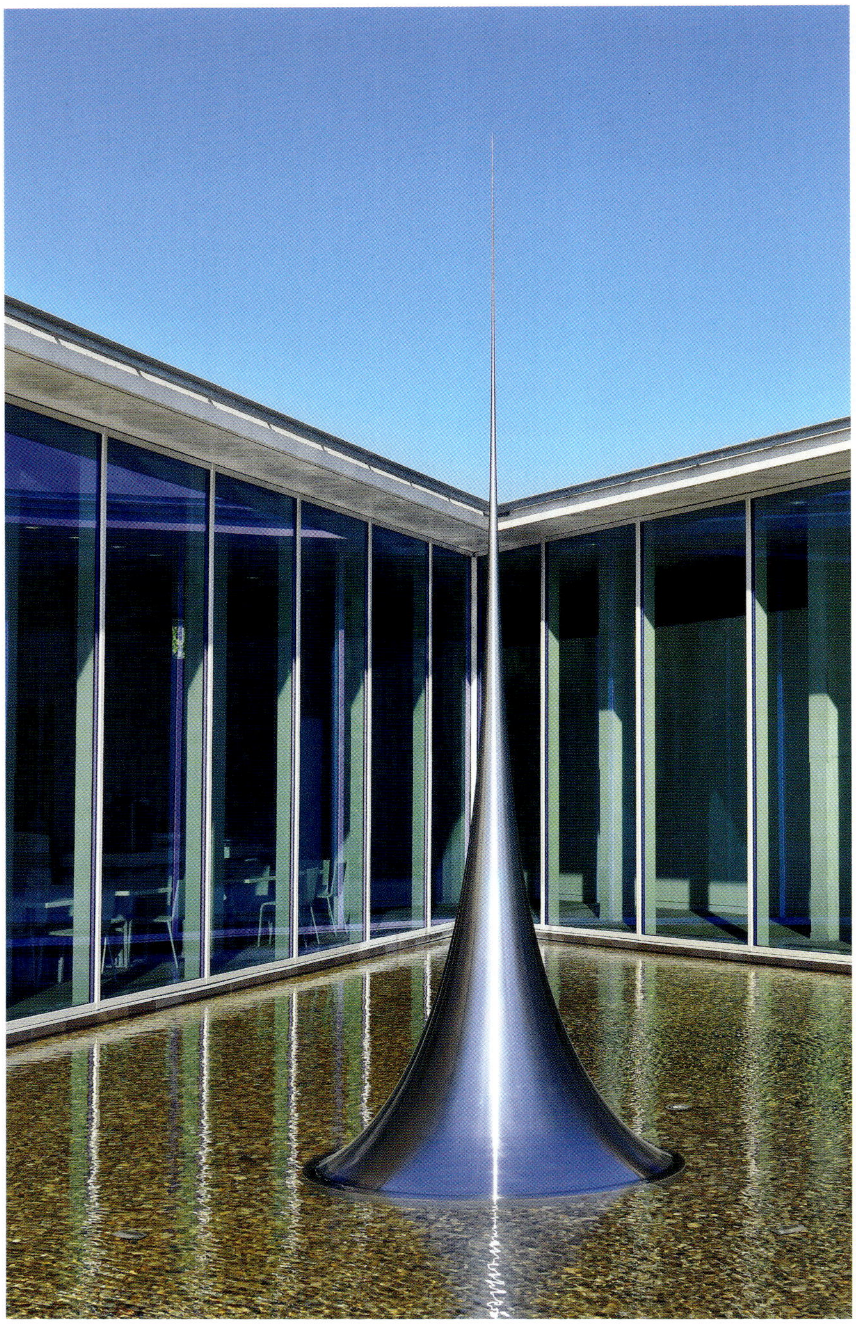

Hiroshi Sugimoto's hybrid version of a basic mathematical model is also a celebration of infinity.

Nouvel, Norman Foster and Renzo Piano. This is the perfect place to study contemporary architecture – exemplified in structures that span the divide between sculpture and architecture. As walk-in installations they occupy the same environment as sculptures by other renowned artists, such as Franz West, Tom Shannon, Tunga and Sean Scully.

Patrick McKillen discovered this vineyard in 2002 on one of his visits to Aix-en-Provence, where his sister Mara has lived since the early 1990s. She now manages the estate, with the assistance of the artistic director Daniel Kennedy and the oenologist Matthieu Cosse. In 2004 McKillen decided to combine first-class wine with first-class art and architecture. In 2008 Jean Nouvel's *Chai* was inaugurated. This two-part work consists of two halls that are linked underground and whose forms are derived from the cross section of a barrel. One half houses the wine press, the other half is used for bottling. Once McKillen, together with Matthieu Cosse, had turned his 300-acre vineyard into a high quality, biodynamic winery, he invited artists and architects to his estate. As a passionate collector he now proposed that they should create works that specifically related to that landscape. "Unlike some others, Paddy McKillen never went to see other sculpture parks in search of ideas," explains Kennedy, "the project grew organically." McKillen has long been friends with most of the artists he has invited to his estate and deliberately does not attach conditions to his commissions. "We give the artists carte blanche. Andy Goldsworthy and Tunga each spent a month at Château la Coste before choosing a site." And now Goldsworthy's *Oak Room* (2009) seems to fit entirely naturally into its surroundings. It is not easy to find this walk-in work of art, which is hidden behind an old wall in the woods and takes the form of a round, dug-out chamber lined with interwoven oak branches. Towards the ceiling these branches form a filigree vault. It is only when the visitor's eyes have adjusted to the darkness that this masterly construction looms into view. "There is not a single nail here. Andy Goldsworthy made the whole thing by hand," remarks Kennedy. In contrast to Goldsworthy's careful handiwork, Richard Serra's sculpture *Aix* (2010) looks like a brutal intervention into the natural setting. It consists of three huge sheets of steel, rammed into the ground at different heights and at irregular angles to each other. They mark the incline of the steep slope in this part of the estate. Meanwhile the British artist Tracey Emin's response to these surroundings is entirely ironic. In her *Self Portrait: Cat in a barrel* (2013) at first everything seems entirely logical: a walkway leads to a wooden platform on stilts, providing a wonderful, panoramic view of the long, fertile Luberon Valley. Right in the middle of the platform there is a closed wine barrel. However, if

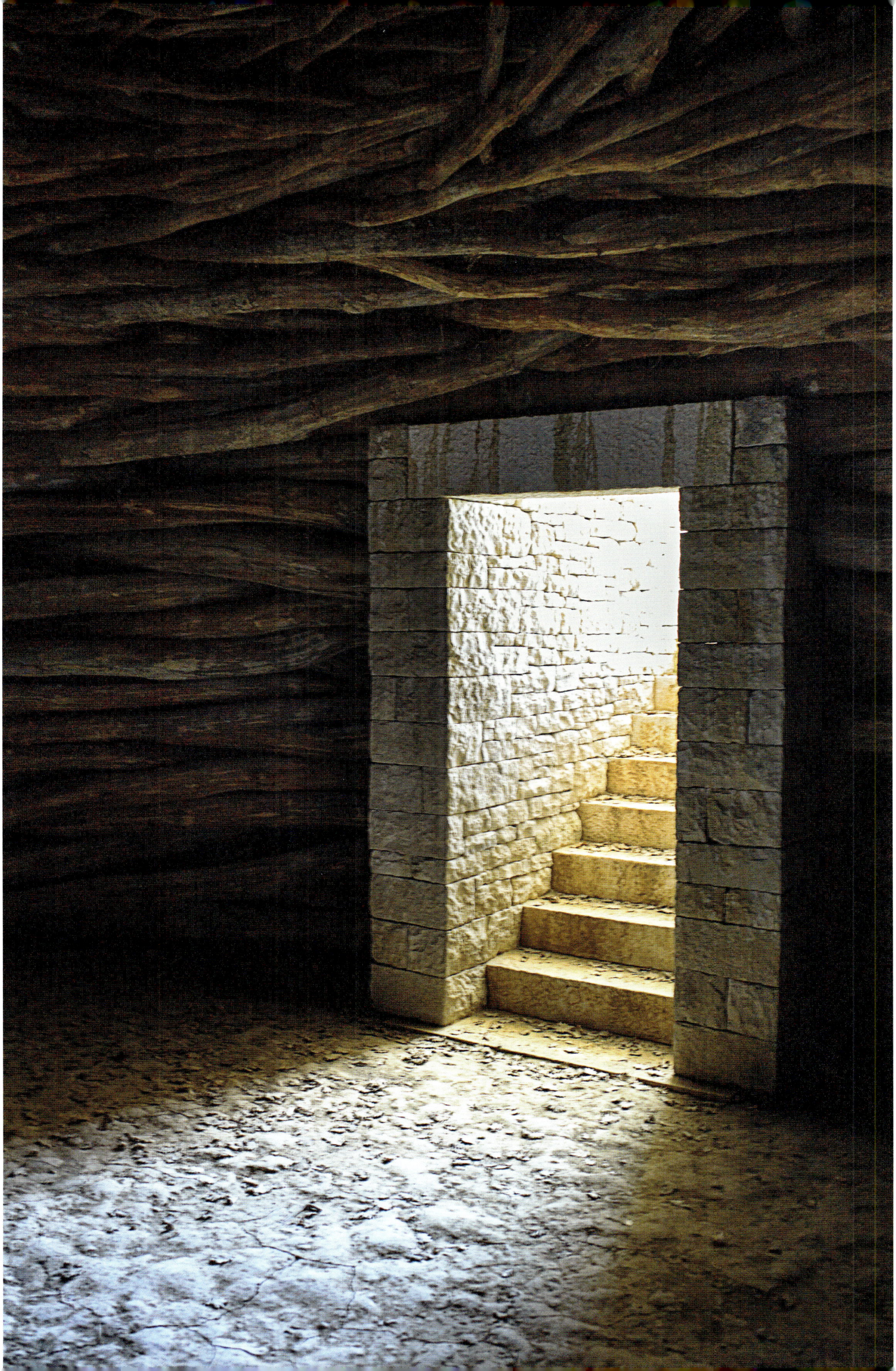

Château la Coste, France

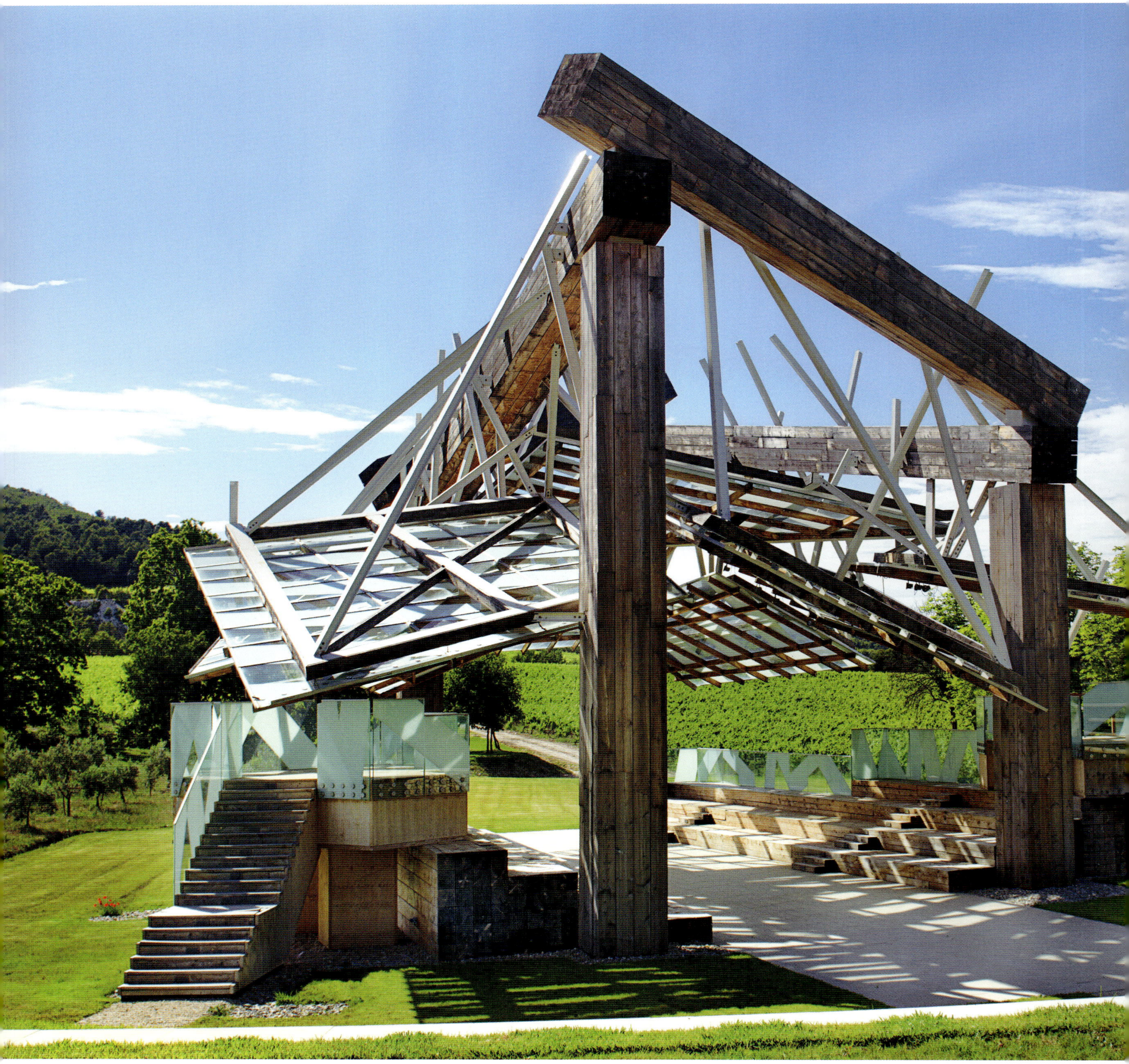

Just four massive wooden beams with a steel core support the overlapping glass roof panels of Frank Gehry's fragile-looking Music Pavilion.

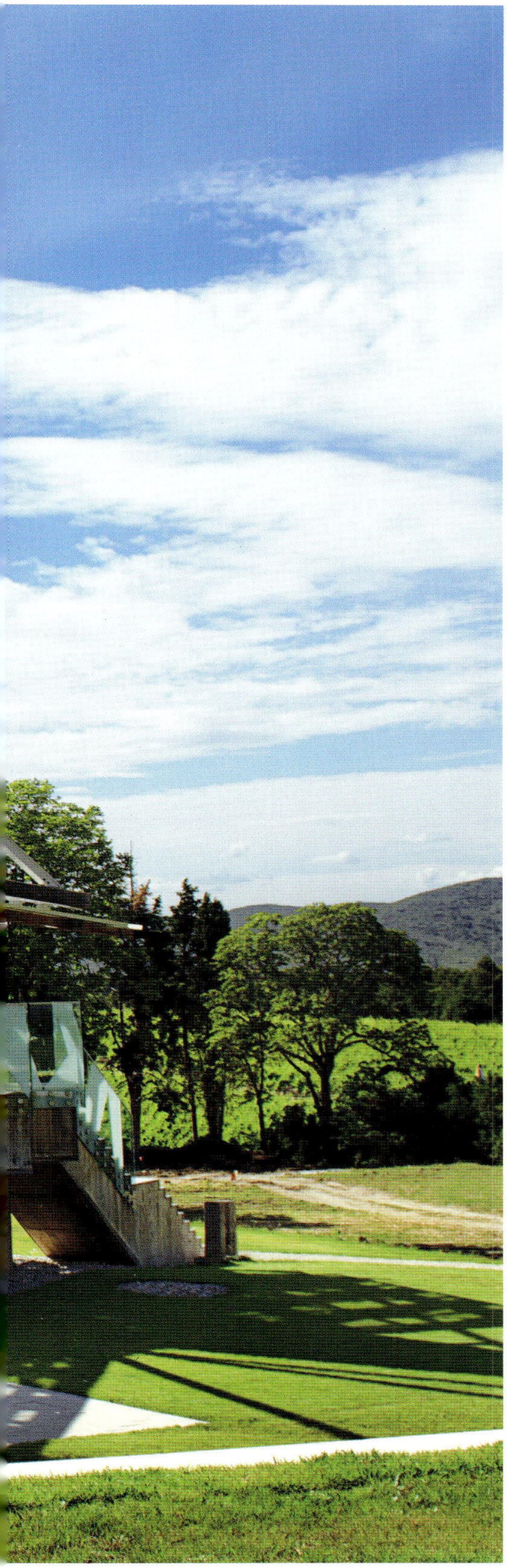

visitors look in through one of the small holes bored into the side of the barrel, they will see a sculpture of Docket, Tracey Emin's cat. At the highest point of the *domaine*, on the top of a hill, is Tadao Ando's *Chapel* (2011), a glass structure around the old stone walls of a Romanesque chapel. The side walls are bricked up. As the heavy wooden door closes behind the visitor, he or she is initially plunged into deep darkness. But then rays of light seep in beneath the door, at the altar and through the roof. It is as though the chapel were floating.

Not far from the chapel a work by James Turrell will soon be in place: "a tunnel, like his *Roden Crater*." That much Daniel Kennedy can tell us just now. Another key work in the sculpture park is Frank Gehry's *Music Pavilion* (2008) – a deconstructivist structure of loosely hung glass canopies that reach upwards and outwards on a simple framework of solid wooden beams. It stands on a wide meadow in sight of the Art Centre. It was originally constructed (with financial support from Patrick McKillen) for the renowned Serpentine Gallery Pavilion series in London, one of the most ambitious programmes for contemporary architecture. Frank Gehry's pavilion set new standards for event spaces in an urban context. At Château la Coste it stands in the midst of natural scenery and toys with views and vistas of the vineyard. The interior is set out like an amphitheatre. The continuous central section is the stage. In summer there are regular concerts, readings and performances here. With the addition of prefabricated houses by Jean Prouvé, McKillen has also made the connection with architecture from the past. Prouvé, who has been a role model for almost all the architects who have left their mark in the *domaine* of the Irish entrepreneur, originally designed these prefabricated structures as accommodation for war refugees in 1945. In so doing he proved the efficacy of building using prefabricated modules in the modern industrial age. With his outstanding talent for construction, Prouvé was also an inspired furniture designer – the European counterpart to Charles and Ray Eames. In the two prefabricated houses at the winery visitors can sit on original furniture or peruse the books in the library. The ambience of alternative domestic architecture is enhanced by a small garden designed by the renowned landscape architect Louis Benech and by an extended dialogue with a seventeenth-century Vietnamese teahouse.

Those who are seeking quietness and contemplation in untamed nature can return to the woods and take the winding path by a small stream. There they will find Tadao Ando's wooden pavilion and the installation *Four Cubes to Contemplate Our Environment* (2008–11) – an urgent appeal for a greater awareness of the world around us. Just a few steps away from it is Paul Matisse's memorable *Meditation Bell* (2012). Reminiscent in its appearance of a gateway to a Japanese temple, this is in fact a sound installation, created by the grandson of the legendary painter Henri Matisse. It consists of a six-metre aluminium tubular bell resting on two supporting columns. A long rope can be pulled to activate four hammers, which then all strike the bell at once. A long-lasting sound, resonating for minutes on end and palpably vibrating, runs right through the listener's body.

McKillen still has many more ideas for his unusual sculpture park, but, as he himself has said, "We don't have a 'master plan'. The nature of the project continues to evolve with the contribution of each artist and architect." And Frank Gehry, Jean Nouvel and Hiroshi Sugimoto have indicated that they already have new ideas for Château la Coste.

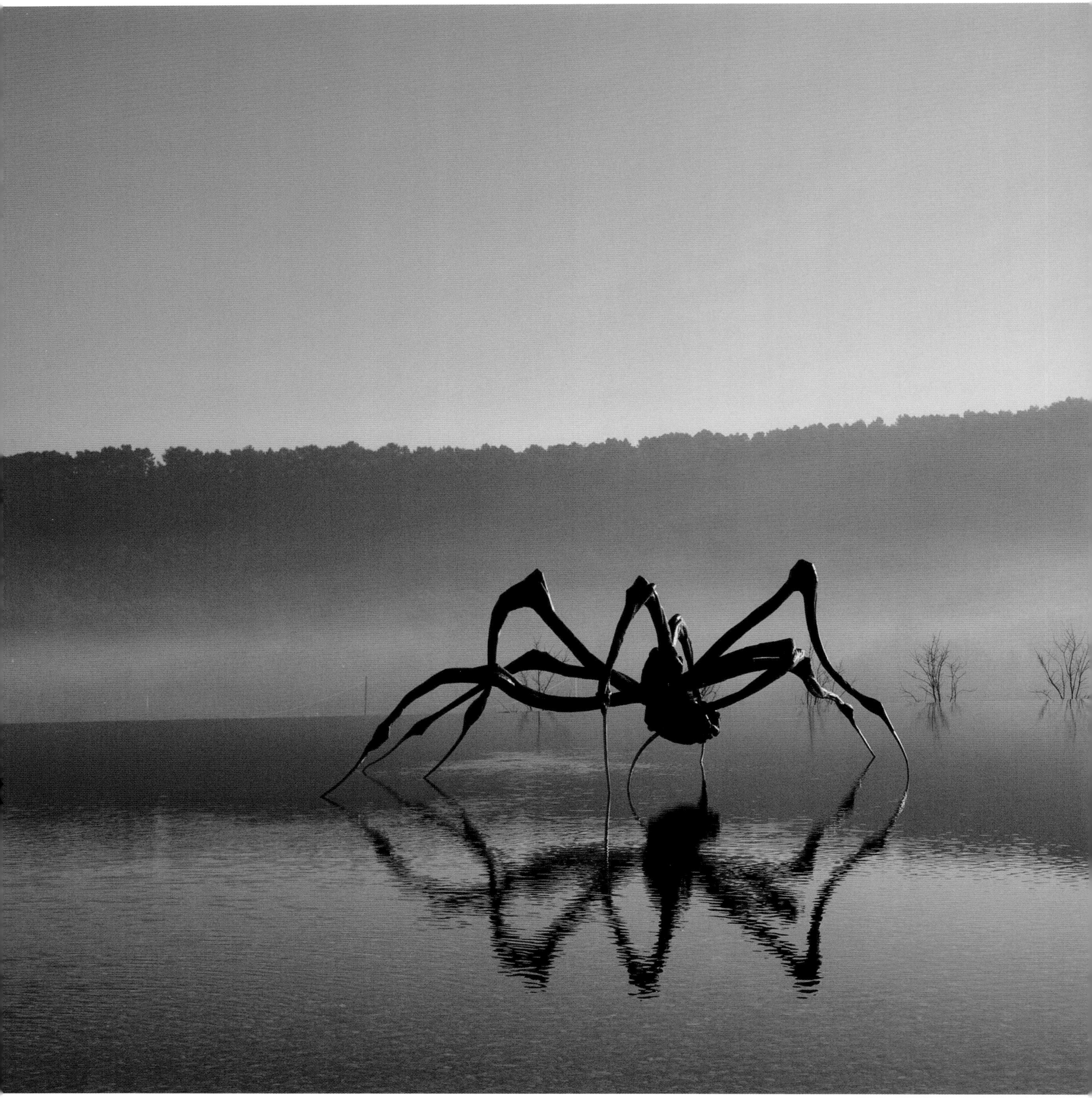

Louise Bourgeois' *Crouching Spider 6695* – spectacularly poised on the surface of the infinity pool.

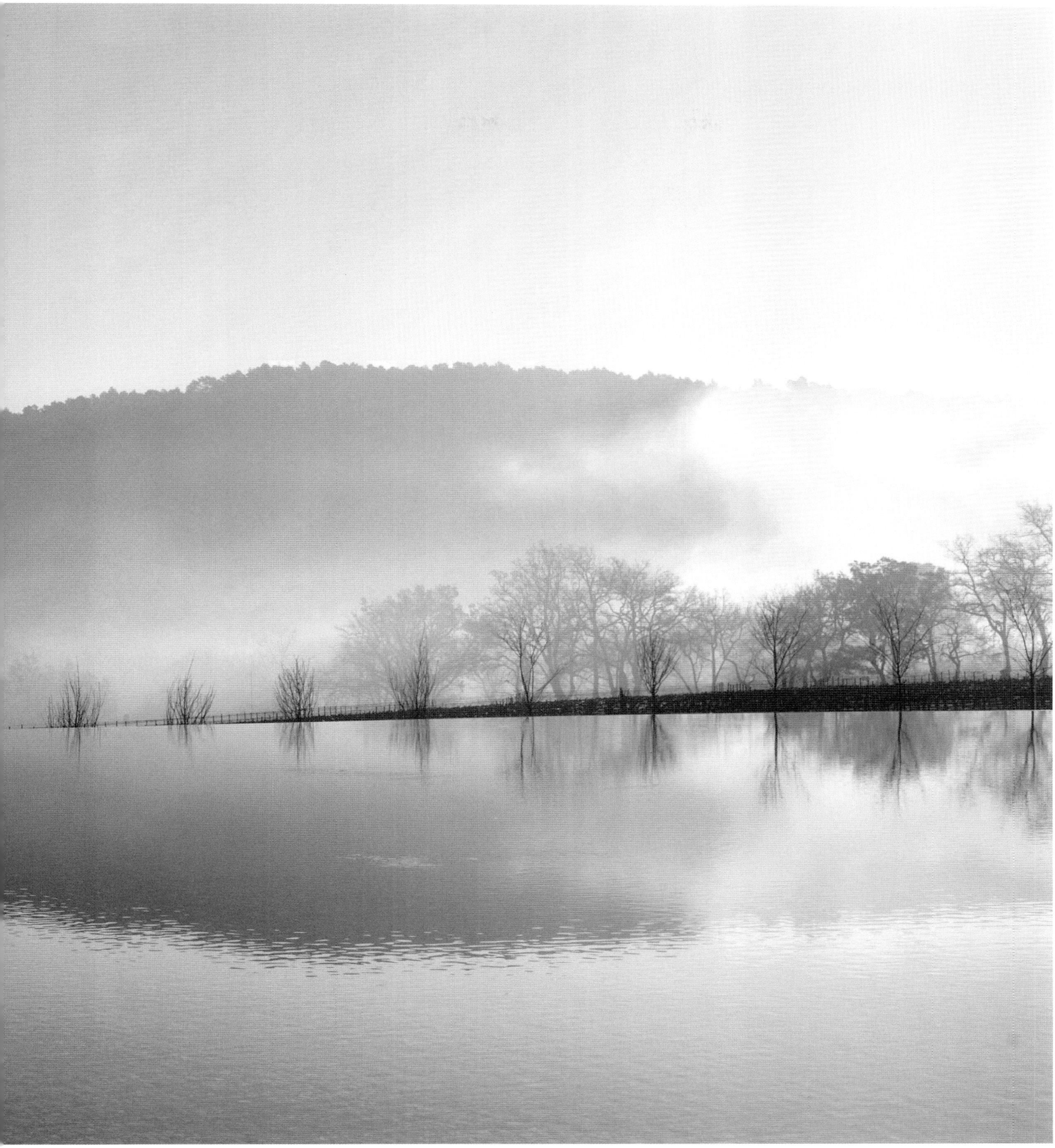

Château la Coste, France

SYMBOLS OF REMEMBRANCE IN THE DESERT – ART MEETS ETERNAL HUMAN MYTHS

ARCHITECTURAL SCULPTURES ON THE PLAINE DE MARHA, MOROCCO

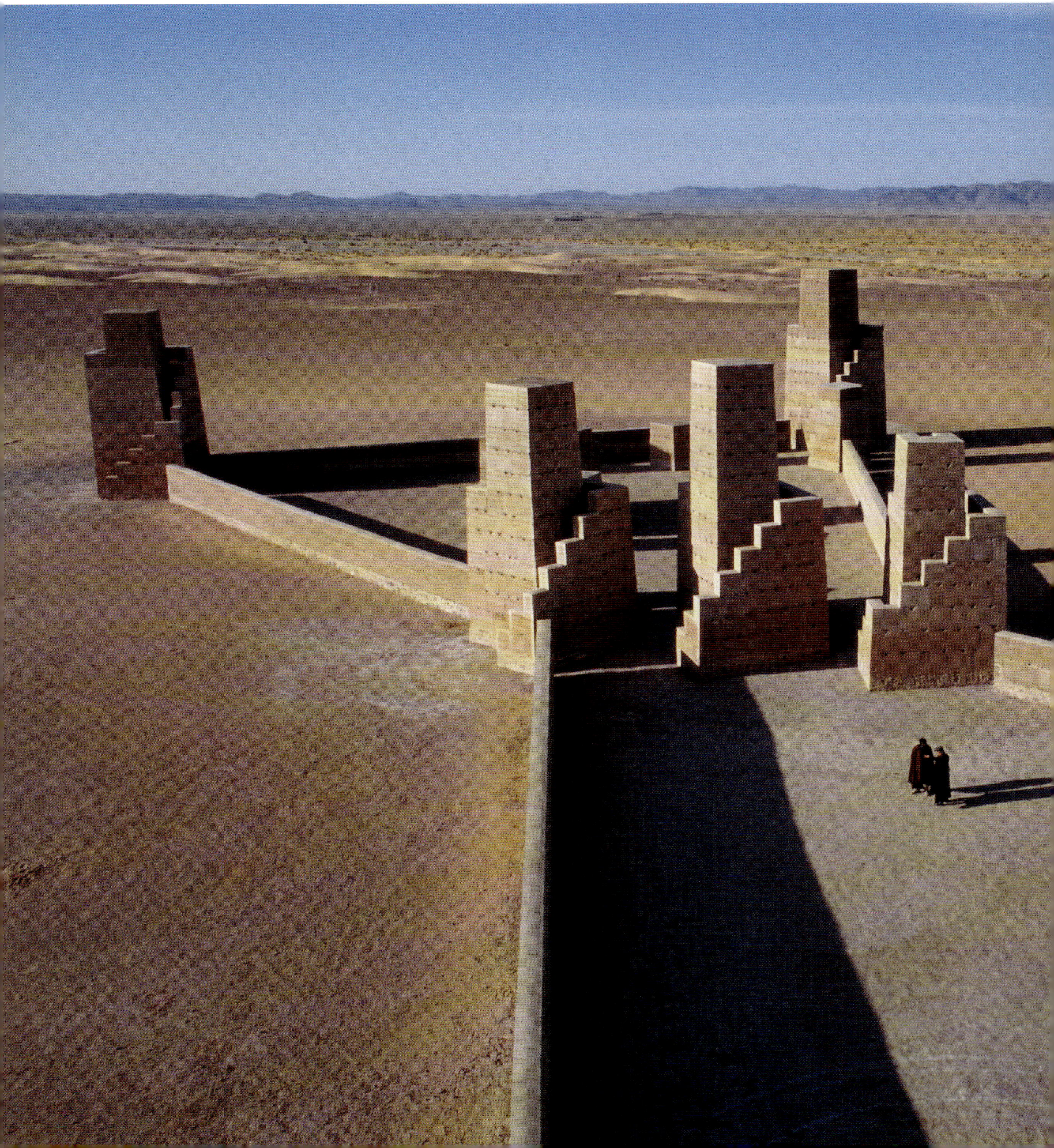

Covering an area of 450 square metres in the middle of the desert, the *City of Orion* is an architectural mirror image of the constellation of the same name.

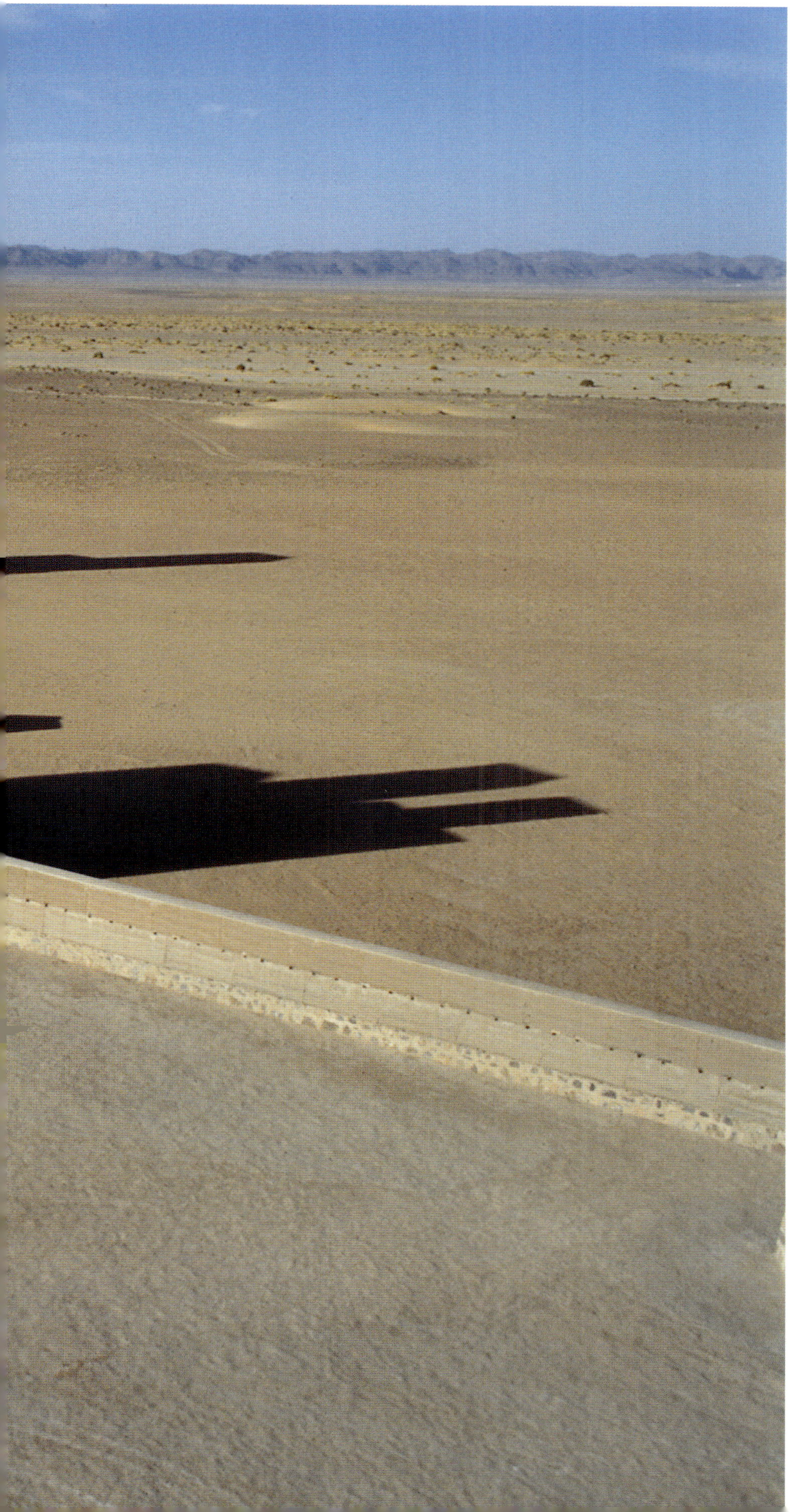

The Plaine de Marha in the extreme south-east of Morocco. Silence, a vast landscape, dazzling light – the sky. Shepherds shelter in their tents by scrawny thorn bushes. A few goats and camels are wandering about in their search for food. Like a Fata Morgana, just three kilometres from here three works of art rise up out of the desert sand – large-scale installations somewhere between architecture and monumental sculpture. *Stairway to Heaven* (1985–87), *Golden Spiral* (1992–97) and *City of Orion* (1998–2003) are all symbols of longing for that which is beyond human cognition. They are built from materials offered up by the desert: stones and clay. The creator of these impressive structures is the German artist Hannsjörg Voth (b. 1940). He prefers to work alone, in endless, open landscapes. He would like to have become a zoologist, but his father – an architect – advised him to become a carpenter, like the men in his family before him. "It's been a useful skill for realising projects," says the wiry man with the striking moustache.

For his best known and most popular project, *Journey to the Sea* (1978), Voth built a raft measuring thirty-two by ten metres, which he and some friends used to transport a gigantic, twenty-metre-long, fictitious 'mummy' along the Rhine, from Ludwigshafen to the North Sea at Rotterdam. The journey was like an archaic funeral procession. The climax was the burning of the figure at sea. The raft was subsequently dismantled and the wood sold off as lumber. In 1981 Voth retreated to a gigantic pyramid that he had constructed as a seventeen-metre-high pile dwelling in the Ijsselmeer in the Netherlands. For this project – *Stone Boat* – he lived in the pyramid and spent his time chiselling a boat from a block of stone from the Dolomites. Ultimately the finished boat sank to the bottom of the Ijsselmeer when pack ice destroyed the wooden piles supporting the pyramid.

The artist now went in search of terra firma and found it in Morocco, where he used traditional clay-construction techniques to realise his own, very individual variant of international Land Art. He created three structures, each with its own freshly dug well, which reactivated ancient myths. Voth's works of art are dominated by geometric figures such as circles, squares, triangles and spirals which he regards as "modes of expression that are deeply rooted in our collective consciousness

The *Stairway to Heaven* symbolises ascent and transcendence.

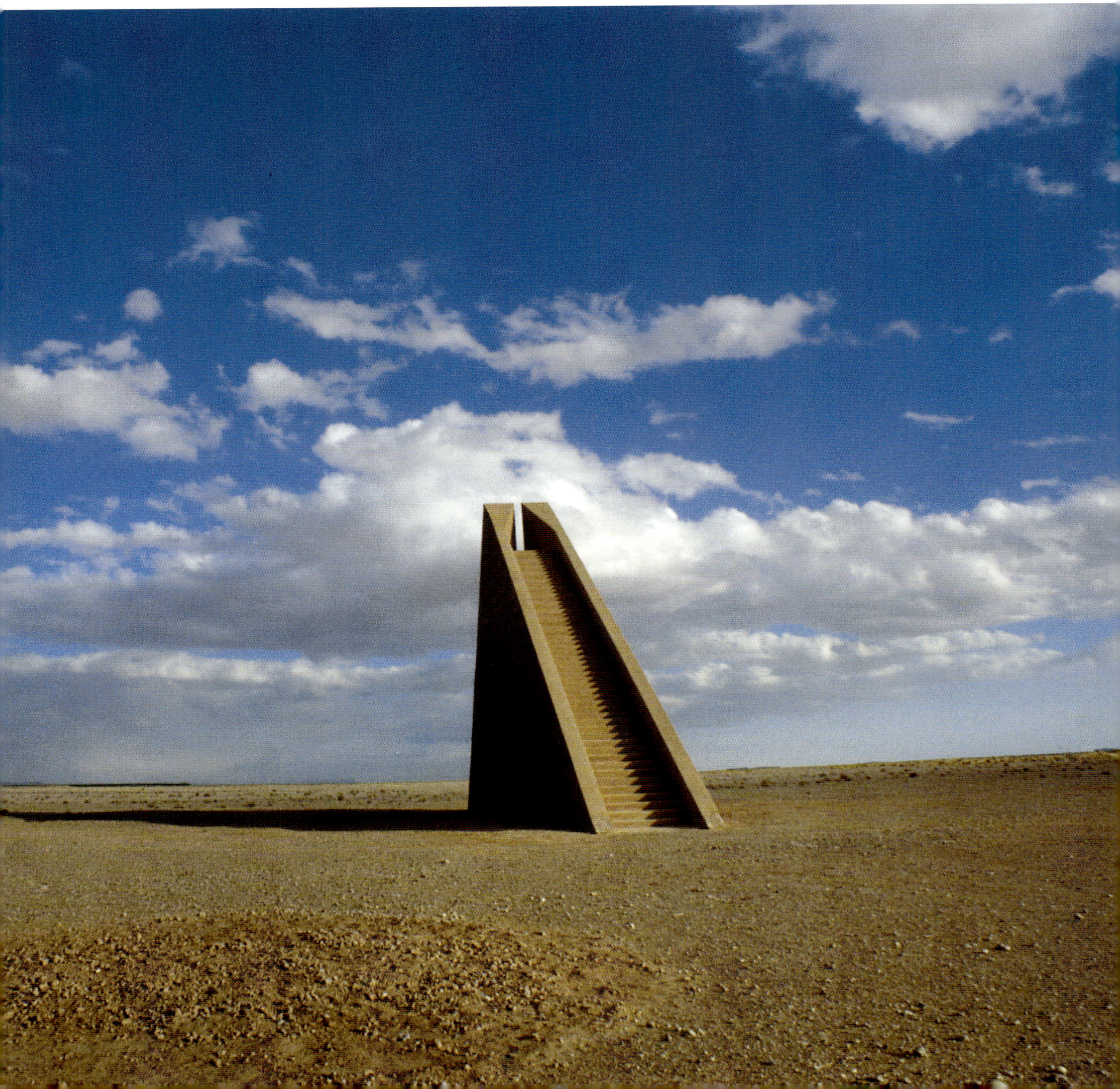

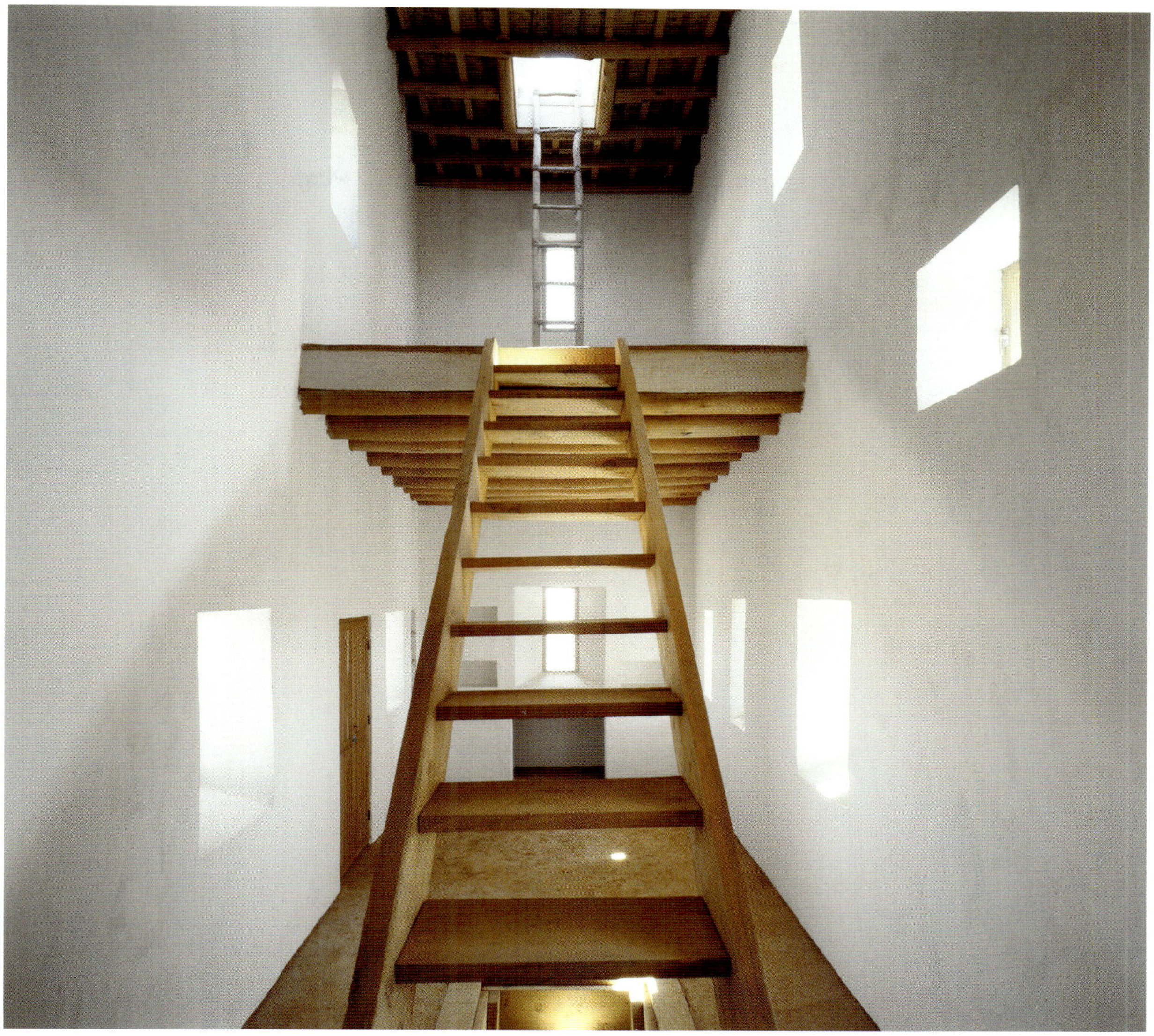

The three-storey interior houses areas for living and working: view from the study to the entrance above.

of forms but unfortunately also often forgotten." For twenty-five years Voth and his wife, the photographer Ingrid Amslinger, spent the winter months living and working at Plaine de Marha in Morocco. "I went in search of a primal landscape," he explains, "as yet untouched by human hand, where you can have a unique cosmic experience and where the stars shine at night like a single light."

For *City of Orion* he created an image of the much-loved constellation on the ground. The realisation of this mega-project made huge demands of the artist. Once again Voth had to take care of the project's finances. He had to make endless visits to government offices before he was at last granted permission to build on the ancestral homelands of the nomads in that region. And then there was the actual structure: "The difficulty of dealing with thirty to fifty Moroccan workers, the complicated logistics of constructing a large-scale project from rammed earth without having recourse to modern, technical aids – in murderous heat and in the freezing cold – meant that I had to draw on every last ounce of my physical and mental power," says Voth, not without pride.

The first of his structural sculptures, *Stairway to Heaven*, was made between 1983 and 1987. "In many cultures a stairway stands as a symbol of ascent and transcendence," explains Voth. From a distance the staircase looks tiny, like a raised finger. From up close, this structure – sixteen metres in height and twenty-three metres in length – is a mighty wedge with a compelling presence. Fifty-two steep steps lead up to a platform. Up here the world is at one's feet and one's gaze travels freely to the faint outlines of the Atlas Mountains on the horizon. At the platform level there is access to two rooms, one above the other, for living and working, where for eight years Voth and his wife spent the winter months. In the room above the living space there is a winged object. Its 'feathers' are made from metal. The wings have a span of three-and-a-half metres and were made by Voth as a symbol of the unfulfilled dream of flying. The long, sharp feather-blades are indicative of the diametrically opposed characters of Daedalus and Icarus. The father was a realist; his son, yearning to fly, was a fantasist.

Just eight kilometres to the west a 260-metre, circular wall slowly emerges – in the form of a huge stone spiral – from the reddish clay ground, symbolising growth and exertion, both upwards and downwards. After the highest point of six metres – in the centre of the spiral – it narrows into a round shaft containing a spiral staircase with one hundred steps leading downwards, first to the living quarters and then further down to the well. Floating on the water in the well is an 'ark' – a precious object made from gold. "The title *Golden Spiral*," as Voth explains, "comes from the geometry of the golden section (in the ground plan of the structure) and the fact that the point of intersection determined the position of the well." Voth constructed the spiral from nine quarter-circles whose radii increase according to the principle of the Fibonacci series: "The reference to this series invokes a set of laws that is found in numerous growth processes in nature." Unlike the *Stairway to Heaven*, the *Golden Spiral* is constructed from lava rock from the surrounding area – once again, everything was worked manually and moved using pulleys.

The climax and end point of Voth's built structures is the *City of Orion*. This consists of twenty-two clay towers – some as tall as sixteen metres – with connecting walls that map out the shape of the constellation Orion on the surface of desert. The central star in the 'sword belt', Orion Nebula M 42, is marked by a tower, which again has a well inside it. Voth has been fascinated by stars ever since he was a small child. "I was always asking my mother about the stars, why they are there and what they are called."

The *Golden Spiral*, which rises upwards above a 17-metre well, is built from desert rocks and incorporates the geometry of the golden section into its design.

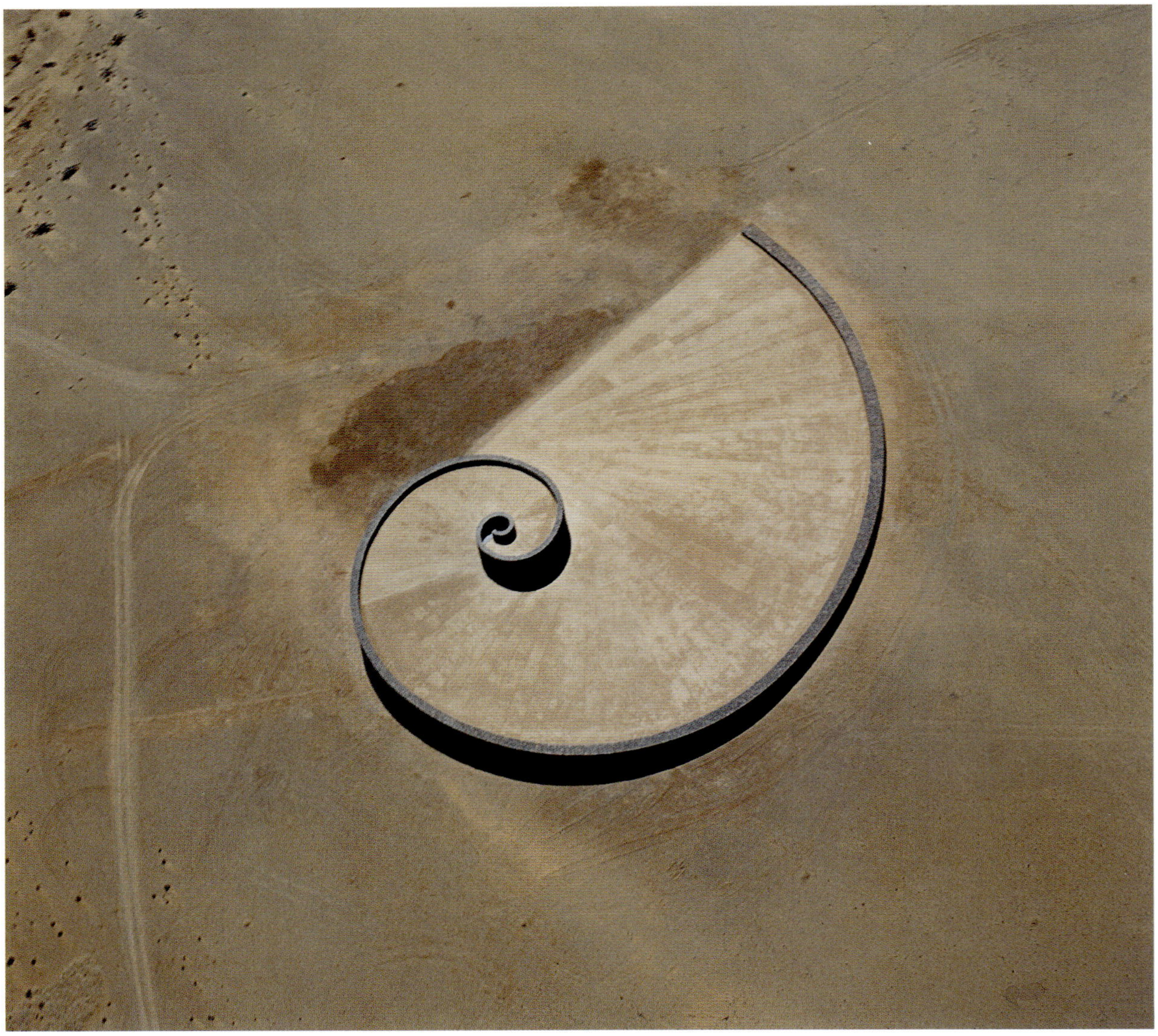

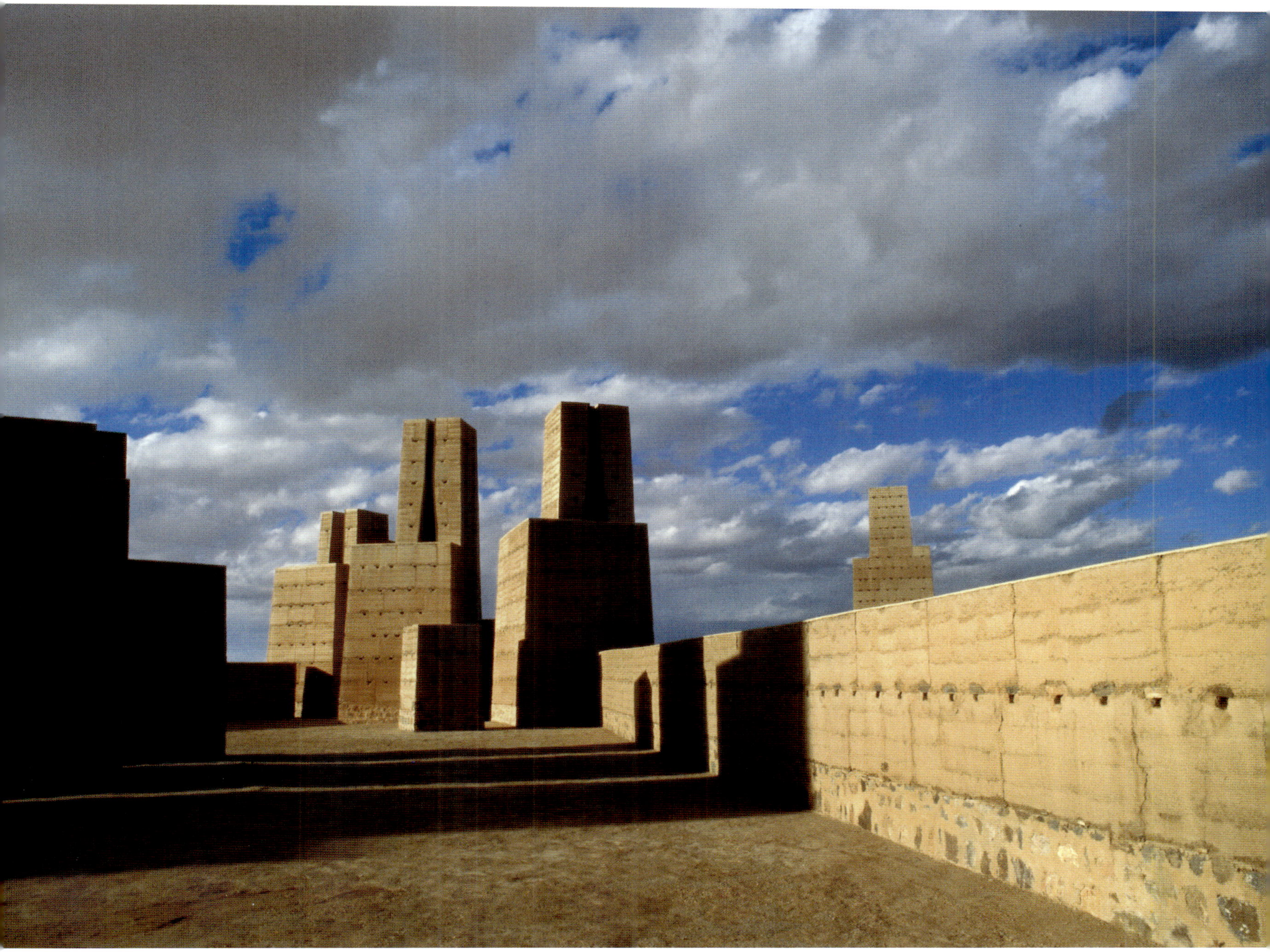

The *City of Orion* with its walls and towers (up to 16 metres in height), which are also observatories, was built by Voth using traditional, rammed-earth construction methods.

He chose the constellation of Orion because it is one of the oldest and most impressive phenomena in the night sky. It was already mentioned in the Sumerian-Babylonian *Epic of Gilgamesh* written in the third millennium BC. The height, breadth and depth of the individual towers were determined by Voth according to the luminosity of individual stars. The towers marking the seven main stars – Rigel, Saiph, Bellatrix and Betelgeuse, along with the three stars on Orion's belt, Mintaka, Alnitak and Alnilam – can also be used as observatories. Steps on the outside walls lead up to seats where, at particular times, the visitor can look through slits in the wall and observe the constellations Canis Minor, Taurus, Gemini, Auriga, Canis Major and Lepus as they progress across the night sky in winter – and of course Orion itself. Voth has in fact expressed the hope that "as people observe these constellations from a scientific point of view, their mythological meaning will also come more to the fore again. After all, it is very much part of the essence of our civilisation."

NEW ZEALAND IN ART AND FAUNA

CONNELLS BAY, WAIHEKE ISLAND, NEW ZEALAND

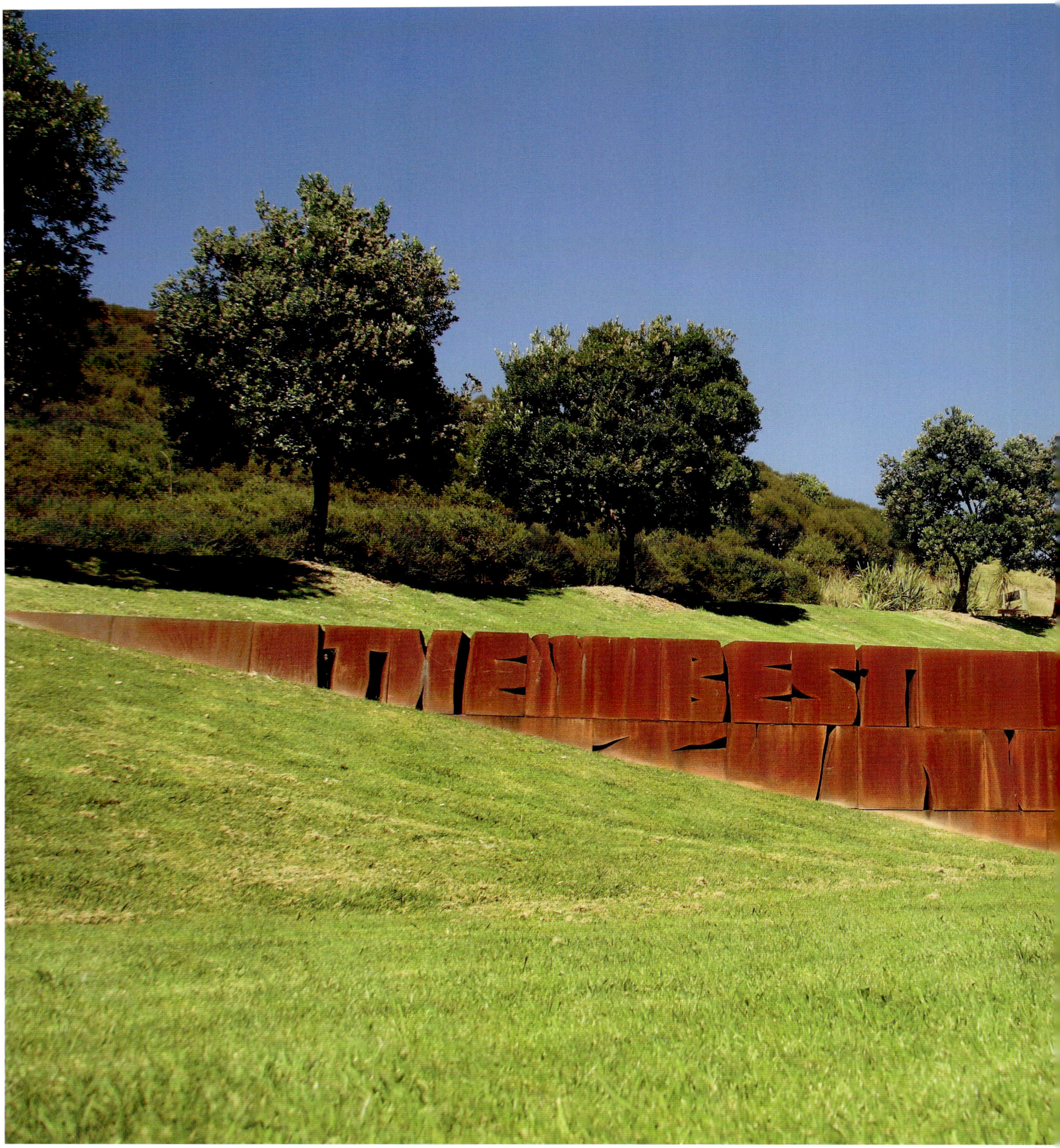

Dave McCracken's ***Best Laid Plans Go West*** **(2009): art in New Zealand need not fear comparison in the international art world.**

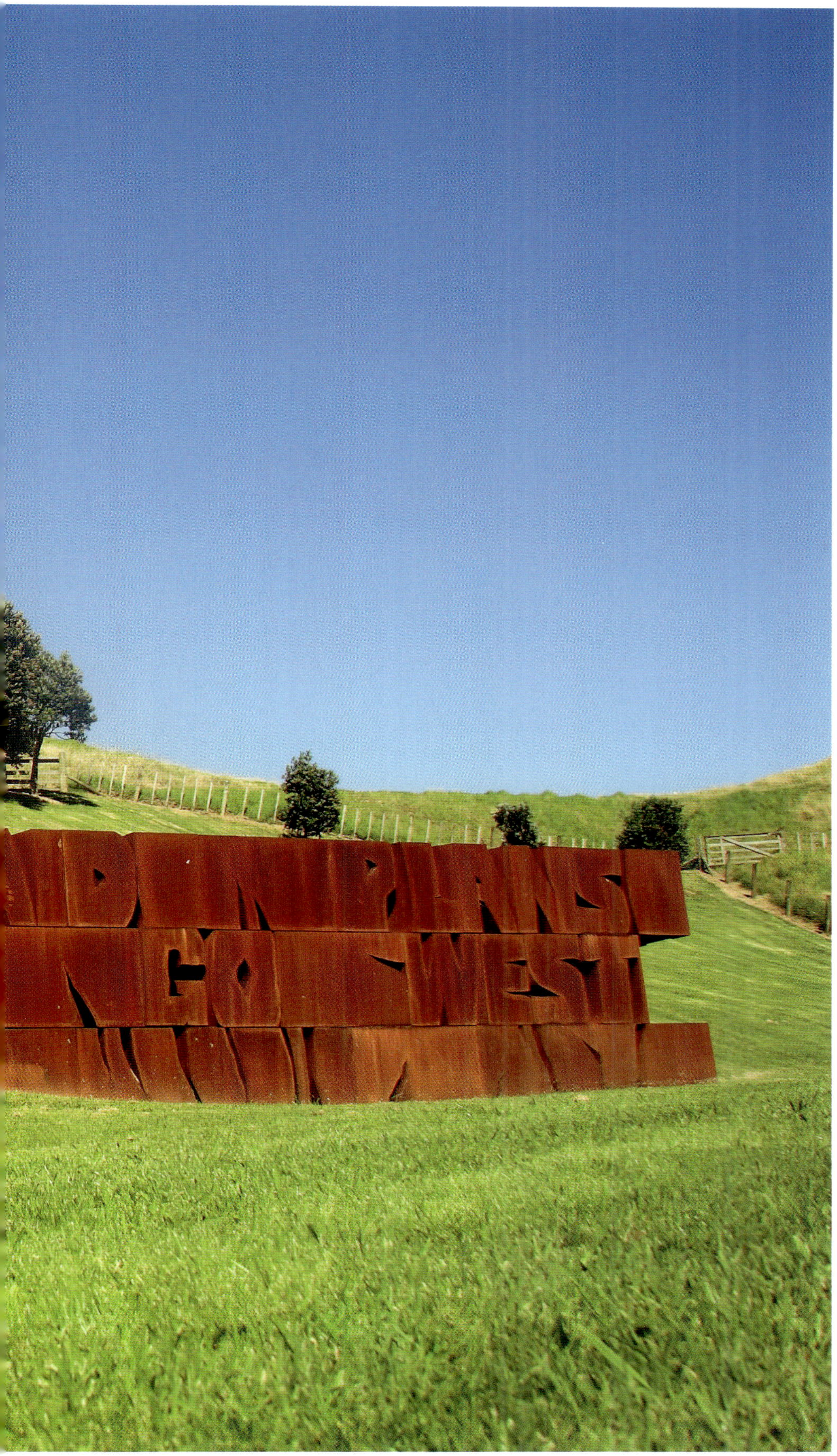

Anyone exploring the contemporary art scene in New Zealand will soon come across the names of John and Jo Gow. As a couple they could hardly appear more different: he is tall and lanky, she is small and wiry. Both are disarmingly open and masters of understatement. They see themselves as foster parents, devoting their entire energy to caring for their charges – particularly for the sculptures from their own native country, namely New Zealand. The Gows' names crop up everywhere: on the sponsors' panel at Auckland Art Gallery, on the list of initiators of the local biennial Sculpture on the Gulf, on the organising committee of the International Sculpture Symposium and in connection with the recent Rotoroa project, for which John Gow and a group of friends created a combination of artist-in-residence programme and eco-tourism on the volcanic island of the same name. The former broker made his fortune by raising funds for hit musicals such as *Cats*, *The Phantom of the Opera* and *Les Misérables*. He and his wife Jo – passionate art lovers and collectors – spent many years in London, during which time they travelled throughout Europe visiting museums and exhibitions. When John withdrew from his business activities due to age, he and his wife decided to return to New Zealand, "and there we saw art that no one knows in the international art market but that could certainly hold its own there," explains Jo.

The opportunity to do something for native artists arose, if anything, by chance when the Gows bought a former dairy farm on the island of Waiheke in the Hauraki Gulf. This island, formed from lava, is just a thirty-minute ferry ride away from Auckland, on New Zealand's North Island, and is a favourite destination at weekends. However, Connells Bay, the former dairy farm that is now the Gows' sculpture park, is at the other end of the island, in the south-east, far away from the buzz of weekenders. It has become a small paradise, hidden away with a private bay, where a young orca may appear and where the penguins come up onto the veranda to sun themselves. "It was just love at first sight when we saw the old farm with the three cottages by the beach," recalls John Gow. That same day they signed the sales contract. And then the work began – the three wooden cottages from the colonial era were in poor condition and the seventy-five acres of pastureland in the valley behind them had completely run wild. "The farmers had planted trees everywhere that were not native to New Zealand," remembers Jo. "We decided to completely reconfigure the entire property. In the end we planted over 20,000 exclusively native trees, ferns, flowers and shrubs!" When workers clearing the ground came across a huge stump of a macrocarpa tree split apart by a lightning strike the Gows asked a friend of theirs, the artist Fatu Feu'u, to carve a sculpture from it. He responded by creating *Guardian of the Planting* (1999) – a gigantic Janus-like head with two faces. From its position on a small, verdant plateau it looks from the steep hillside out over the entire narrow valley. This striking sculpture whetted the Gows' appetite for more works of art on their extensive property. "What we had done more or less intuitively when we were replanting suddenly struck us: we had created all sorts of different 'rooms' that would be perfect for sculptures." And since they had decided to only plant native fauna, it made sense only to invite New Zealand artists to make works for the newly restored estate. This focus gives Connells Bay its unique identity as a place offering an overview of works made by leading sculptors in New Zealand over the last twenty years. The Gows now decided only to commission site-specific works. "The artists have an entirely free hand in the locations they choose for their art. We invite them here, show them the place and tell them about the history of the farm. All the rest is up to them, although we do take a keen interest in the evolution of the works of art," explains John. Besides the art itself, the Gows also greatly appreciate the contact they have with the artists. The artists not only stay in one of the three delightful cottages, there is also an opportunity to get to know one another in this isolated spot. "And most of all we enjoy the meals we have with the artists, the profound discussions about God and the world, which have led to real, deep friendships," adds Jo. "That accounts for at least 50 per cent of the joy this project brings us."

In their various ways the sculptures and installations all engage with the natural setting. Peter Nicholls's *Tomo* (2005), a red, wooden band that winds its way like an artery through a grove of kanuka trees, bears the names of all four settler families that previously lived on the farm. Meanwhile Virginia King's *Oioi Bridge* (2005) not only makes the transition from flat pasture to grassy slopes visible, she has also turned it into a physical experience. This kinetic work of art, made from aluminium, is set in motion as soon as the visitor steps onto it, which in turn starts up a wild concert. The planks are loosely

Peter Nicholls's *Tomo* (2005): a red wooden band wends its way through a copse of kanuka trees like a pulsing artery.

Right: Fatu Feu'u carved the head of the *Guardian of the Planting* from the trunk of a macrocarpa tree that had been struck by lightning.

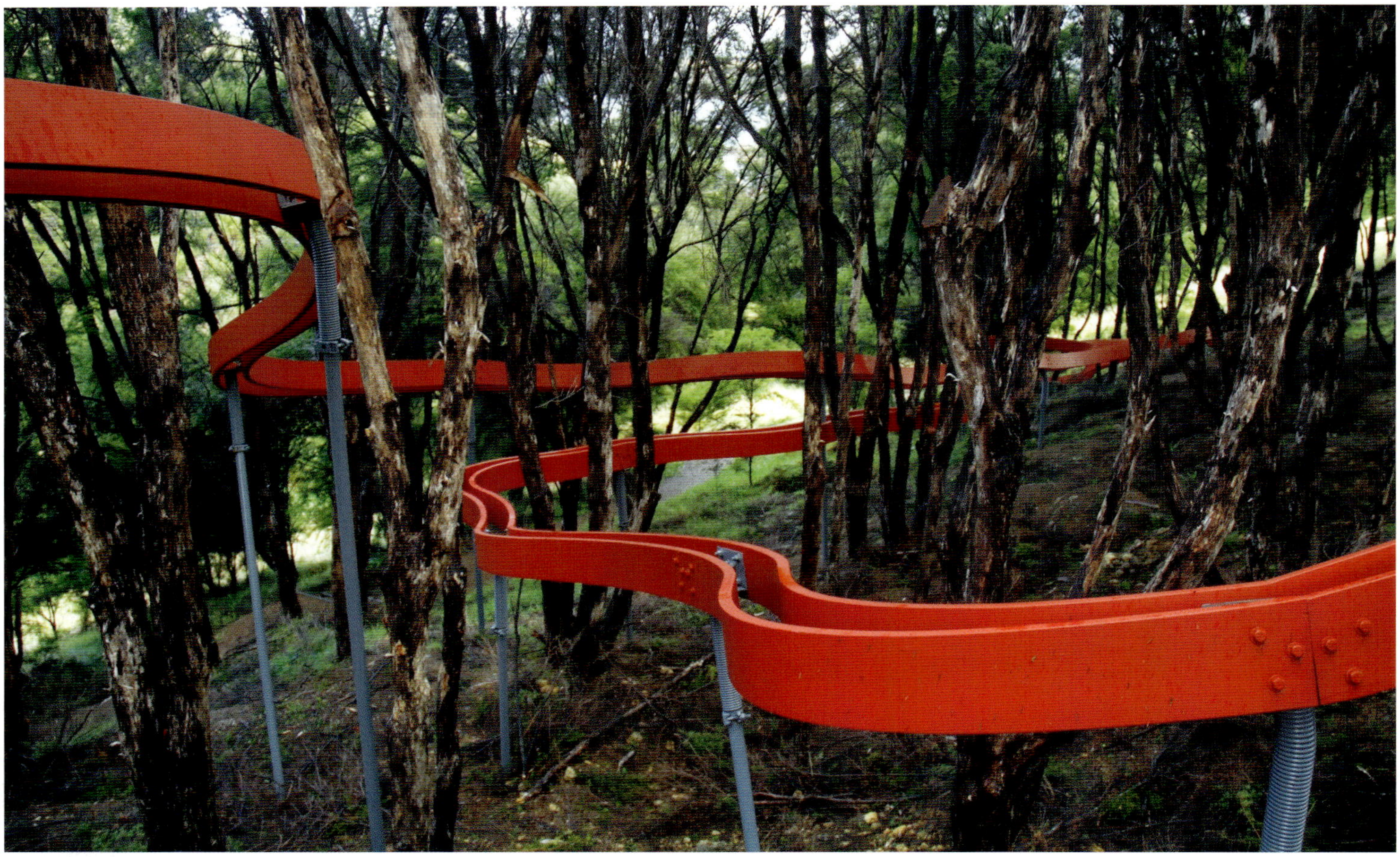

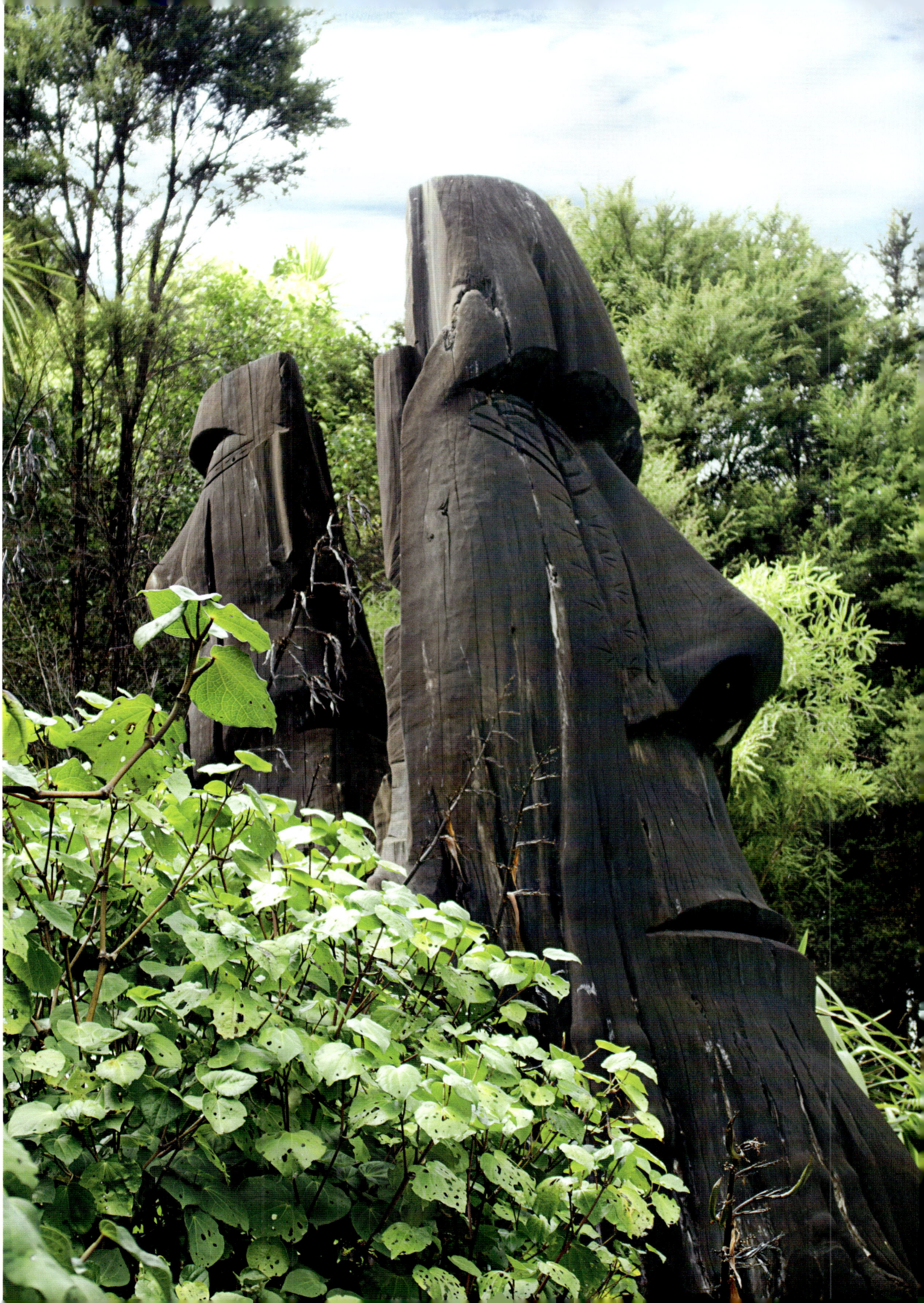

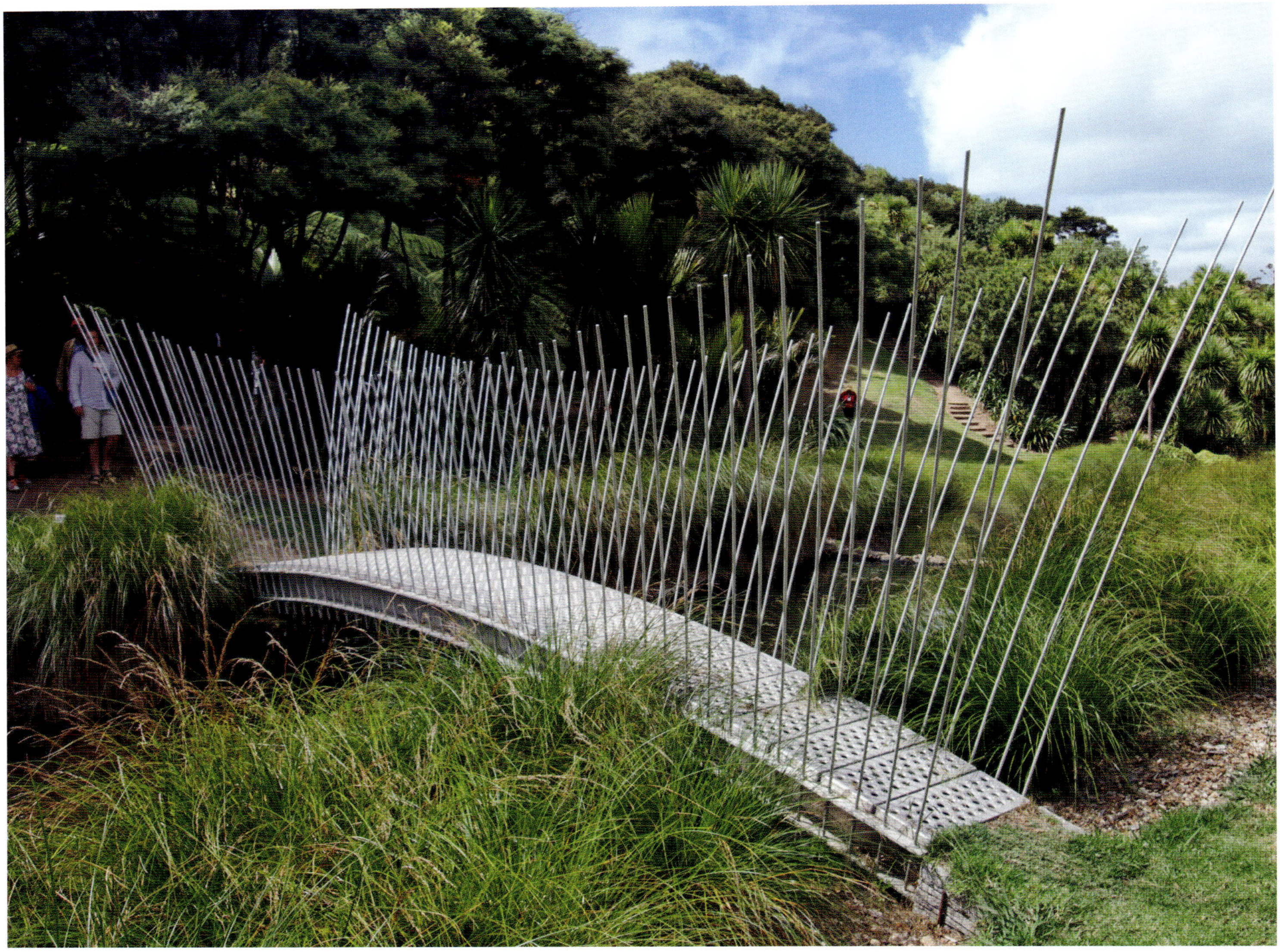

The design of the railings of fine vibrating aluminium rods on this bridge by Virginia King echoes the oioi grass that flourishes in this area.

connected and dangling underneath them are coins that noisily jingle and rattle. The idea of making a 'handrail' from tall, fine sandblasted aluminium rods came to King from the oioi grass, which abounds in that area. Phil Price's *Dancer* (2003), with its round, rotating golden-yellow discs made from carbon fibre, refers to the sea of yellow narcissi that surround this sculpture in spring. Sometimes even a catastrophe can lead to a work of art, as in the case of *Slip* (2003–04), an installation by Chris Booth. "When Chris was here a storm caused a major landslip on a hillside. Chris is a spiritual person, who is acutely aware of the vulnerability of nature. He had just made a work for the Kröller-Müller Museum in the Netherlands, which 'healed the land', as he put it, and so he created a related work for Connells Bay," explains John, pointing to the five baskets on the hill. "Technically it was an extremely problematic work, but now it's one of the best of all thirty!" Booth used between two and three kilometres of steel wire to create large baskets, which he then filled with greywacke rocks. The baskets were anchored in the ground – as a symbol of the section of land that had slipped away and as a warning of the ecological consequences of humankind's increasing manipulation of nature. And there is a similar connection in the case of the artificial *Skeleton Trees* (2006) by Regan Gentry that suddenly loom into view in the middle of a small area of woodland. Gentry made these from the fencing wire which farmers in New Zealand used to use to fence off a field once they had cleared a patch of land.

The numerous stories and issues that are worked into these sculptures and installations are of crucial importance to the Gows. "As well as being the basis for the close relationships

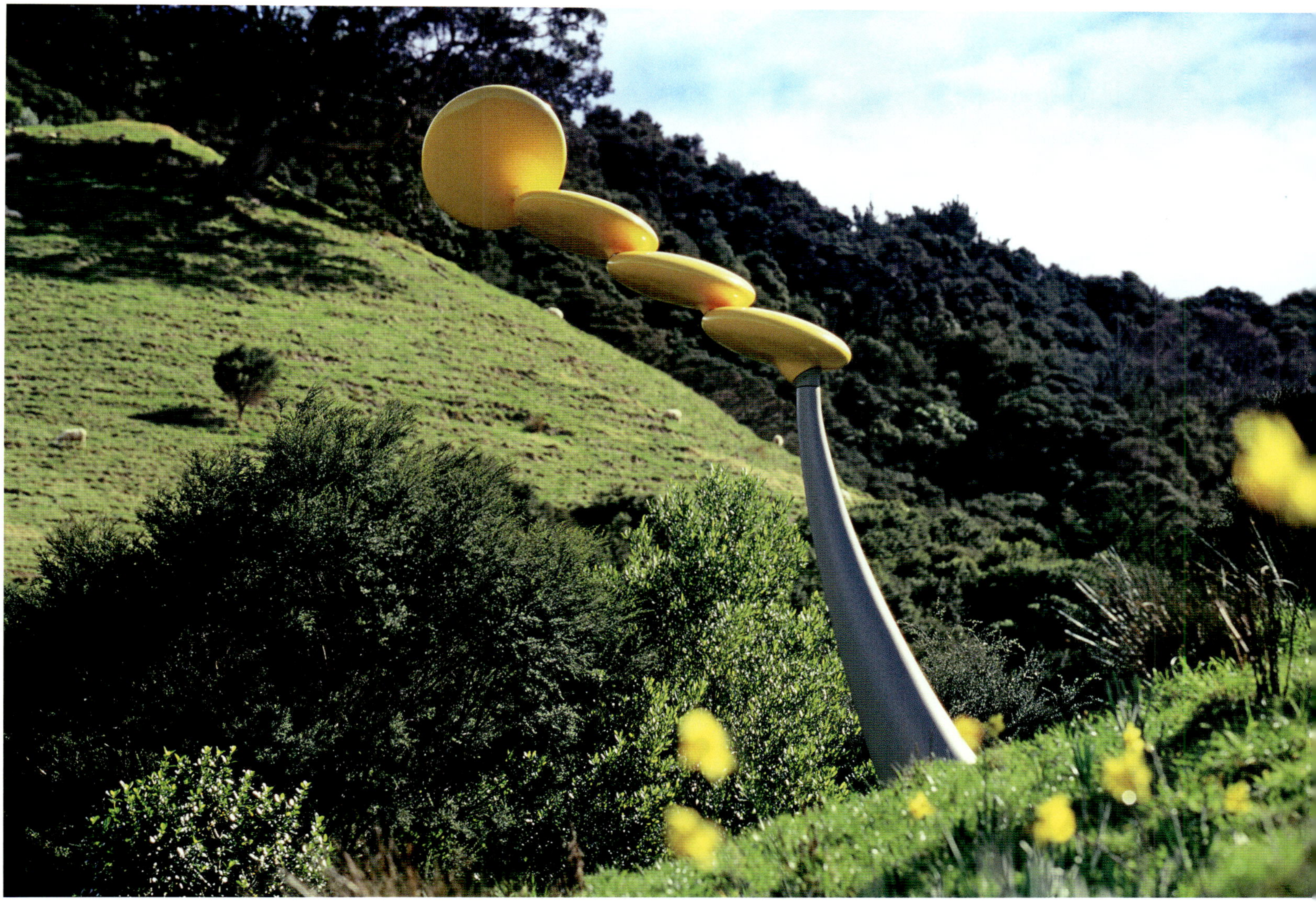

Phil Price is known for his kinetic sculptures. His *Dancer* is poised above a sea of flowers in the same colour.

we form with the artists, they are also a real point of contact with visitors," says Jo Gow. In order to experience the visitors' reactions to the works of art and to discuss their ideas, the Gows take the visitors on guided tours themselves, by arrangement. Some visitors rent the guest cottage and take the opportunity to revisit individual works or to enjoy the magnificent views of the sea and the many little islands in the area. "We have met incredibly interesting people that way, too. Some have sculpture parks of their own, others might be inspired to start one – and in the end we all sit together at our dining table as new friends," laughs Jo, looking happily towards the oversized kitchen plug, *Bung* (2008), that is bobbing about on the waves in the bay – an ironic commentary on climate change by the young artist Julia Oram.

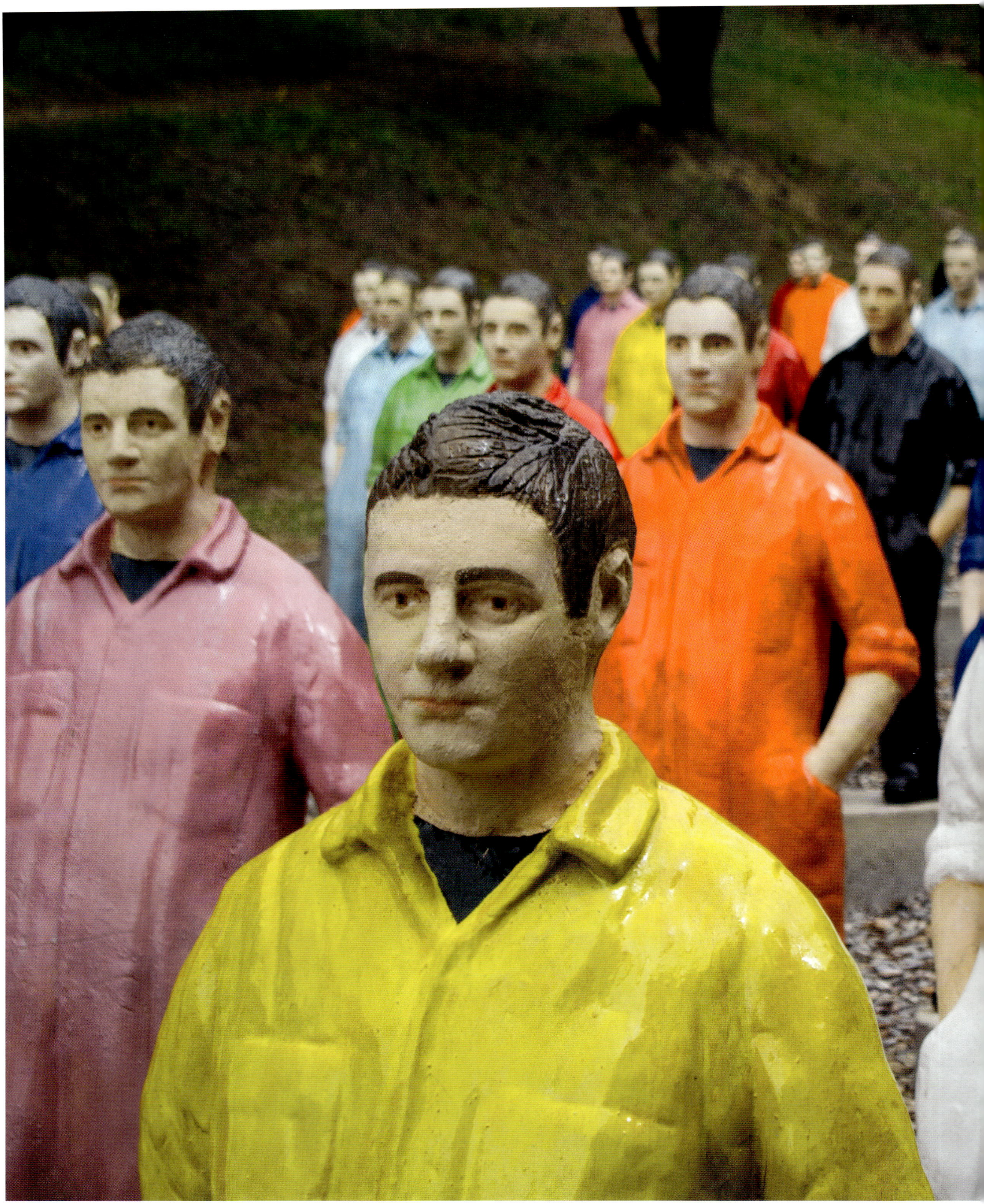

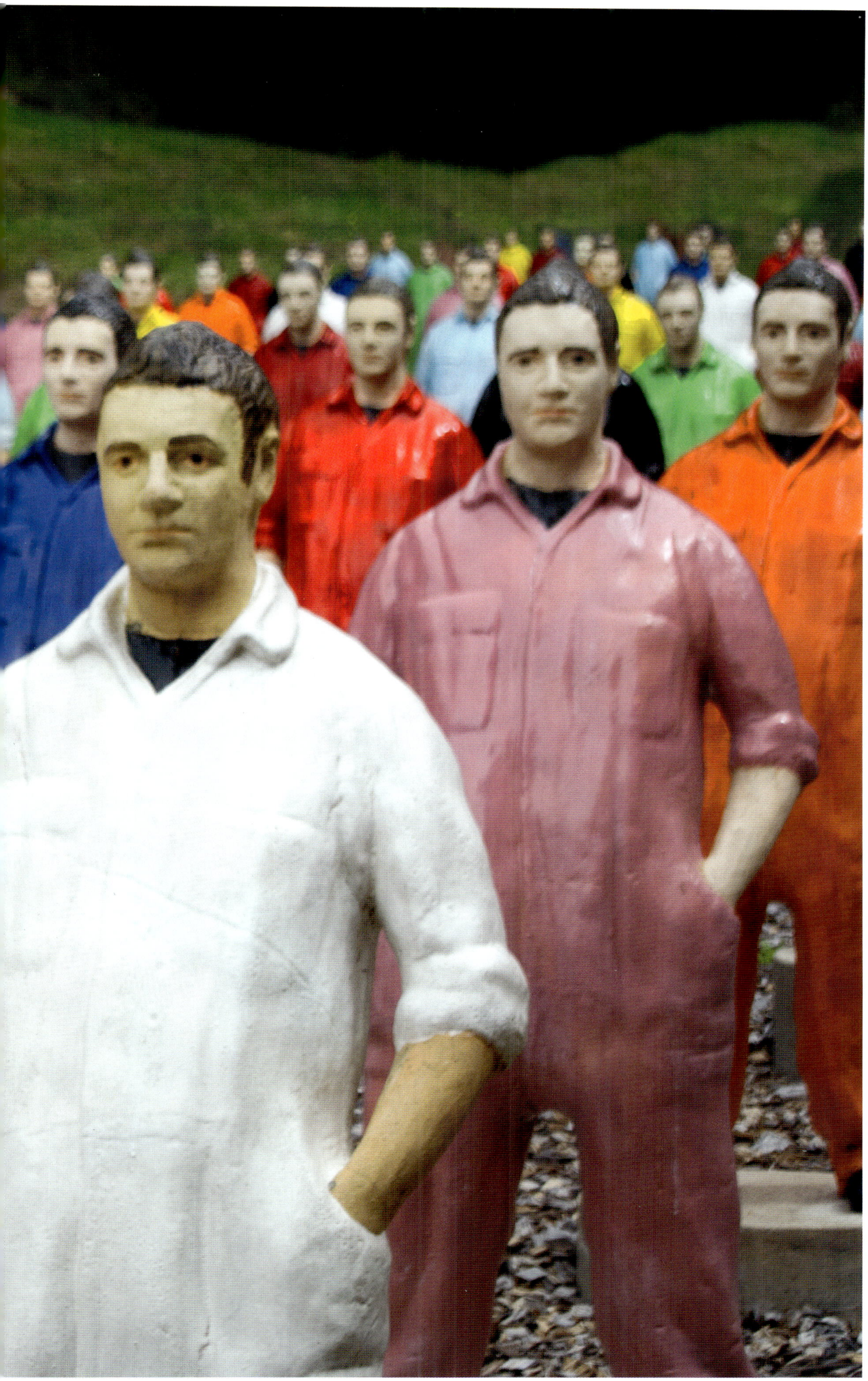

Vanish (2008–09): an army of 160 brightly coloured models of the artist Gregor Kregar fills the valley floor in the park.

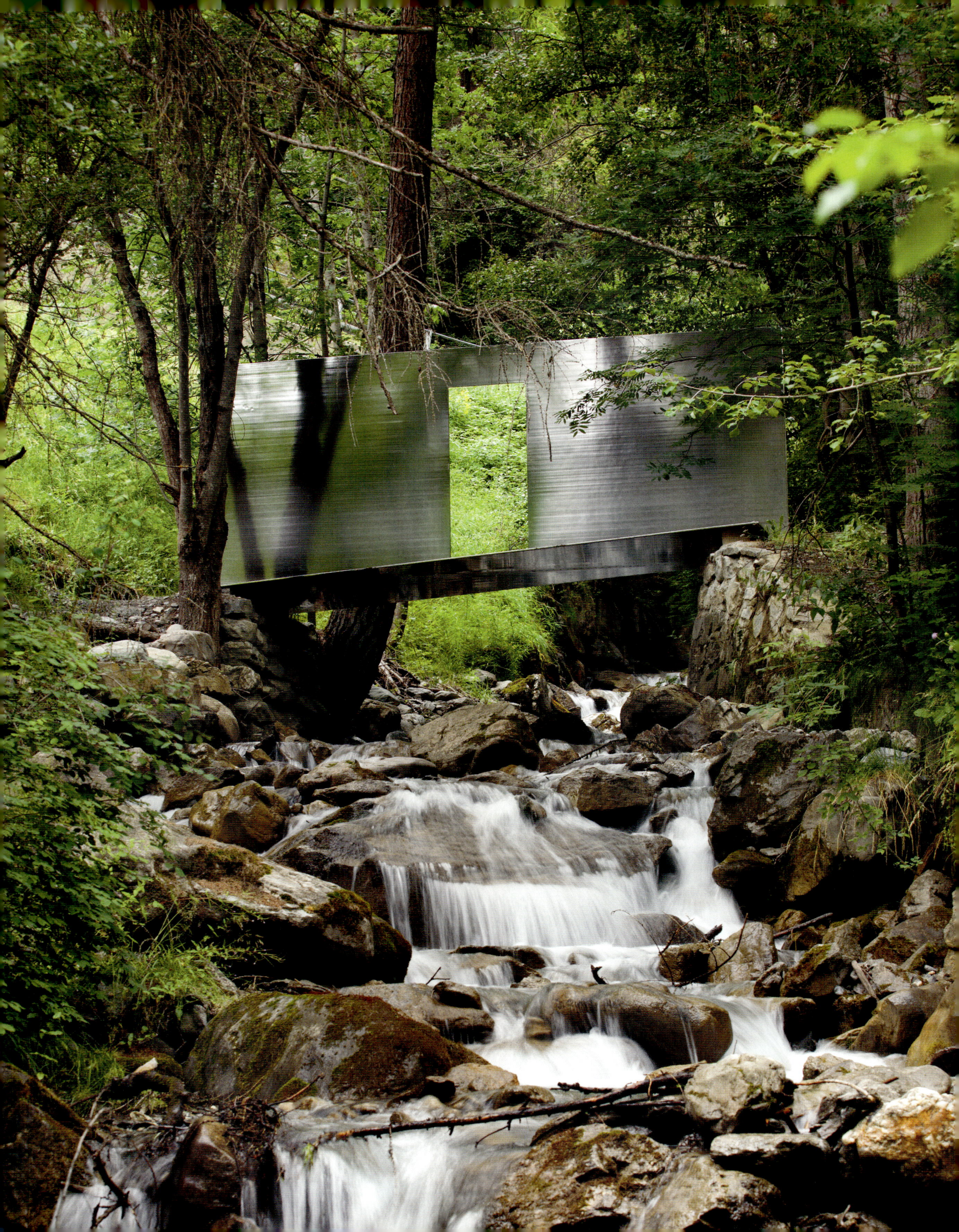

FANCIFUL ENIGMAS IN THE SWISS MOUNTAINS

FUNDAZIUN NOT VITAL, SENT, SWITZERLAND

A balancing act is needed to cross this mountain gorge on donkey heads. The donkey notably figures in Rhaeto-Romanic myths.

Randolinas, Rhaeto-Romanic for "swallows", is what the locals in Sent call emigrants who earn their money abroad but keep returning to their native town. Not Vital is one of these, deeply rooted in his own culture. The world is his studio, but each summer he goes home again. The people of Sent have a special loyalty to their small mountain village in the Lower Engadine. Only a minority still speaks Rhaeto-Romanic, or Romansh, as it is also called. It is the original language spoken in Switzerland. "The people of Sent are always homesick, even when they are at home in Sent," says Vital, with an inscrutable smile. He deliberately uses his native language in the titles of his works. He is acutely aware that Rhaeto-Romanic culture is threatened with extinction and, in response, has built up a rare collection of Romansh literature. He is mindful of his responsibility as a Romansh speaker: "As a minority we have to take care to preserve our own language, our myths and traditions." His family has lived in Sent since the fifteenth century. Life in the mountains, with its rugged landscape and long winters, has always been harsh and has never provided enough to feed everyone. So for centuries the people of Sent have gone out into the world. All the little, Italianate *palazzi* between the solid farmhouses in the centre of the village have been built by locals who have returned home – having made their fortune in neighbouring Italy as pastry chefs and café proprietors.

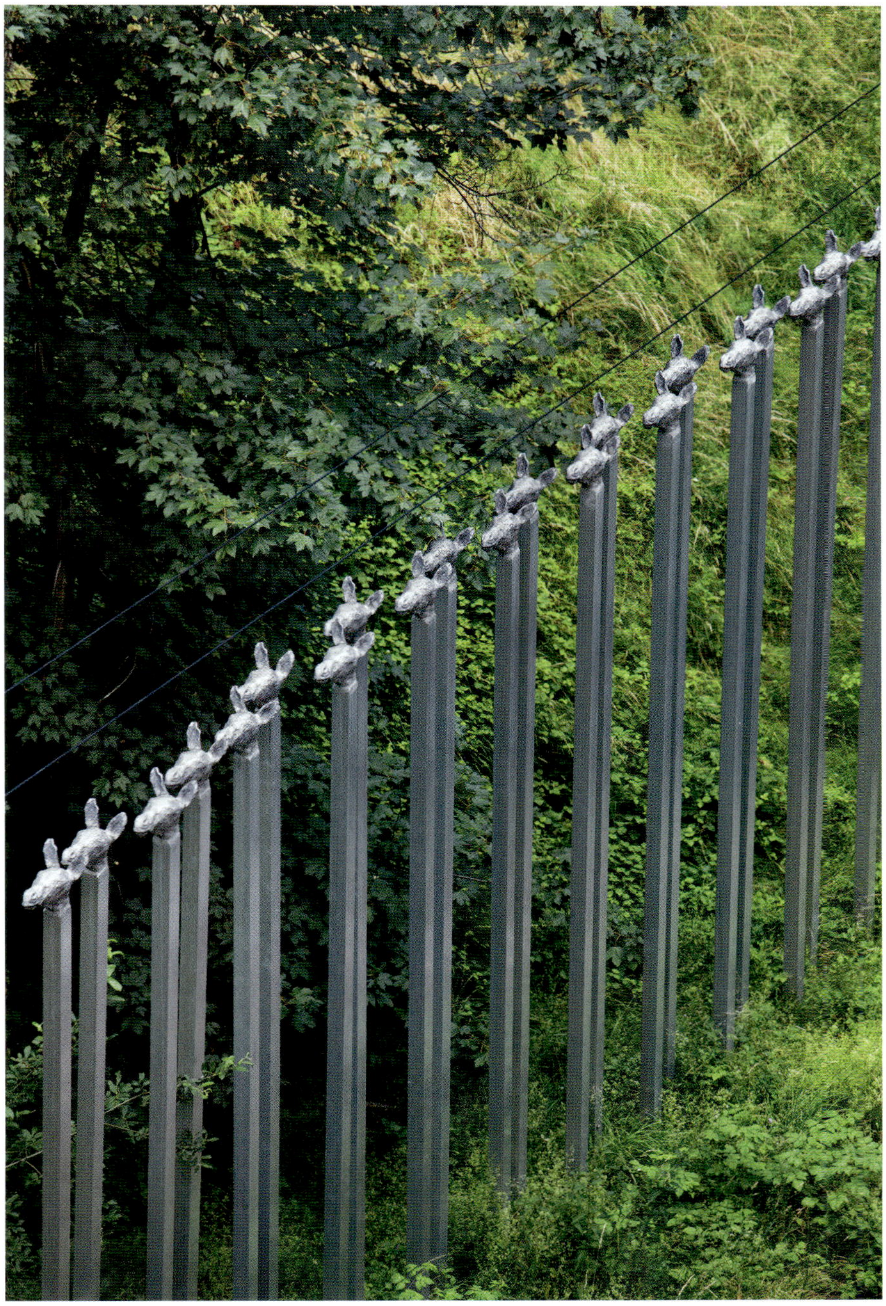

Left: Humans, art and nature – fluid transitions ensue at *Punt*, a bridge with a wall of highly polished stainless steel.

Not Vital has built something rather different in his birthplace: a whole realm of unique structures. Each is a work of art in its own right, created from his positively inexhaustible fund of ideas. Vital, a self-styled nomad, is constantly on the move and takes inspiration for his own work from locations all over the world. He is particularly drawn to extreme landscapes with intact cultural identities, of the kind he has seen in Africa, Indonesia and Brazil. By now he has built structures on almost every continent: unusual clay edifices, pyramids, towers and recently even a cave in Patagonia – "to watch the sunset.... Dwellings are a basic human need. At home our summer holidays used to be five months long and we were forever building huts in the forest."

In 1998 Vital bought an area of steep woodland on the edge of his native village of Sent. During the summer months, little by little, he has constructed extraordinary fantasy structures and installations, including bridges made from cast donkey heads, a tree with legs of ham and big bars of chocolate hanging in the branches, a tower with a hirsute exterior and a house that disappears into the ground at the push of a button. A realm that seems to have its roots in the wildest childhood dreams. And that is precisely what is happening here – Not Vital is making repeated forays back into his own childhood: "I can shut myself away here and experiment to my heart's content." This large area of parkland, home to an unusual concept and with its own history, is the perfect location for this. The original owner, Luzio Crastan (1880–1965) – as much a *randolin* as Vital – who made his money in Italy by trading in sugar and coffee, dreamt of creating a grand home for himself to retire to in Sent. In the 1920s he transformed the steep woodland into a magnificent park – with rare plants, such as mulberry trees and Douglas firs from Canada, with flower beds, topiary hedges, elaborate stairways and an extensive system of paths. He created a wide terrace to accommodate a semicircular swimming pool and a garden pavilion halfway up the grounds. And he planned to build a villa up above that, as the crowning glory of his estate. But due to a lack of funds and the outbreak of the Second World War it never came to pass. The parklands ran wild and became a meeting place and adventure playground for the village youths, including the young Not Vital, who remembers that "the park was always a magical place for us children." It was a place where they told stories and dreamt up fantastic ideas. And that is what Vital is tapping into with his intriguing sculptural edifices and installations, which all relate to particular aspects of this special place: unspoilt, intact nature, the close connection with the local population and its Romansh culture in which sagas and myths play an important part, and the artificial character of this park, which sits like an alien body in the midst of an otherwise entirely open, grandiose mountain landscape.

Together with his brother Duri, a well-known architect, and craftsmen from all over the world, Not Vital has been realising his fantasies in this secluded Alpine valley known as Val da Muglins: works of art somewhere between architecture, nature and sculpture. And Vital frequently uses the materials that are already at hand in the parklands: a wooden shed, *Chamonna süll'aua* (2002), was built around two trees and placed above the fast-flowing torrent in the valley; a huge, hand-woven nest, *Tuor da silenzi* (2003), has been installed in the crown of a twenty-metre fir tree, creating a place to enjoy the sunset or just to take in the spectacular view from the perspective of one of the now rare golden eagles that like to nest here. Directly next to it, a free-floating stage, the *Büna libra* (2011), made from dark red Corten steel, extends outwards above the slope. The audience for dance performances, readings and concerts sits on the steep grassy slope, as though in a "natural amphi-theatre", as Vital puts it. But even when there are no performances, at any time of day or year the panorama in the distance, with its snow-covered mountain peaks, provides a highly dramatic backdrop.

The extremely steep slope of the park makes considerable demands on the visitor. But even that is not enough for the artist: he insists that visitors interact with the art in ever-new ways. In the case of the donkey bridge, *Punt dals asens* (2001), visitors have to make their way above a ravine by balancing on the cast-aluminium donkey heads. And in the case of *Tuor per in pella bos-cha* (2001), in fact a tower-plus-bridge construction with dark red, artificial hair, the visitor climbs up from the valley floor inside an eighteen-metre-high narrow stairwell with endless steps. And anyone who decides to climb the ladder leading up a fir-tree trunk to the eagle's nest must have the necessary head for heights. Quite the opposite applies in the shed *Chamonna süll'aua*, in which an animal skin has been laid out. This is where

The centrepiece of the park is the free-floating *Büna libra*, made from Corten steel, with a breathtaking view of an unspoilt mountain landscape.

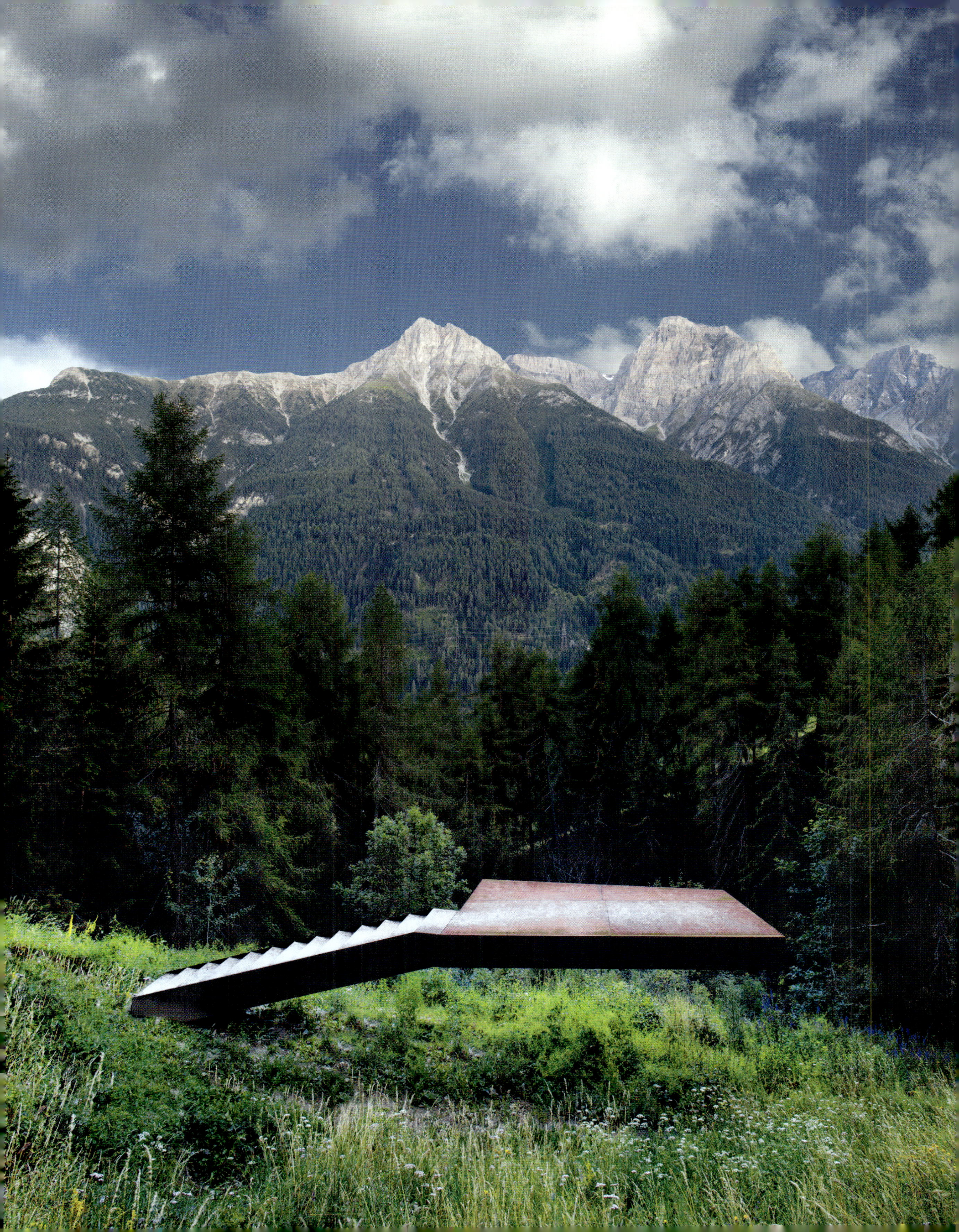

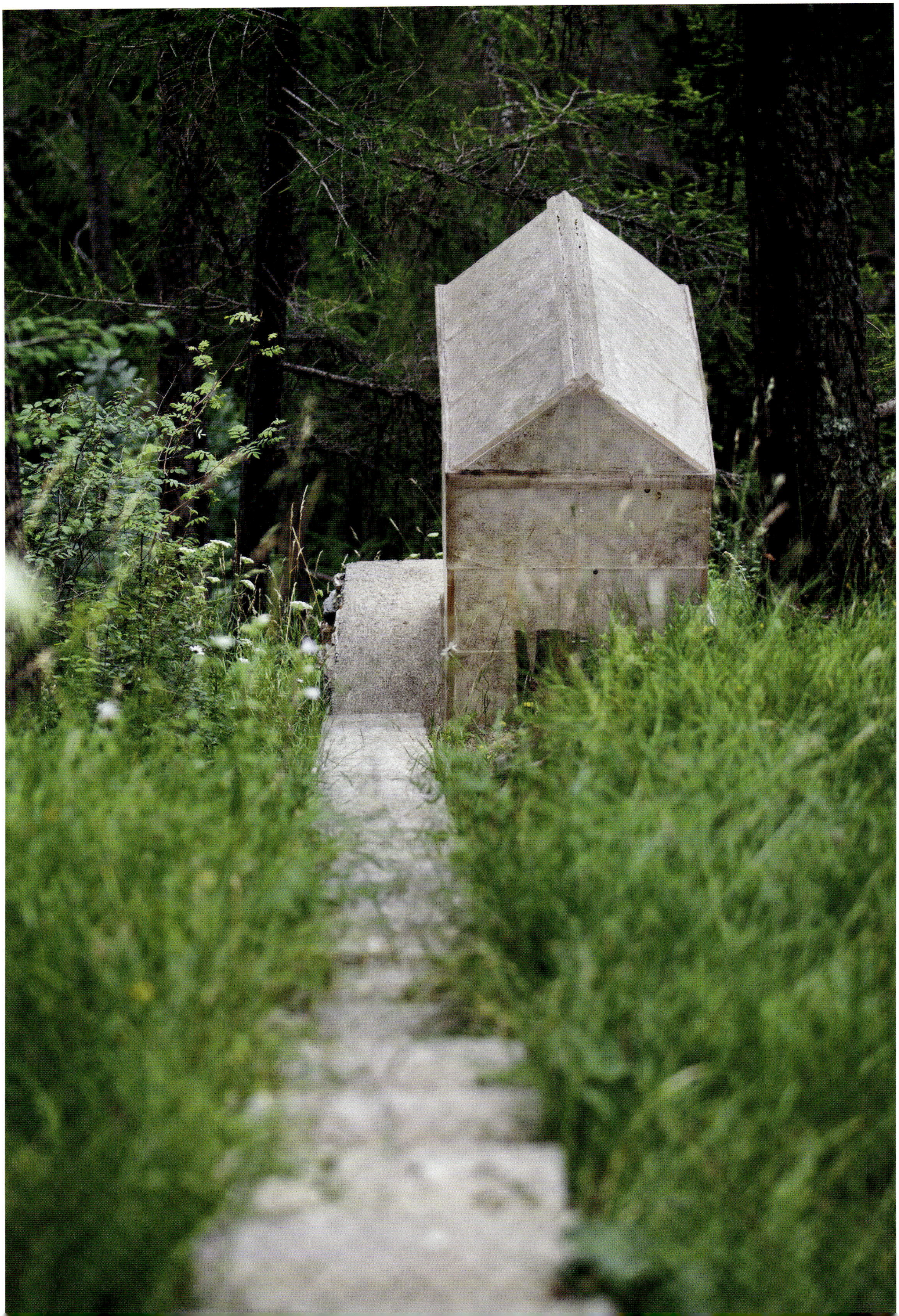

Left: Not Vital loves craftsmanship: the little chapel on the steep mountainside is built from satin glass that was hand-blown in Murano

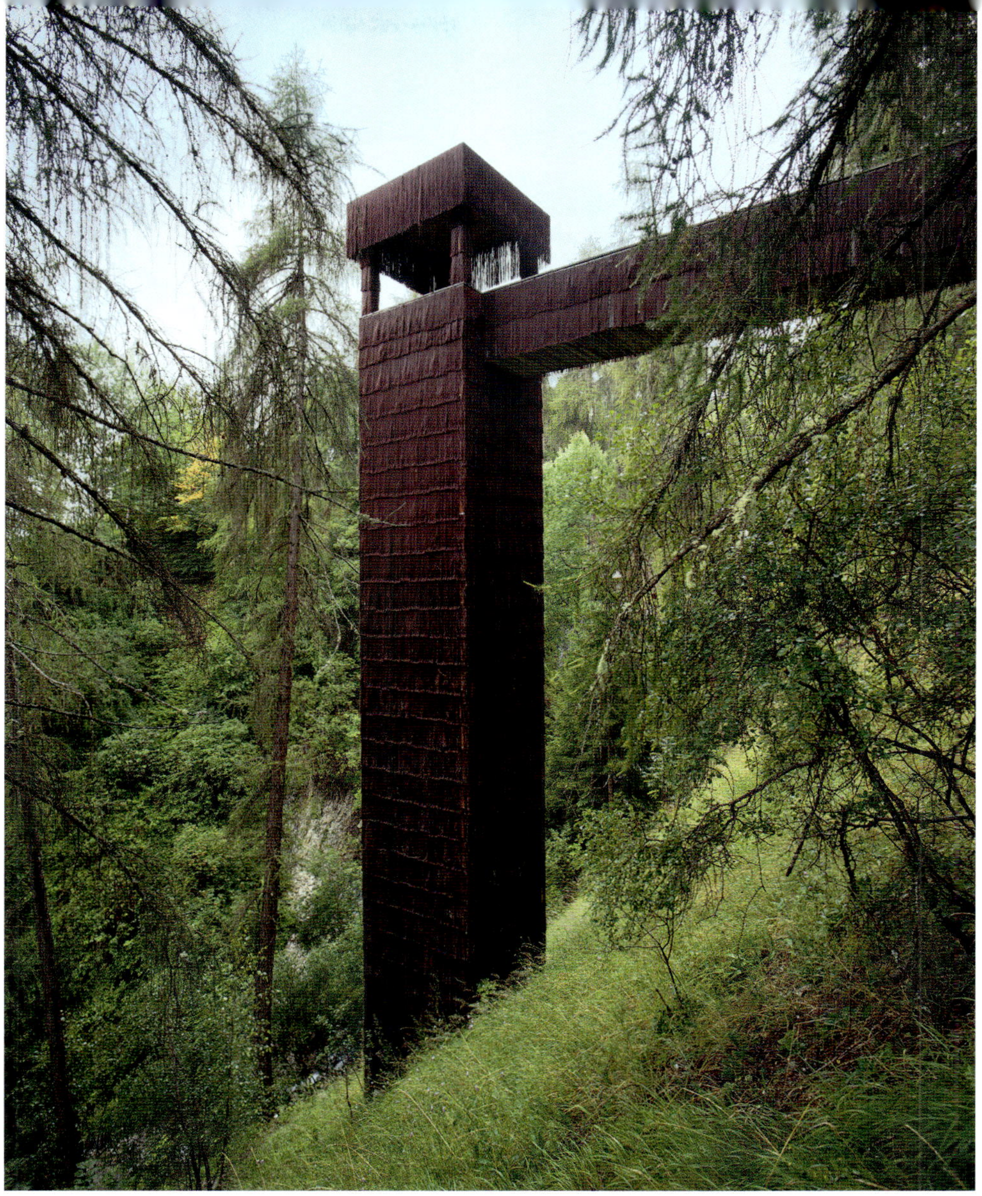

When the wind blows, *Tuor per ir pella bos-cha* – a bizarre fantasy structure clad with artificial hair – looks more like a kinetic sculpture.

Not Vital lies down, looks down to the water through the glazed opening and loses himself in the sound of the rushing stream: "Nature, my alternative to psychotherapy for people with burnout," says Vital. "The walls are soundproofed so that all I can hear is my own heartbeat and the rushing water. And as time passes my heartbeat slows – it's my way of relaxing." Much higher up in the parkland there is a small, white, chapel-like structure, *Chamonna da glatsch* (2002), clinging to the slope. In amongst the dark trees it gleams like an ice cube in the sunlight. This building, like the steps that lead to it, is constructed from satinised white glass – made by a famous Venetian master glassblower. "With this work I wanted to show what it is like if you fall into a crack in a glacier." Vital loves to come up with absurd surprises. He takes devilish delight in the sight of a visitor drenched with a mighty jet of water released from a camel's head at the push of a button, and he loves it when, in the case of *Josujo* (2007) – Romansh for "up, down" – a remote-controlled house suddenly disappears in its entirety, like a Fata Morgana, in the freshly mown meadow. Vital's comment, not without a touch of sarcasm, is that "that's what we should do with all the holiday homes around here, which are only occupied for a few weeks each year."

Using man-made materials such as glass, steel, aluminium and even synthetic hair, Not Vital underlines the dysfunctionality of his structures and their parallel existences as sculptures that seem to merge into nature. With its splendid, dark red hair, *Tuor per in pella bos-cha*, for instance, almost appears to float in the wind. Its solid structure dematerialises between the trees. By this means Vital creates a harmonious connection between nature and 'artificial' works made from non-organic materials. Another particularly impressive example of this is the 'invisible' bridge *Punt* (2008), that is to say, a wall made from highly polished stainless steel, with a doorway cut into it, that reaches across the river like a bridge. As the visitor crosses he or she becomes invisible, disappears. The reflections on the surface of the wall blur the boundaries between reality and fiction. The human being and the work of art are either swallowed up by nature – or lose themselves in nature. The perfect metamorphosis.

Not Vital's *Lotus* and the swimming pool created for the previous owner, an émigré who made his fortune abroad.

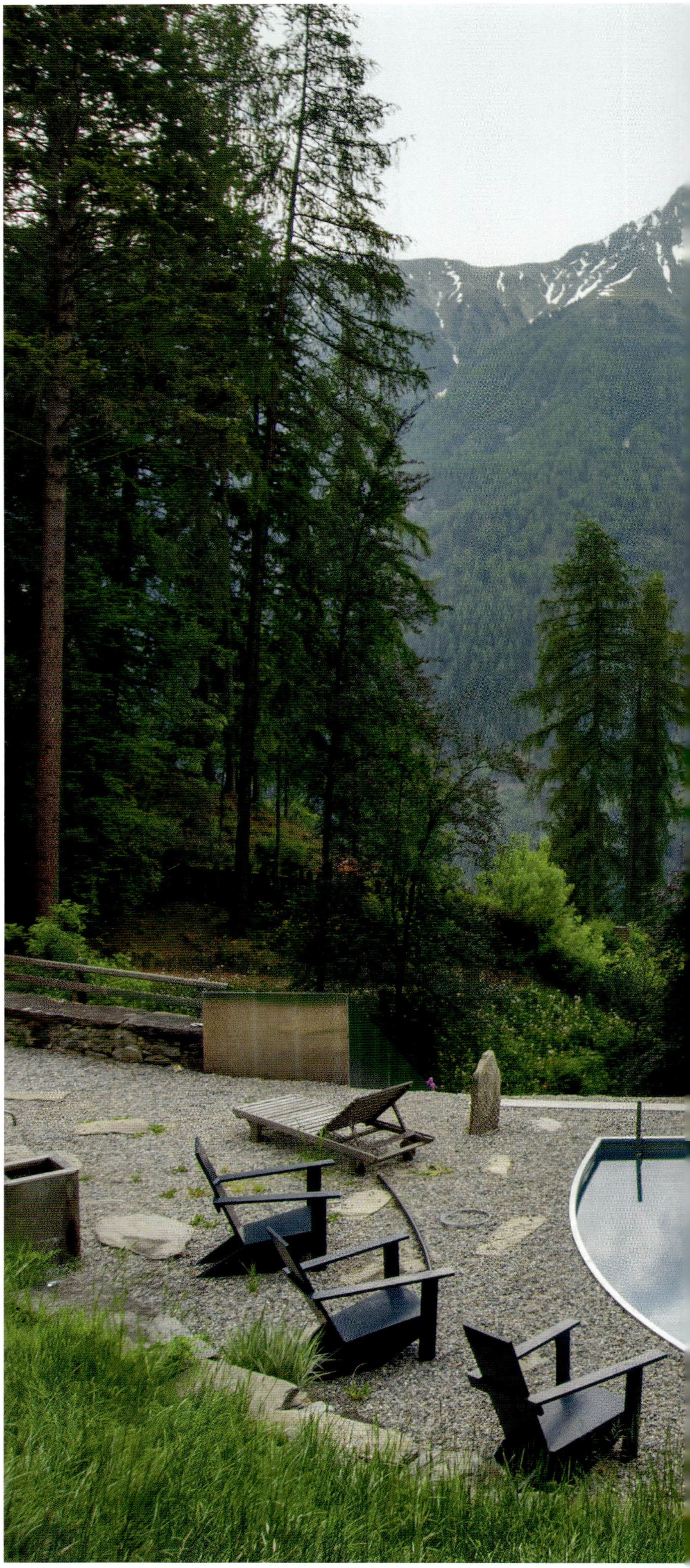

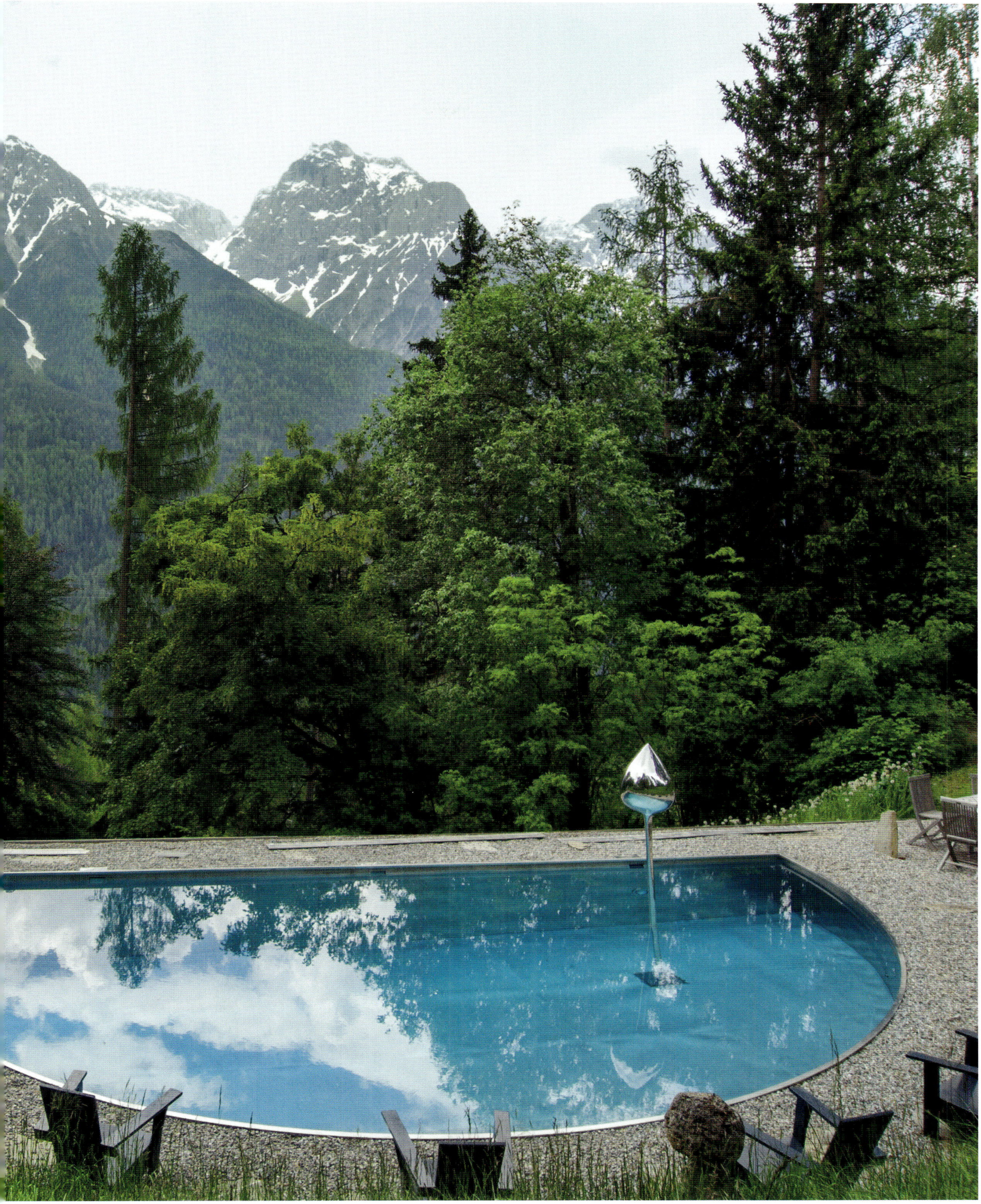

Fundaziun Not Vital, Switzerland

A SURREAL GARDEN OF EDEN
LAS POZAS, XILITLA, MEXICO

Even as a child Edward James (1907–1984), the son of an American railroad magnate and a Scottish aristocrat, was something of a misfit in British society with his wild dreams of rooms that can fly. When he came into his vast inheritance at the age of twenty-one he decided that his residence – Monkton House on the West Dean Estate in southern England – should be painted lilac. Trompe l'œil banners 'hung' from the windows and he embellished the façade with tall bamboo plants. The English upper classes were shocked but his Surrealist friends were thrilled: "He is crazier than all the Surrealists put together. They act it, but he is the real thing," enthused Salvador Dalí, who designed his famous *Lobster Telephone* (1936) for James, his friend and patron. The Surrealists flocked around him. In 1937 René Magritte painted a portrait of Edward James entitled *La reproduction interdit*. This wealthy bird of paradise supported the Surrealists' cause by helping to fund their journal, the *Minotaure*. He also financed legendary productions by the choreographer George Balanchine for the latter's new company Les Ballets, founded in 1933 – not least partly for the sake of his own wife, the dancer Tilly Losch, who also performed that year in *The Seven Deadly Sins*. James was not only a close friend of the Surrealists, he was also one of the most important collectors of their work. And yet these same friends did not appreciate the poetry and paintings that he himself produced. When his marriage failed after just a few years and the Second World War broke out some years later, James decided to leave Europe for good.

Having first travelled to the United States, James subsequently settled in Mexico. In 1947, not far from the little mountain village of Xilitla in the northern province of San Luis Potosí, he found what he already knew from paintings by his Surrealist friend Max Ernst: a wild, abundant tropical landscape with exotic animals – ocelots, jaguars, birds, butterflies and snakes. He bought a completely overgrown estate where there had once been a coffee plantation and named it "Las Pozas" – after the sequence of nine pools fed by a spectacular waterfall. This was the perfect site for cultivating orchids, which he started to do in this tropical wilderness with the help of his friend Plutarco Gastélum. James had met Gastélum some months previously

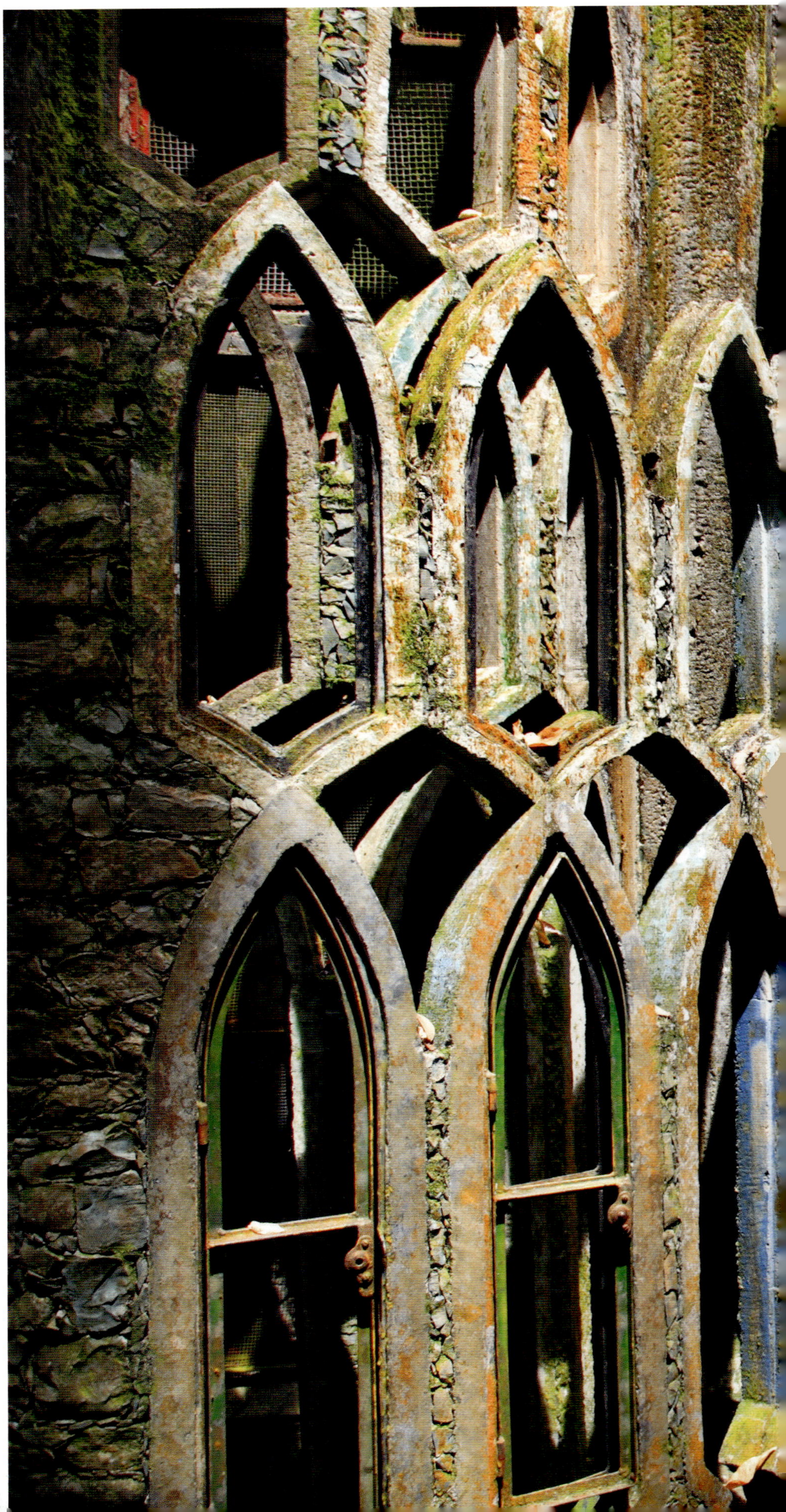

Edward James built palatial residences for his birds and animals, such as this *House of Birds* with its echoes of Gothic churches.

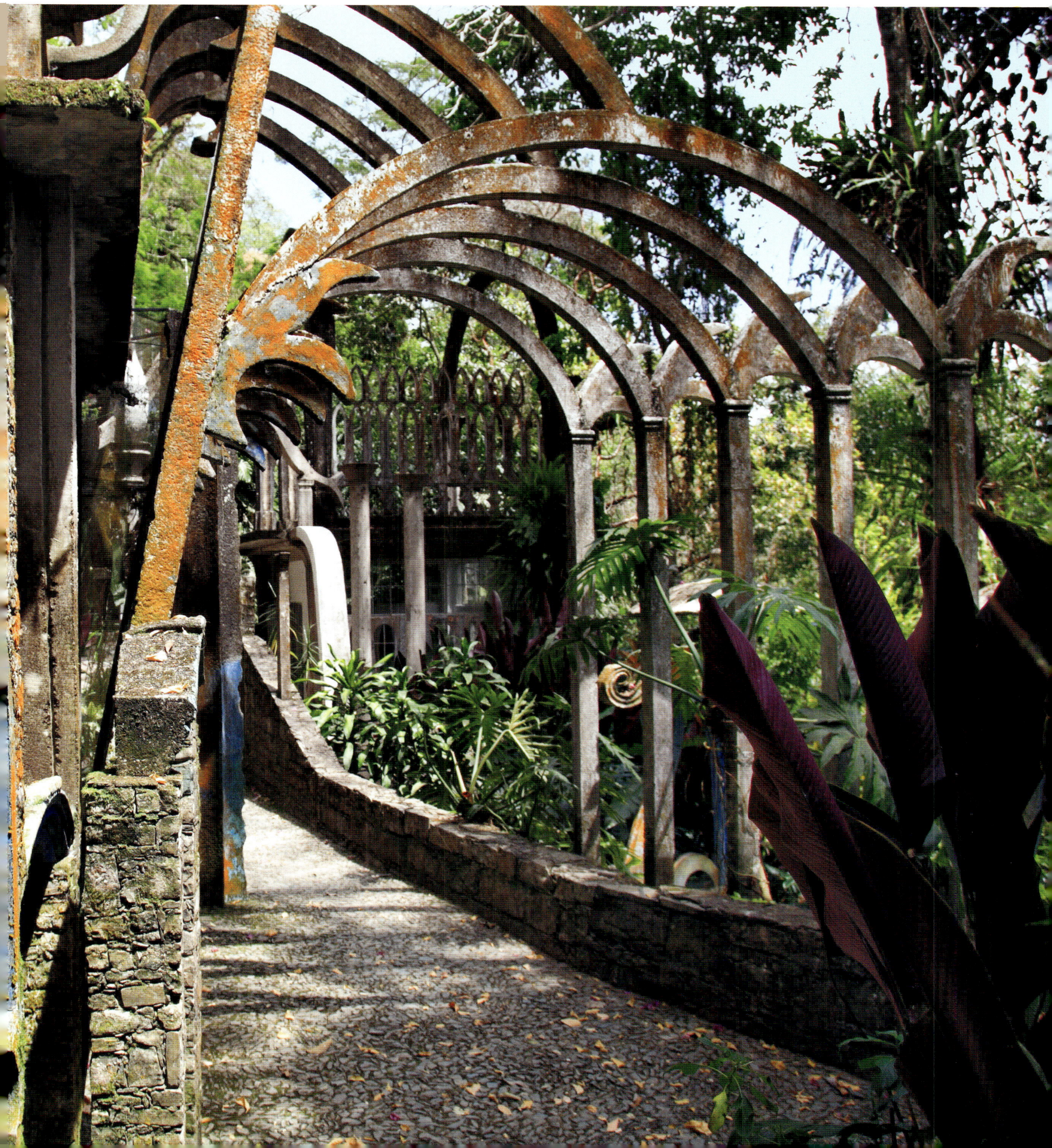

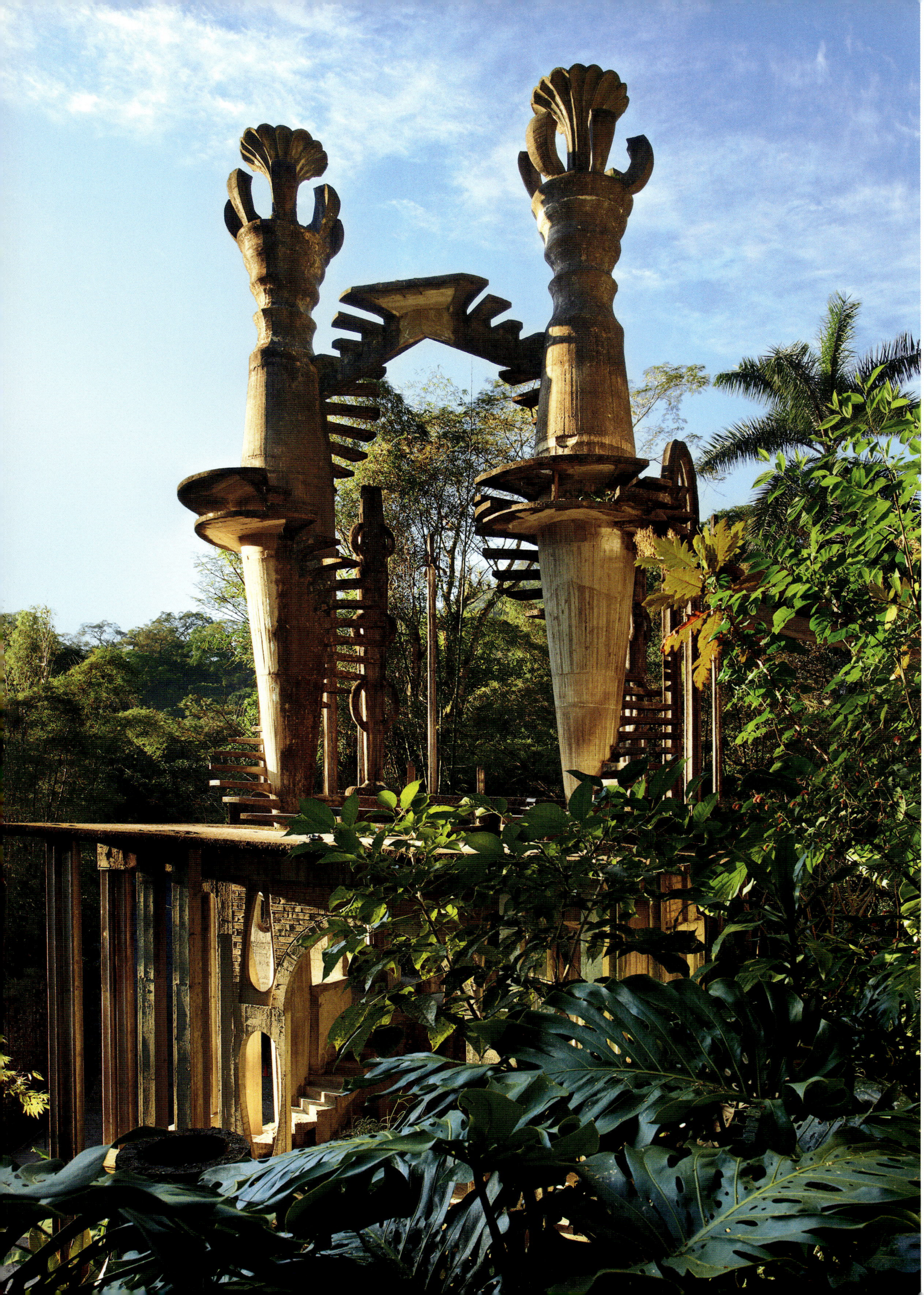

Left: Surrealism cast in concrete: ***Stairway to Heaven*** **with spiral staircases going upwards into thin air.**

when he had been staying in a hotel and found himself dictating telegrams on a daily basis to Gastélum, who was employed in the telegraph office. This developed into such a close friendship that Plutarco Gastélum decided that he and his wife, along with their four children, would move to Xilitla with his new European friend, who was determined to cultivate orchids. What began as friendship soon became the basis for an extended family. With Gastélum's help James built a home in Xilitla, which he named El Castillo – a house with bizarre towers, staircases and open rooms with plant-like columns. The Gastélum family lived there with their eccentric "Uncle Edward" until his death.

For years the orchids flourished in the nearby rainforest until, in 1962, an unusually harsh frost in early winter ruined all of James's hard work. And it was at this point that he decided to make casts of rare plants, which he could install in nature for all time. This soon led to the creation of autonomous, surreal architectural sculptures, some as much as thirty metres in height – open structures with spiral stairs leading into nothingness, free-standing door frames, upside-down columns, 'meaningless' terraces and oversized sections of bizarre ornaments. Fragmentation became a principle here. James set about creating an exotic landscape of ruins, overgrown with moss and wholly integrated into the tropical vegetation, which future archaeologists would see as the puzzling remains of a lost civilisation. Multitudes of workers transformed his fantasies into abstruse buildings and idiosyncratic sculptures – if necessary, by night. But James paid his workers well and they deeply admired his strange ideas and his generosity. Little by little James invested almost his entire fortune in his dream. Plutarco Gastélum became his closest ally and coordinated all the construction projects in the park, generally with no more than a sketch as a guide to what James had in mind. "Sometimes when James was travelling he would just send a postcard with a particular detail encircled – a Gothic window in a French cathedral that had caught his attention and that he wanted to have at Las Pozas," recalls Plutarco's daughter Gabriela Gastélum. Her father was the only person who could understand the ideas of his "crazy friend" so that, with the help of the local craftsmen, they could be realised as architectural sculptures. James was not only active as an artist. He also installed a power station in the wilderness so that he could create a magical atmosphere in the park at night. Part of his elaborate lighting system even included a device that could create 'coloured rain'.

Labyrinthine, narrow paths snake along artistically layered stone walls through the steep site with its thirty-six sculptures, columns, pagodas, temples, fountains. These cover an area of ten acres hidden in a wilderness in an estate comprising two hundred and fifty acres in total. Some of these structures have become part of their surroundings to such an extent that it is almost impossible to find them. When trees fell over James devised supports and re-laid the paths in that area. Ever the Surrealist, it was his aim that everything at Las Pozas should be free – from nature to the wildlife to the architectural structures, which have no function and are only there for aesthetic reasons. The titles of these structures sound like the names of fairy tales: *The House with a Roof like a Whale, The House on Three Floors Which Will in Fact Have Five or Four or Six.* James used to go to the park every morning at dawn and spend the entire day in the world

After a sharp, early frost destroyed his orchids, Edward James replaced them with painted poured concrete exotic flowers.

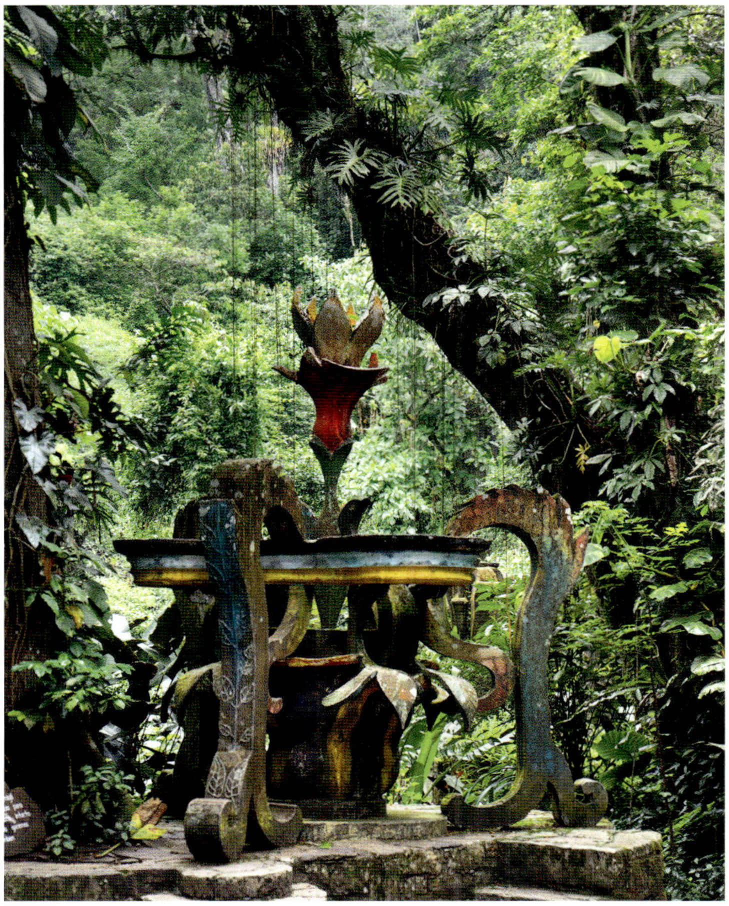

he had created just for himself, the birds and the animals. With parrots on his shoulder and a pig by his side he would spend hours walking through the park. "With his flowing robes, beard and a long hiking pole in his hand he looked like Saint Francis, the patron saint of the animals," says Zaira Linan, a native of Xilitla, who now has overall responsibility for the park. "It was how you would imagine life in paradise." James used to lie for hours in a stone sarcophagus listening to the sounds of the birds in the rainforest. He would meditate at the top of a hill in the mist of low-lying clouds or bathe naked in a pool that looked like an eye. And while he sat at the middle of the pool, in the 'eyeball', fish in the outer pool would swim around him. Meanwhile peacocks would walk proudly around the wide edge of the pool, displaying their splendid plumage.

James had a passion for the birds and animals that he lived with. He built palaces and pagodas with filigree columns and Gothic windows especially for these wild creatures. When his alligator was close to death he engaged a composer to write a requiem for him and his friend José Horna fashioned a wooden chamber for his boa constrictor. Directly above it James had a small room where he would work on his poetry and take his siesta – with the snake wrapped around him and his favourite birds in a half-open aviary by his side. Sometimes Plutarco's wife Marina had to prepare sumptuous banquets for his guests, "but the guests at his table were not human beings, they were creatures from the jungle," Gabriela tells us.

When Edward James died in 1984, he left his park to his 'substitute family' – Plutarco and Marina Gastélum and their four children, with whom he had lived for over twenty years. "We loved him for all his wonderful ideas. He was so kind to us, he took us with him on his trips. We learnt so much from him," says Gabriela with deep gratitude. For some years the family tried to maintain the park themselves, but this became increasingly difficult due to a lack of funds. Exposed to the vagaries of the tropical climate the surreal world of sculptures at Las Pozas was in danger of falling into decay. In 1991 the park was opened to the public for the first time. In 2007 the Pedro and Elena Hernández Foundation took the park over and, together with Cemex (Mexico's leading cement manufacturer) and the regional government, set up the Fondo Xilitla, which now oversees the conservation and maintenance of Las Pozas.

Edward James left a poem for posterity, which he wrote at Las Pozas, in which he describes his life in a heavenly paradise created by human hand from one man's vision:

"I have seen such beauty as one man has seldom seen;
therefore will I be grateful to die in this little room,
surrounded by the forests, the great green gloom
of trees my only gloom – and the sound, the sound of green.
Here amid the warmth of the rain, what might have been
is resolved into the tenderness of a tall doom
who says: 'You did your best, rest' – and after you the bloom
of what you loved and planted still will whisper what you mean.
And the ghosts of the birds I loved, will attend me each a friend;
like them shall I have flown beyond the realm of words.
You, through the trees, shall hear them, long after the end
calling me beyond the river. For the cries of birds
continue, as – defended by the cortege of their wings –
my soul among strange silences yet sings."

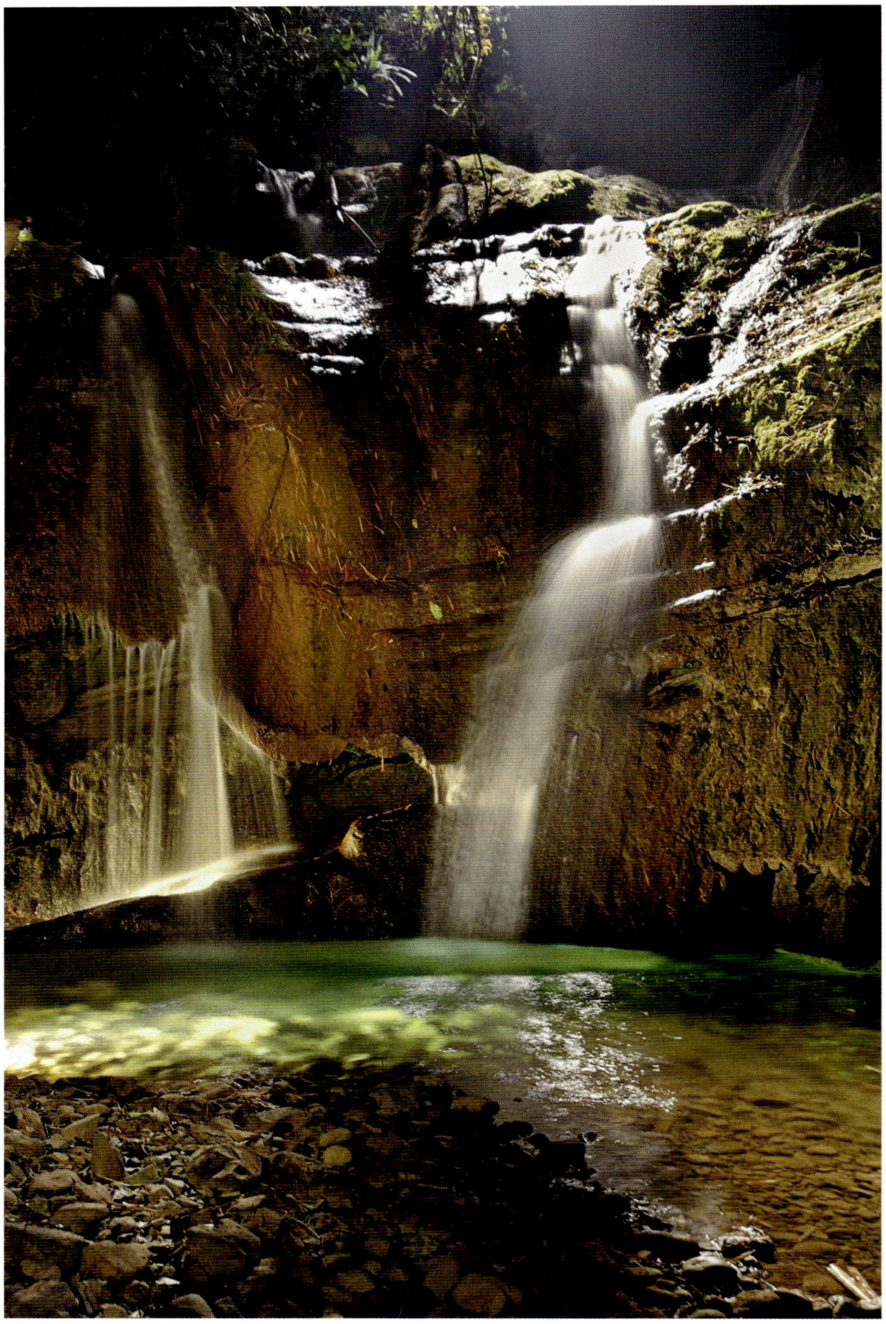

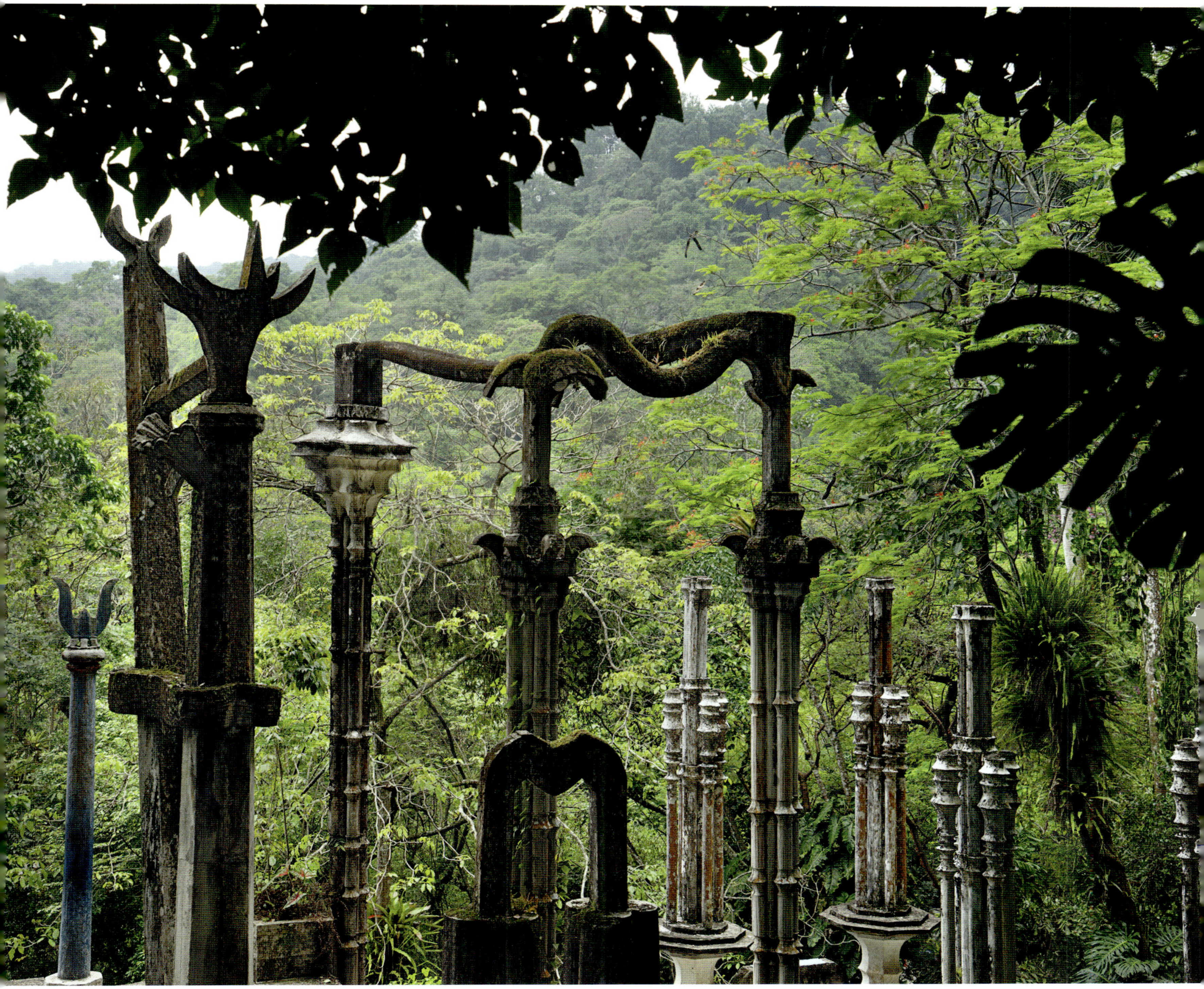

The *House with Wings* emerges in the jungle like an apparition. Far from supporting anything, the columns mutate into bizarre structures.

Left: *Las Pozas*: the many natural pools beneath the cascading waterfall not only gave the park its name, they were also home to James's alligators.

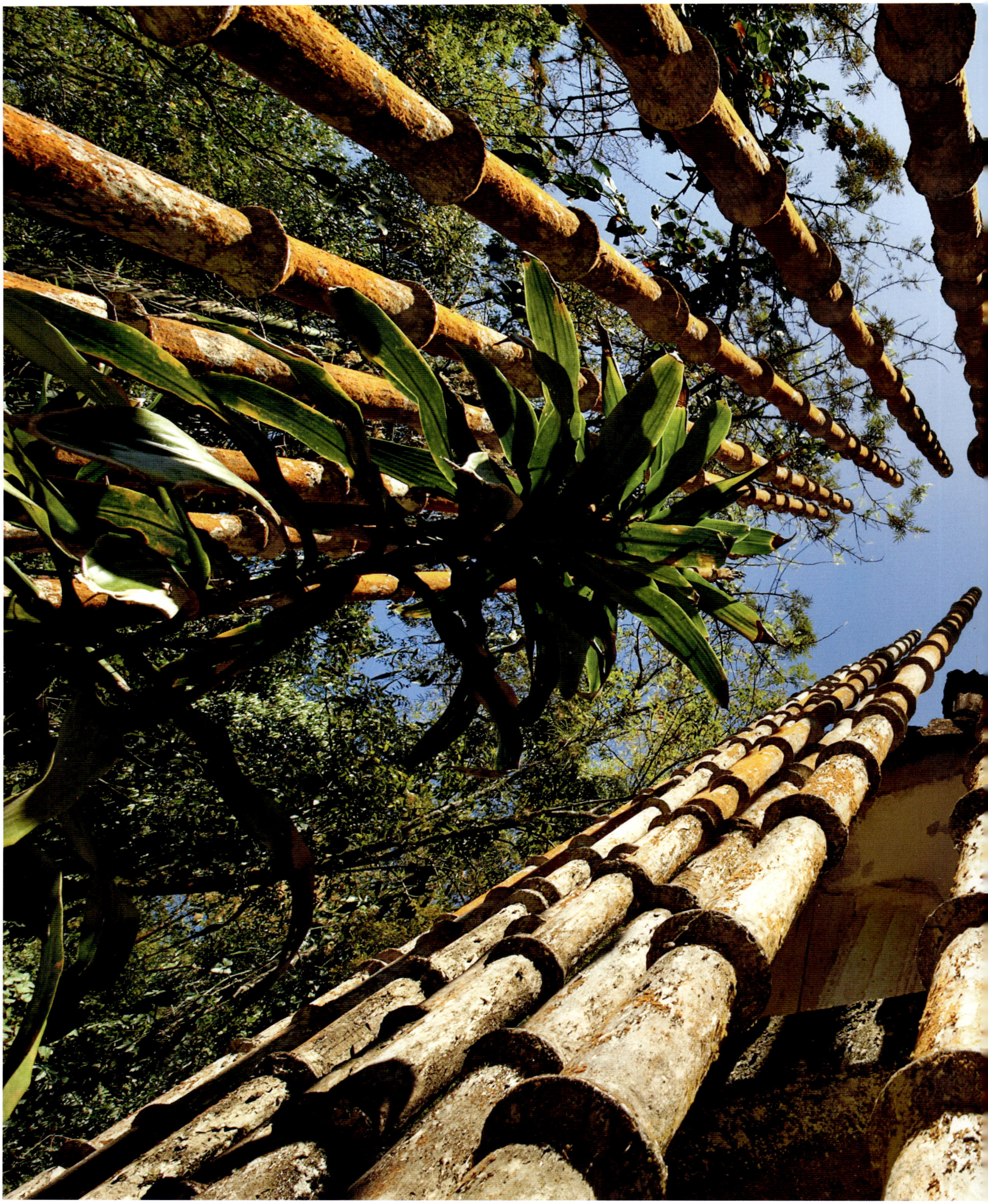

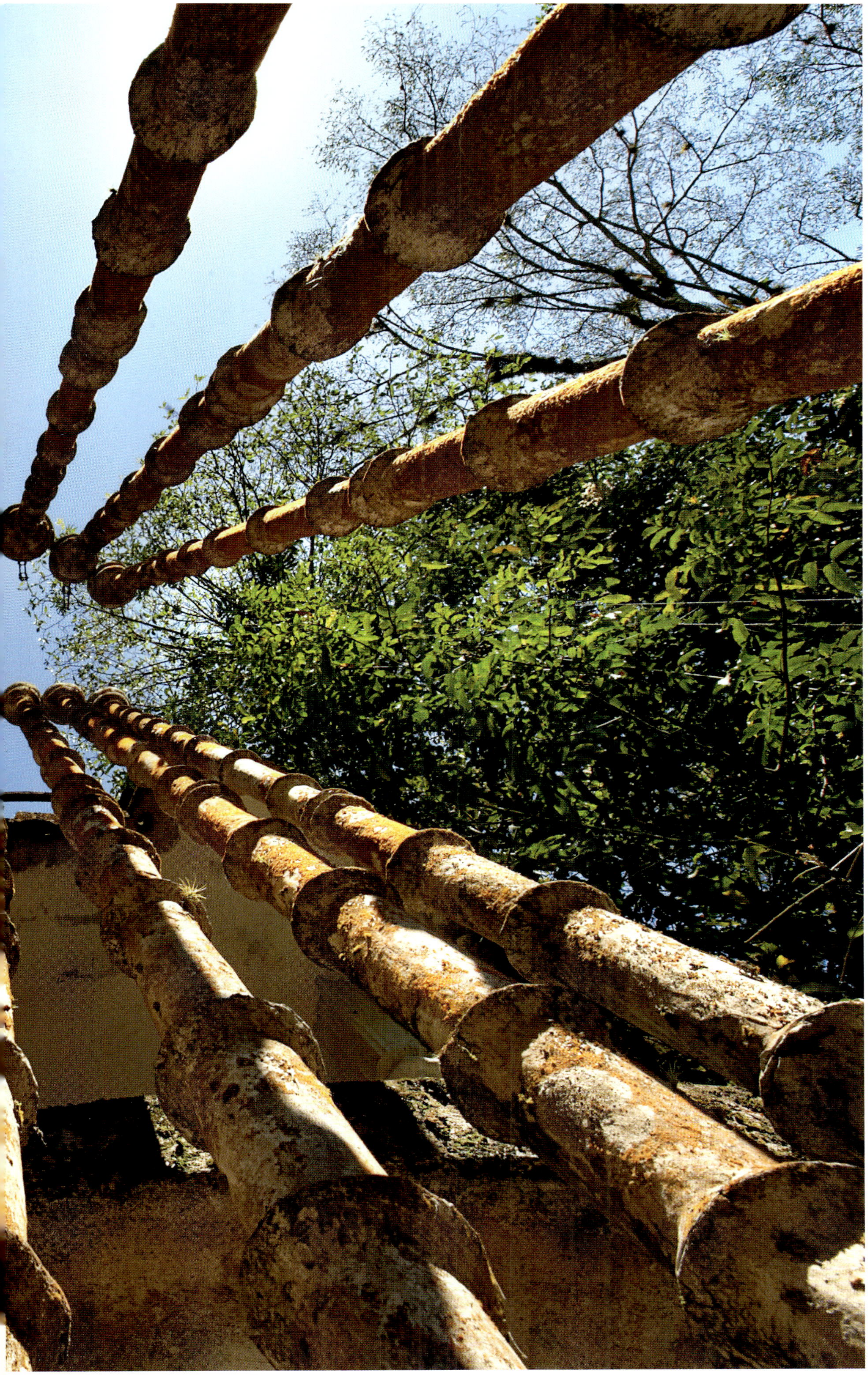

A forest of artificial bamboo posts 'grows' by the *Bamboo Palace*, a good 15 metres in height and rising up past all four storeys.

REVIVING TRADITIONS
FATTORIA DI CELLE, SANTOMATO DI PISTOIA, ITALY

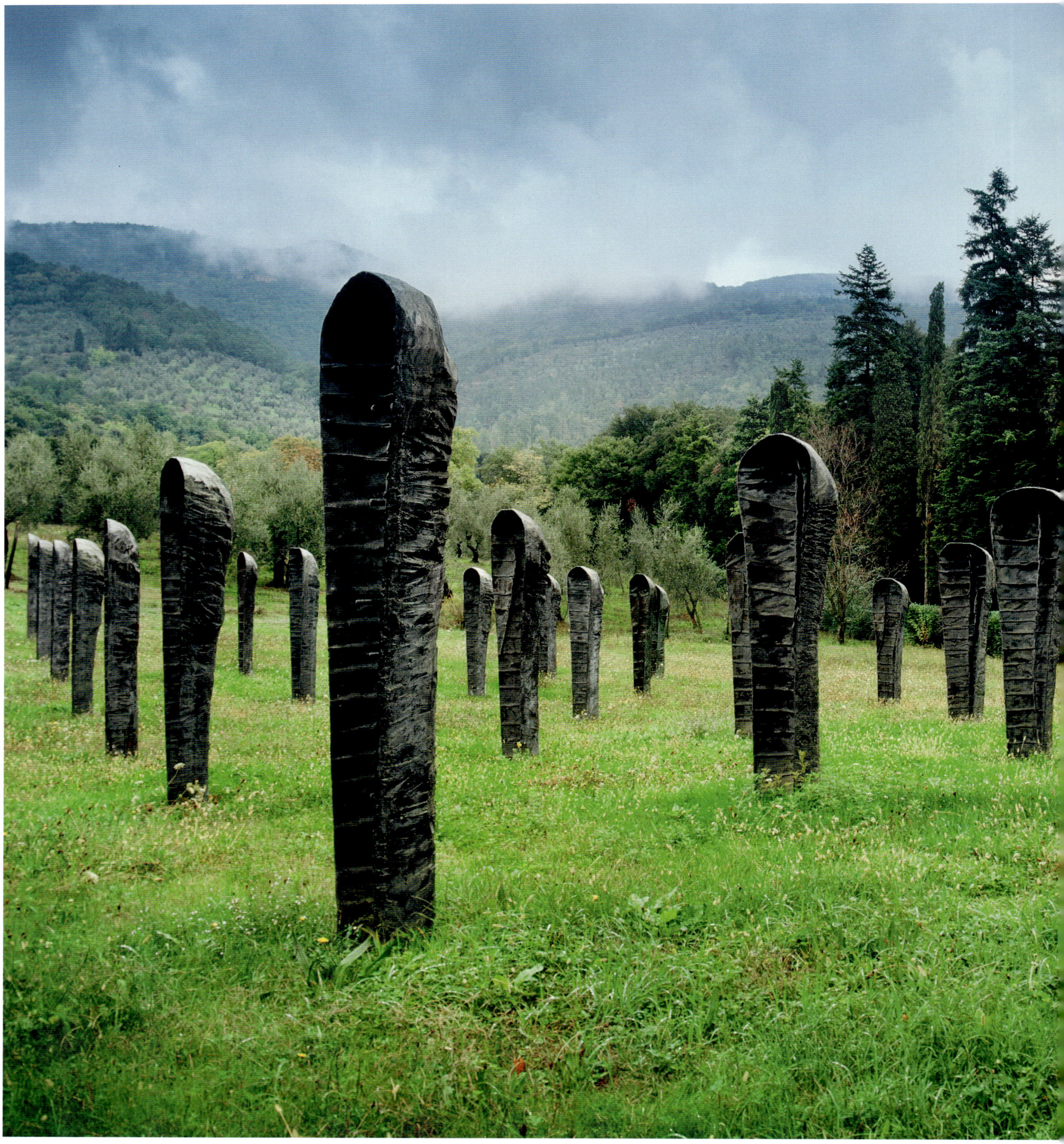

Magdalena Abakanowicz, ***The Catharsis***: **a stele-field of life-sized figures with neither heads nor limbs which seem more like upright burial caskets.**

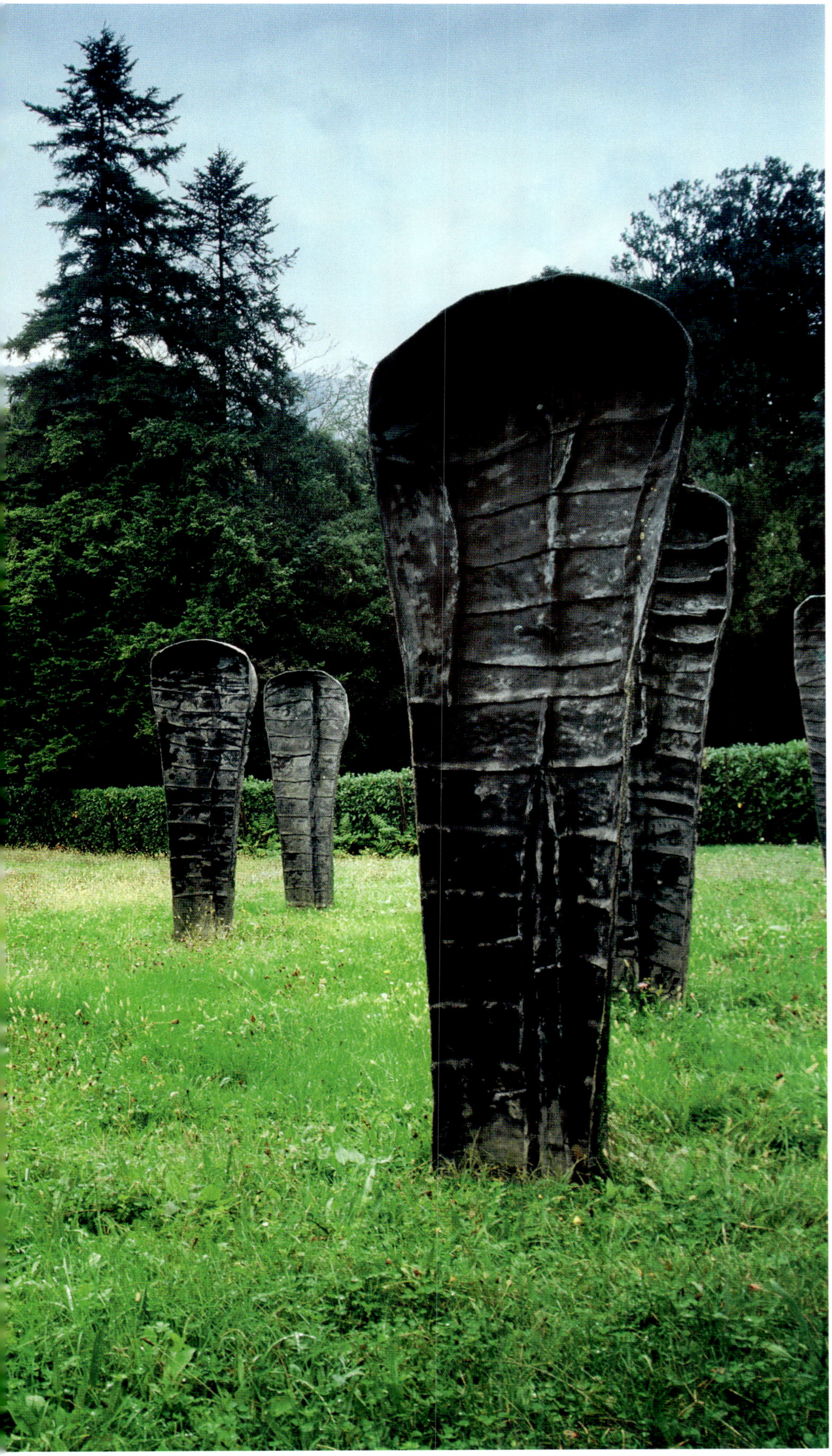

In 2012 Fattoria di Celle celebrated its thirtieth anniversary. This private sculpture park owned by the textiles manufacturer Giuliano Gori in the hills above the little Tuscan town of Pistoia was not only the first of its kind in Europe, it is still one of the most spectacular in the world. Giuliano Gori early established the principle of site-specific sculpture as a means of connecting nature and art. But Giuliano Gori has no interest in attracting large crowds; he prefers only to admit those who are really interested in art to his park. Visitors therefore have to make an appointment, in writing, and must be prepared to walk for three to four hours. This is the minimum length of time it takes to see all of the historic grounds that now contain seventy extraordinary works of art.

When the collector Giuliano Gori bought this fine estate in 1970 he was in fact merely seeking a home for his ever-growing collection of outstanding works by leading twentieth-century artists. The villa and chapel, with a formal garden in the Baroque style, were built by Cardinal Carlo Agostino Fabroni (1651–1727) from Pistoia. He was an important patron of the arts and an influential advisor to Pope Innocent XII. The estate also contained farm buildings (the *fattoria*), landscaped parklands and the adjoining feudal lands with olive groves and vineyards. Gori converted the villa and the farm buildings into a private museum for his collection. In the villa he reserved the top floor for Arte Povera, with one of the farm buildings dedicated to works by international artists. These artists, such as Sol LeWitt or Dmitri Prigov, were able to design entire rooms there. But then Gori realised that the historic, landscaped parklands, which extend around the house for over eighty-five acres, could be a very special exhibition site for contemporary art. In the mid-nineteenth century a local architect, Giovanni Gambini, was commissioned by the then owners – the Caselli family – to landscape the grounds in the English style. A skilfully devised system of paths now gives access to the different parts of the estate with its areas of woodland, meadows and copses. The typical features of a Romantic landscape are seen here in abundance: artificial lakes, waterfalls, rocky outcrops and follies – in the form of an Egyptian monument, a neo-Gothic teahouse, a grotto, half-timbered buildings in the rural

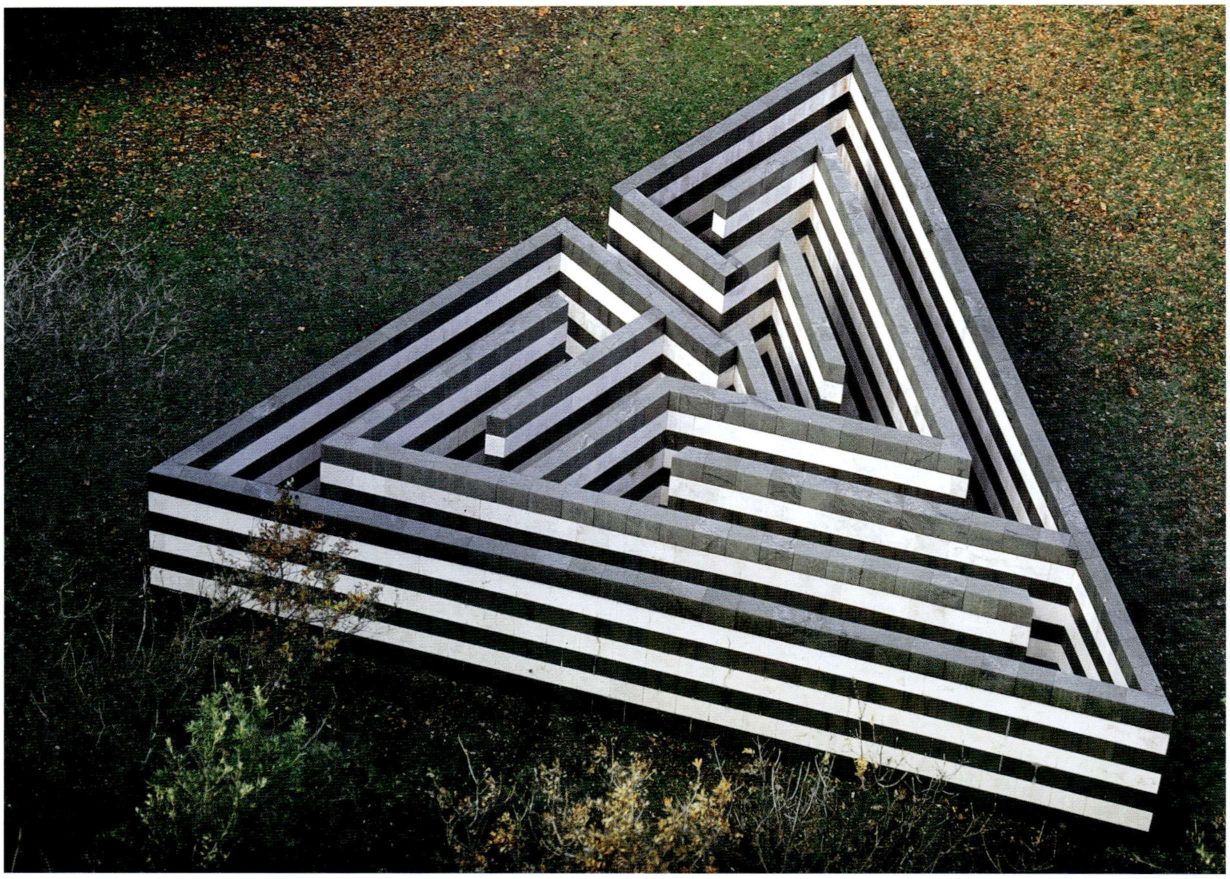

style (serving as grain stores) and a splendid, architect-designed aviary. All of these works of art, the most recent of which dates to the early twentieth century, were commissioned for specific locations on the estate. Gori wanted to revive this tradition. As he himself says, "I saw the possibility of continuing this idea, of making a direct connection between art and nature – of offering artists somewhere that they could create a work specially for this place." It was also at exactly this time – in the 1970s – that he had first seen the then very new, site-specific installations in Kassel and Venice – although, in view of the unusual size of these installations and the temporary nature of these exhibitions, the artists had used transient materials. By contrast, Gori wanted any works of art in his parklands only to be made from resilient materials that could stand up to the weather conditions.

Gori already invited the first nine artists to his estate in the early 1980s: "Courage was required on both sides. It was needed from the artists because some of them, for example Anne and Patrick Poirier, had no experience with outdoor sculptures," he recalls with a smile. "For me, too, it was a radical step – to go from a collection that had hitherto only been about the private desire to have works in one's own home to a collection that is about art that bears fruit in a much larger-scale context and that is much more open to debate." It was important to him that "in their works the artists would always respect the natural setting, not engage in crass interventions or change the character of the estate." Compared to some other sculpture parks this is clearly a constraint. However, it has ultimately ensured that the works of art and the natural surroundings at Fattoria di Celle relate especially closely to each other. From the outset Gori only wanted the best possible works and allowed himself to be guided by an international advisory board. This included renowned art experts from his circle of friends, such as the Israeli art critic Amnon Barzel; Knud Jensen, the founder and director of the Louisiana Museum in Humlebæk (Denmark); and Manfred Schneckenburger, the director of Documenta in 1977 and 1987. It is therefore hardly surprising that the list of artists whose work is represented at Fattoria di Celle is illustrious, to say the least, and goes from Magdalena Abakanowicz, Daniel Buren, Ian Hamilton Finlay and Bukichi Inoue to Dani Karavan, Richard Long and Richard Serra. Some of the artists – for instance Alice Aycock and George Trakas – were spotted by Giuliano Gori on his intensely concentrated explorations of biennials in various parts of the world.

When artists are invited to create a commissioned work, as a rule they spend some months on the estate with their families. Not only does this create a close connection, generally it also leads to the artist making additional works when the commission is finished, as in the case of Robert Morris. But these collaborations with artists also have a major impact on the farm managers and the workers on the estate. "At first our people were somewhat put out by the artists' ideas, but after a while they were all for it. After all, they are the ones who work with the artists as they devise a new, unique artistic language. And that makes everyone proud," Gori tells us. The artists are always allowed to choose their own locations for their installations. "Richard Serra ran all over the grounds until he came to a steep slope that was completely covered with weeds and bushes. He knew straight away that that was the place for his installation *Open Field Vertical Elevations* (1982). And he also knew straight away that instead of working with metal he wanted to work with the local stone – which is actually unusual for him. He

Left: An art space for visitors to explore: Robert Morris's 12 × 12 × 12 × 2-metre *Labyrinth*.

took hundreds of Polaroid pictures of the site. He had decided that the installation would relate to the topography of the hillside, so he needed the photographs as 'visual filters'." While the topography was crucial to Serra's artistic concept, other artists engaged with the philosophical backdrop of Romanticism and the Enlightenment that is intrinsic to English landscape gardens focussed on the botanical features of the natural setting (such as Richard Long, who created his *Grass Circle* in 1985) or concentrated on the history of the estate. Roberto Barni's *Mute Servants* (1988) is a good example of the latter. However, all the artists were keen to work for Gori because of the potential for interaction here. Consequently visitors can enter most of the installations; many even take the form of complicated architectural designs. Robert Morris's *Labyrinth* (1982) initially looks like a large triangular cube, with the broad green-and-white stripes running along its sides recalling the façades of famous Tuscan cathedrals. Anyone entering this structure discovers that they have entered a labyrinth of narrow, two-metre-high passages, which make it almost impossible for the visitor to find his or her orientation. This feeling is intensified by the work's position in a sloping field, because the incline makes the stripes appear distorted. The visitor's senses of visual perception and balance are disturbed. Beverly Pepper also chose a sloping site for her sculpture, which she dedicated to the great Italian landscape architect Pietro Porcinai (1910–1986). Downhill from the neo-Gothic teahouse she created a mighty work in the form of an earth pyramid, cut open and faced with cast-iron panels to form a stage. Wide stone steps in the grass form an auditorium that can hold up to 300 people for music, dance and stage performances at the *Spazio Teatro Celle* (1992) in the summer months. At

Outside the historic villa: Roberto Barni's *Mute Servants*.

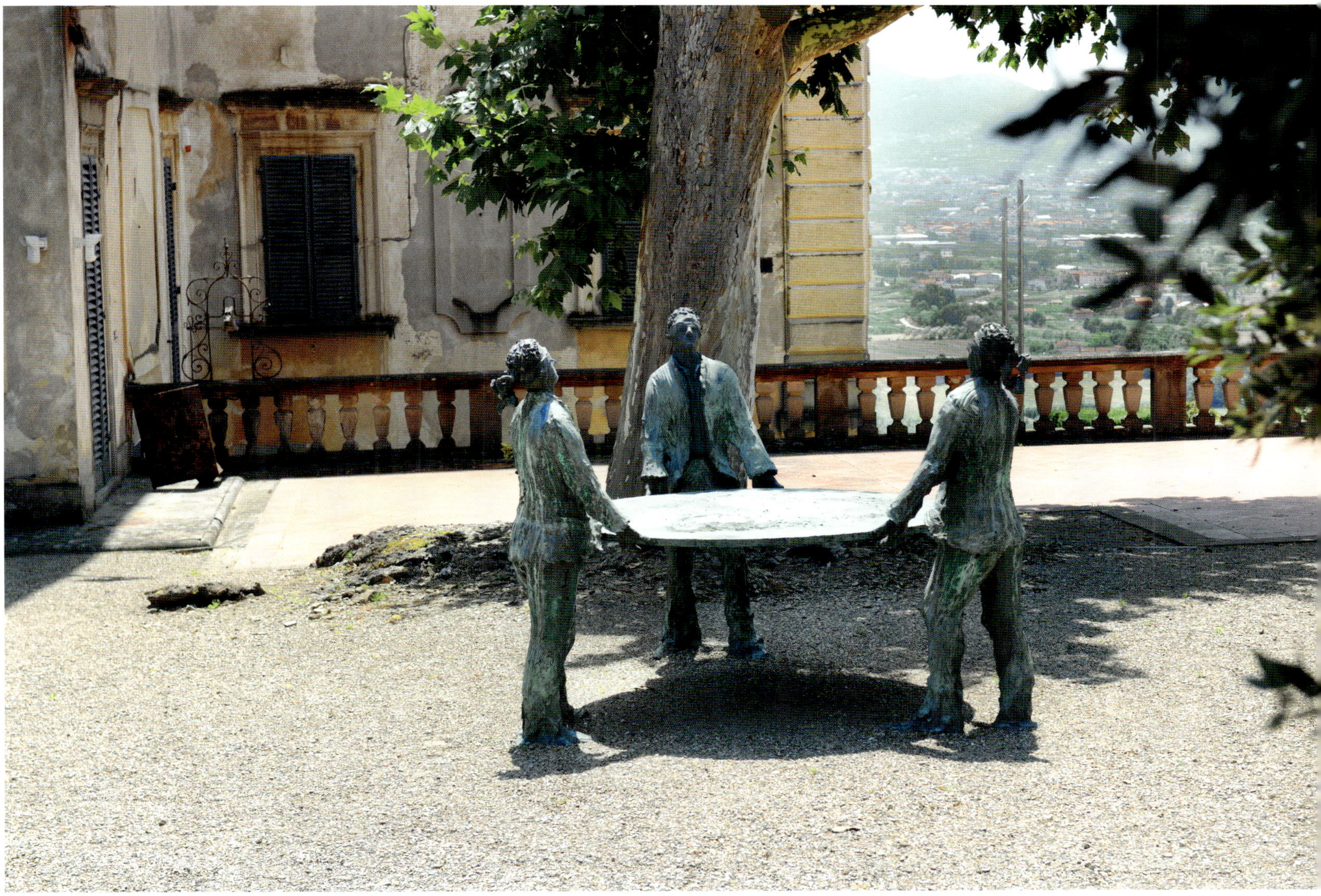

the top of the amphitheatre the two cast-iron prongs of a tuning fork stand guard. The artists who have worked here were inspired both by the setting and its architectural features, the follies – such as the teahouse and the aviary – which have taken on new meaning through the juxtaposition with contemporary art.

By 1985 the 85 acres of the historic parklands were no longer sufficient, so Gori invited his artists to avail themselves of an additional 110 acres directly adjoining his estate. Now the artists enter into dialogue with olive groves and meadows and rise to this new challenge in their different ways. Magdalena Abakanowicz chose a fenced-in field for her installation *Catharsis* (1985), which comprises thirty-three life-sized figures, with neither heads nor arms, arranged in four rows as though they were enacting a ritual of some kind. This was her first work in bronze. The hollow forms seem reminiscent of sarcophagi. Although they initially appear identical, closer examination shows that each is unique. This subtle, disconcerting work questions the role of the individual in society. Bukichi Inoue made a particularly daring move with his work *My Sky Hole* (1989). He sends the visitor on a meditative journey through his installation, much of which is below ground, under an olive grove. A gate of two eleven-metre columns guides the visitor towards a long, narrow passage between two stone walls that leads literally into the hills. A small fountain and marble benches provide an opportunity for reflection before the visitor reaches a spiral staircase leading upwards. Once again the visitor senses the close connection here between the art and the site. These works of art do not occupy positions in the landscape, they are part of the landscape.

Daniel Buren, *La cabane éclatée aux 4 salles*: the exterior is uninterrupted mirror glass; the colourful interiors are reflected in the doors outside the building.

Right: Jaume Plensa's glass-brick cube, with two identical internal spaces and inscriptions, becomes a magical light sculpture as night falls.

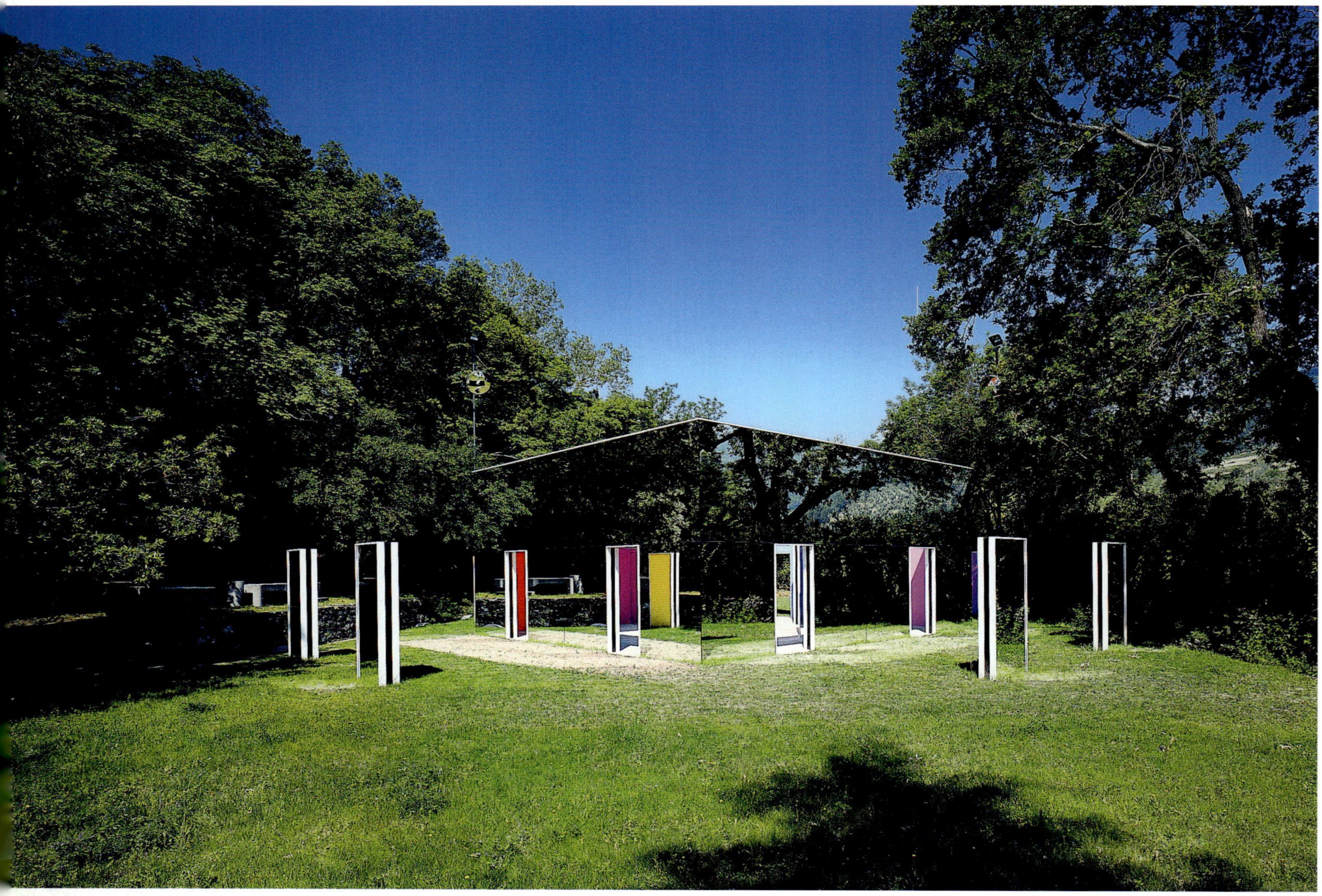

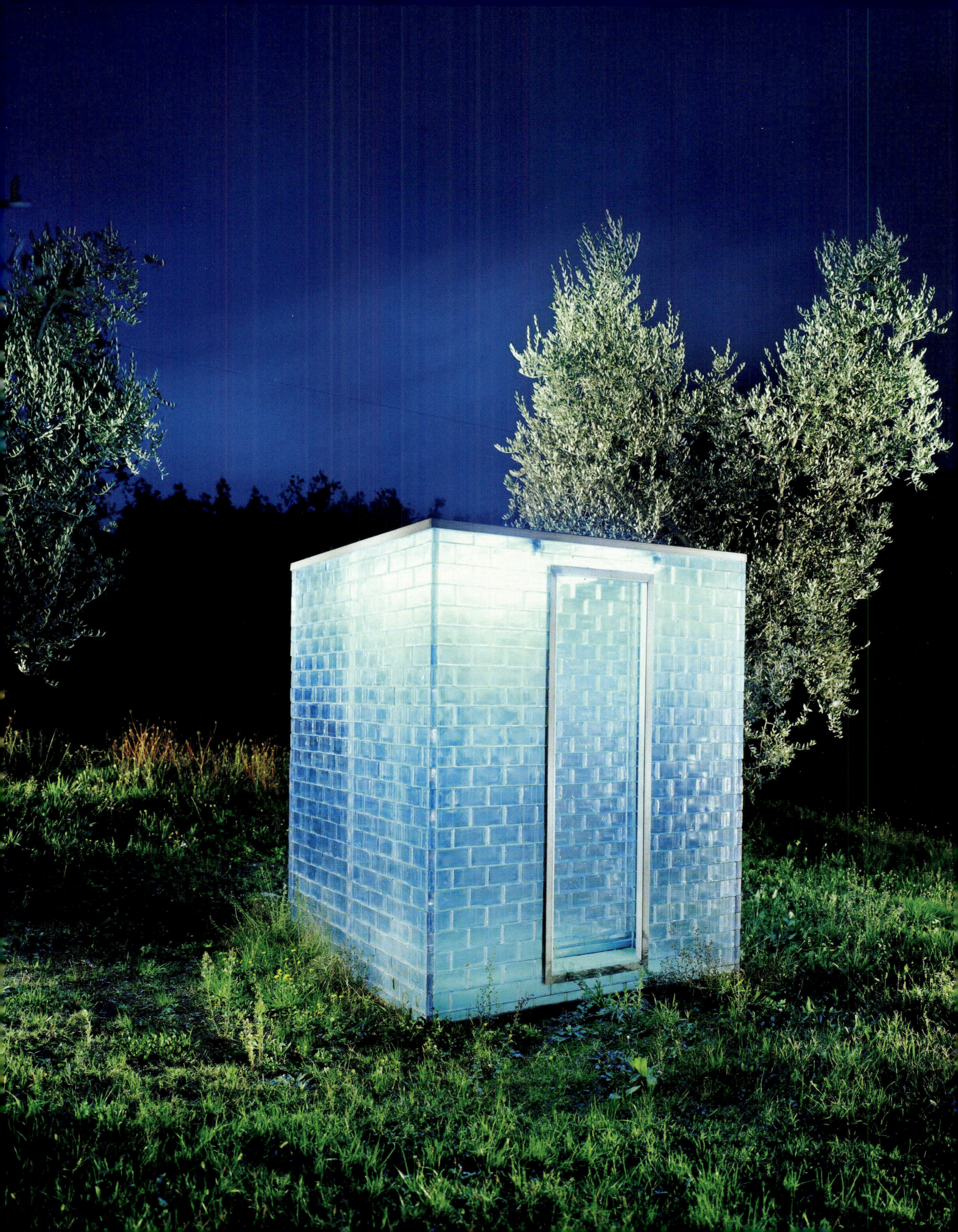

EXPLORING THE ORIGINS OF EXISTENCE
THE GARDEN OF COSMIC SPECULATION, DUMFRIES, UK

Scotland is known for its archaic landscapes, its silent lochs, barren hillsides, fields edged with stone walls. Nature here is still largely intact – and provides the perfect backdrop for Charles Jencks's (b. 1939) interest in the theories of the origins of the universe. But not only that. Since 1988 this renowned American architectural historian and passionate scientist has also been developing a unique concept in his Garden of Cosmic Speculation, which is about nothing less than the universe. In his garden he gives visual form to complexity theories and to existential issues in human life: fundamental natural phenomena such as DNA, selfish genes, the distortion of space and time in black holes, the Big Bang. Jencks expresses these as tangible metaphors in nature, as earthworks, sculptural arrangements and garden designs.

Things began in a rather less spectacular manner. Jencks's wife Maggie Keswick (1942–1995) wanted to redesign her parents' garden at Portrack House, north of Dumfries. "Initially Maggie and I just wanted to create somewhere for our children to swim," recalls Charles Jencks with a laugh. "We started to dredge the Nith, a small watercourse in the grounds. But then we saw the huge mounds of earth and the pools, and we wanted more." As an expert on Chinese garden culture, Keswick, who had partly grown up in China, came up with the idea of creating 'borrowed scenery', an important aspect of Chinese gardens where the designer devises an idealised imitation of the surrounding landscape – in this case the lochs and rolling hills of the southern Scottish Lowlands. According to Taoist geomancy the hills and the mountains are the "bones of the Earth", which are energised by *chi*, the breath of subterranean dragons. One of the aims in Chinese gardens is to give visual form to these forces of nature. Keswick designed three *Slug Lakes*, which lie like curved mirrors at the foot of the 120-metre-long, boldly sweeping *Snake Mound* and the fifteen-metre-high *Snail Mound* – both designed by Jencks.

Shortly after that Maggie Keswick was diagnosed with cancer. From then on the design of the cosmogenic garden around Portrack House was overseen by Charles Jencks alone and he is still working on it today, realising his ideas. In the meandering zigzag of *Snake Mound* Jencks used abstract forms for the two mounds of earth. The basic form of the wave or spiral is found throughout

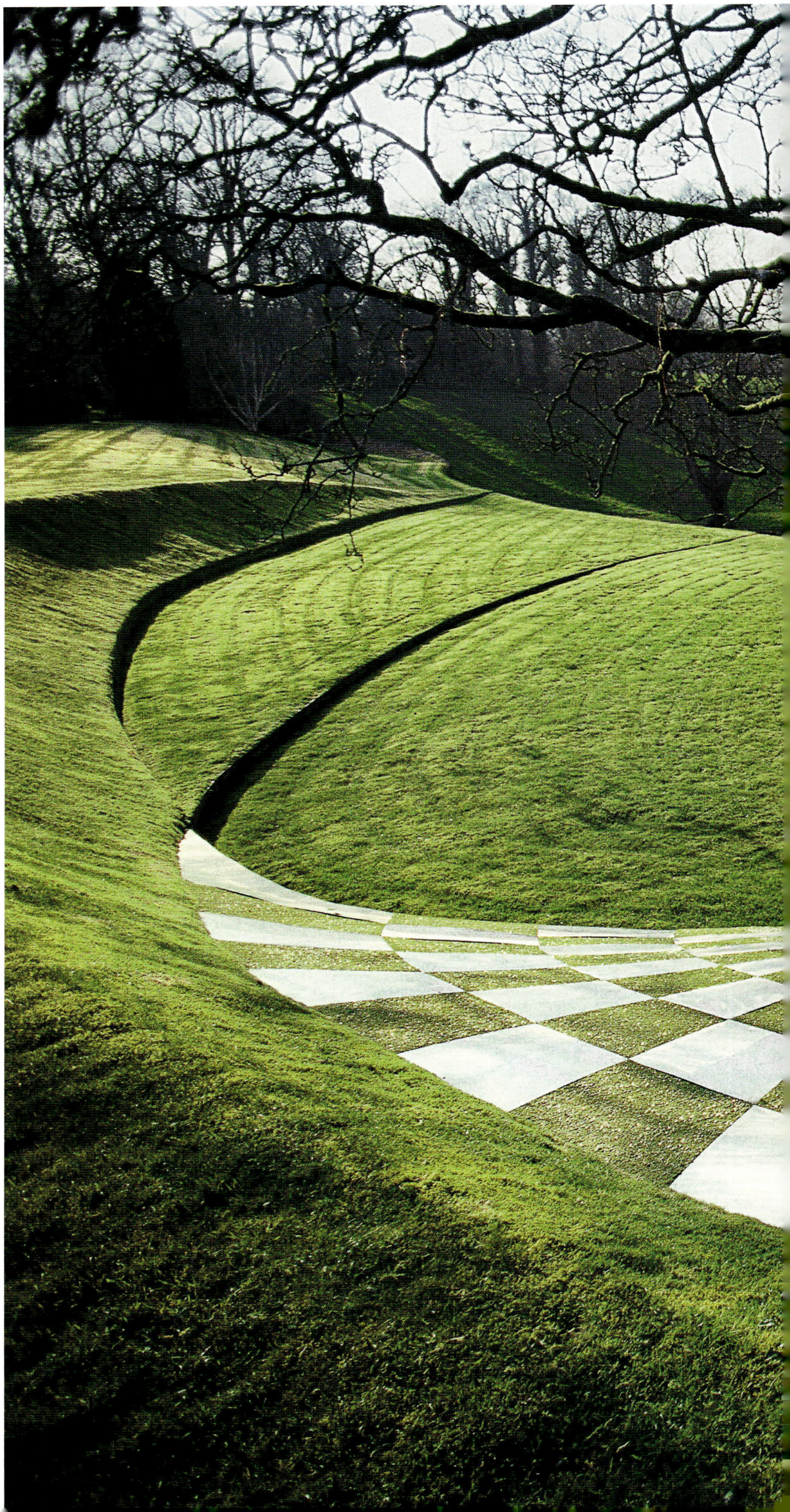

The *Black Hole Terrace* conveys a sense of the inescapable pull of the gravitational forces inside a galactic black hole.

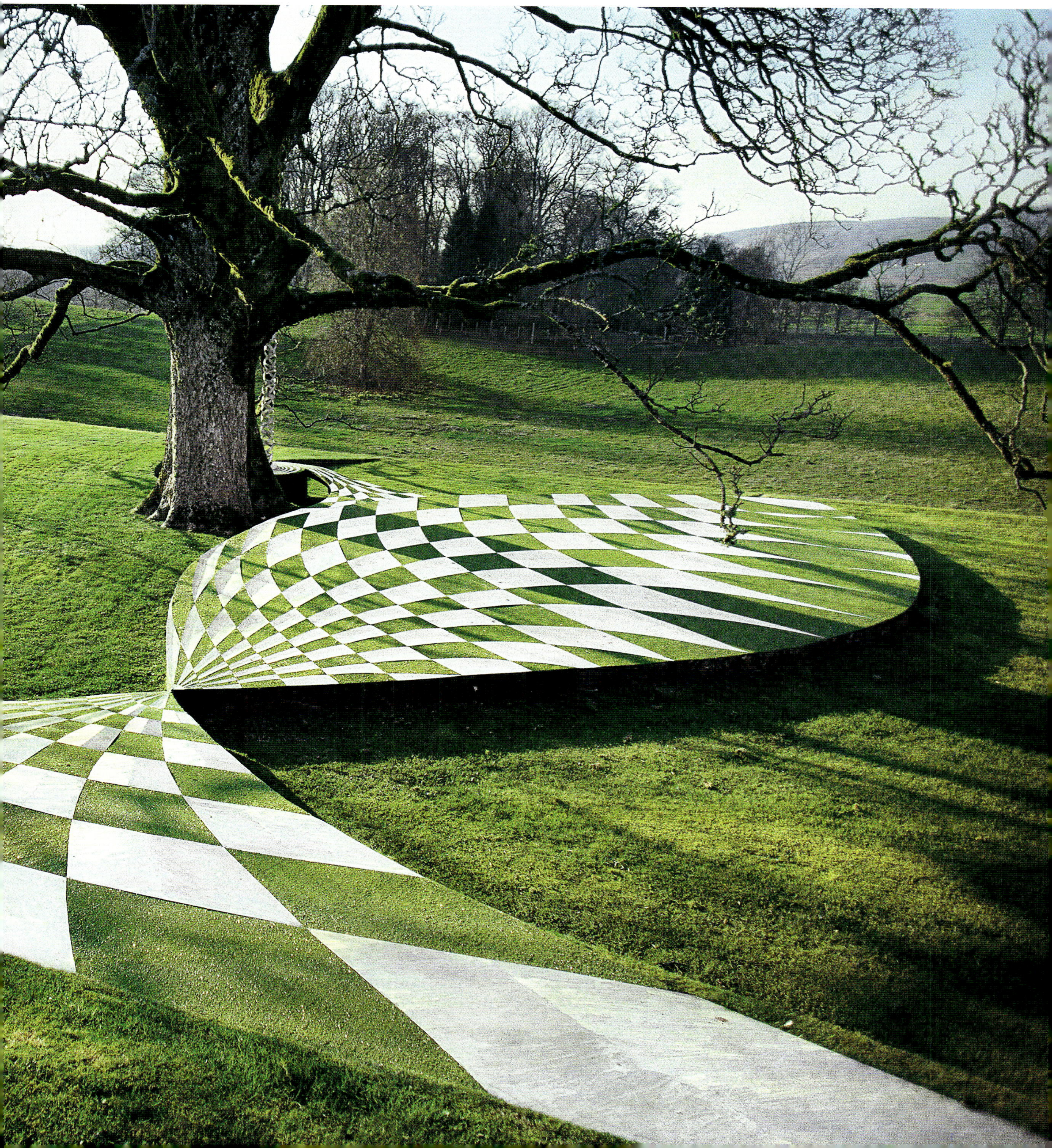

nature in the form of a double helix – from the structure of chromosomes to hurricanes to the shapes of galaxies. It is the ordering principle of creation. According to chaos theory it is the "nonlinear dynamic" that determines human existence. Waves therefore abound in the garden: in staircases, walls, curved ponds, in bizarre bridges, winding paths and installations, as details in the design of fences, gates and terraces, or as parts of the waterfall. Jencks talks of a "landscape grammar of waves" that he has applied to his garden, since, as he puts it, "Brain waves organise our bodies, waves order the Earth and unleash earthquakes. They are the foundations of life."

Jencks's intense study of cosmology and cosmogenesis led him to develop his own contemporary concept of a garden that embraces new themes, which relate to the ongoing debate concerning the origins of the universe. For Jencks the garden is the ideal place to engage with the great questions that face humankind. And he wanted to reflect the latest, revolutionary scientific discoveries of the twentieth century in the design of his garden as a work of art that is both natural and created by human hand. He wanted advances such as the discovery of DNA to be given visual expression in the landscape of the garden – in order to promote understanding, debate and, above all, a new mode of aesthetic observation.

The extended wall in the upper section of the garden is the longest visible wave here. It consists of two intersecting curved retaining walls in the form of soliton waves – which maintain the same shape and energy over long distances. In this structure Jencks also created a reinterpretation of a classical ha-ha. In traditional British landscape design this is an edge or an extended ditch that separated the formal garden from any adjoining pastureland in such a way that the view is not interrupted. Different sections of the landscape appear to merge seamlessly into each other. Jencks combined the notion of an edge with that of a wide terrace outside the main house. The *Symmetry Break Terrace* is a metaphor for the most important jumps that define the history of the universe: the progress from energy to matter, then to life and lastly to consciousness. Jencks presented this scientific model as a distorted ellipse of offset bands of grass and pebbles. Contrary to the traditional teachings of religion and science, Jencks takes the view that the universe is not a precise mechanism but a process that advances in jumps. In 1995 he published a highly acclaimed book on this topic, *The Architecture of the Jumping Universe*. He also discusses

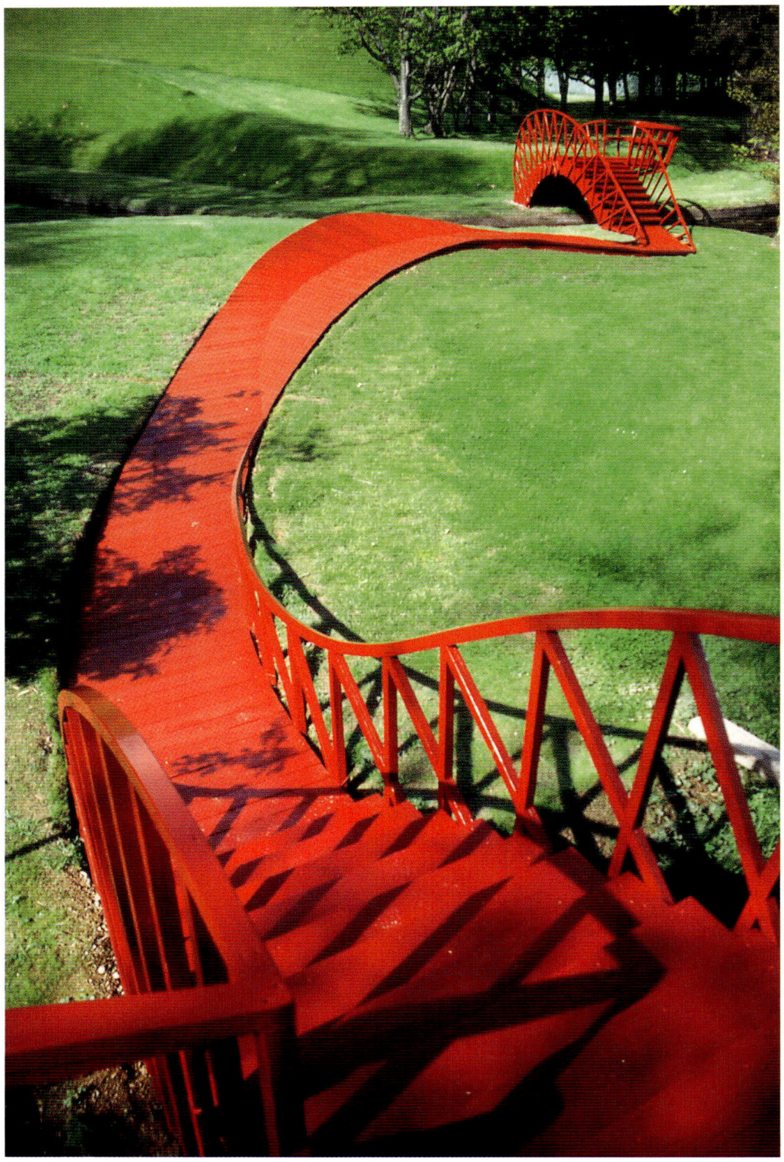

The bridge meanders through the garden, symbolising irregularity and fragmentation in the natural world.

Right: View of *Snake Mound*, looking from *Snail Mound*: a world shaped by waves.

the influence of chaos theory and complexity theory on contemporary architecture in the lectures and talks he gives worldwide.

Not far from the *Symmetry Break Terrace* there is another important installation, the *Black Hole Terrace*, which explores the galactic phenomenon of the same name, in other words, collapsing stars, with a mass much greater than that of our sun, which swallow up everything that comes their way. Their gravitational force is so powerful that even particles travelling at the speed of light could never escape. In Jencks's garden this phenomenon is represented as a whirlpool of units of silvery aluminium and green artificial grass, with the black edges representing space and time. "If you fell into the whirlpool, into the black hole – space is stretched there, but time is compressed, until in the end it stops altogether – that would mean, metaphorically speaking, that gravity would elongate you downwards, to a breaking point, like a string of spaghetti," as Jencks puts it.

Apart from giving visual form to complex natural phenomena, this exposed spot was also a favourite place for Charles Jencks and Maggie Keswick to enjoy a sundowner. Sadly these evenings came to an end in 1995 when Maggie died of breast cancer. Jencks now turned her formal kitchen garden, where she had planted vegetables and herbs, into a *Physics Garden*. Everything here is about DNA and our senses. In six beds with low box hedges there are several large sculptures – a DNA double helix made of aluminium, a large ear, an oversized nose, a hand and an accessible grotto full of eye motifs – all metaphors for the different senses of perception: hearing, smelling, tasting, touching and seeing. And Jencks added a sixth sense: intuition. In the beds he planted herbs that stimulate particular senses – thistles for the sense of touch and aromatic herbs such as oregano and lavender for the sense of smell. In addition the paved paths are embellished with "ambigrammi" – words that can be read from two sides.

Beyond the onetime tennis court is the *Universe Cascade* – a waterfall and flights of steps in the form of a gigantic double helix – descending from the house down a steep slope to the lower part of the garden. "The DNA double helix is the basic structure of chromosomes and hence the basis of all life on our planet. The individual steps are jumps in the evolution of the universe," Jencks explains. In the same way that the strands in a DNA molecule are coiled around the nucleus of a cell, each of the steps contains

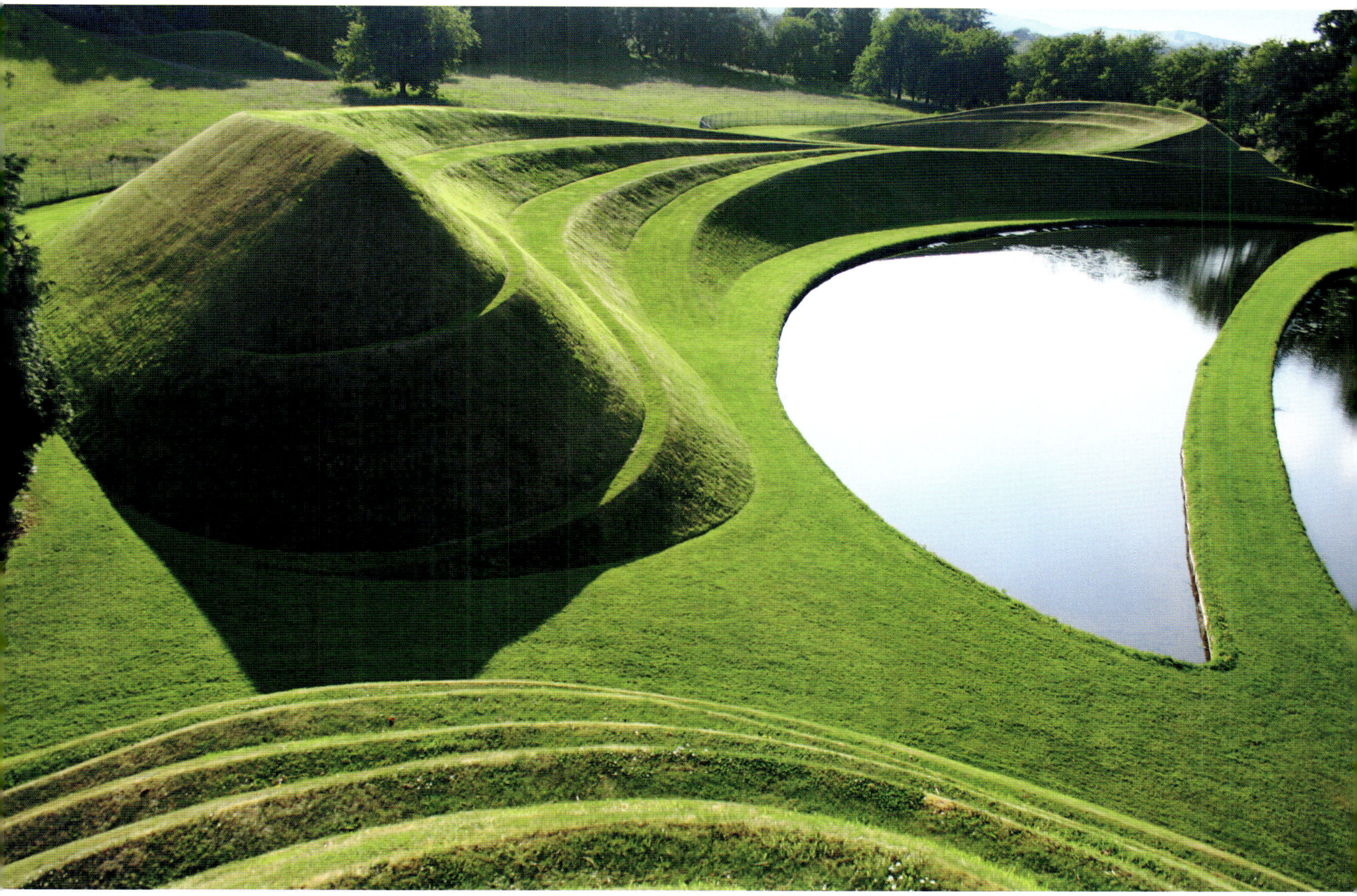

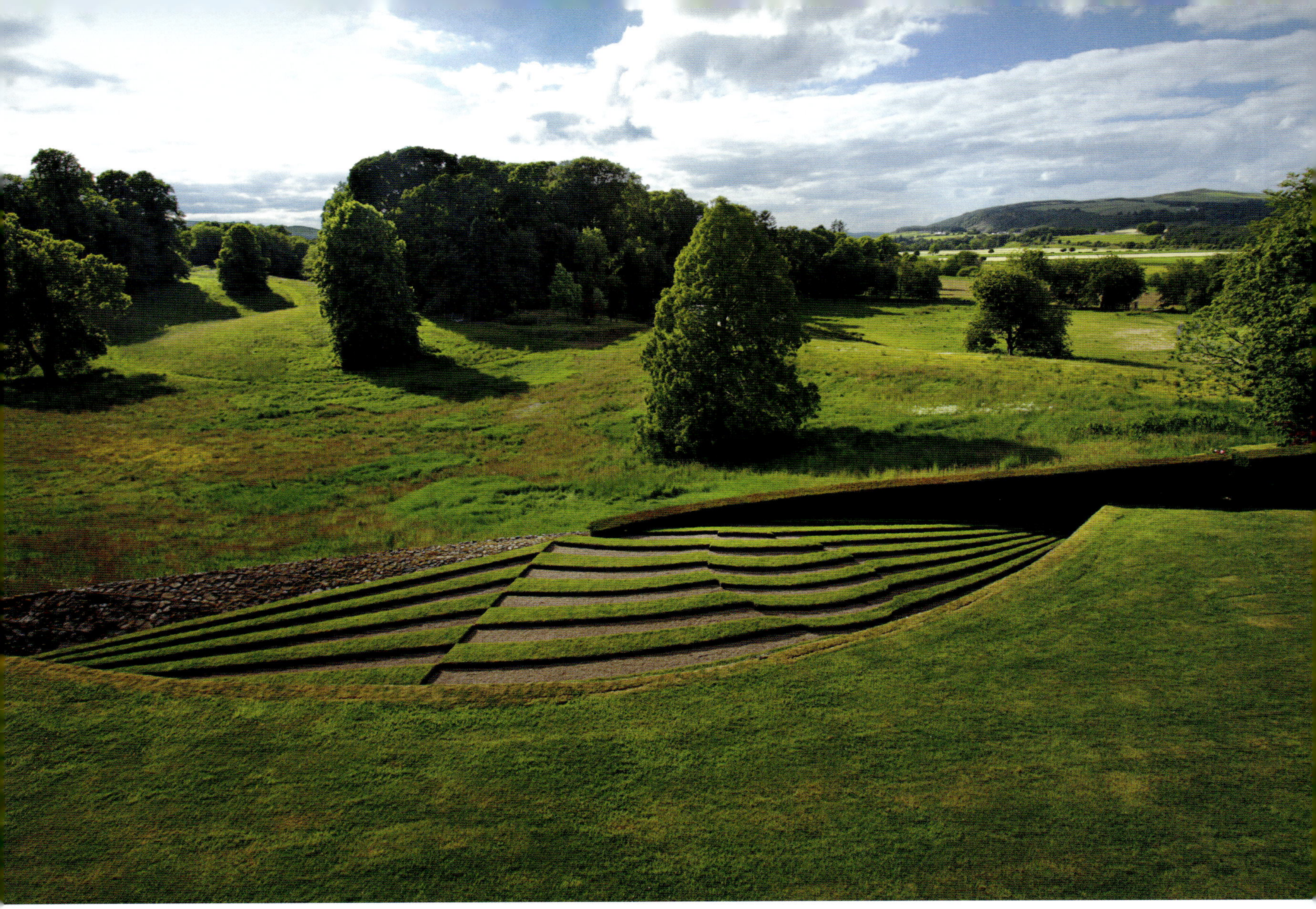

a stone symbolising Gaia, Mother Earth, as the starting point of all life. "About 530 million years ago, during the Cambrian Period, there was an unusual increase in the number of species, which much later on led to the emergence of the human species. It is not until the penultimate step that we get to the development of religions and civilisations," says Jencks. "That is the step that separates humankind from the rest of nature," he continues, "we are the creations of nature, but not the same as nature. You can see that in the fact that nature does not change the laws of nature in the way that we do." Jencks is highly critical of the irresponsible way that human beings treat nature, which is also why he wants people to understand the connections in nature. The zigzag, as a representation of our level of civilisation, also stands as a symbol of this sorry state of affairs.

Another area of scientific research that Jencks has engaged with is particle physics, particularly the phenomenon of quarks. In the early 1960s the physicist Murray Gell-Mann postulated their existence as the fundamental stable constituents of other particles such as the protons and neutrons that make up atomic nuclei. On this basis he proposed that they could be described as the fundamental building blocks of all matter – a revolution in atomic physics. In the northern part of the garden, where a small stream broadens out into a *Water Dragon* (appropriately shaped), Jencks created a *Quark Walk*, with sculptures and scientific formulae on wood, stone and metal, symbolising the debate surrounding the existence and grouping of elementary particles. They are all reflected, together with the viewer and the clouds in the sky, in the surface of the stream – images of fleeting traces and of the search for the still-elusive proof of the existence of quarks as another essential building block in the great question of existence.

Each of the scientists, philosophers and artists with whom Charles Jencks debates the latest scientific findings in his Garden of Cosmic Speculation comes in a spirit of enquiry, but also in sheer amazement. Because not only does Jencks's extraordinary garden present them with visual interpretations of scientific phenomena and issues, it also does so in an entirely new, aesthetic language of forms for art in nature. As Jencks himself has said: "If artists and architects want to portray the new world in all its dynamism and fertility, they either have to find new languages or develop existing languages. Life in the forms of art is the measure of cosmogenesis.... It is the task of the artist to provide people with sensory equivalents."

Left: ***The Symmetry Break Terrace*** **as a metaphor for the most important organisational jumps in the evolution of the universe.**

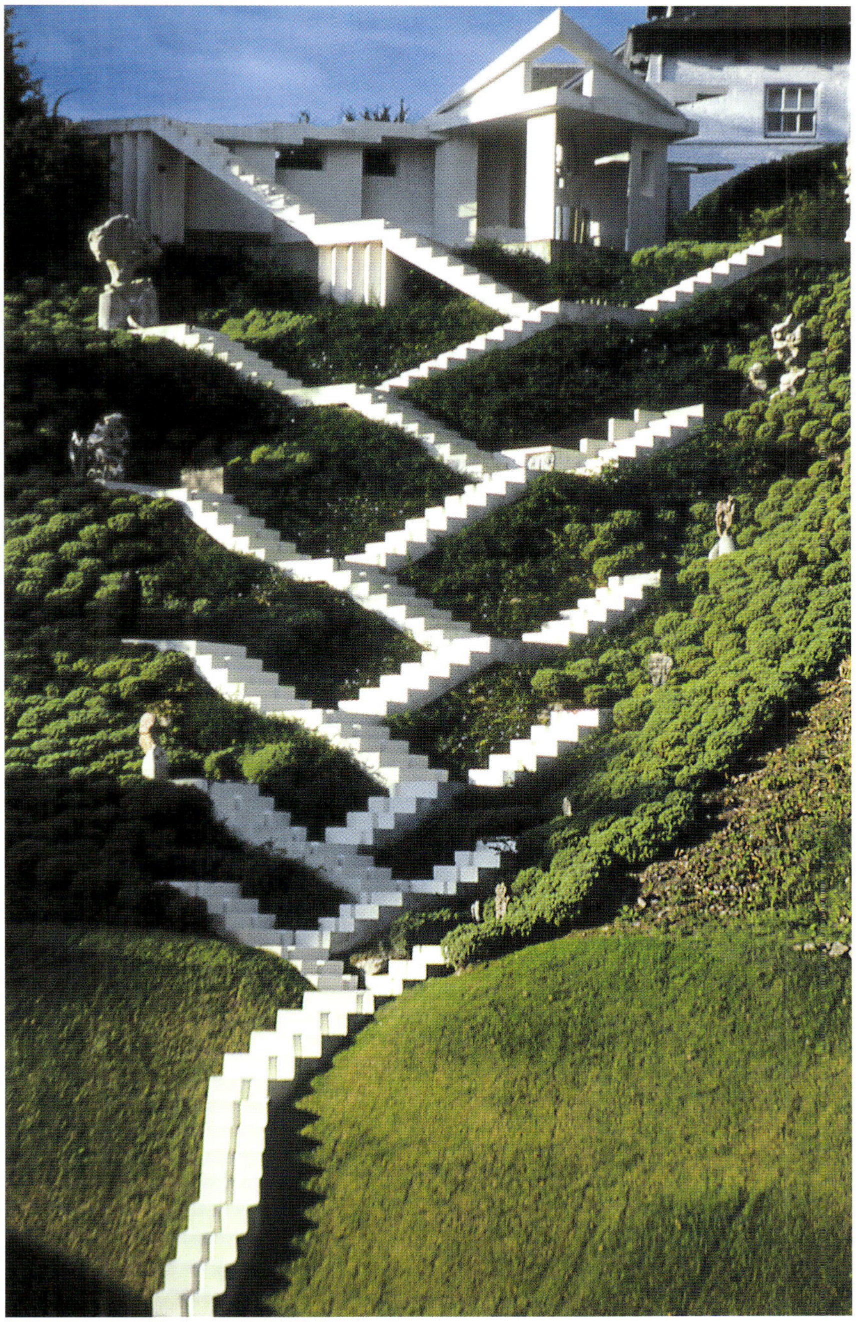

The spectacular ***Universe Cascade*****: a double helix of steps and watercourses explains the history of the universe.**

Hidden inside the *Eye Mound* there is a realm of vision, with bizarre patterns, telescopes, eye motifs and a 'dome of eyes'.

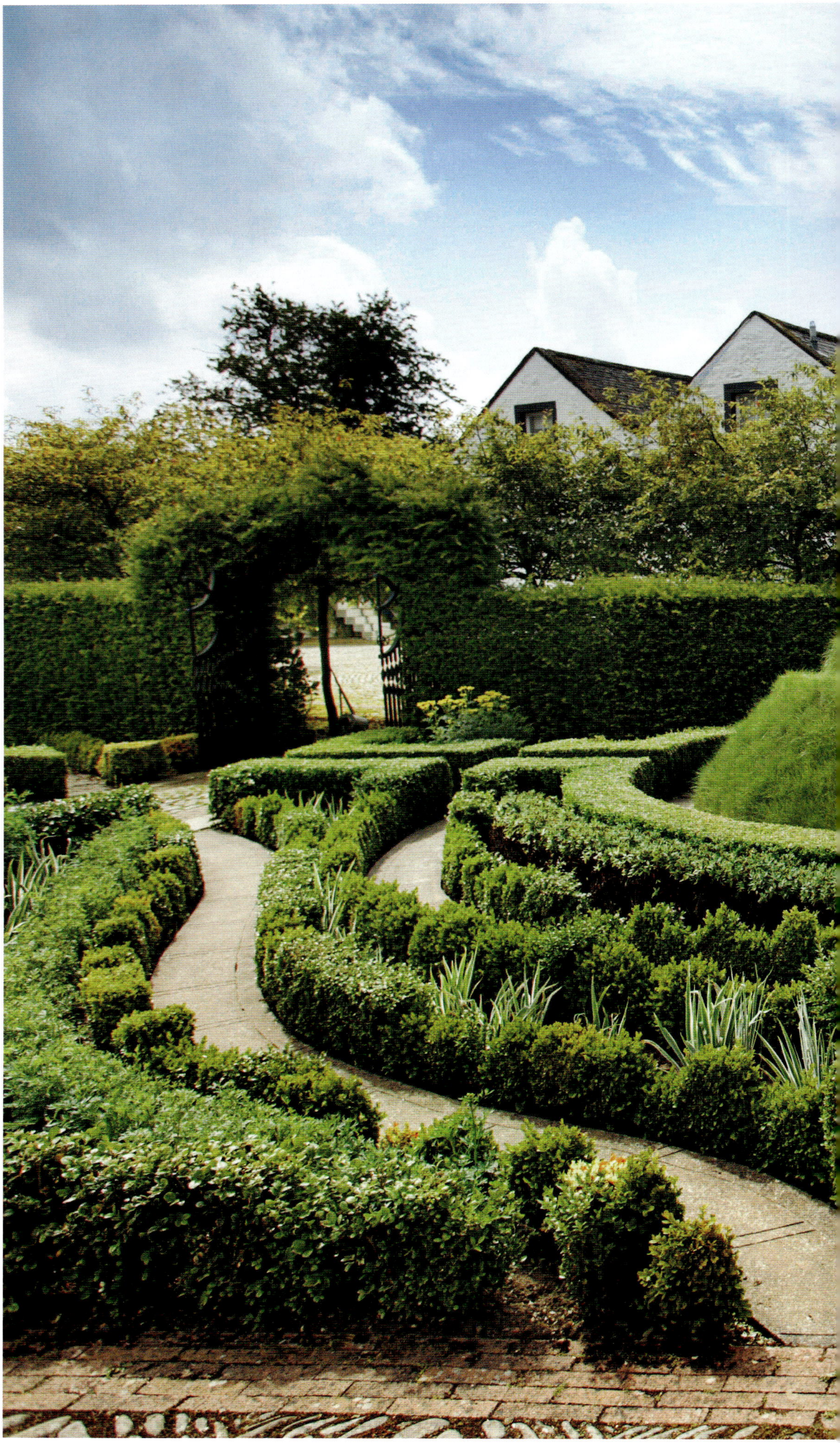

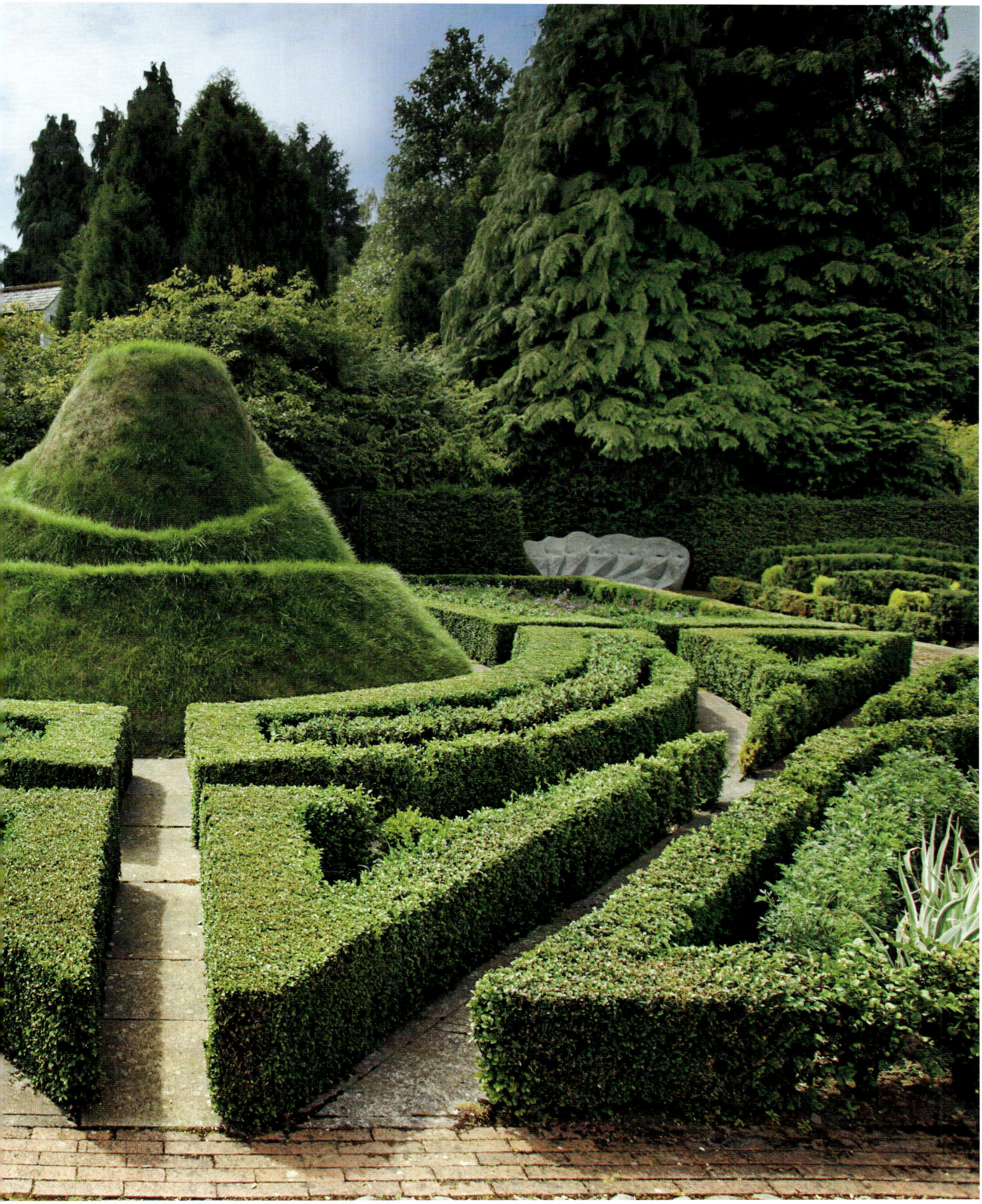

The Garden of Cosmic Speculation, UK

THE PLACE THAT BECAME A SCULPTURE

JUDD FOUNDATION AND CHINATI FOUNDATION, MARFA, USA

Marfa, Texas. The New York artist Donald Judd (1928–1994) could hardly have got further away. This small town, with a population of two thousand, is situated just short of the border with Mexico at the foot of the Chinati Mountains in an endless, open landscape. With the increasing aridity of the land in recent decades cattle ranches are now few and far between. Only the trim buildings in the main street recall better times when there were still cowboys tending large herds. Just once, in 1955, the town briefly came back to life when it became a shooting location for the movie *Giant*, with James Dean in his last role. After that Marfa fell back into oblivion. But that was exactly what fascinated Donald Judd – the great master of Minimal Art – on his first visit to the town in the late 1960s and what made him decide to settle there later on.

This quiet, abandoned military base from the Second World War, in a rough, empty landscape with astounding starry skies, had unlimited space for art and artistic ideas. And it provided Judd with a way of countering the superficial art elite and the exhibition practices in American galleries and museums that were entirely unsuited to contemporary art. In his view the art world was far too heavily oriented towards the viewer's taste, as opposed to the art and its contents. Judd, accompanied by his two children, leased one of the old Army barracks and started to set up his own Minimalist installations. In 1974 he bought the other buildings on the same compound, including the onetime headquarters and the vast storage sheds. Living, working and showing his work in one and the same place – that was his idea of being an artist. In the end Donald Judd had his own vast property with a range of different buildings and at last realised his dream. As a nod to its original function he called it *The Block*, or *La Mansana* in Spanish. This compound was like a microcosm, where Judd could lead a completely autonomous existence. He had everything he needed – from a vegetable garden to a chicken run to his own library with over 10,000 books on art and architecture. He even made his own furniture from wooden planks and boards – in chunky, geometric designs. But these were not just functional items for Judd, they were also art.

These works of art became the focus of his household in a home that was also

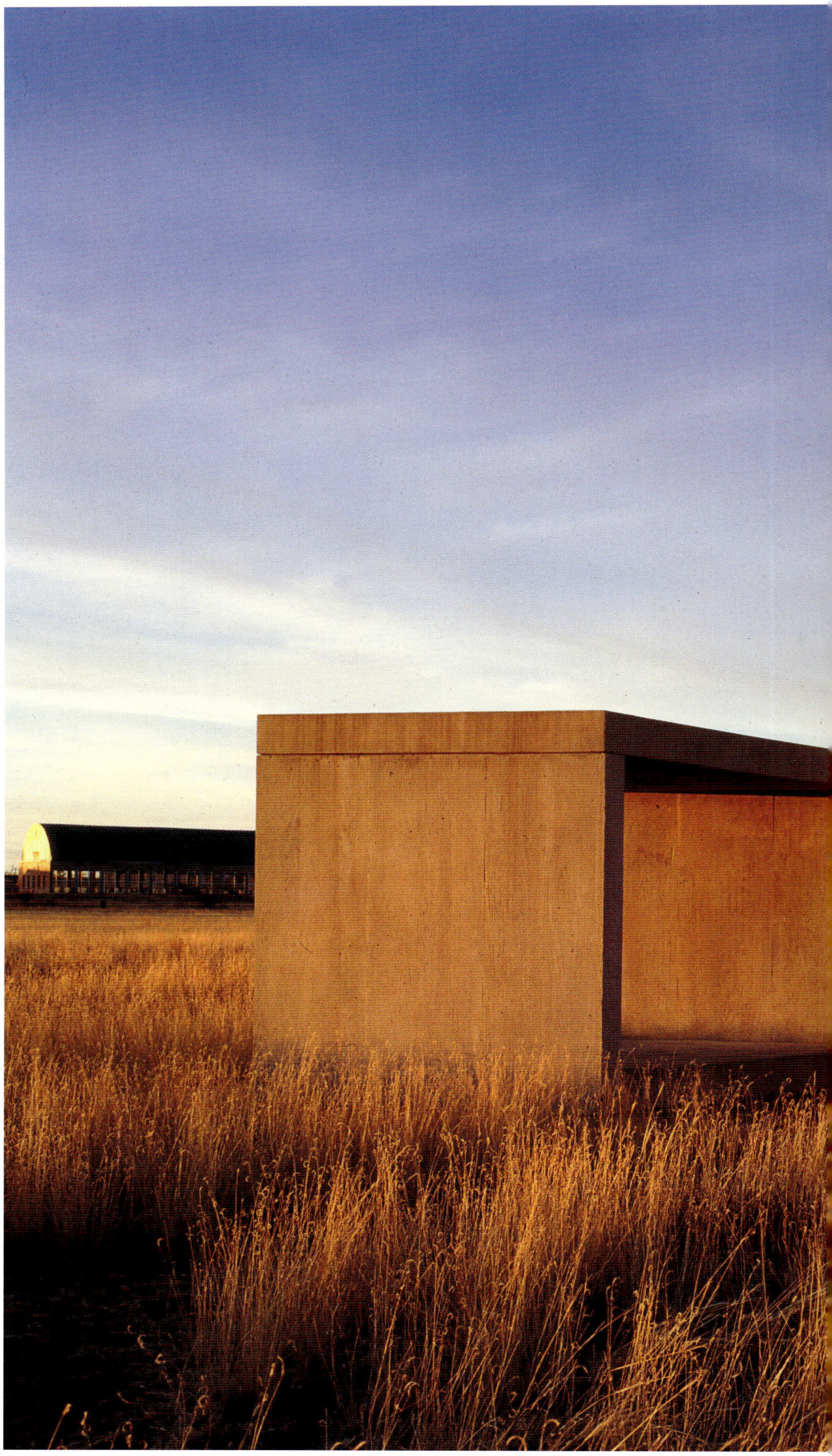

Far away from the American art business –
Donald Judd's *15 untitled works in concrete*.

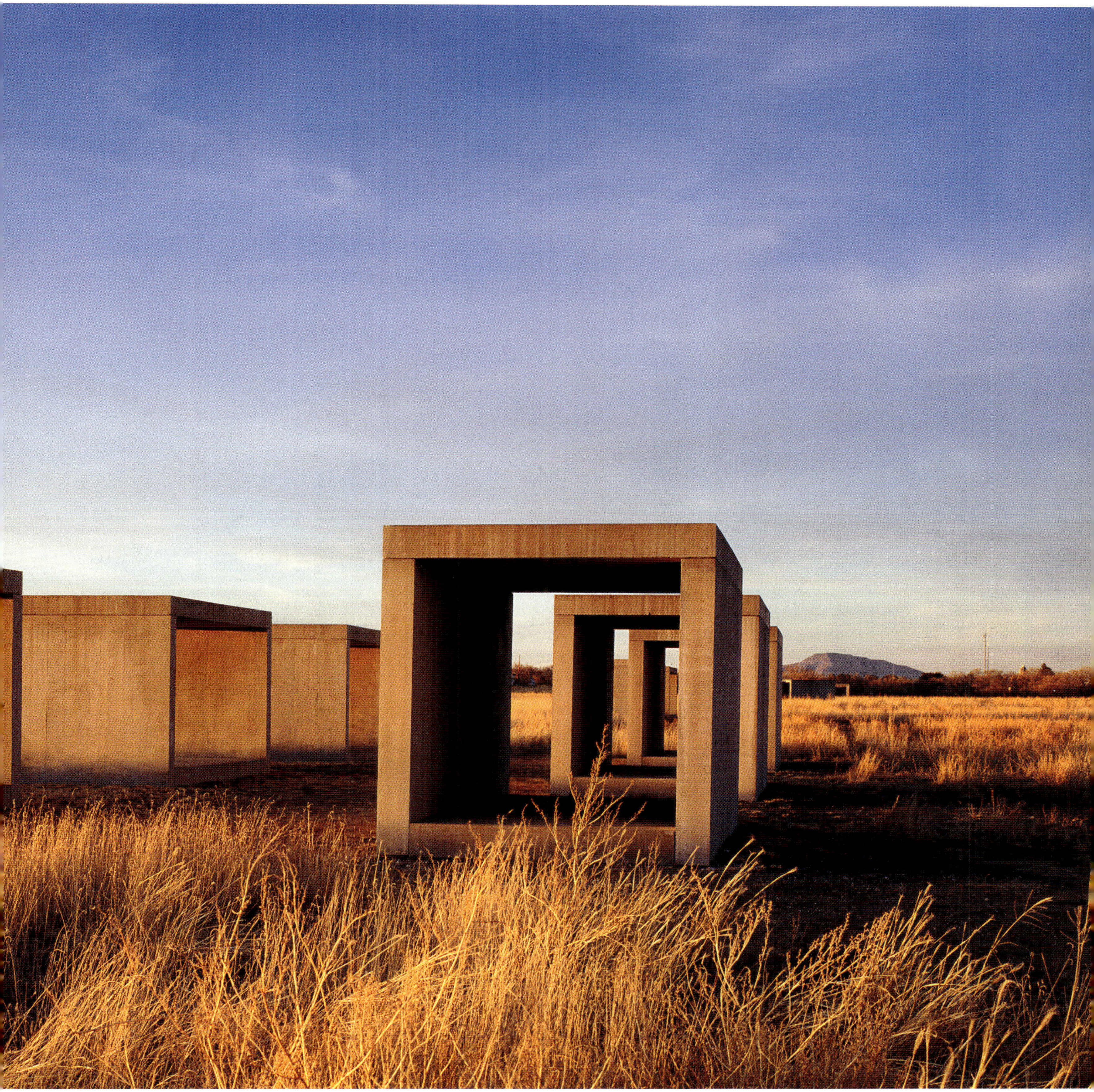

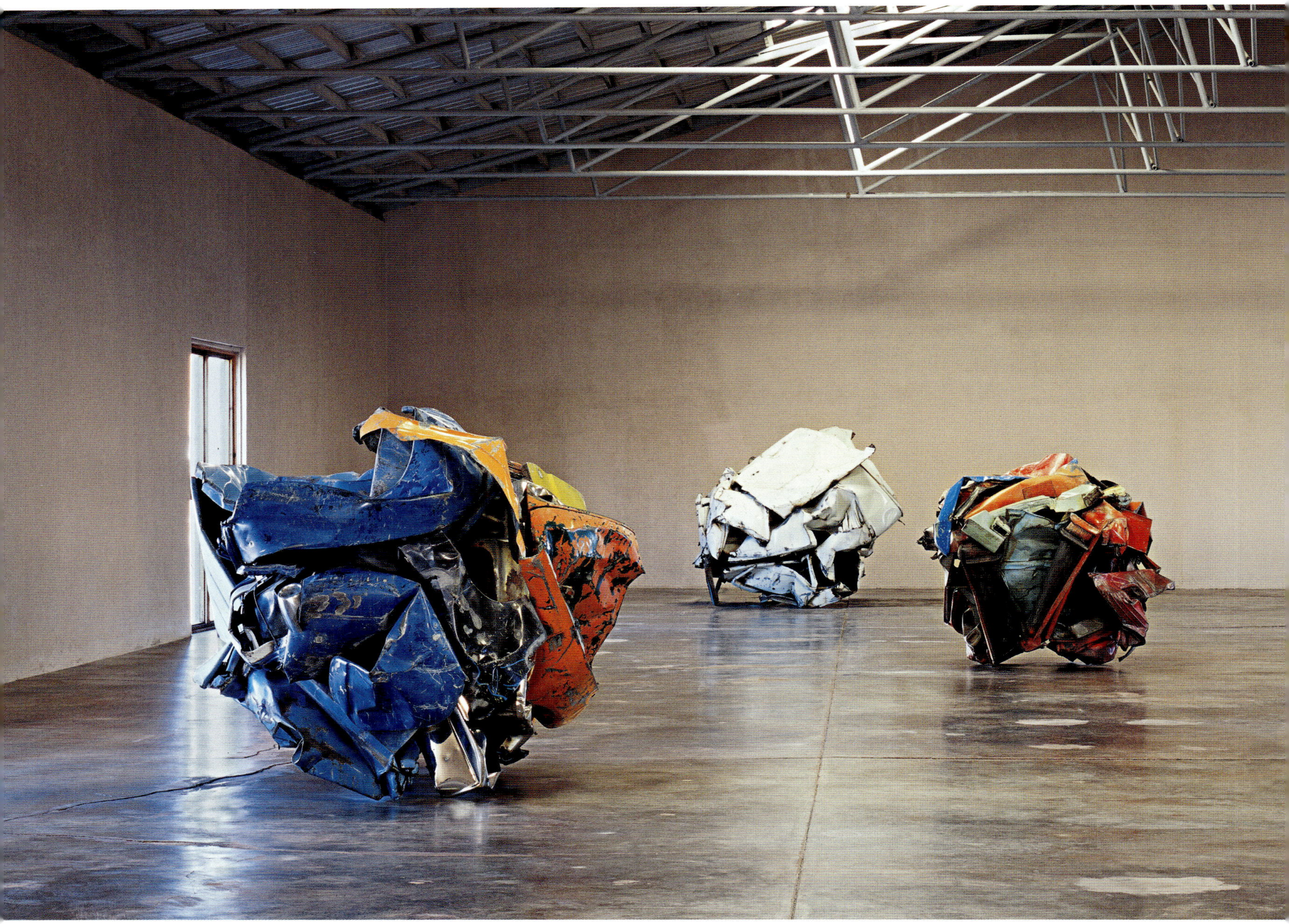

a museum. Like presentations in museum spaces, Judd placed his art-furniture in amongst everyday functional items. The bed was of particular importance. Judd lived, worked and slept in all the rooms. His entire environment – furniture, living quarters and grounds – was designed down to the millimetre according to a single mathematical concept, from the entrance door to the height of the mud walls surrounding the property, to the size of the internal yard and the summerhouse with seating to the distances between the various buildings and the works displayed in the two exhibition halls. A recurrent motif is the revolving door in the form of a floor-to-ceiling quartered window that relates not only to the windows in the halls but also reconciles the difference between inside and outside and at the same time – very practically – increases the air circulation in the hot Texan climate. Although Judd had already embarked on the idea of turning his previous home in New York, on Spring Street, into a *Gesamtkunstwerk*, it was only at Marfa that he could fully carry it through.

After *The Block* Judd extended his activities as an architect and landscape architect, furniture designer, craftsman, painter, sculptor, writer and scholar to the

Existing buildings become art spaces: storage sheds once used by a wool company now house large-format sculptures by John Chamberlain.

What used to be hangars on a military base are now a museum where art, architecture and nature enter into a fully symbiotic relationship.

whole area. Little by little the town of Marfa also became one large *Gesamtkunstwerk*. He reconfigured empty shops and three ranches as studios that also could always serve as exhibition spaces. The old bank was turned into a museum for his art collection with works by friends of his. Judd gave his fellow artist and friend John Chamberlain the huge storage spaces that had once belonged to the Wool & Mohair Company for his large-format sculptures. Every cent Judd earned was ploughed back into his projects in Marfa. But without financial support from the Dia Art Foundation he would not have been able to continue to develop his idea of an entire town dedicated to art.

In collaboration with the foundation Donald Judd ultimately realised his last mega-project, which was also his most spectacular work: the transformation of Fort D. A. Russell, near Marfa, into a museum founded on an entirely new concept – a symbiosis of art, architecture and nature. This was to be the beginning of the Chinati Foundation, which now has its headquarters here. This huge military site with two storage sheds, an extensive array of barracks and a gigantic riding hall perfectly matched Judd's vision of venues for new, large-format contemporary art which could not be adequately accommodated in conventional museums where it was only ever temporarily on display. Initially Judd wanted to present works by just three artists: John Chamberlain, Dan Flavin and himself. Later on, however, installations and large ensembles by other artists in his circle of friends were also presented here: Carl Andre, Ingólfur Arnarsson, Roni Horn, Ilya Kabakov, Richard Long, Claes Oldenburg and Coosje van Bruggen, David Rabinowitch and John Wesley. Some of the buildings here proved to be ideal for multipart, site-specific works such as Dan Flavin's *Marfa Project* (1996),

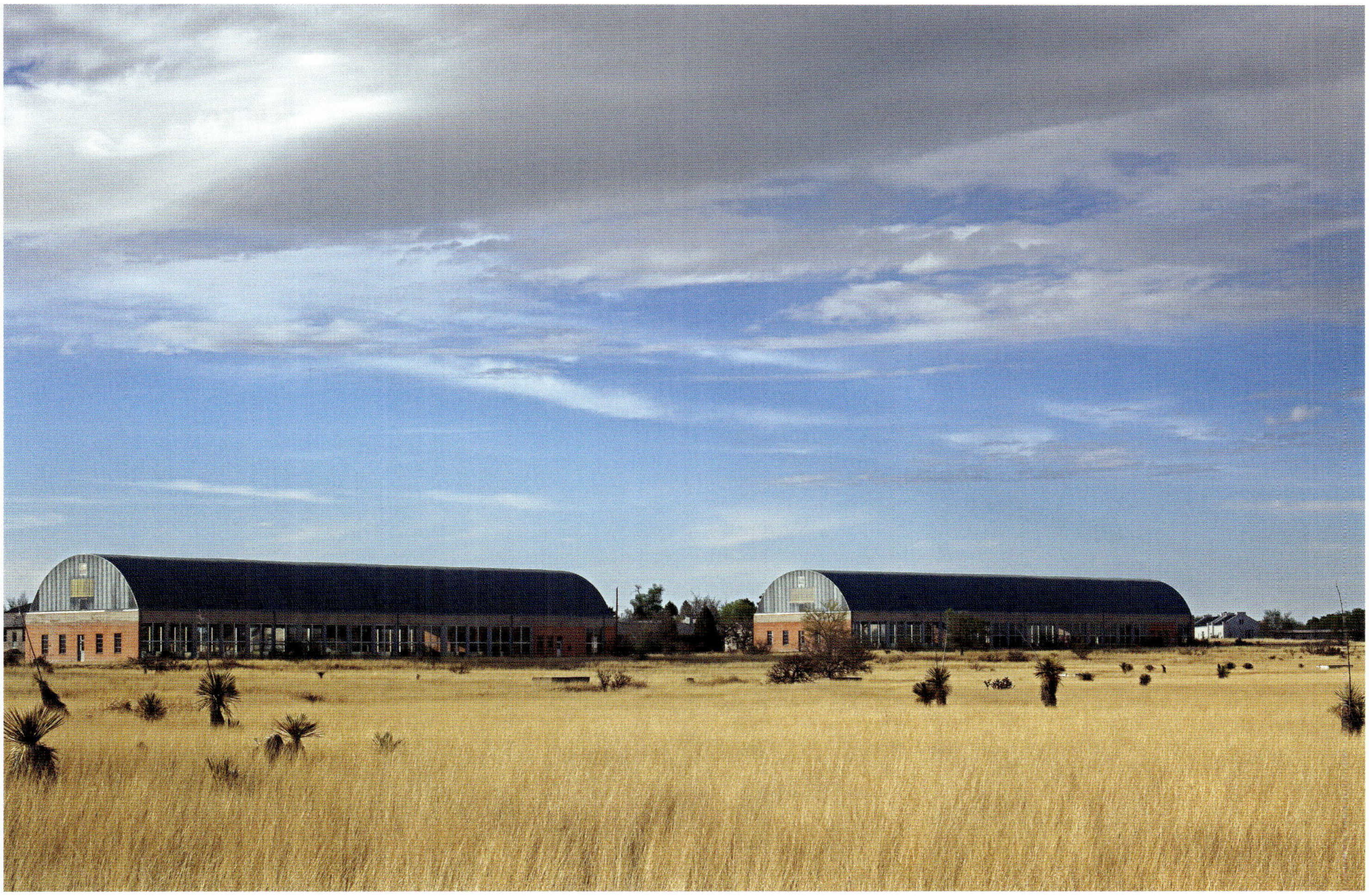

Judd Foundation and Chinati Foundation, USA

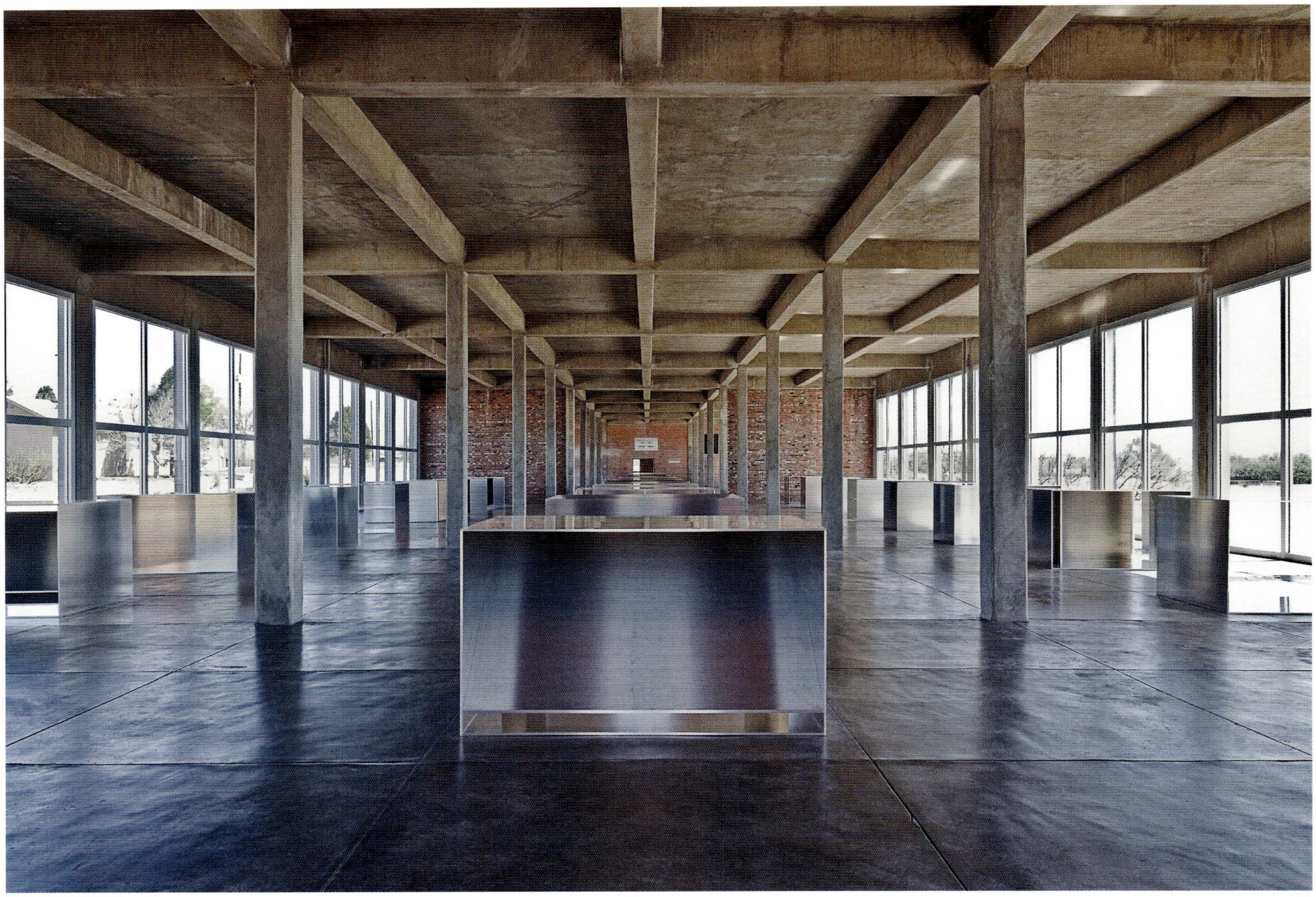

which comprises twelve spectacular light installations with fluorescent light in the long corridors of military barracks.

Judd's boldest artistic leap in his oeuvre and the highpoint of his artistic activities in Marfa came in his experiments with space: the space around an object, space in relation to light that defines the dimensions of the space. In two major, site-specific installations – *100 untitled works in mill aluminum* (1982–86) and *15 untitled works in concrete* (1980–84) – he took two different approaches: one spatial experiment in an internal space and another in the open air. The two installations connect through the long glass walls of the exhibition spaces. "The installation of these works in the Building should be planned so as to form a unified entity of works and space," as Judd explained in one of his letters to the Dia Art Foundation. In the case of his *100 untitled works in mill aluminum* he placed the highly polished, aluminium units – each measuring 41 × 51 × 72 inches (104.1 × 129.5 × 182.9 cm) – in two former artillery sheds, according to a carefully calculated spatial plan. As before, when he had been working on *The Block*, Judd ensured that the building perfectly matched the dimensions of the works of art so that together they would become a single work of art. Judd therefore changed the proportions of the sheds: he replaced the flat roofs with vaulted roofs in galvanised iron thus doubling the height of the building, replaced the side walls with continuous squared and quartered windows and had the concrete floor polished to give it a high sheen. He now positioned the gleaming metal units – with the utmost precision – in this aesthetically charged

The size and proportions of the architecture and the light entering from outside have been precisely adjusted to suit this installation of 100 aluminium boxes with identical external measurements.

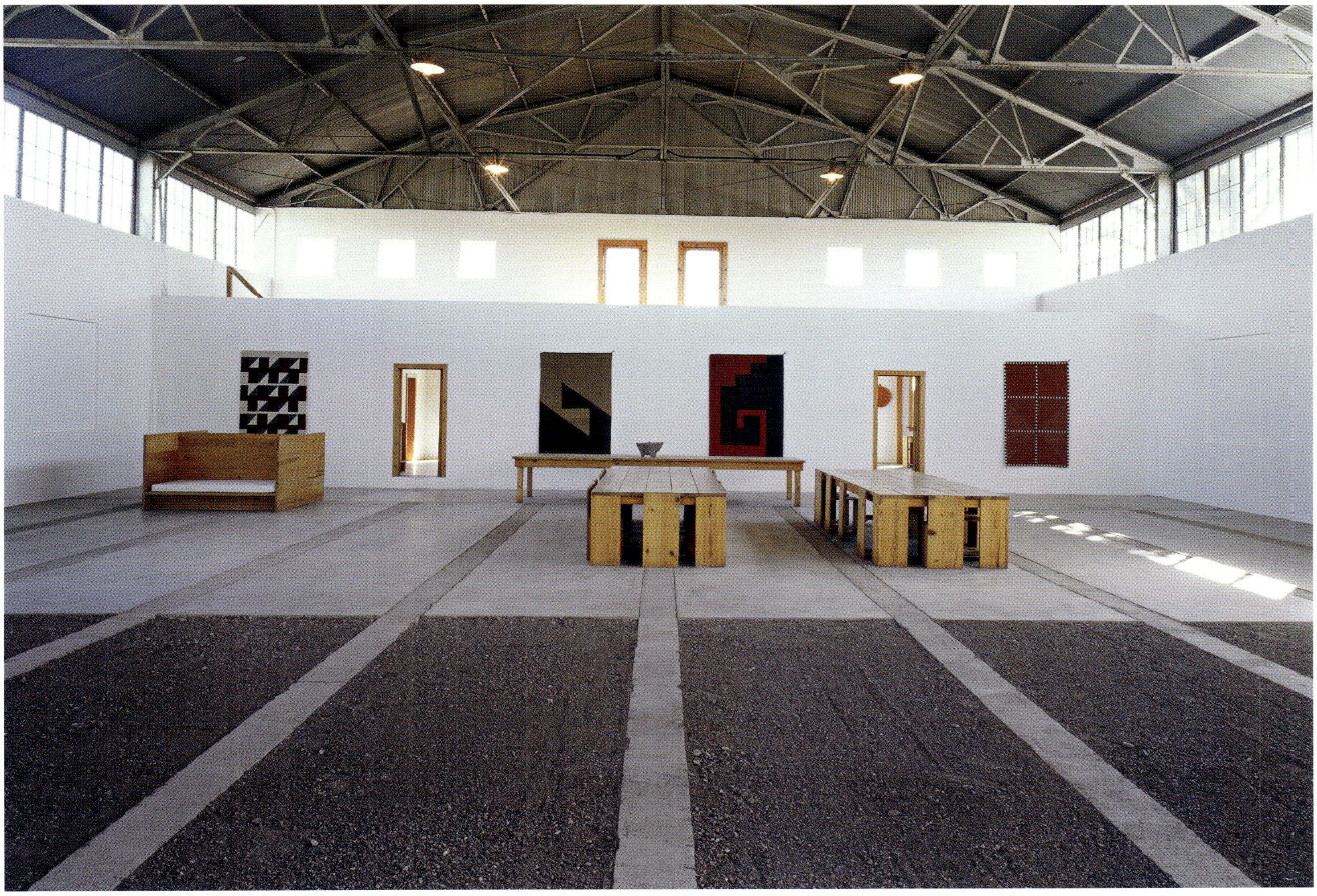

The *Arena* – previously used as a riding hall – where everything, including the furniture made by Judd himself, is a work of art that plays its part in defining the space.

setting. The interior space of each unit is divided differently, using horizontals, verticals and diagonals to create one hundred unique variants. In addition to this the distances between the units and their relationship to the space are calculated with equal precision. Judd worked on this piece – the most radical of his installations – for four years. Light played a crucial part in his experiments, creating unusual reflections, shadows and highlights on the metal surfaces of the units and thus shaping the viewer's perception of the space. Some units suddenly seem to be quite transparent, others appear to be closed. The rigorously hieratic concept for this installation and the space it occupies produces an immensely dynamic effect. And the glass walls allow the spatial interconnections to escape the limits of the interior and continue outside, where Judd placed his *15 untitled works in concrete*, consisting of sixty open, free-standing concrete boxes in total. Each of the fifteen groups is configured differently – as triangles, rectangles or L-shapes – and they are all placed along a straight line with fixed coordinates running parallel to the hills on the horizon. The groups are positioned at intervals of sixty metres and form individual spatial configurations that are perceived differently depending upon the light; at the same time they can also be defined in very different spatial terms as a single installation in a seemingly limitless landscape.

Judd Foundation and Chinati Foundation, USA

WOMEN IN ART

EKEBERGPARKEN, OSLO, NORWAY

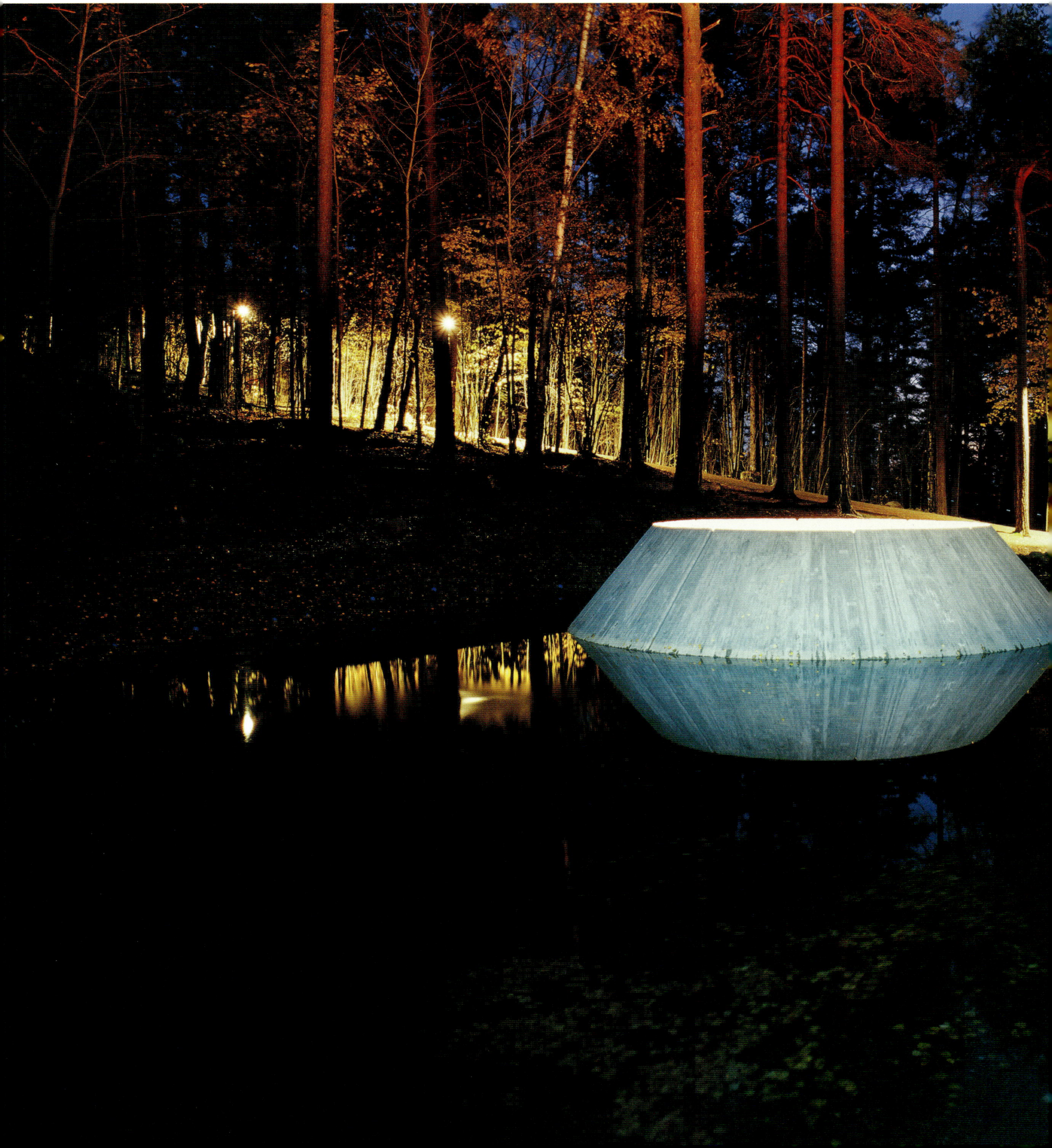

Ideal for observing the bright night skies in the summer in Oslo: James Turrell's Skyspace *Double Vision*, surrounded by water.

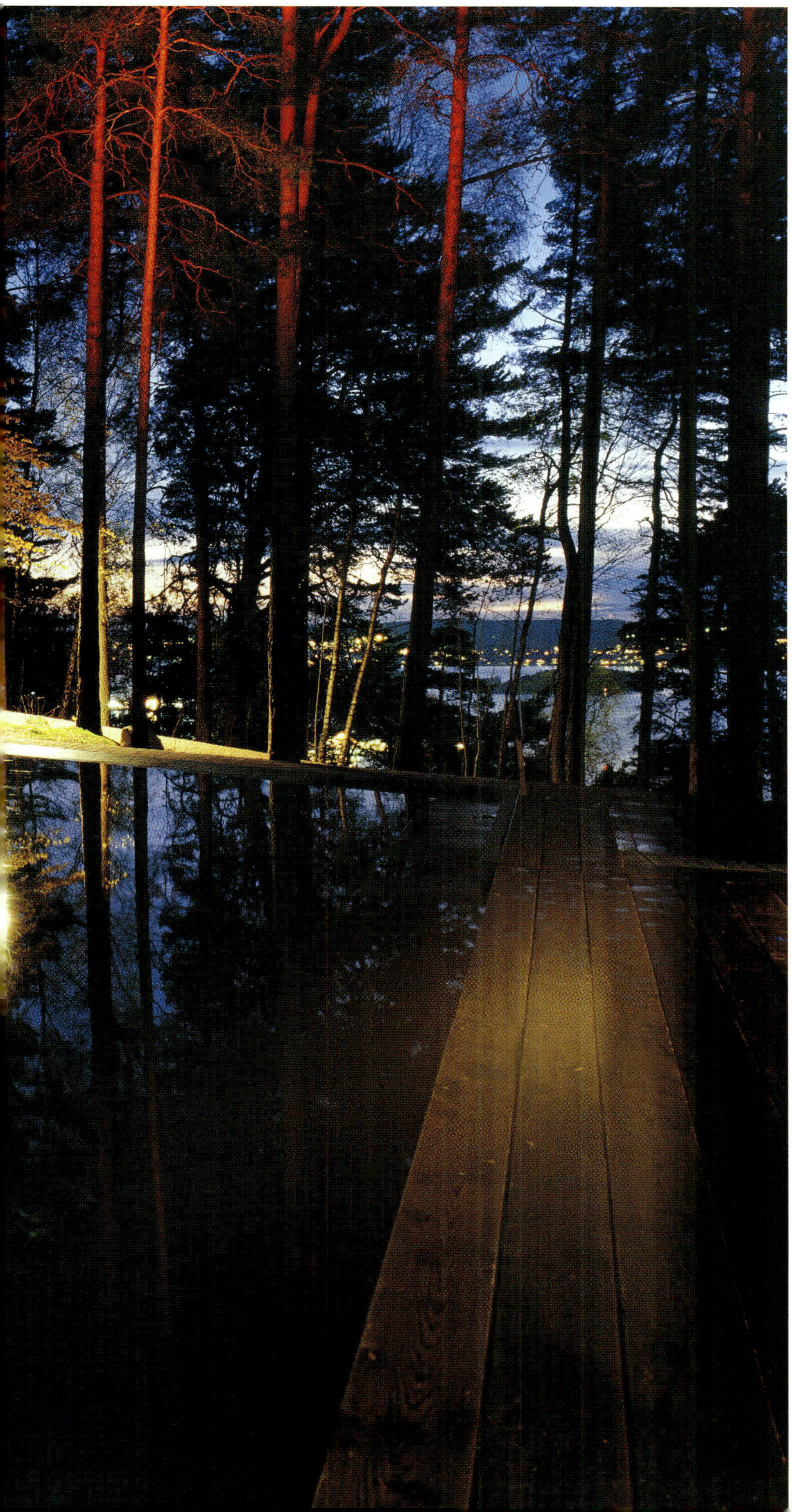

When Christian Ringnes (b. 1954) proposed to the city of Oslo in 2012 that he should turn the badly neglected grounds of the once much-loved Ekebergparken in the south-east of the city into a carefully tended sculpture park he was astonished to meet with such determined resistance. The papers were filled with eye-catching headlines: "Awful: Ringnes to Destroy the Ekebergparken", "Art Instead of Nature", "A Women's Park Made by Men". But Ringnes's intentions were entirely honourable. After all, he had already rescued the now popular Ekeberg Restaurant in the park at great cost to himself and had in effect saved the park from ruin. For ten years this architectural jewel from the 1930s, with spectacular views out over Oslo Bay, had stood empty. When it was being renovated Ringnes had often taken walks in the park, which was in an equally poor state. "Wherever you looked there were used needles and condoms. The paths in the woodland were uncared for, steps were rotting," he recalls. He wanted to change that – by creating a park where art would also be on view. In the end a cooperation agreement was reached between Ringnes and the city. But there were numerous conditions attached to the contract, since the city – as the park's owner – also had to take account of reservations voiced by archaeologists, environmentalists and local historians opposed to the scheme. Above all the archaeologists were worried about the petroglyphs and burial and cult sites from the Stone Age and the Iron Age on this site. For their part the environmentalists and local historians were afraid that Ringnes would alter the layout of the park to accommodate the art. Their concern was the fact that the Ekebergparken had been laid out in the late nineteenth century as a people's park, as a 'green lung' for the workers in the area, who those days were exposed to high levels of industrial air pollution. In addition, the wooded hillside above Oslo Bay had been of great strategic importance to the defence forces during the Second World War. There is still a vivid reminder of this in the imposing staircases for a onetime military memorial that were intended to remain visible for future generations.

Ringnes had to agree not only to cover all the costs for the restoration of the park including any important remains but also

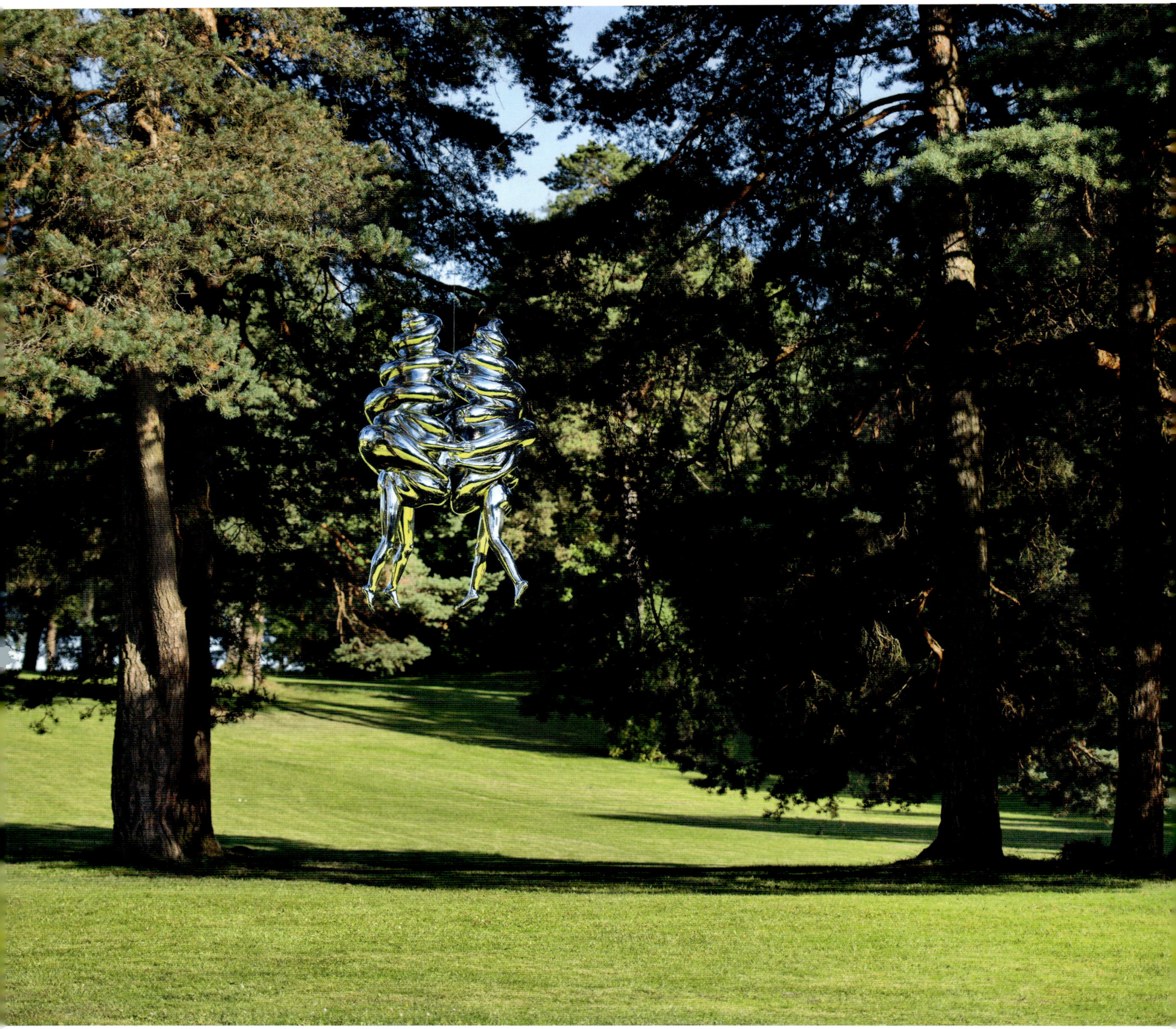

The Couple by Louise Bourgeois: the entanglement of the sexes above the heads of visitors to the park.

to take responsibility for their maintenance. The park's trees could only be touched in so far as was necessary for ecological reasons. In return Ringnes was granted permission to install sculptures in the park for the next fifty years. "But the worst thing was – and is – that we always have to drill boreholes at the sites where we want to install sculpture", he complains, "always in the presence of archaeologists, anthropologists and geologists who see to it that works of art are not installed where there could be prehistoric finds." Ringnes rolls his eyes. "It was so frustrating." Despite all the conditions he had agreed to, up to the park's opening in September 2013 there was a constant hail of protests. But he never lost heart and pursued his project despite all these obstacles. "And now the people of Oslo are proud of the park", he concludes, not without a tinge of irony. As a "documentation for all those who come to the park", he has papered the walls of the smart visitors' toilet at the entrance to the park with newspaper cuttings of the many protestors' calls to action. There is a certain satisfaction in his words now – which is entirely justified, because all his critics have fallen silent, including the feminists. They had objected to the idea that Ringnes's chosen theme for the sculpture park should be "womanhood", even if it was for the best of reasons. "I didn't only want the art to be high quality, I also wanted the park itself to be unique," he explains. And there were other reasons why he chose that theme: "Here in Oslo we already had the Vigeland Park by Gustav Vigeland [1869–1943], with its collection of monumental figures in stone and bronze. It needed a female counterpart. Added to which, Oslo is the city that awards the Nobel Prize for Peace, and in my mind peace has feminine attributes. And lastly the grounds of the Ekebergparken are largely left to grow naturally; this and the notion of creation are symbolic of the feminine."

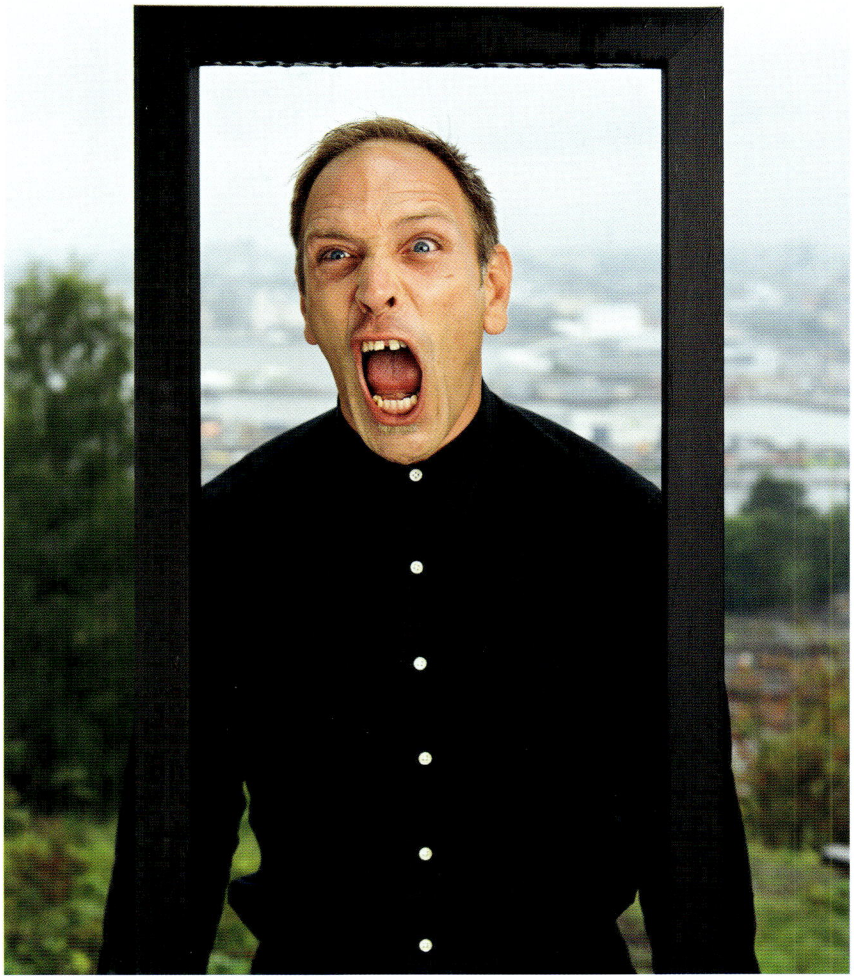

In *The Scream* Marina Abramović invites visitors to release their own primal screams in a homage to Edvard Munch's world-famous work of the same name.

After just one year the Ekebergparken, with (at present) thirty-two sculptures and installations, is already well established as a favourite destination for the people of Oslo – especially for the art. Works by world-renowned artists such as Auguste Rodin, Salvador Dalí, Aristide Maillol and contemporary stars such as Jenny Holzer, Marina Abramović, Louise Bourgeois and Tony Oursler explore a wide range of themes on the subject of womanhood. All the works had to enter into a dialogue with their natural surroundings in this park where there are no gates shutting people out, no opening times and no security guards. "I had never counted on it, but people have shown great respect for the art. We never have problems with vandalism or theft." Quite the opposite – many visitors make a point of thanking Ringnes personally. They come from the city or from the nearby campsite and explore the park with their children, or go jogging, or have picnics on the grass under Louise Bourgeois' gigantic, polished aluminium sculpture *The Couple* (2003), dangling loosely in the wind: a couple entangled in the same cocoon, at the mercy of fate and each other, for better or for worse. And that is what Ringnes particularly enjoys about his sculpture park: unpretentious, spontaneous encounters with art, moments of discovery, the effortless absorption of new ideas. Everywhere there are visitors reading labels. As Ringnes recounts, "Recently someone looking at Auguste Renoir's *Venus Victrix* (1914–16) suddenly said to me, 'Why would you put art like that in a park? She should be in a museum!' So I said, 'But wouldn't that mean that only a handful of people would see her?' And that's how people start to think about art." A similar

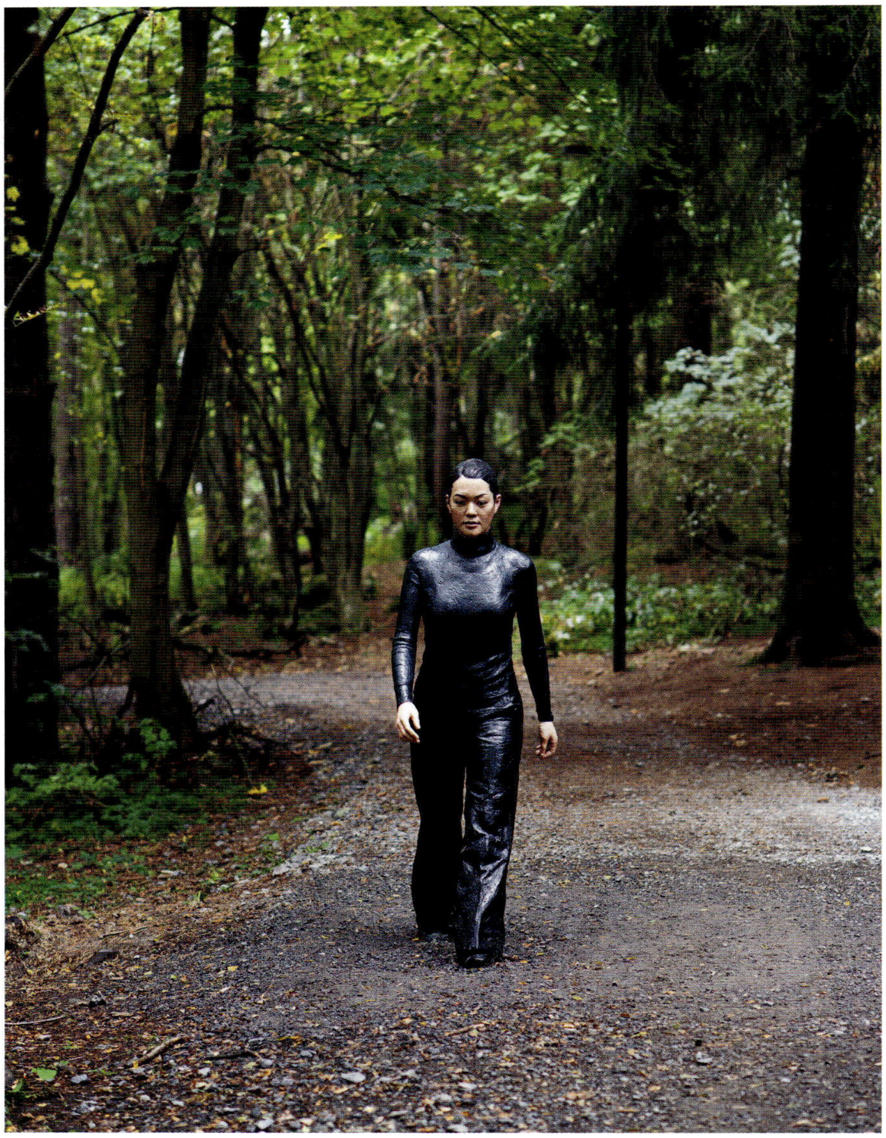

Sean Henry's larger-than-life ***Walking Woman*** **on one of the paths serves as a reminder of the unrestricted public access to the park – even at night.**

Right: As though in the primal cave: a former underground water reservoir is now a mystical, poetic Ganzfeld in this installation by James Turrell.

effect is achieved by *Indre rom VI – livsløpet*, a pavilion by the Norwegian artist Per Inge Bjørlo in the form of an arched space with a huge sculpture under the ceiling with an udder-like appearance. Even though the particular archaeological importance of the park means that there are certain constraints on the artists' choice of location, some have already made outstanding site-specific works. Dan Graham has created a wonderful glass pavilion on the site where there was once a dance pavilion in the original people's park. There is no band playing there any more, but instead visitors interact with their reflections and those of the surrounding woodland. Meanwhile Marina Abramović responded in 2013 to the 150th anniversary of the birth of Norway's most famous artist, Edvard Munch, with a work combining sculpture, performance and film that refers to his painting *The Scream*. At a viewing platform situated in the same place where Munch supposedly discovered the landscape that became the background of his painting, she invited three hundred locals to let out their own primal screams. Ringnes recalls that day: "It was moving; many of them wept afterwards." Abramović's video of that event is already touring the world and will soon be on show in the little museum below the restaurant. But visitors to the park can still similarly rid themselves of all the things weighing on their minds by releasing their own almighty screams.

The most spectacular work in the park is James Turrell's Skyspace *Double Vision* (2013), which is in fact a combination of a Ganzfeld and a Skyspace. A tunnel leading into a steep slope takes the visitor to what was once an underground reservoir. The light space with its two Ganzfelds is initially entirely in darkness – "like a primal cave, a womb," says Ringnes. And then all of a sudden the visitor is bathed in a sequence of coloured glows. It almost seems as though one could reach out and touch the colours. Beyond the double Ganzfeld space a short passage leads to the Skyspace, where the visitor can look out through the open ceiling and watch the constantly changing sky as the sun sets. In Norway, with its light nights, sunsets are very gradual. "Usually I'm an impatient person, but the sunsets here are like meditation for me," says Ringnes with a smile. But *Double Vision* in fact combines sound and space. If visitors stand in the centre of the space and talk in a loud voice, they can feel the sound waves encircling their bodies. The Skyspace itself is set in an artificial pool above the reservoir, embedded in an area of mixed woodland. Long benches invite visitors to gaze at the sky above them and to reflect on the universe.

Sean Henry's *Walking Woman* (2010) has come to symbolise the Ekebergparken – this modern woman, dressed in black, strides confidently and calmly along a woodland path. The extent to which works of art become part of life here is evident in the number of children who immediately want to take her hand. The comment on this achievement that most pleased Ringnes came from a father, who said, glancing at his daughter, "Her first encounter with art – let's hope it's not the last."

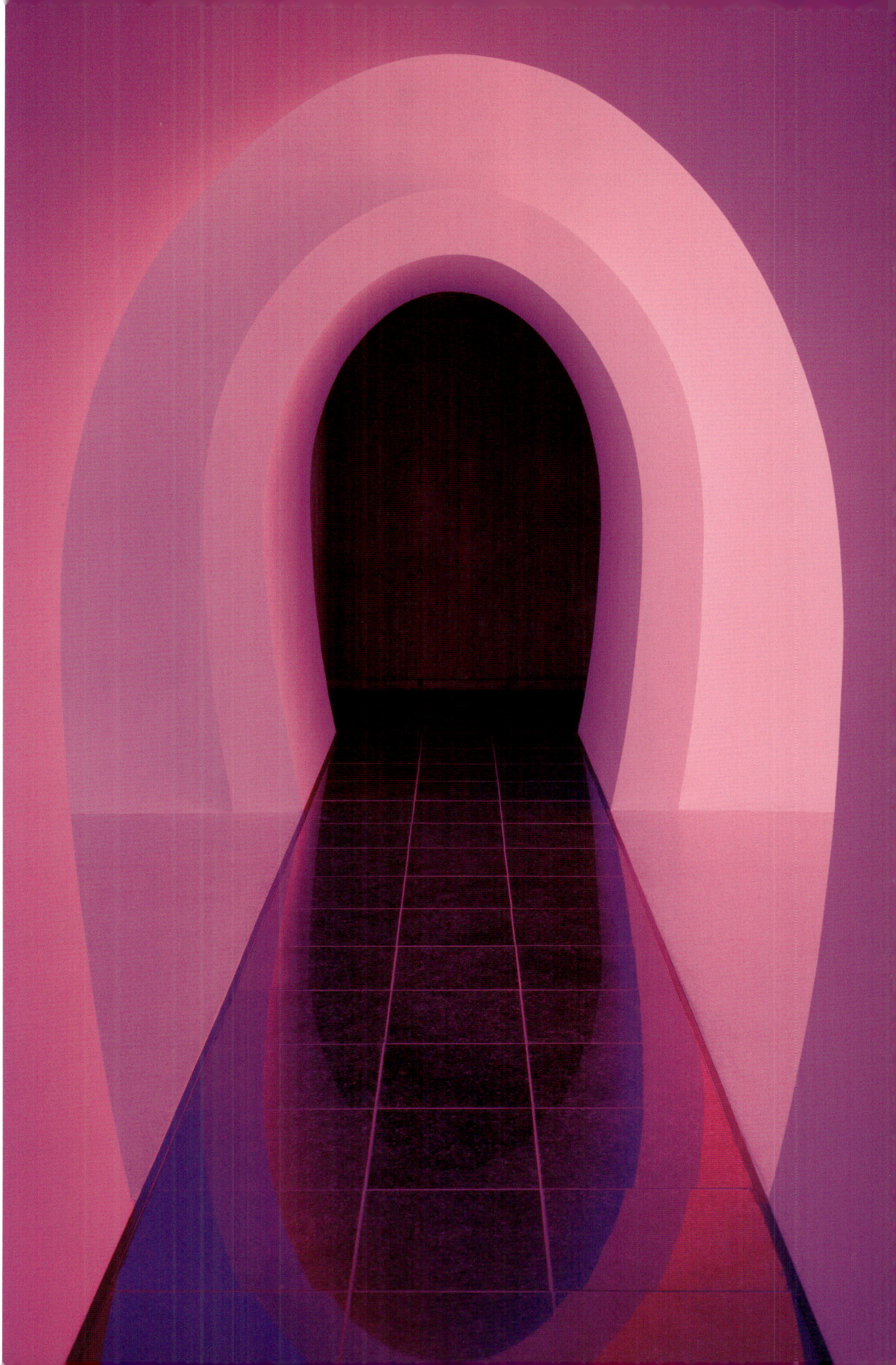

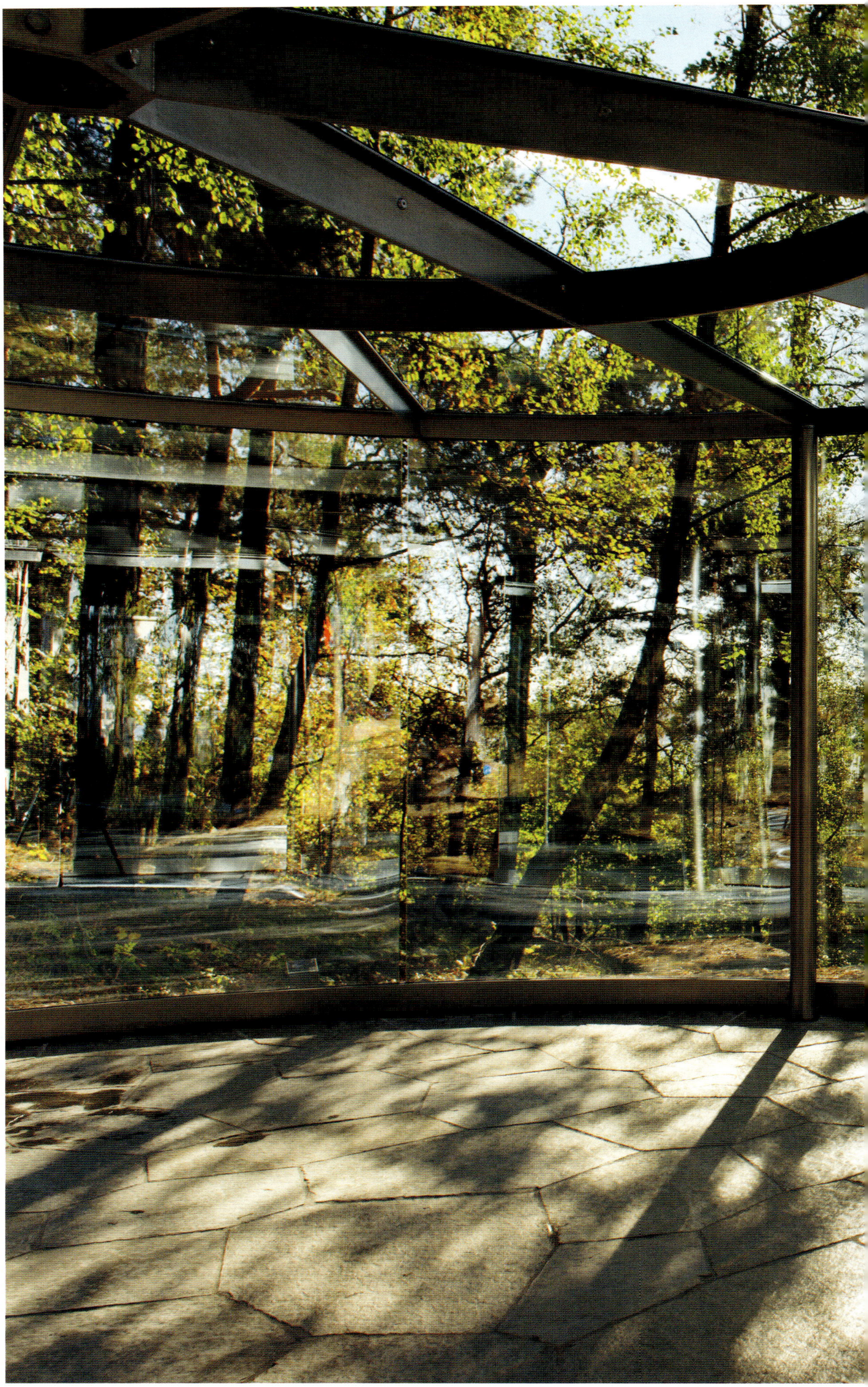

Dan Graham's *Pavilion* creates a twofold reflection of nature: as the female component in the creation myth on the outside and as its own mirror image on the inside.

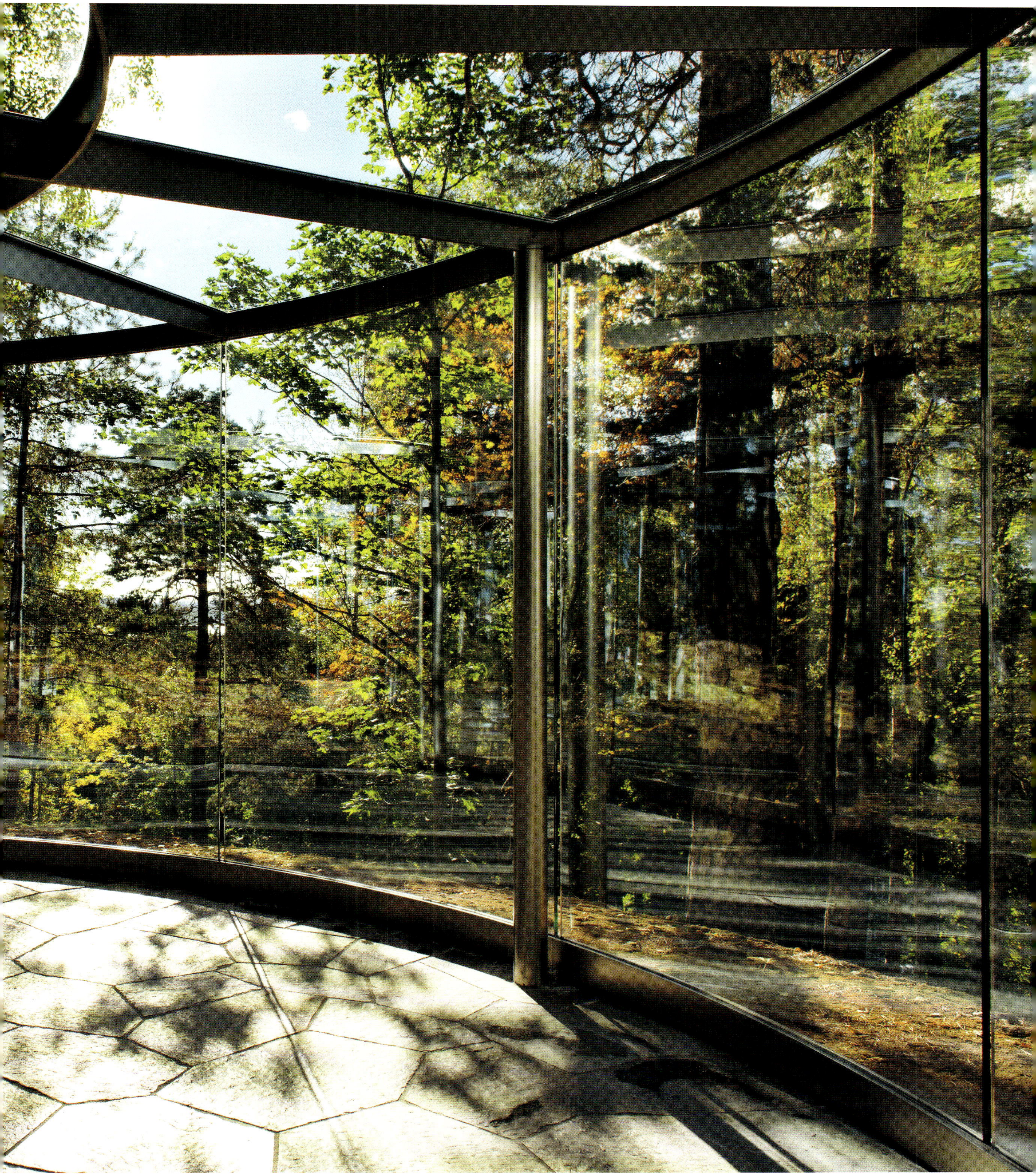

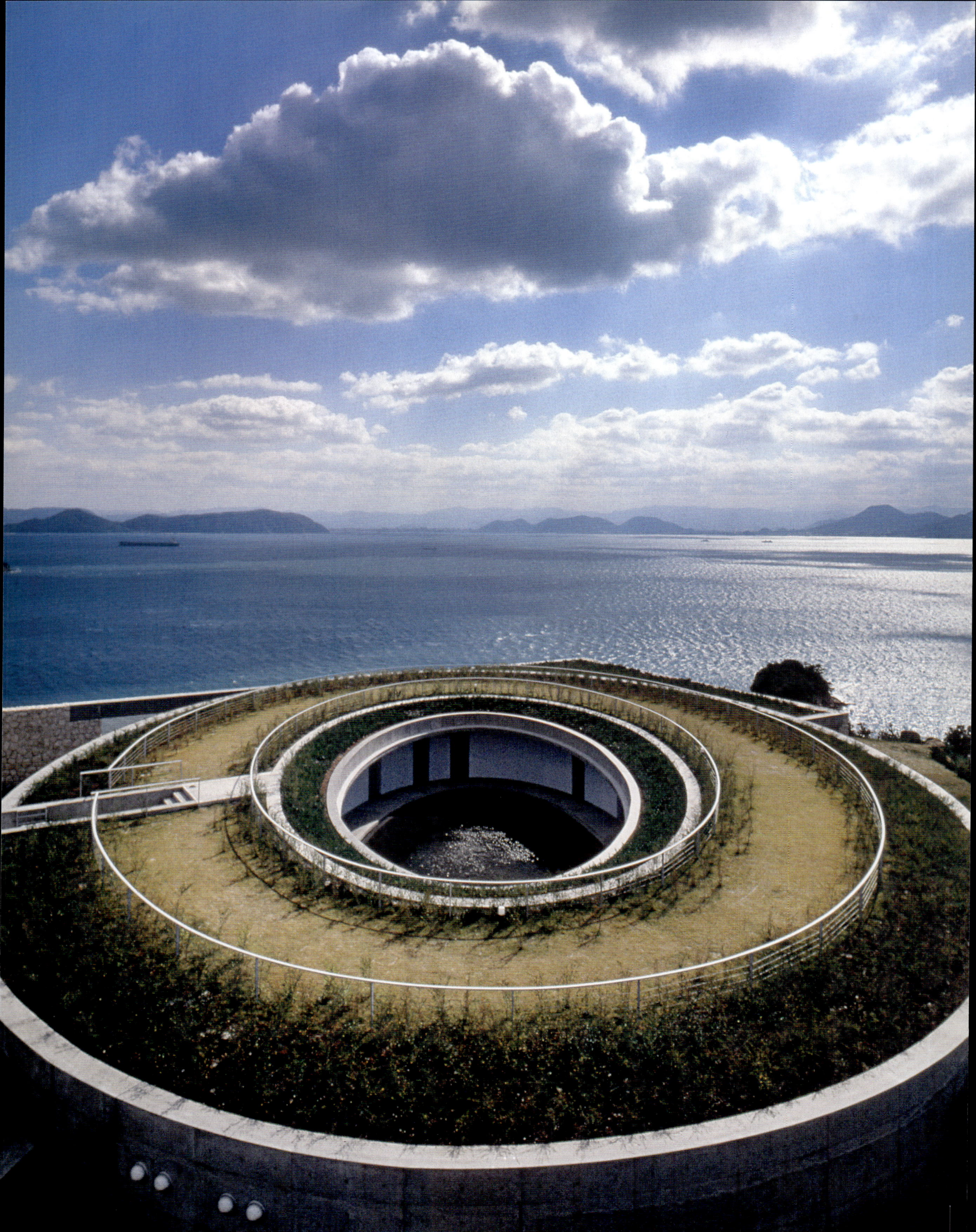

A VISION OF A BETTER LIFE

BENESSE ART SITE NAOSHIMA ON NAOSHIMA, TESHIMA AND INUJIMA, JAPAN

"Good art is like a good life. And a good life makes you happy," says Soichiro Fukutake (b. 1945) smiling as he gazes into the evening sun. This is why the art-obsessed entrepreneur, patron of the arts and visionary not only renamed his business (Fukutake Publishing) Benesse Holdings Inc., he also chose this same name (derived from the Latin *bene* ['well'] and *esse* ['to be'] for his art project: Benesse Art Site. He has created an entirely new, ultimate art experience on three islands – Naoshima, Teshima and Inujima – which form part of an archipelago in the Seto Inland Sea. Fukutake's aim is to create a single entity consisting of nature, architecture and contemporary art. "I want visitors to engage directly with the art and to think about what the phrase 'a good life' really means," he explains with evident determination. In his view nature is the right setting for art – this is where the viewer can truly experience it and feel it.

The journey to the islands is not uncomplicated. Visitors travelling from Osaka have to make a number of connections before finally boarding the ferry to Naoshima. And even then they still have to cross the island to its southernmost tip. This particularly beautiful stretch of land is part of the Setonaikai National Park. And this is where the visitor finds a highly unusual mix of intact nature, a hotel, museums and a sculpture park. After the sudden death of his father in 1986, Soichiro Fukutake not only took over his publishing house in Okayama, he also inherited a project that was very close to his father's heart: an international tented camp on the island of Naoshima for city children who had never had a chance to connect with nature. Through this project he realised how the very considerable urbanisation of so many people in Japan had led them away from their own culture, which is in fact closely linked to a deep appreciation of nature. And, looking at the Seto Islands, which were once renowned for their beauty, he saw the damage that had been done by industrialisation. Environmental pollution and industrial waste had left their mark: paddy fields had run wild, derelict industrial sites disfigured the landscape, villages were falling into ruin – developments that are seen in all highly industrialised societies. And with ever-decreasing employment opportunities, the young people were leaving for the city. But Fukutake had a vision of how to solve these problems, how to reverse the course of civilisation, diverting it from destruction and realigning it towards the optimisation of the resources on hand.

The idea of using art in the landscape to reconnect people with nature came to Fukutake not least through his friendship with the leading Japanese architect Tadao Ando (b. 1941). And it was Ando who developed the concept for the *Gesamtkunstwerk* at Benesse, namely that the visitor should be aware of the connection between nature and art at all times. In the vast entrance hall of Benesse House, which is both a museum and a hotel, the 'weeds' that seem to be growing out of the smooth, seemingly perfect concrete walls are in fact virtuosic carvings by the artist Yoshihiro Suda. In the exhibition spaces Ando's huge windows give as much importance to the spectacular views out over the inland sea as to the works exhibited inside the building – by world-renowned artists such as Jannis Kounellis, Yves Klein, Jasper Johns and Richard Long. An oversized yellow pumpkin with black polka dots by the Japanese artist Yayoi Kusama sits proudly on the island's pier. At the beach, free of deck chairs and sun shades, there are large-scale installations, such as the seemingly foundered *Shipyard Works: Cut Bow* (1990) by Shinro Ohtake. The Chinese artist Cai Guo-Qiang has installed a hot tub in the middle of a field by the sea for hotel guests. Mighty *taihu* rocks are placed according to the principles of Feng Shui around this *Cultural Melting Bath* (1998); their bizarre shapes relate to the rocky outlines of the Seto Islands. Walter De Maria's installation *Seen/Unseen – Known/Unknown* (2000), under the first tread of a gigantic stairway (another work by Tadao Ando), consists of two huge spheres of polished granite that catch the rays of the rising sun and thus mark the easternmost tip of the island. The stairway itself is a huge sculpture: *l'art pour l'art*.

The other two museum buildings on Naoshima – Chichu Art Museum and Lee Ufan

Architecture and sculpture: Tadao Ando's *Benesse House Oval*. A building designed as several ovals which sits on the top of the hill like a bird's nest.

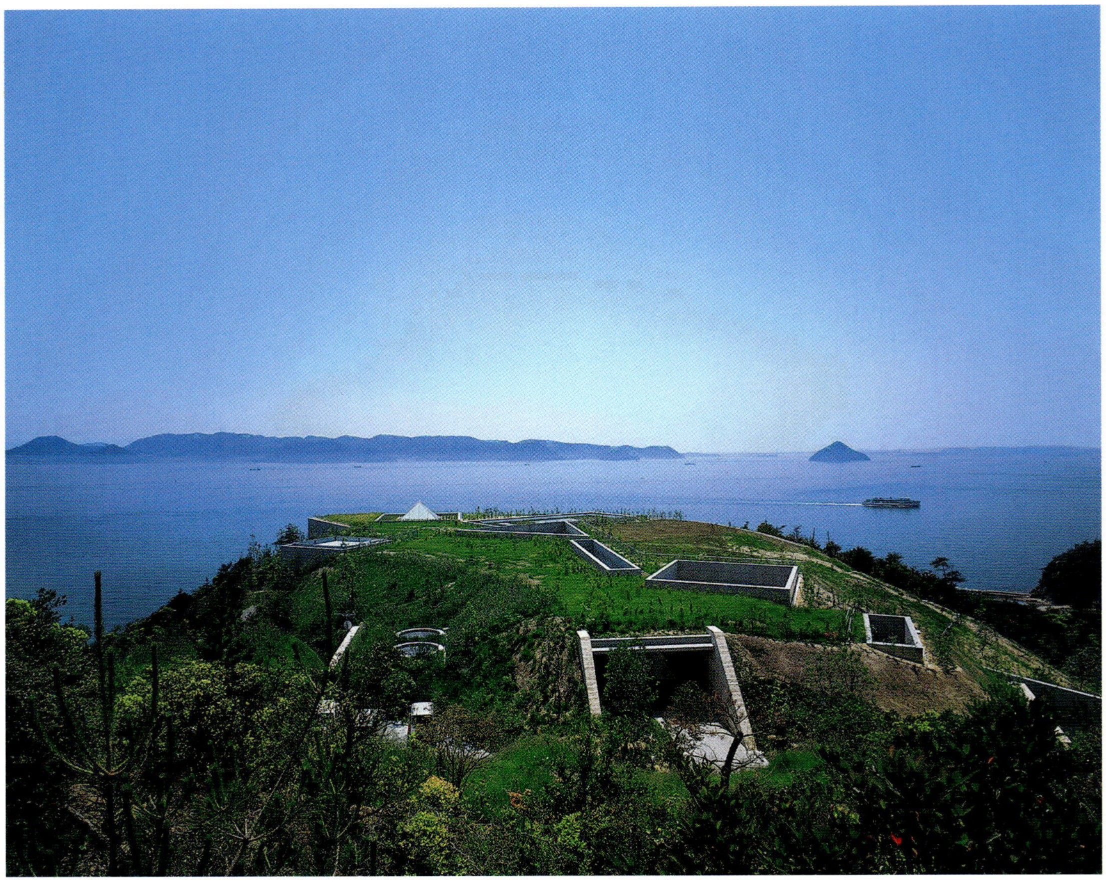

The Chichu Art Museum is mostly underground and reflects the relationship of humankind and nature in a new way.

Right: *Art House Project, Go'o Shrine*: For *Appropriate Proportion* (2002) Hiroshi Sugimoto reconfigured the old shrine with an underground stone chamber and steps made from optical glass.

Museum – are also architectural sculptures. Tadao Ando's interest is in the internalisation of art, in the truest sense of the term. The entire structure of Chichu Art Museum is hidden inside a rocky hill high above the sea (*chichu* means "in the earth"). A cave-like, underground museum-labyrinth for works of art by just three artists: Claude Monet, Walter de Maria and James Turrell. Friendly but strict museum personnel ensure that people either speak very quietly or not at all. Visitors who want to see the water lilies by Claude Monet have to remove their shoes and put on slippers. There is no artificial lighting, just soft, diffuse daylight entering through the light tunnels in the ceiling. The rooms are entirely white. Everything seems to be floating because the viewer does not have the usual reference points, such as the clear definition of the floor. As a result one's senses are heightened. The almost sacred ambience created by Tadao Ando celebrates these sublime works of art. And there is an air of deep mysticism surrounding the light installations by James Turrell, including his *Open Field* (2000) – a room in which visitors enter only to find themselves entirely surrounded by light. Following this a small staircase, in complete darkness, leads the visitor up to an approximately five-metre-wide fluorescent-blue rectangle. But a surprise awaits, because what looks like a huge wall painting turns out be an entire room filled with fluorescent light. Lee Ufan Museum, with its sparse interiors and courtyards, has a similarly labyrinthine layout. The minimalist architecture is in perfect symbiosis with the radically reduced art of the Korean-Japanese artist Lee Ufan. The visitor finds tranquillity and emptiness here, nothing more and nothing less. In one of the rooms Lee Ufan applied one huge brushstroke directly to the wall.

In 1998 Soichiro Fukutake realised it would be a mistake to concentrate solely on making the islands attractive to art lovers in need of rest and recuperation. He therefore founded his *Art House Project*, on the basis that art should be integrated into the daily lives of local residents so that they, too, would be sensitised to the unique qualities of their landscapes and culture, to the "good life" here. "I want them not to leave the islands for the city," he says and adds vehemently, "Urbanisation is the cause of all the alienation and environmental damage in Japan!" Through the Benesse Foundation he bought or leased abandoned houses on all three islands and had them restored in the traditional regional style. But that was not all. Artists were commissioned to work with the local villagers to create art sites. "The locals should be proud of their villages and their culture," says Fukutake emphatically. And they are proud – above all the residents in Honmura, one of the three villages on Naoshima. In what used to be the kitchen in *Kadoya* (1998), a 200-year-old farmhouse, the artist Tatsuo Miyajima – with the help of local residents – created the light installation *Sea of Time* (1998): 125 blinking digital counters floating in a pool of water counting from one to nine at different speeds. The speed of each sequence of numbers was decided by the locals and they also explain the work of art to visitors. With his remodelling of a derelict Shinto shrine the artist Hiroshi Sugimoto created a striking work of art and

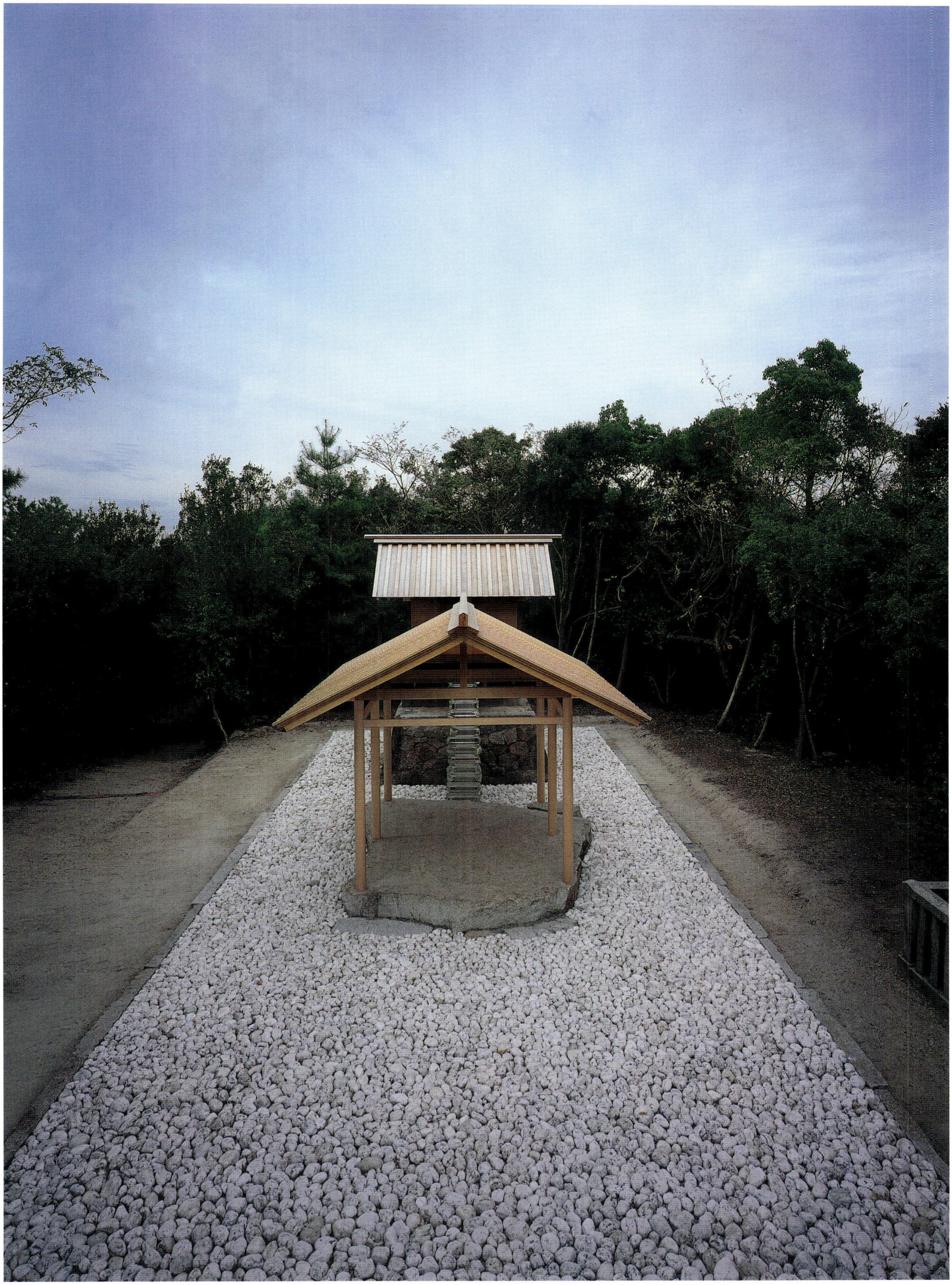

Benesse Art Site Naoshima, Japan

an important new place of worship. A staircase of large, optical lenses connects the main building with an underground chamber – symbolically linking Heaven and Earth.

In order to encourage communication between visitors and the locals, the artist Shinro Ohtake was commissioned to create a *sento* – a public bathhouse: the *Naoshima Bath "I Love 湯"* (湯, *yu*, means "hot water"). In the traditional Japanese *sento* bathers soak and chat in hot water, which can be as much as 56 degrees Celsius. In his *sento* Ohtake used fantastic found objects he had collected all over Japan: brightly coloured columns, a ship's hull on the ground floor, an aeroplane cockpit between palms on the roof – and all sorts of kitschy mosaic pictures in the interior, along with a large elephant from an erotica museum, which now watches over the bathing pool.

As in the Lee Ufan Museum, tranquillity and emptiness are also paramount in Teshima Art Museum, which was opened in 2010 on the island of that name. Since the 1980s this island and its once flourishing paddy fields had been used as a dump for industrial waste, with blatant disregard for the relevant laws. But now it has become a

Ryue Nishizawa and Rei Nato created the Teshima Art Museum in shape of a droplet of water lying on the ground. Inside it visitors hone their perceptual responses to nature.

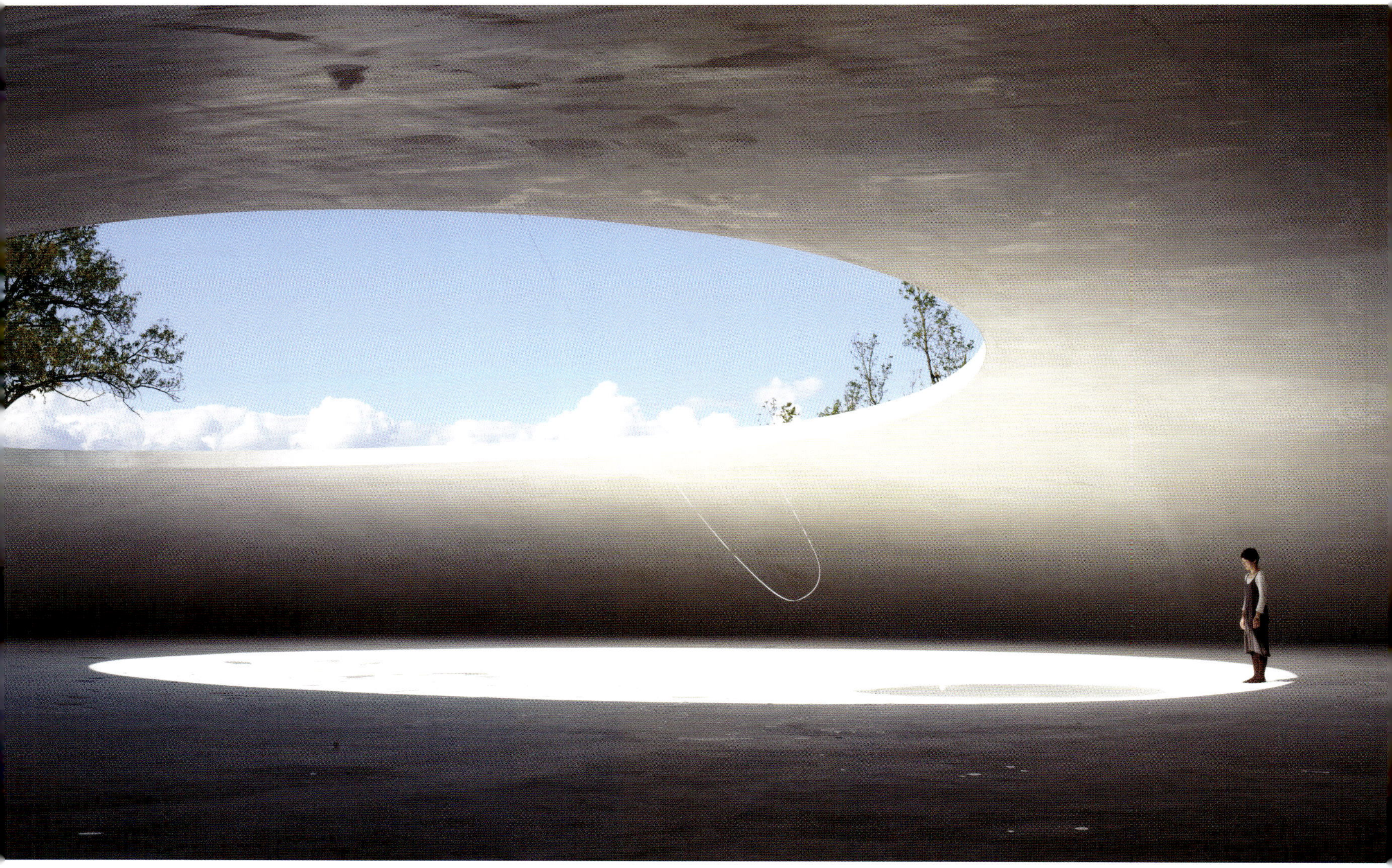

Inujima Seirensho Art Museum: Yukinori Yanagi and Hiroshi Sambuichi have turned the former copper refinery on Inujima into a *Gesamtkunstwerk*.

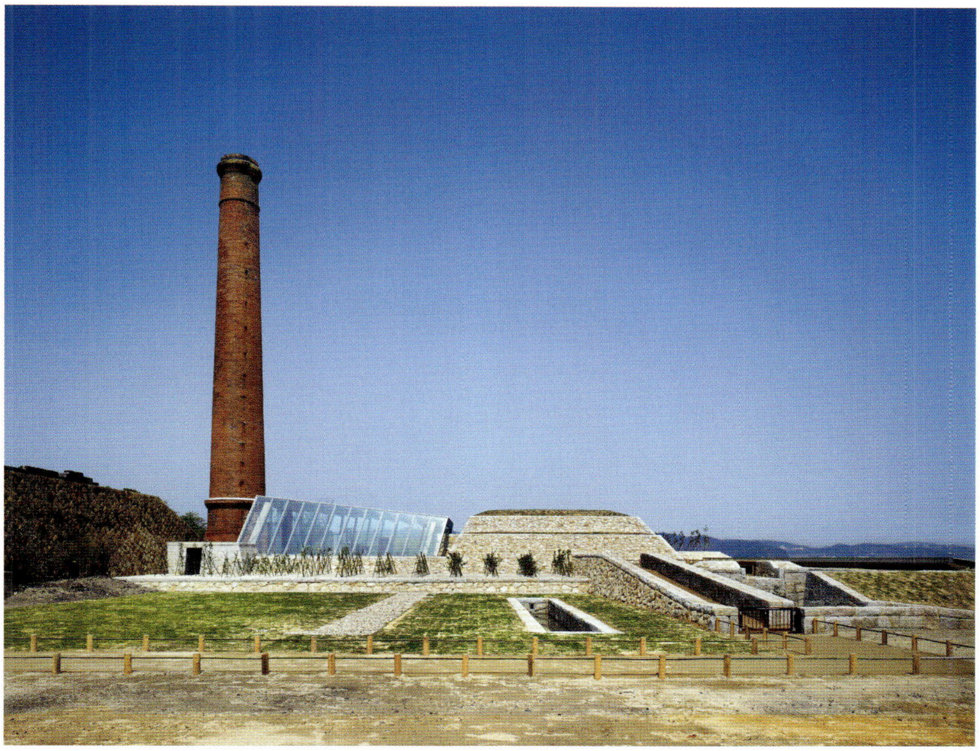

place of pilgrimage for art lovers from all over the world who come to gaze upon one of the most extraordinary architectural sculptures: a museum that consists of a large, empty shell covering an area of forty by sixty metres. It looks like a huge raindrop that has landed on a hillside. In the ceiling there are two elliptical apertures, one at either end, which expose the interior to the rain, the wind and storms. It was this interplay of water, wind and light that interested the architect Ryue Nishizawa and the installation artist Rei Nato. Visitors to this museum are again asked to refrain from conversation and to concentrate fully on the drama of the natural forces entering the space. Suddenly one hears the trickling of droplets of water. These are pumped up through the ground into the interior, where the wind catches them and blows them into bizarre little rivulets, which run to and fro on the smooth, polished surface of the floor. With this minimalist water installation, *Matrix* (2010), Rei Nato makes reference to both the architecture and its position on an island. Around the museum Soichiro Fukutake had the rice terraces reinstated and now the previously mistreated land is fertile again. He wants "people to become familiar with our ancient culture of rice cultivation."

Finally, Soichiro Fukutake linked his art activities on the three islands – Naoshima, Teshima and Inujima – with the Setouchi Triennale, which had originally been initiated by the Kagawa Prefecture in order to highlight the unique features of the individual islands in an era of globalisation. Fukutake widened the remit of the Triennale "in order to create something akin to Documenta in Kassel – but in a place that is famous for its environmental sins," as he himself put it. Like the great art exhibition in Germany, every three years since 2010 different Seto islands host exhibitions for one hundred days and once abandoned locations become temporary venues for art by younger artists. The *Art House Project* on Inujima is also part of this: old houses, gardens and the centre of the village become works of art in their own right. However, the main attraction on this island is Inujima Seirensho Art Museum. Here Fukutake deliberately chose the remains of a copper refinery as the centre of his latest activities. This vast site, with brick walls and chimney stacks up to forty metres in height, serves as another dramatic demonstration of the wounds inflicted by industrialisation. In 2008 the young architect Hiroshi Sambuichi from Hiroshima and the artist Yukinori Yanagi transformed this industrial skeleton into a spectacular museum building. At the same time Sambuichi created a prime example of sustainable construction, making use of the existing substance of the building and deploying environmentally friendly practices such as solar energy, geothermal energy and ventilation. This vast work of art is a labyrinth of dark corridors where the visitor is partly guided by mirrors. In *Hero Dry Cell* (2008) by Yanagi, the visitor's way through the darkness into hall-like spaces is lit by a single light source: a projection behind the visitor's back. The work reflects on the life and work of the renowned Japanese writer and cultural critic Yukio Mishima (1925–1970), an artist and political activist whose dramatically staged suicide was intended to alert his fellow citizens to the loss of Japanese culture through overly rapid industrialisation and Westernisation. In other parts of the museum Yanagi created eerily poetic spatial installations comprising original items from Mishima's home in Tokyo.

At Inujima Seirensho Art Museum, its founder Soichiro Fukutake once again presents the world with a striking example of the questionable legacy of modernity, but he also offers a solution in his demand for a new society that is oriented towards sustainability and aesthetics. In his own words, "I hope to create a society with 'well balanced values', where art helps to put a smile on the locals' faces again and city dwellers are filled with envy." He wants people to discuss the concept of *benesse*, to question existing social systems and to strive towards new ways of living; in short, he feels that a new philosophy is needed for civilisation in the twenty-first century. And he has already proved that this is possible with his extraordinary art projects on once ravaged islands in the Seto Inland Sea.

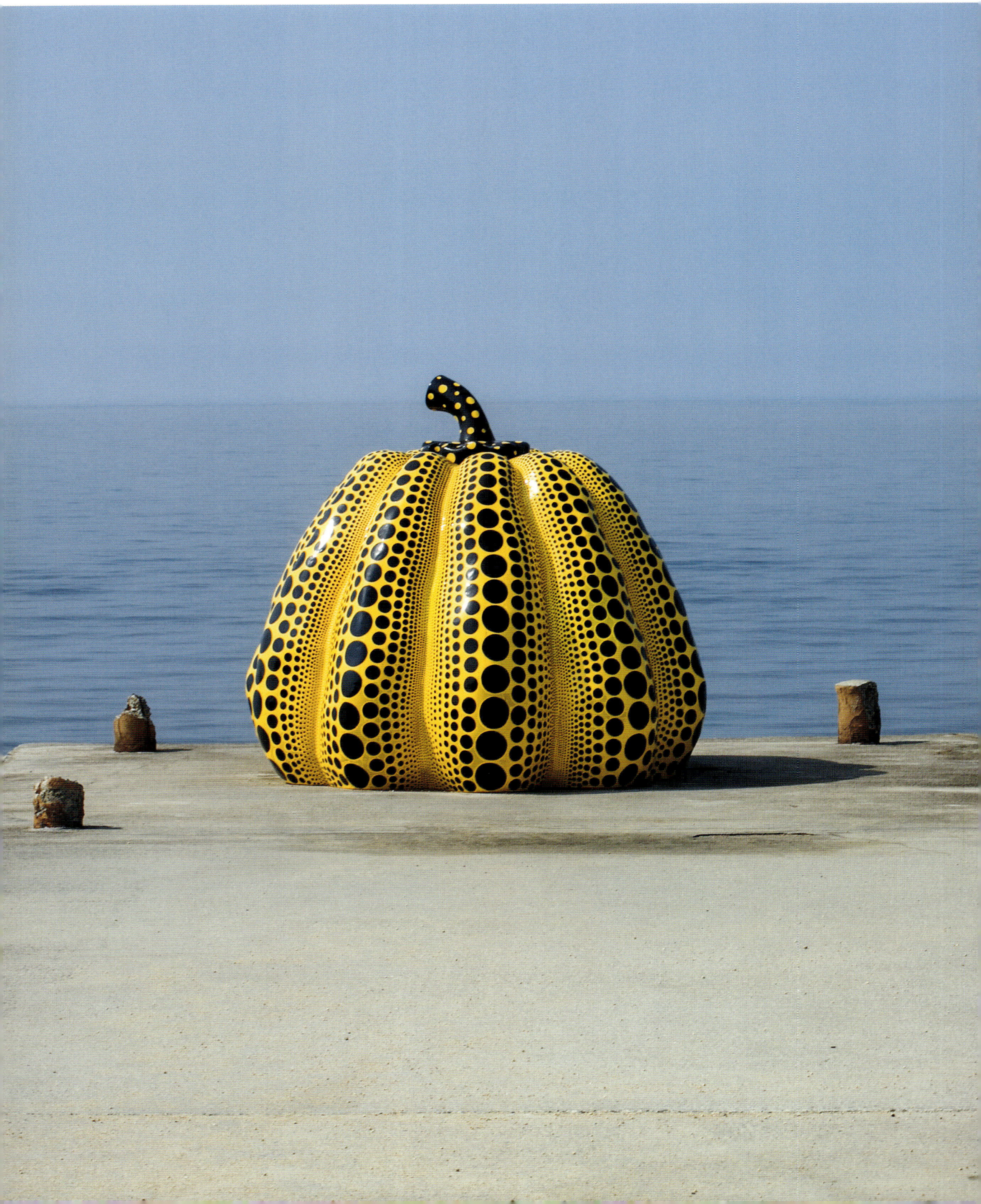

By the sea: large-format sculptures like this *Pumpkin* by Yayoi Kusama.

FROM ART ISLAND TO CULTURAL REALM

STIFTUNG INSEL HOMBROICH, NEUSS, GERMANY

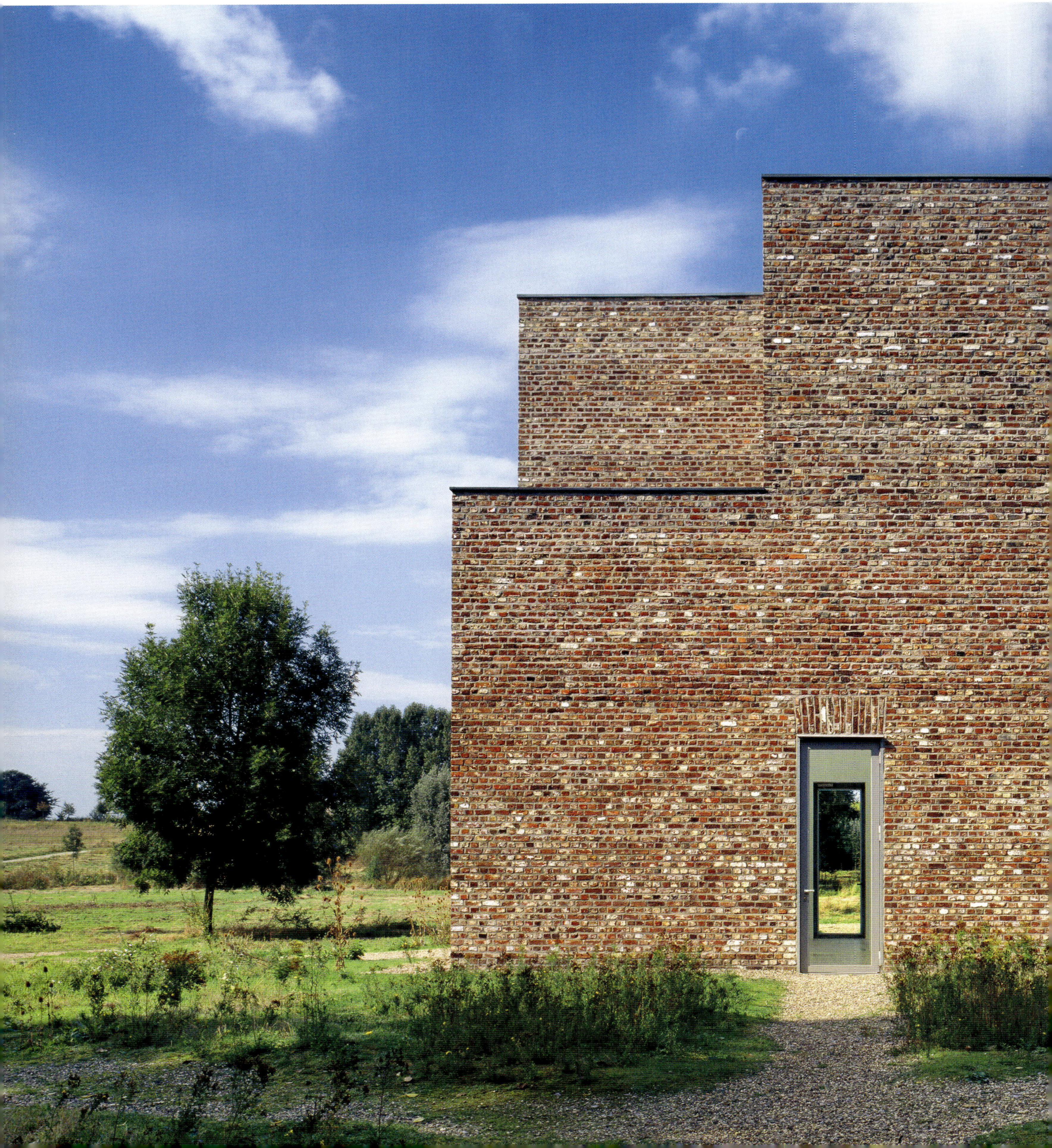

Art and nature: Erwin Heerich's *Tower* is an architectural sculpture – an empty space with four doors leading out into the landscape.

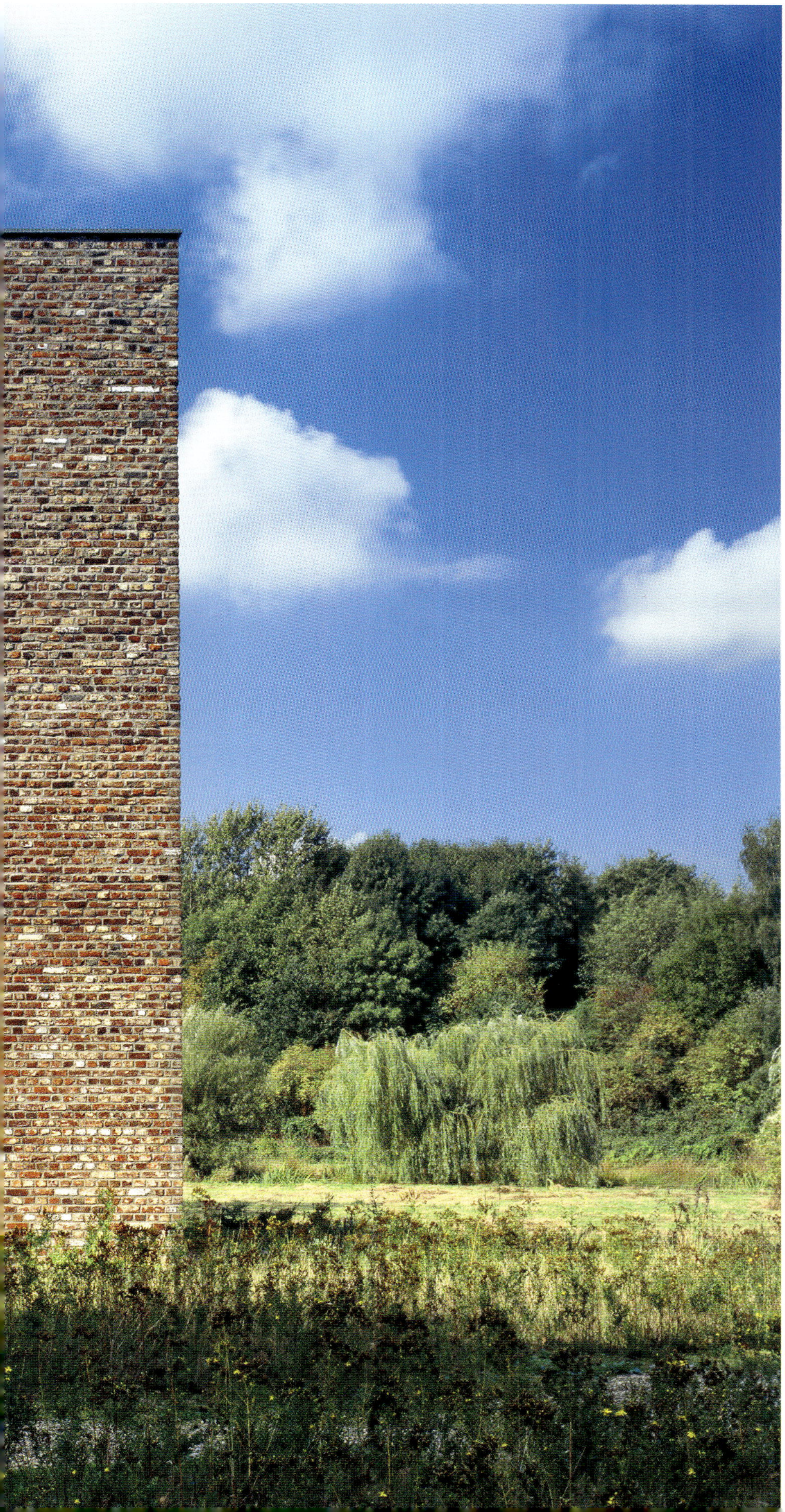

Smoke rising from factory chimneys, motorways and a decommissioned military base. The highly successful property developer Karl-Heinrich Müller (1936–2007) could hardly believe his good fortune that it was here, right outside his home town of Düsseldorf, that he found the perfect piece of open country for his unusual museum concept. Ever since the 1970s, when he had had to start stacking his pictures under beds because of a lack of space, he had dreamt of creating a private museum, outside the city, where he could exhibit art, as Paul Cézanne once said, "parallel to nature" – with exhibition pavilions in amongst natural vegetation, in an intact landscape, where art and nature would be seen on equal terms, as a single entity. It was an idea that quickly turned into a visionary project on the grand scale, even a new life philosophy, in which art, culture and nature are equals.

In 1982 he acquired Insel Hombroich for this purpose: a site with a grand villa, outhouses and parklands. In the early nineteenth century the Wuppertal entrepreneur Peter de Weerth built an idyllic summer retreat for his family in the midst of marshy pastures. However, visitors to the site after the Second World War found that the villa, the Rosa Haus, had fallen into disrepair, the parklands were running wild and the pastures had been ploughed up for crops. Little was to be seen of the island the house had been built on. The curve of the river Erft had long since silted up. Müller had it dredged. His plan was to exhibit his own collection in one part of the villa, while the outhouses were renovated for two good friends, the sculptor Erwin Heerich (1922–2004) and the painter Gotthard Graubner (1930–2013), providing each with his own studio and exhibition space. The sculptor Anatol Herzfeld converted a barn into a studio for himself. Now the core of Müller's 'island family' all had their own spaces. These were his closest companions, with whom he was in constant contact as he developed yet more ideas for his museum project in the countryside. At the same time, the renowned landscape architect Bernhard Korte started to reinstate the original layout of the parklands. He studied the old drawings and turned the surrounding fields (which Müller had also acquired) back into pastureland – with artificial ponds, slim black poplars and

Stiftung Insel Hombroich, Germany

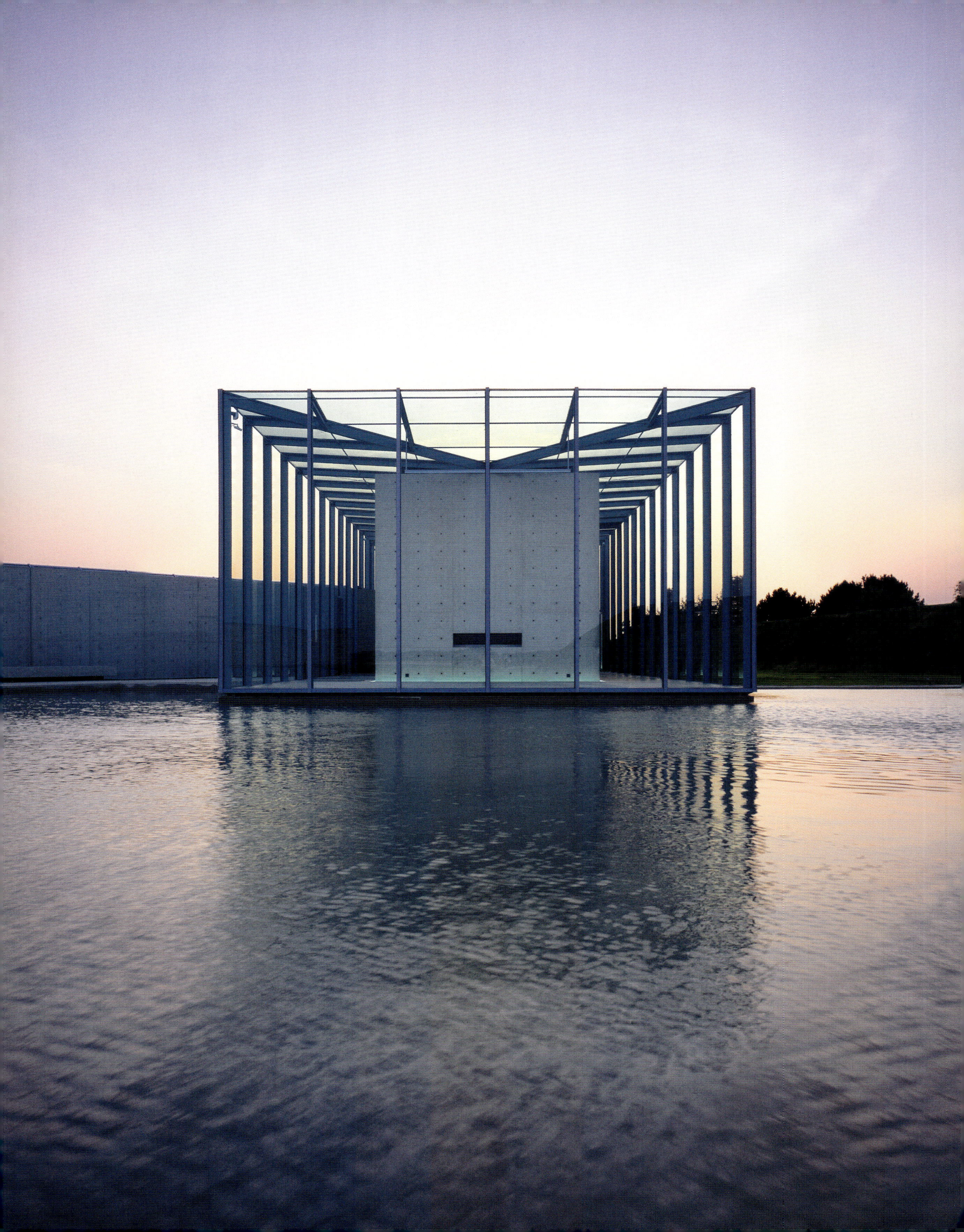

wind-tossed pollard willows. Alongside the fruit trees a country garden was laid, with perennials between the vegetable patches and the fruit bushes. And up above a ridge in the nearly sixty-acre grounds, terracing with meadows was created. Müller wanted a natural-looking landscape, a balance of design and natural vegetation. Any interventions were to be "as few as possible and as many as necessary."

Meandering paths invite the visitor to explore the grounds, benches allow for moments of quiet repose. There are ten pavilions with brick façades distributed through the expansive landscape, their simple forms and meditative presence having been described as "chapels in the landscape". Designed by the Heerich, he based his designs on geometric forms such as circles, rectangles and squares, from which he developed minimalist cuboids: the *Snail*, the *Labyrinth* and the Twelve-Room House. They are autonomous, walk-in sculptures, built as display rooms for a large part of Karl-Heinrich Müller's art collection.

Karl-Heinrich Müller was, in the best sense of the word, obsessed with art. By the age of nineteen he already had several thousand slides with images of works of art from the Middle Ages right through to classical modernism. Thanks to his early professional success, he was soon in a position to start acquiring art in all genres and from every epoch. And he proved to have a good collector's instinct. Early on he realised the importance of artists such as Yves Klein, Eduardo Chillida and, above all, Kurt Schwitters. But he also collected prehistoric objects that had not yet been studied by scholars in the field. Driven by an insatiable curiosity for all things new, Müller constantly sought out interesting people with whom he could exchange ideas and from whom he could learn. Gotthard Graubner was his most important adviser in all he did. "He was the motor," as Müller once said. Together the two men travelled all over tracking down unusual art objects: heads from Cambodia, Chinese sculptures from the Han dynasty, archaeological finds from South America, etchings by Rembrandt, furniture by Gerrit Rietveld, paintings by Lovis Corinth. The overriding criterion for any purchase was the timelessness of the item in question. Regardless of their style, time and cultural origins, the objects and works of art Müller acquired had to work together. It was through Graubner that Müller learnt to identify the internal connections between different cultures. And Graubner combined widely diverse artefacts to create autonomous, artistic installations rooted in the formal and tonal affinities of different works of art and that create spatial and thematic connections between them: Rembrandt drawings juxtaposed with works by Alberto Giacometti, protohistoric sculptures from Luristan with pictures by Hans Arp and Jean Fautrier, works by Kurt Schwitters and African objects, Gotthard Graubner's own meditative cushion pictures together with Buddha sculptures from the Khmer Empire. "Every painting, every sculpture, every object must be allowed to speak for itself, so that it can come fully into its own," as Graubner himself said. His installation has been retained; it is a permanent feature of the exhibition building. In the largely windowless, whitewashed rooms there is an almost sacred atmosphere. The only lighting for the works of art is daylight from above. The colours change depending on the position of the sun and the time of year. With neither labels nor security guards to be found anywhere in these exhibition spaces, visitors are given the opportunity to experience these works in a pure, unadulterated form – without being biased by dates and written information. They have to rely entirely on themselves and on their own perception. Similarly, in the grounds there are neither route markers nor explanations. Visitors find their own way. Suddenly one comes across an object by the renowned sculptor Alexander Calder in the orchard. Or a path leads to a secluded spot with a wooden bench and a view of the quiet waters of the river Erft. Along another path one finds Herzfeld, intently welding a sculpture

Left: Karl-Heinrich Müller engaged the architect Tadao Ando to redevelop the rocket station. Ando's buildings are poised on the cusp between architecture and sculpture.

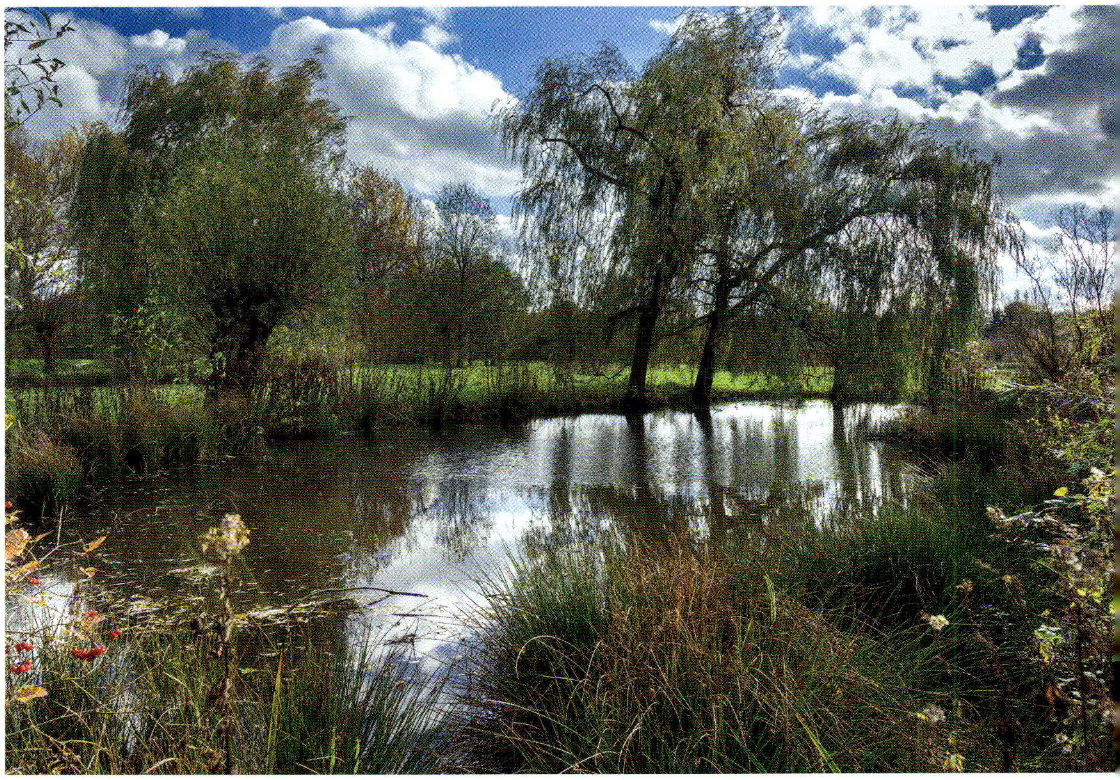

The pastoral landscape looks untouched but is in fact the work of the immensely skilled landscape architect Bernhard Korte.

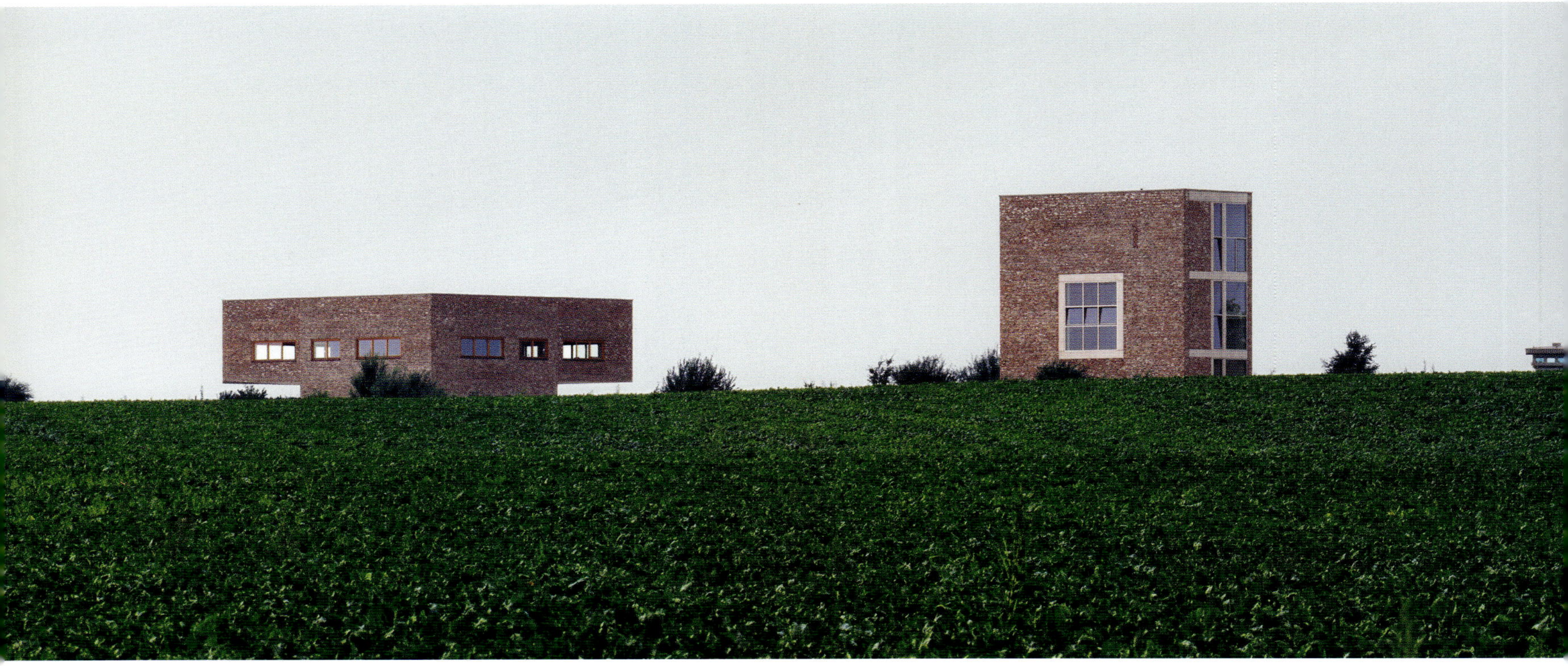

Buildings for the 'culture lab': an accommodation block and a library at the rocket station for a new spiritual life surrounded by art and nature.

in his outdoor studio. Walks at Hombroich are full of surprises and discoveries. In the café there are refreshments and a Rhenish buffet, where visitors help themselves and are free to decide how much they will pay.

Müller was not keen on rules and regulations; he preferred individual responsibility and freedom. Mindfulness and slowing down were important factors in his concept of an individual's experience of art, nature and architecture. The pavilions are deliberately built far away enough from each other for visitors to consciously take in the natural setting as they walk from one to the next. Visitors should have enough time to gather their thoughts, to reflect on what they have just seen. It is only then that they can understand the analogies between art, as something made by human hand, and nature's creative forces. To this end Heerich positioned 'transformation spaces' between the various natural spaces, that is, buildings that visitors have to pass through on their way to the next section of the grounds. The work *Tower* (1987–89) is the most radical realisation of this idea: an empty cuboid structure with four glass doors, aligned as opposing pairs, with pastureland around it. The door frames work like picture frames, with the view of nature seen through the glass door as the work of art. Müller wanted to make these grounds a place of 'inner cleansing', not unlike the experience visitors to a church may have. With his experience of monasteries in Europe and Asia, he wished for Insel Hombroich to "grow into a place of spiritual practice and religious dialogue."

In 1994 Karl-Heinrich Müller had the opportunity to considerably extend his project, both spatially and conceptually. He thus purchased a nearby site – previously a missile base – as well as the fields between it and his own land. This area was subsequently named Kirkeby Field, after Danish artist Per Kirkeby, who created a series of brick buildings there, in a similarly minimalist style to those of Heerich. There, and at the one-time missile base, where NATO concealed Pershing and cruise missiles in bunkers behind high earth walls during the Cold War, Müller now set about creating a new laboratory for wide-ranging interdisciplinary dialogue and encounters – "with cells from all the realms that humans come into contact with," as Müller described it. Aircraft hangars, observation towers and bunkers were turned into studios and living quarters for yet more artists. Writers, composers and academics came to work and live here. Soon after acquiring the site, Müller invited ten architects and artists to draw up plans for futuristic buildings or works of art that would be in harmony with the natural setting: Tadao Ando, Raimund Abraham, Katsuhito Nishikawa, Alvaro Siza, Eduardo Chillida, Erwin Heerich, Anatol Herzfeld, Oliver Kruse, Claudio Silvestrin, Rudolf Finsterwalder and Heinz Baumüller. In 1996 their designs, all positioned somewhere between sculpture and architecture, were shown at the Architecture Biennale in Venice. At a stroke Insel Hombroich became internationally known as a future-oriented art project in which art merges with life. One by one the buildings were realised, not least thanks to the immense positivity of the project's inspired initiator, Karl-Heinrich Müller. He was always able to find new sponsors for his project. Particular mention should be made of three very different examples of visionary, contemporary architecture on this rough site with its bunkers, sheds and observation towers, namely the impressive Langen Foundation museum building (2002–04) by Tadao Ando, the Siza Pavilion (2006–08) and the futuristic Abraham Building (2006–09).

The one-time missile base, Kirkeby Field and Insel Hombroich had now become an autonomous cultural space where it was possible, and still is, to experiment with new ways of living and thinking. As Müller had originally stipulated when he first established his museum project on Insel Hombroich, the general public was also welcome to participate in all the various activities on site. Müller insisted that all the creative artists should also pass on their knowledge and skills to those who were interested – in lectures, workshops and retreats. In addition to this, all three locations host concerts, readings, exhibitions and the large-scale Insel Festival with classical and new music. These diverse events facilitate cultural encounters, encouraging debate and continuing Müller's original concept of an 'island family'. Even children are catered for in his concept. In 1999 the artist Oliver Kruse constructed a kindergarten, the Kinder Insel, on Insel Hombroich, in sight of the Tadeusz Pavilion, which was built to show works by the painter Norbert Tadeusz.

Karl-Heinrich Müller died very suddenly in 2007 – his death came as a shock to all those involved in his project. But the seed had been sown. What had started as an unusual museum had become a forward-looking environment where art, culture, science, religion and nature can flourish through and with each other, in a process that fosters spiritual living – "an open experiment," as Müller once modestly described his vision. A new accent is now being added to the Kirkeby Field by the internationally renowned sculptor Thomas Schütte, who is creating a Sculpture Hall, which – with an elliptical exhibition space and a sloping ceiling – will also be a sculpture in its own right.

A place of deceleration: like a chapel the closed architecture of the *Snail* demands inner composure and circumspection from the visitor.

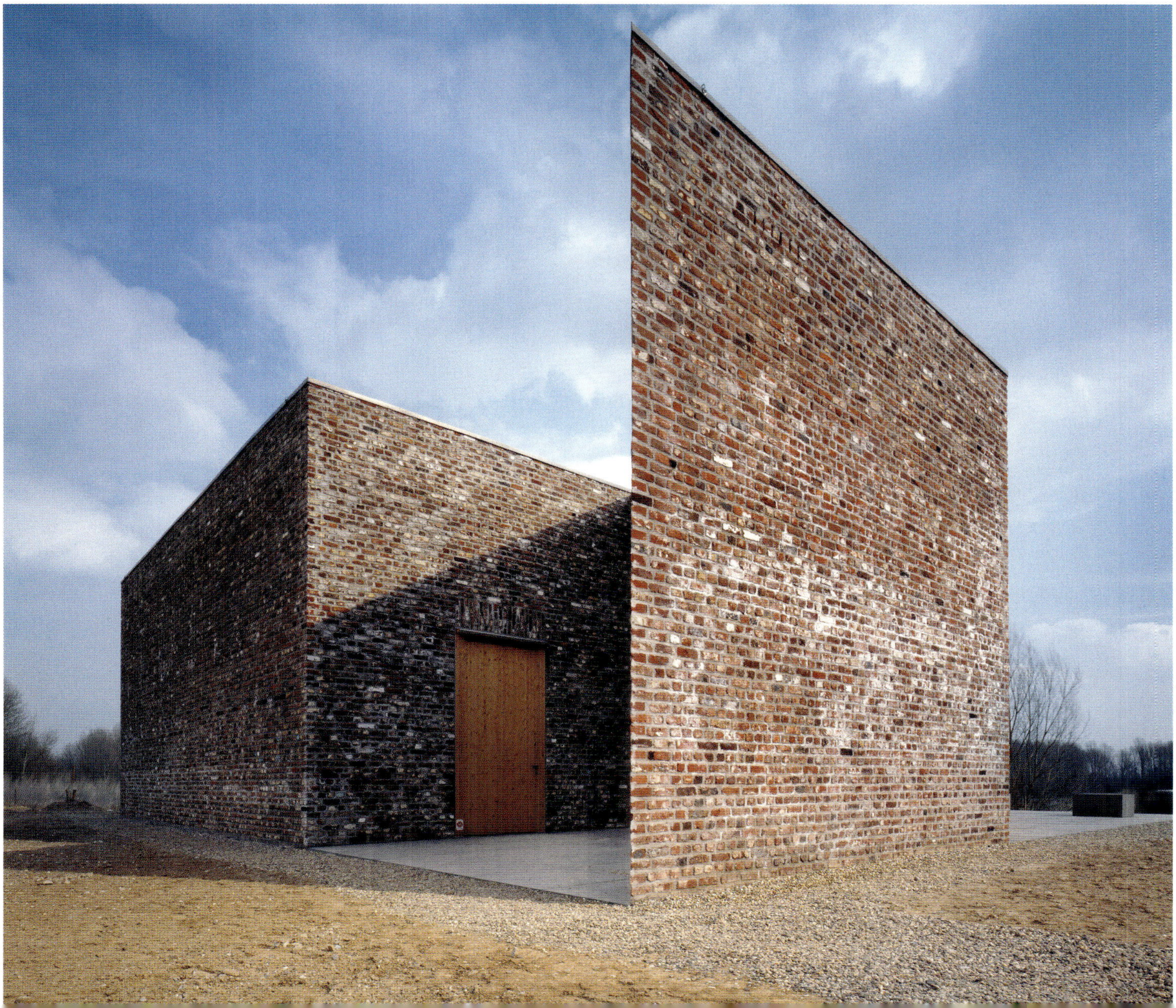

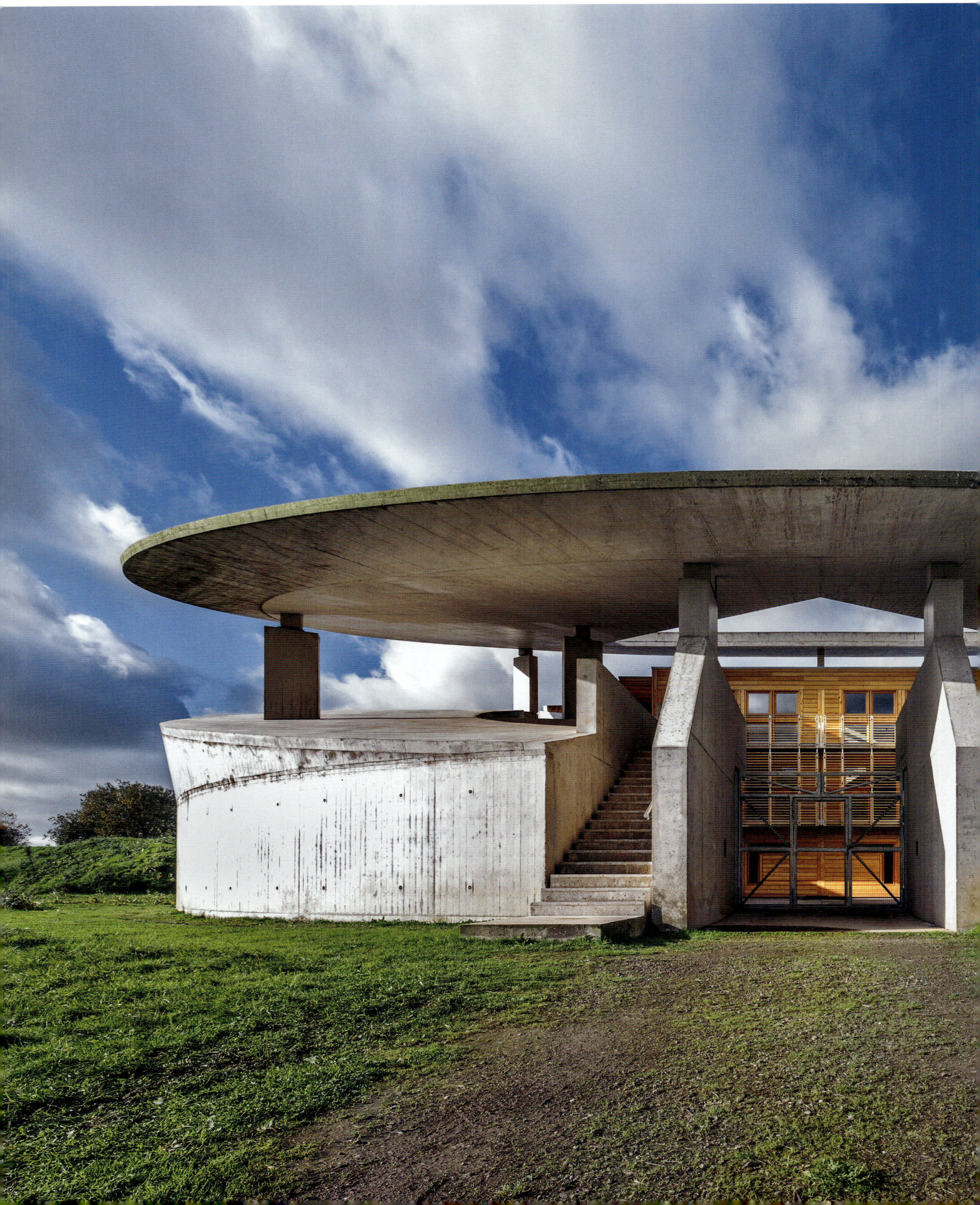

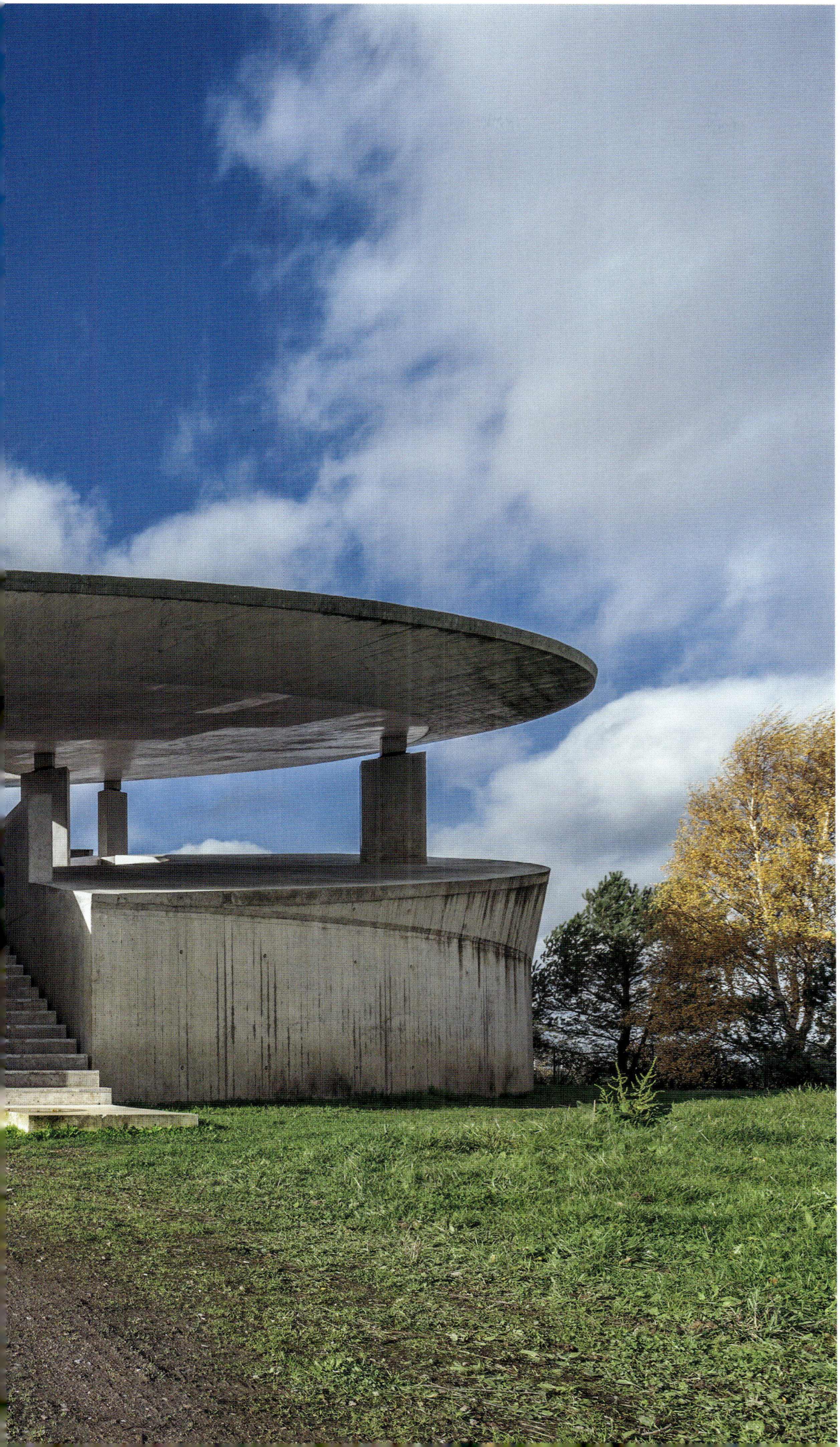

Raimund Abraham's futuristic-looking House of Musicians, with a circular roof that seems to be floating above the building.

Stiftung Insel Hombroich, Germany

FUNDRAISING WITH AN ART FARM
OLIVER RANCH, GEYSERVILLE, USA

It all started in the 1980s with the purchase of a sheep farm and a heated discussion at dinner with friends. Nancy and Steve Oliver of San Francisco, owners of a major construction business and keen art collectors, also love country life and built up an organic sheep farm in Sonoma, north of San Francisco, in an area renowned for its vineyards. The farm became a favourite weekend retreat for the Olivers and their family. But that evening the conversation turned not to sheep but to their other passion – contemporary art and their own art collection. With the upsurge in the art market their collection had hugely increased in value. "A close friend accused us of collecting art not because we love it but as an investment," recalls Steve. "That did it, as far as I was concerned. So I said, 'Okay, then we'll do something here on the farm with art that has no value whatsoever. Art that can't be sold and moved elsewhere without destroying it – we'll show him.'" No sooner said than done.

The first commission went to Judith Shea, a young artist who was already a friend of the family. "At first it was rather a painful experience," remembers Steve Oliver, "she had never made an outdoor sculpture before, and during the first year we just didn't like the sketches she came up with. It was always the same thing, only from a different perspective. All we wanted was something like what we had seen in her museum show. But she completely refused and in the end challenged us to just trust her." So that is what the Olivers did, *nolens volens.* "Although secretly I did think that if we didn't like it we could just bulldoze it," admits Steve Oliver with some amusement. But it never came to that: her *Shepherd's Muse* (1985–88) worked perfectly. It has become a key work for Shea and a point of reference for later works, such as *Without Words* (1988) in the Sculpture Park of the Walker Art Museum in Minneapolis. Her multipart work *Shepherd's Muse*, down below the house, was originally placed on two sides of a cattle gate – a special place in the sense that this is where the lambs were collected together after they had been separated from their mothers. Shea designed an empty man's coat, cast in bronze, which is surrounded by fragments of columns; from up on a rock it could 'survey' the pasture with its bleating sheep on the other side of the gate, gathered around an oversized female head. Six years

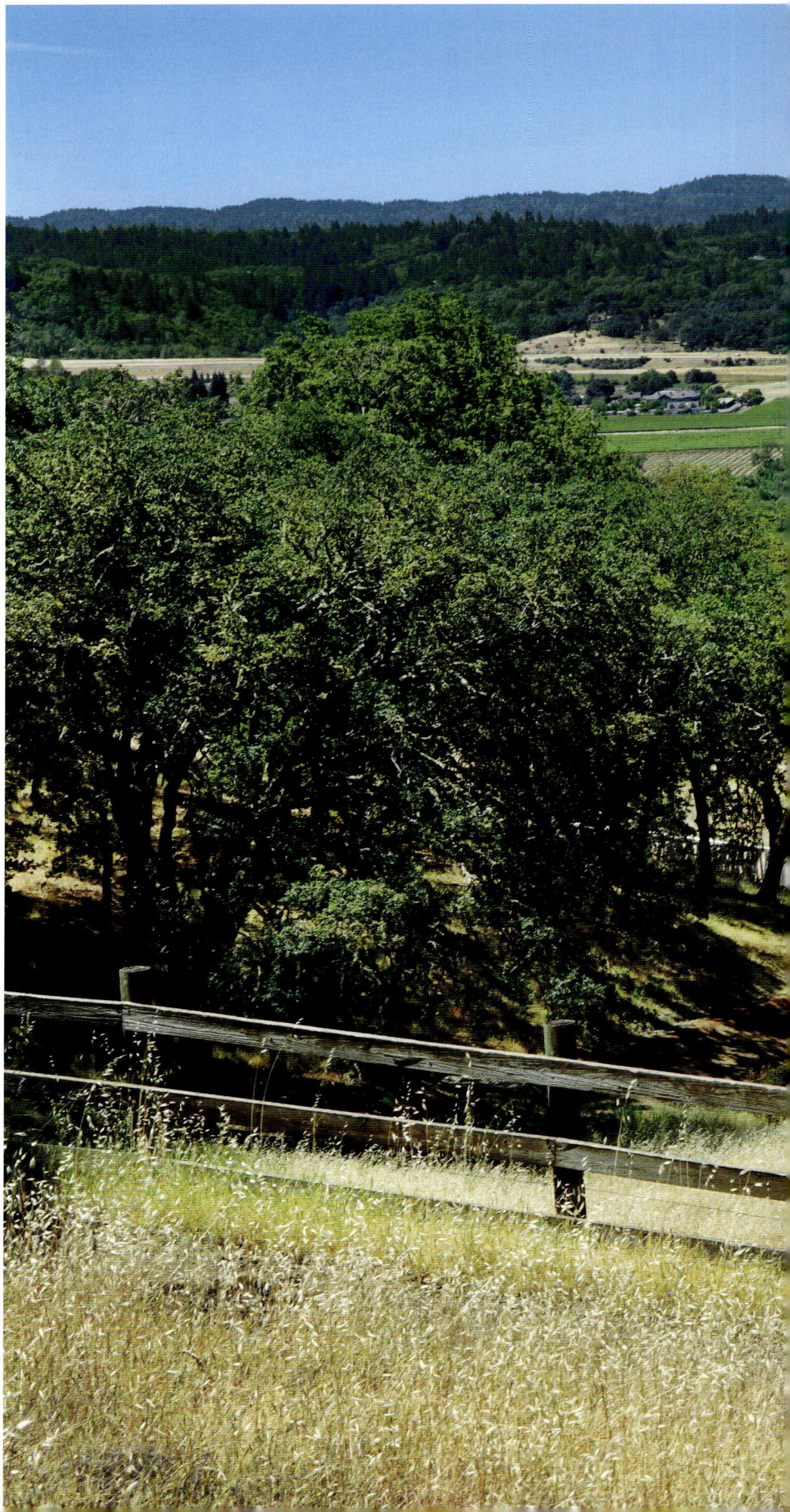

Each year new concert programmes, poetry and dance performances are commissioned for Ann Hamilton's ten-storey *Tower*.

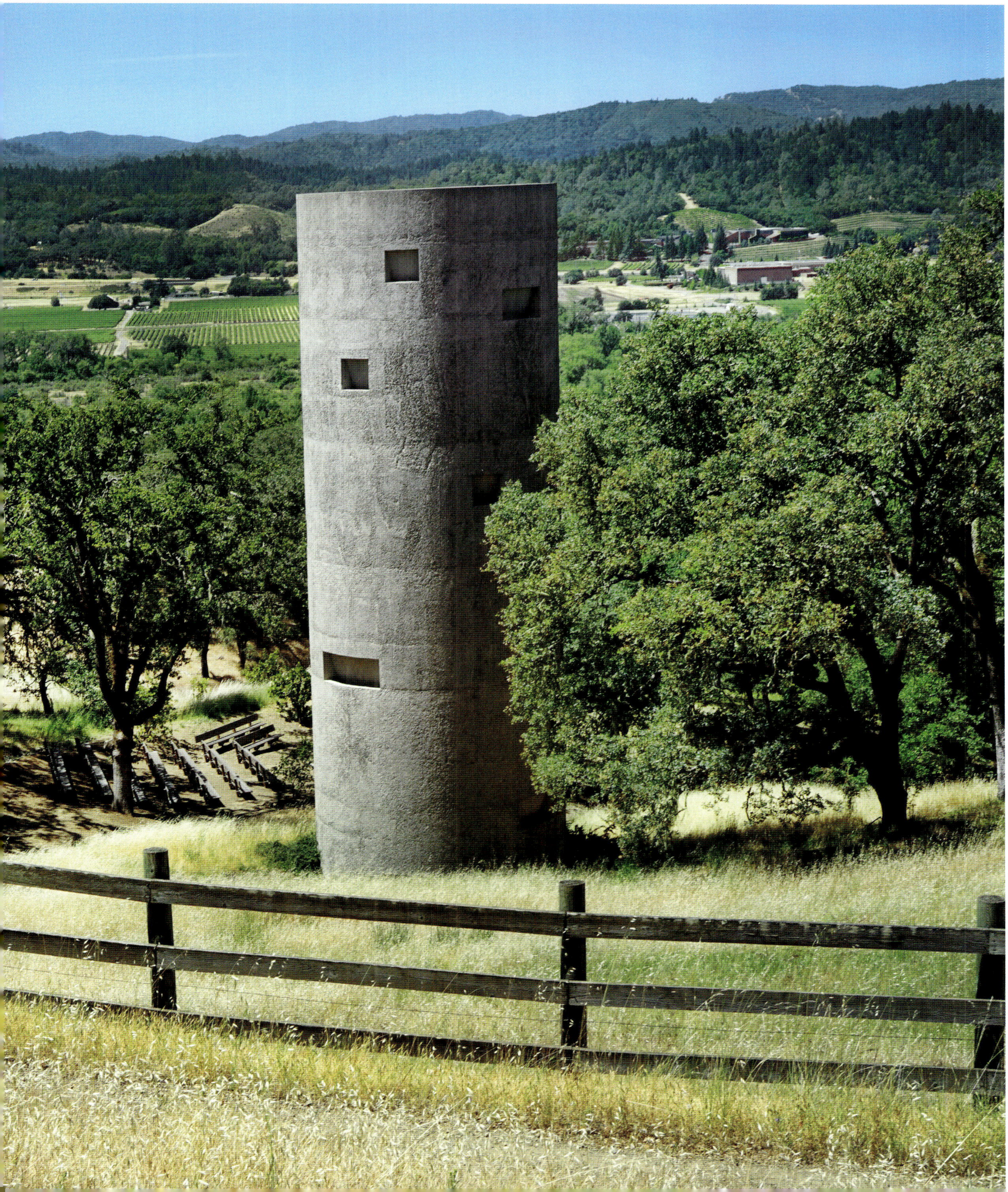

Oliver Ranch, USA

ago, however, the decision was taken to stop breeding sheep, and now the sheep are gone, but so too is the gate.

"We learnt from our experience with Judith Shea how important it is not to meddle in commissions," says Oliver. Shea soon felt very much like a family member to the Olivers. "When she was no longer there at the dinner table we realised something was missing, so we commissioned the next work, from Roger Berry." This work, *Darwin* (1988–89), is a split arch made of Corten steel which spans a small gully and is all about light and shadows. "By now we had realised that we had left the realms of garden art far behind," explains Steve Oliver. And the couple continued to commission new works. To date they have installed eighteen site-specific works on their sixty-acre property. This hilly landscape with its gnarled oak trees and arid pastures has an almost Mediterranean feel. "All the works are immovable," Oliver says once again. The idea of permanently installing art in the landscape on a working ranch – putting it beyond the reach of the art market – captured the artists' imagination. "Bruce Nauman was immediately hooked. He's an avid farmer himself." And Nauman then persuaded Richard Serra to make a work for the Olivers. Serra responded with his *Snake Eyes and Boxcars* (1990–93): twelve solid steel cubes and blocks distributed across a valley.

All the artists have to visit the farm three times before embarking on their proposals – in summer, winter and either spring or autumn, whichever they prefer. Ann Hamilton came up with a very special solution to the challenge, in the form of a thirty-metre *Tower* (2003–07), which is also a venue for experimental projects. "It extends downwards as far as it rises upwards," explains Oliver, indicating the elaborate anchors in the ground.

Steve Oliver raises money for good causes by charging for admission to cultural events in the *Tower* – the audience sits on the 125 steps of the spiral staircase.

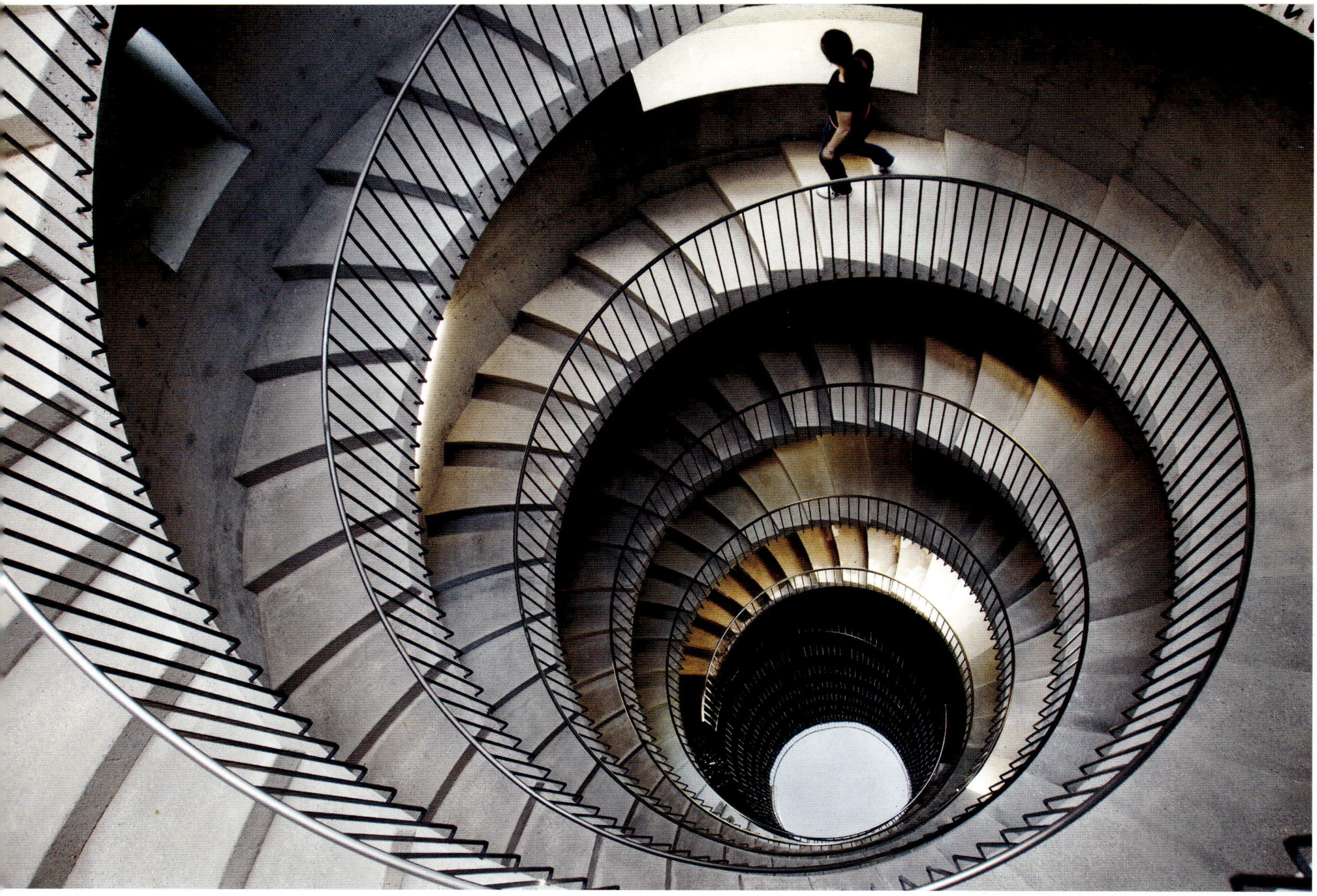

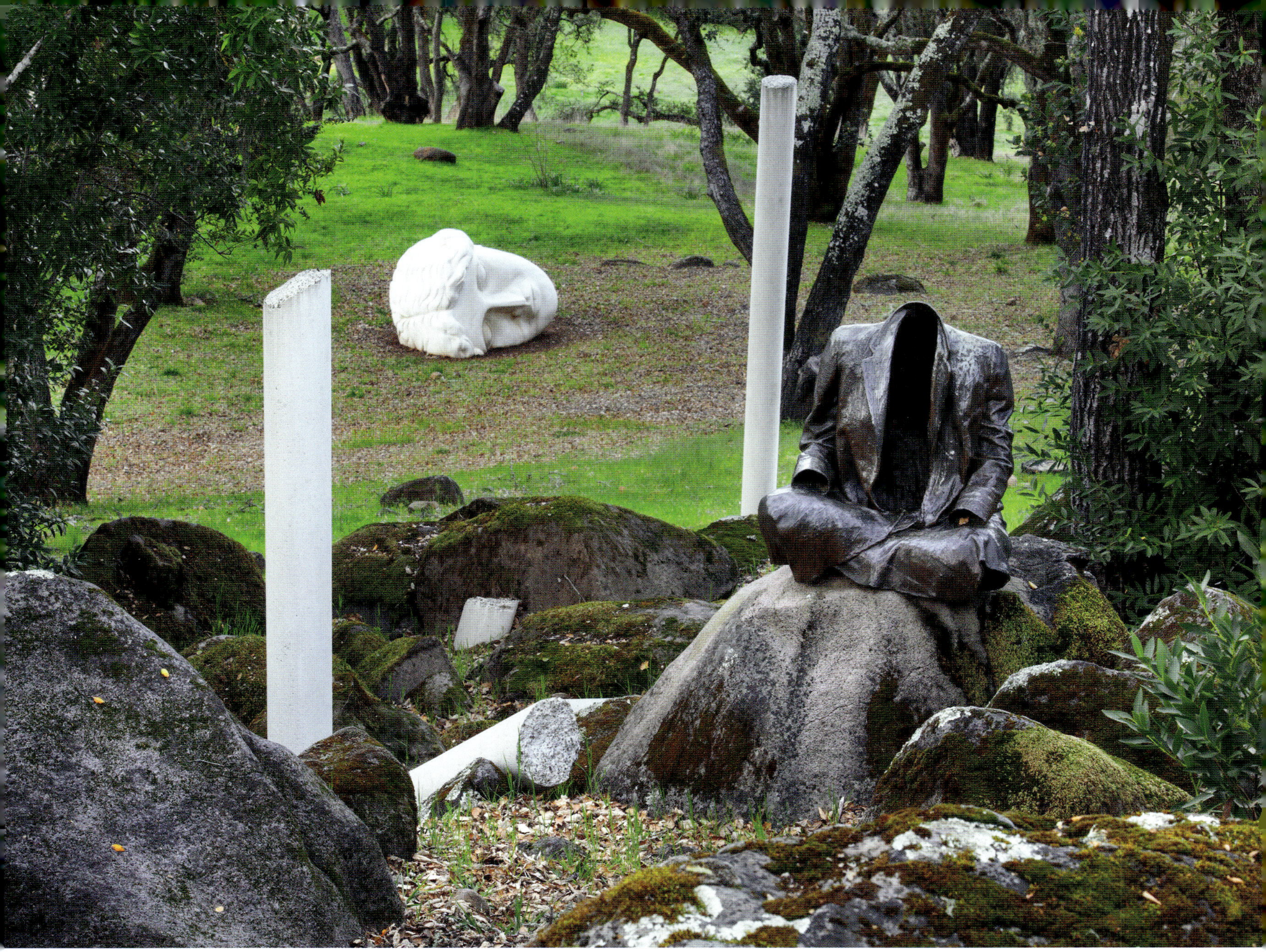

The first work in the sculpture park: Judith Shea's ***Shepherd's Muse*** recalls the beginnings of art in amongst sheep.

In his capacity as the owner of a construction company Oliver has access to the materials and skills needed to resolve complex technical challenges of this kind. "As an engineer and a professional in the construction business I'm naturally particularly interested in this side of things. And then I'm not so much a client as the artist's 'studio assistant'." Ann Hamilton's tower is now regularly used for performances and concerts, with works commissioned by the Olivers from musicians, poets and dance companies. The opening concert in *Tower* was given by Meredith Monk who sang her specially composed *Song of the Century* to an audience of over a hundred. The narrow interior of the eight-storey tower, which has an open roof, houses two staircases that spiral upwards in opposite directions to the full height of the building, one for the audience and one for the performers.

This unusual art project within easy reach of San Francisco soon became known to the art community there, particularly since Steve Oliver is one of the most influential patrons of the arts in the city where he was president of the board of SFMOMA for many years. In his role as board president he frequently took wealthy art lovers on a tour of his property in return for a donation to the consistently underfunded museum. Ever the entrepreneur, he created an entirely new concept: a sculpture park as a fundraising project. "I'll give anyone who is interested a guided tour of the grounds on condition that they (verifiably) donate at least two thousand dollars to any non-profit organisation of their choice – not just art-related projects or institutions." Fundraisers can purchase individual tickets for a tour or can auction a tour at a benefit event.

The heights of the treads on this staircase sculpture by Bruce Nauman vary according to the incline of the landscape.

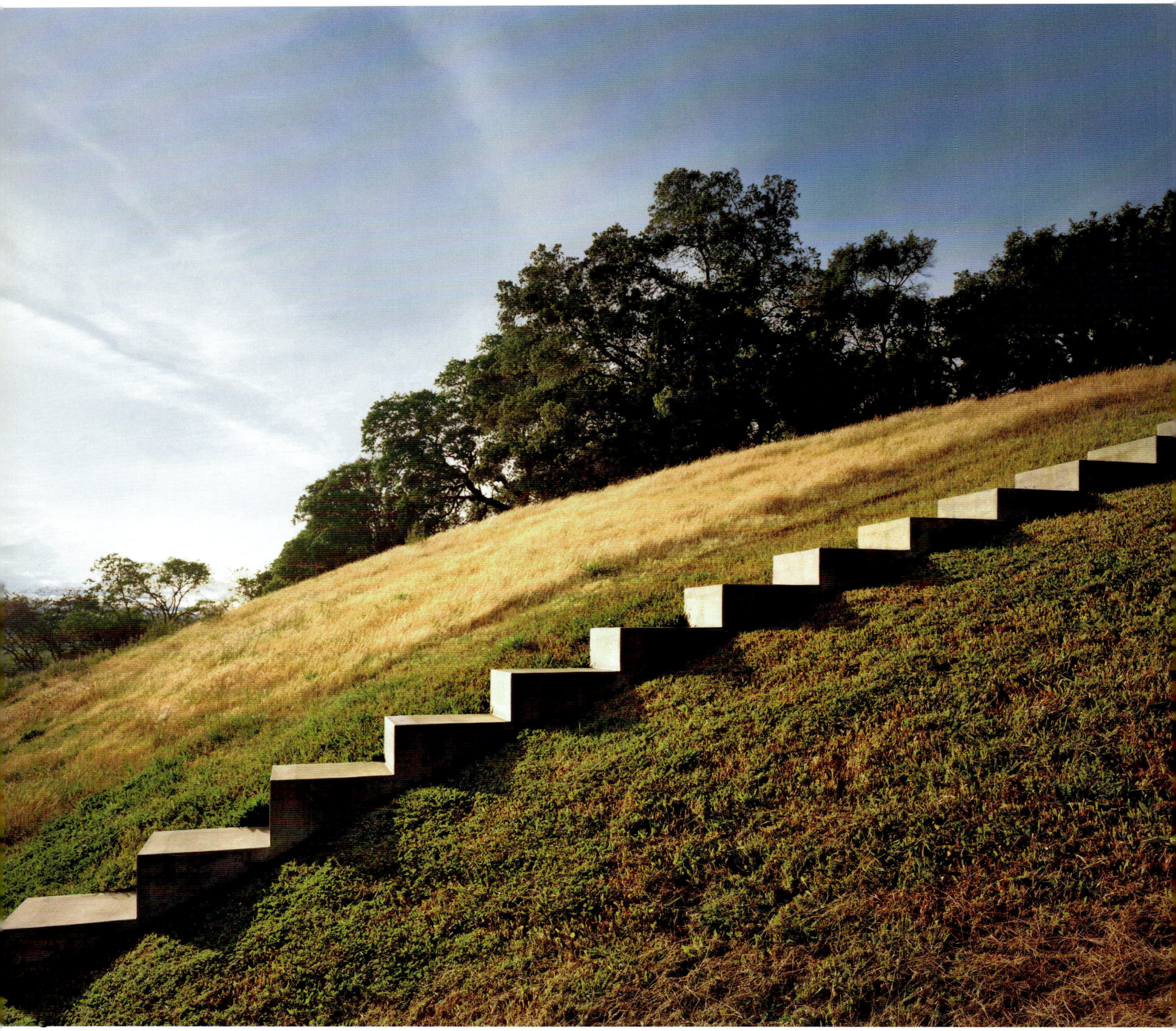

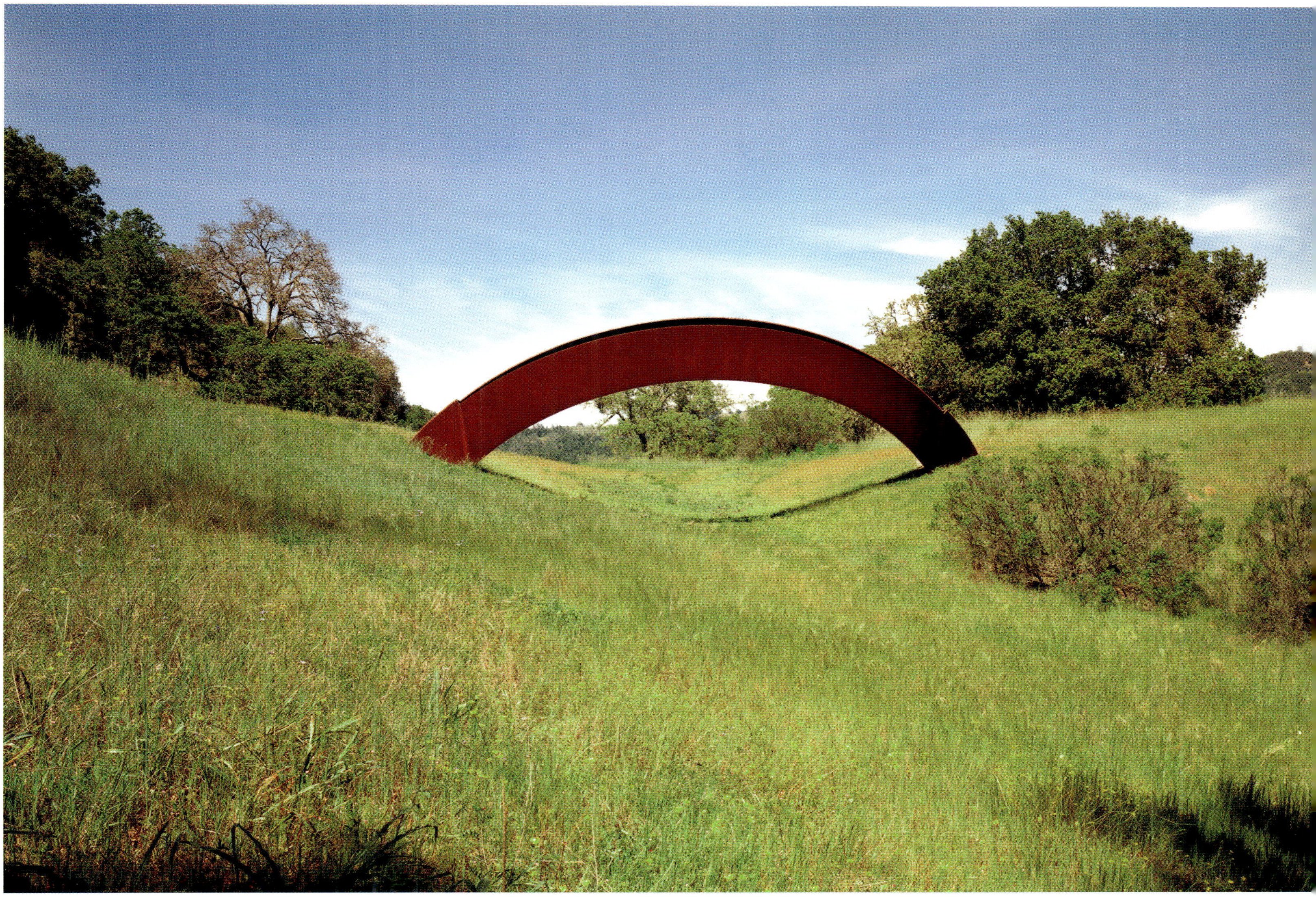

Roger Berry's *Darwin*: the top of this split arch of Corten steel marks the course of the sun in winter, the lower edge its course in summer.

This means that sometimes a coachload of sixty visitors might arrive at one time – or just two. "Recently a couple came who had bid fifteen thousand dollars at an auction," recounts the philanthropist in delight. This scheme, together with admission fees for performances in Ann Hamilton's *Tower*, has by now raised over three million dollars for a whole range of projects – from art exhibitions at the Centre Pompidou to a foundation dedicated to the care of the homeless. "It also means that I meet all sorts of people when they come here to visit. Sometimes they might be wealthy art collectors who round off the day with dinner at one of the famous wineries in this area, sometimes it's a group of people who have never had anything to do with art and would in fact rather be at a baseball game. And if someone in one of those groups suddenly gets it and sticks right by me for the rest of the tour, then that – aside from the knowledge that the tours are supporting so many good causes – is my greatest joy." Whatever the case, Steve Oliver is in no doubt that "the next time they go to a museum, these people will have a very different way of looking at art."

RESCUING THE SEA WITH UNDERWATER ART
MUSEO SUBACUÁTICO DE ARTE, CANCÚN, MEXICO

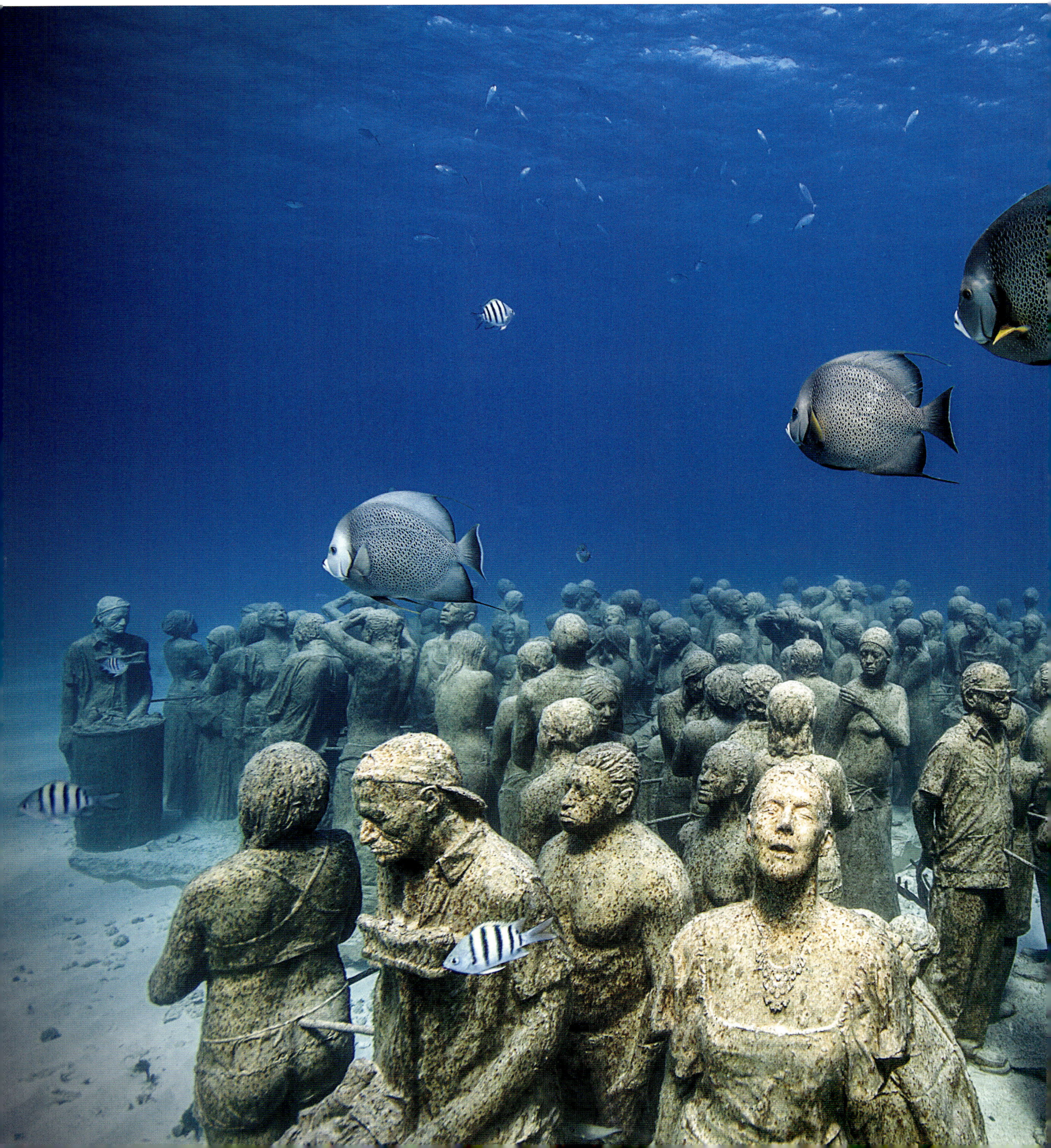

A sunken world on the floor of the Caribbean: the descendants of the lost Maya civilisation as an artificial coral reef.

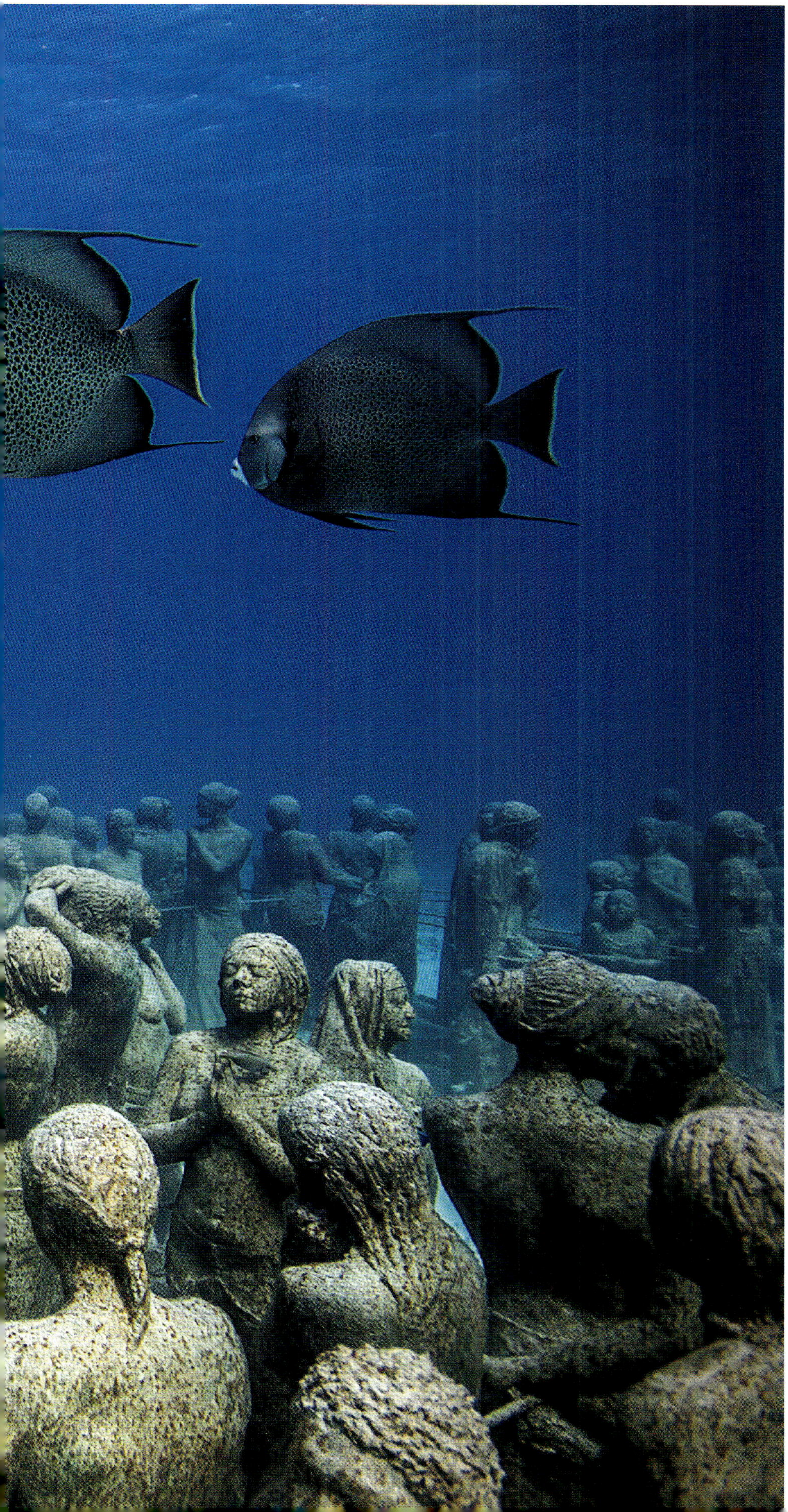

Sandy beaches as far as the eye can see, turquoise water with dazzling fish and glowing coral reefs – the Caribbean at its best. The sea around the Yucatán Peninsula in Mexico is an El Dorado for divers and snorklers. In the magical underwater realms of the second-largest reef in the world there is a vast array of marine creatures: bright corals, sponges, jellyfish, whale sharks and numerous rare fish such as blue parrotfish and neon tetra. But this unique ecosystem is at risk grave due to the effects of climate change, overfishing and the ever-growing numbers of divers in the area.

"Forty per cent of the natural coral reefs have already been irrevocably lost," says the British artist Jason deCaires Taylor (b. 1974), who is also a keen diver, "and scientists reckon it is likely that this will rise to 80 per cent by 2050. Fish and sea creatures are facing an extreme existential threat." The urgency of this situation gave the sculptor an unusual idea – anchor sculptures of his own to the seabed in order to distract recreational divers from the endangered natural reefs. As a result, during the course of a few years the largest underground sculpture park in the world was created off the shore of Cancún, between the Punta Nizuc and the small Isla Mujeres. It has been known as MUSA (Museo Subacuático de Arte) since 2009. This thousand-acre site, which is part of the National Marine Park of Isla Mujeres, Punta Cancun and Punta Nizuc, now contains almost five hundred sculptures by Taylor in two 'underwater galleries': the works of art in Salon Manchones, at a depth of six to nine metres, mainly attract divers, whereas the sculptures in Salon Punta Nizuc, at a depth of four metres, are specifically intended for snorklers.

In the deeper Salon Manchones there are impressive, often ominous groups of figures: five *Bankers* (2011) have literally put their heads in the sand in response to the financial crash. This group was made in direct response to the global economic crisis, and the humble posture of the figures is also intended to kindle hope of a new, binding code of standards for politics and the financial industries. Underwater visitors may also be prompted to reflect on the state of the world today at the sight of Taylor's *Silent Evolution* (2010), consisting of four hundred life-size sculptures of everyday

Museo Subacuático de Arte, Mexico

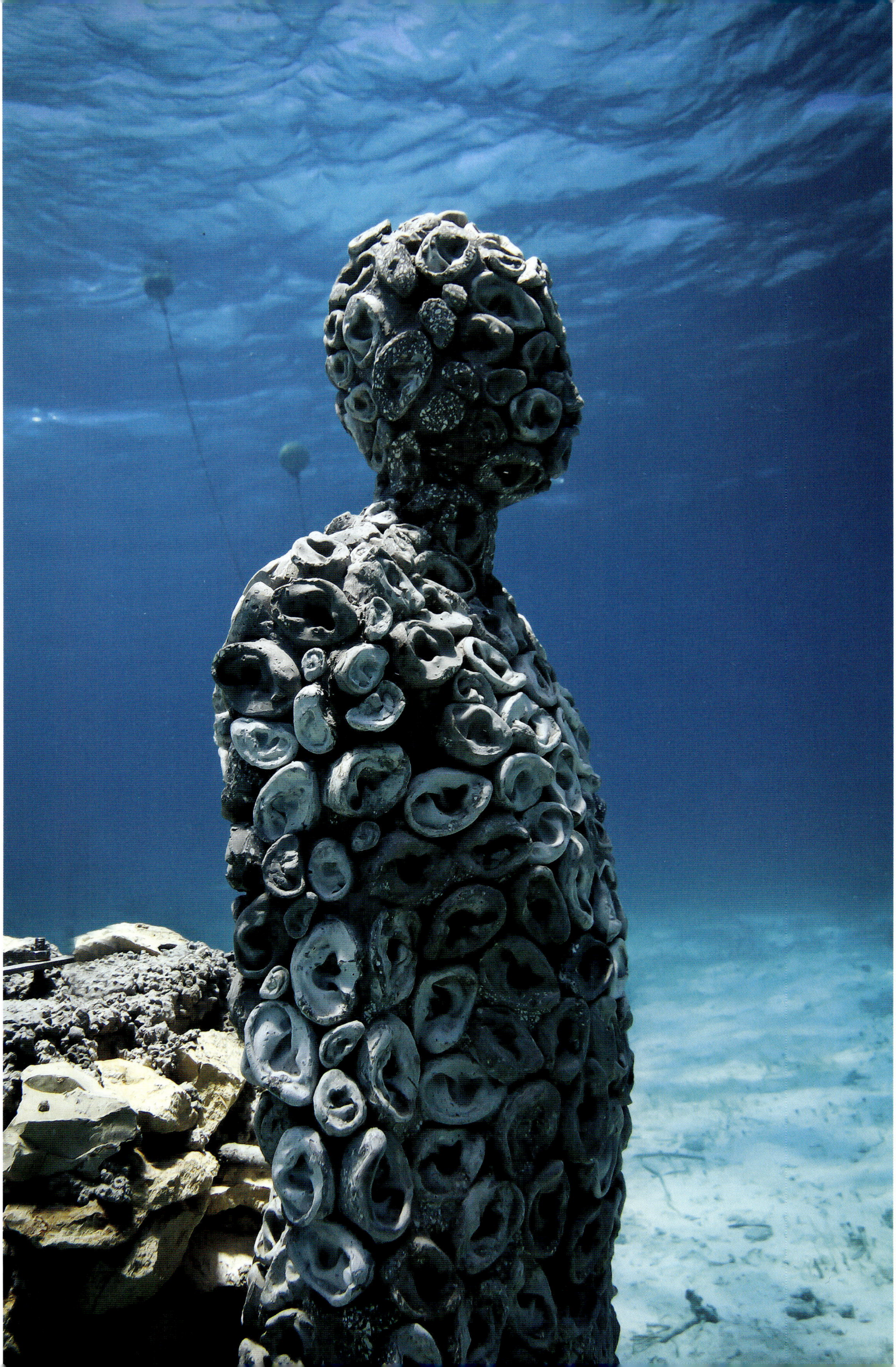

figures in that region – old people, children, pregnant women, teachers, nuns and fishermen – surrounded by shoals of fish. The figures are all descendants of the legendary Mayas in Mexico, whose sophisticated civilisation fell into decline and disappeared. Like their forebears, today's populace is still dependent on natural resources, but these are increasingly under threat. This unspeaking throng of human beings has an immense presence, particularly when the diver suddenly encounters them during an exploration of the seabed. At every turn there is something new to discover – a child on the bonnet of a VW Beetle, *Anthropocene*, a man at a desk with a dog by his feet, a bicycle close by, a table set for a meal in the distance. It is a hushed, sunken parallel world that Jason deCaires Taylor has constructed on the seabed; yet it also seems alive, accepted by the marine creatures – above all the fish – which live on and under the sculptures. Human beings and nature are harmoniously united here in the cycle of life.

In the human figure of *The Listener* (2012) the artist once again points out how very little we know about life in the oceans. "People always say that the world is silent underwater, but that's not right," says Taylor. "There's an astonishing variety of noises, some very loud, because sound travels around four times faster underwater: the cracking of crustaceans, the sound of fish feeding, breaking waves or the chug of a motorboat on the surface." The figure of *The Listener* is covered with ears that Taylor made in a workshop with schoolchildren aged between eight and twelve. This sculpture is also equipped with a hydrophone – an underwater microphone – to record the noises of the sea, which are then stored on a hard disc. Taylor consistently highlights specific issues concerning the world's seas and oceans in his works. In the case of *Urban Reef (House I and House II)* (2012), a series of small cast-concrete houses, Taylor worked with marine biologists to create new homes for reef dwellers: artificial breeding chambers with open doors and windows as a refuge for juvenile fish, a home for crabs and lobsters and a good hiding place from predator fish such as barracudas.

The British sculptor's love of the marine world partly dates to the time he spent in Malaysia as a child. At weekends and in the holidays his parents, who were both English teachers, would hire a boat and go exploring Thailand's islands with him. "We went to places where no one had ever been before – isolated, completely unspoilt

Left: The underwater world is not silent and the *Listener* is covered with ears. A hydrophone in his body records the sounds of the ocean.

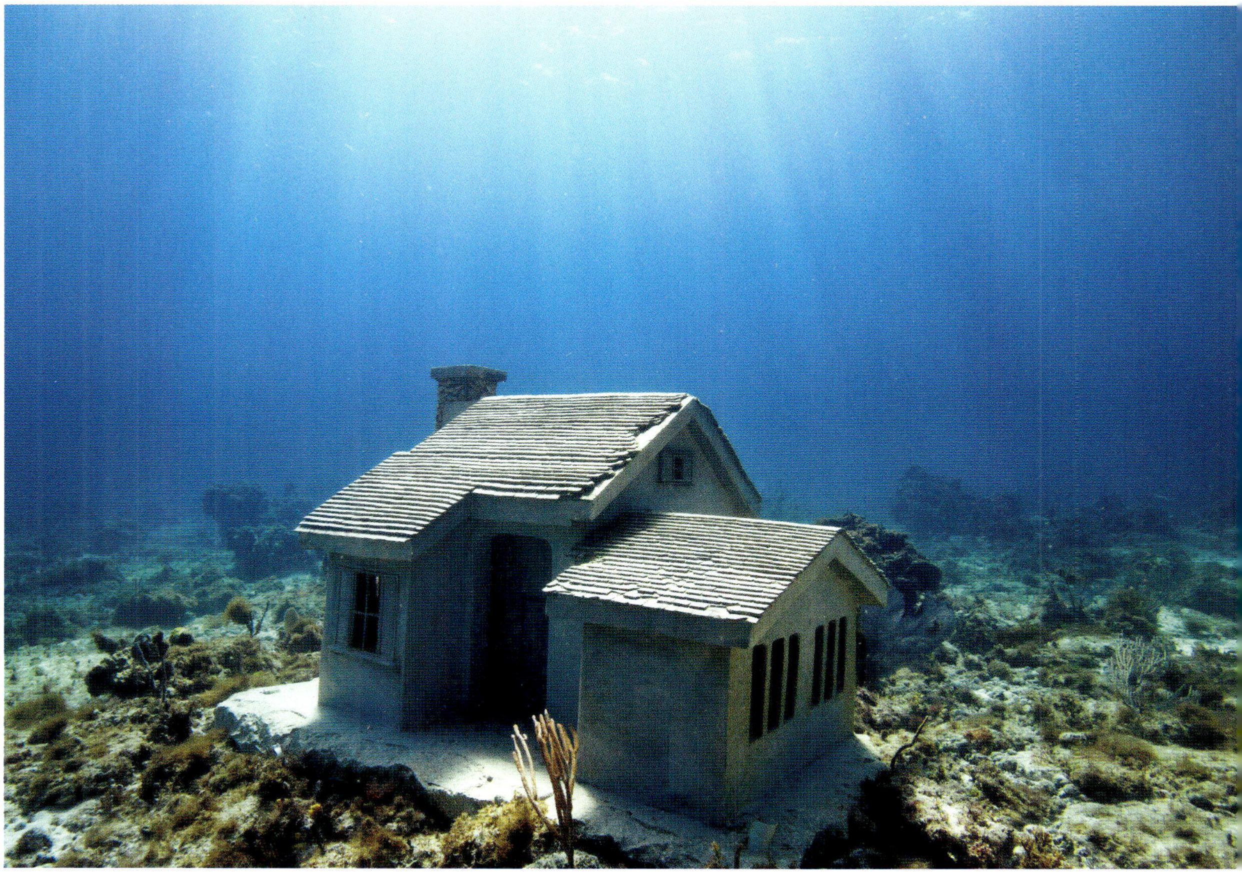

The *Reef House* was created by Jason deCaires Taylor with advice from marine biologists as a safe place for endangered fish species to spawn and take refuge.

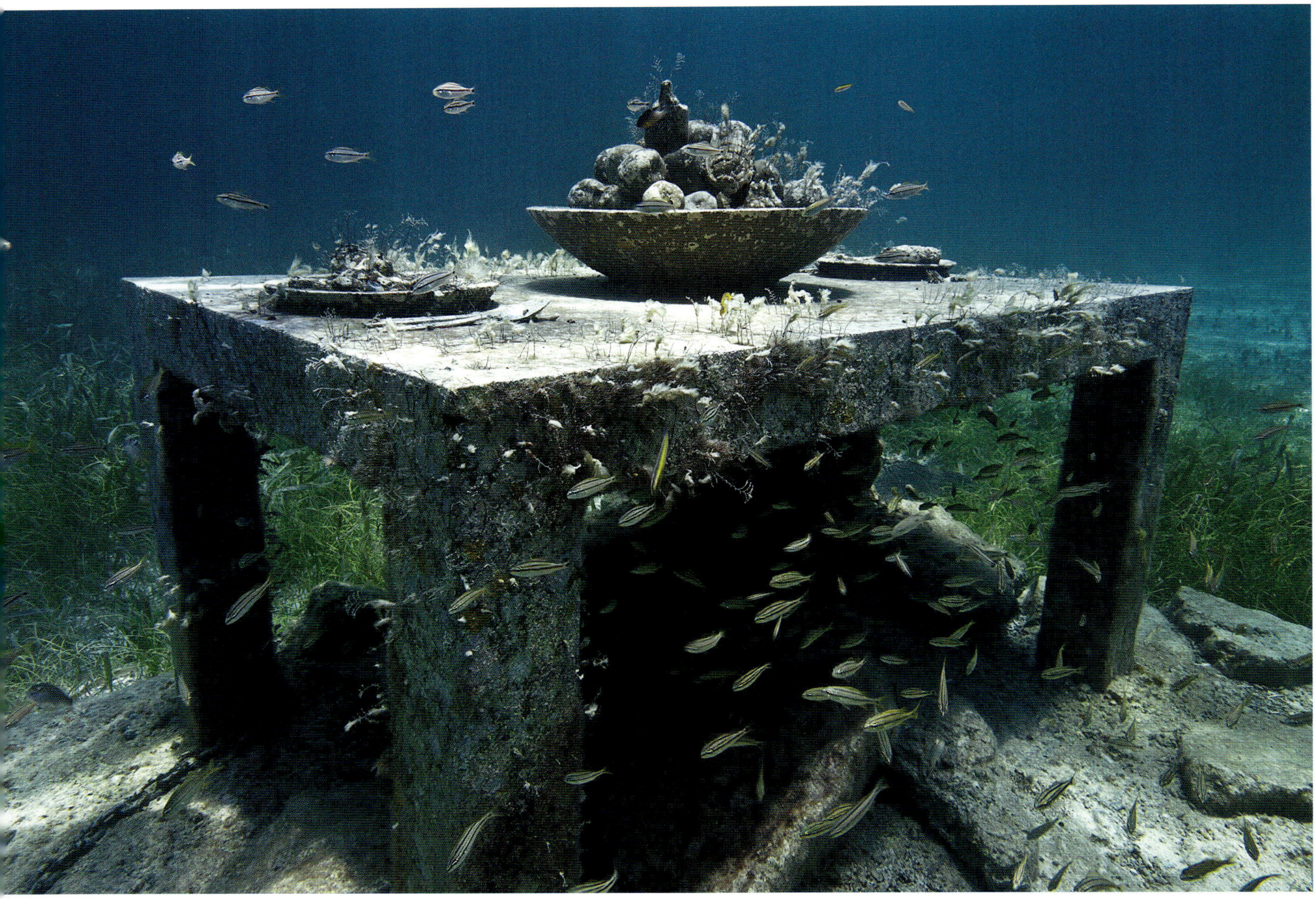

***Last Supper*: a last exhortation to humankind before the ecosystems of the world's oceans collapse.**

islands with untouched beaches," he recalls. Since then he has always had a longing for the sea. Following his training as a sculptor in London, he just wanted to get back to the sea. "I knew I wanted to do something with that never-ending realm – the Earth is two-thirds water – something sustainable. I found artistic work frustrating. You work towards an exhibition and then take the work away again. Such a waste of resources." So Taylor decided to earn his living in a different way – as a diver. But as a divemaster on Grenada he soon had to face the other side of his passion. Following violent tropical storms in the Molinere Bay area in 2004 and 2005, only a restricted zone was accessible to divers. "Pretty soon I hated the crowds of divers everywhere, destroying everything." So Taylor turned his back on the diving business and in 2006 little by little started to populate another part of the bay with sculptures on the seabed. And even though the installations were largely hidden in rocky crevasses, they soon became an insider's tip in diving circles.

Soon the problem of reefs being damaged by the growing numbers of recreational divers was also affecting other regions. Therefore in 2009 Taylor transferred his idea of an underwater sculpture park to the extremely popular National Marine Park of Isla Mujeres, Punta Cancun and Punta Nizuc. Around 750,000 divers come to the national park every year. MUSA offers them an alternative diving and snorkling experience: the natural world as an underwater museum, with sculptures as artificial coral reefs. "I take art away from the white walls of a gallery or a museum and give visitors an opportunity to engage in a new kind of discovery and

Encouraging corals to grow: the surfaces of the sculptures are pH-neutral. Fragments of broken coral have been fixed to this figure.

a feeling of participation – and the chance to extend their concept of planet Earth," says Jason deCaires Taylor. At the same time he can also sensitise divers to his main concern, namely, the need to maintain the Earth's ecological equilibrium. Many of his sculptures in the two underwater galleries have thought-provoking titles alluding to the destruction of the natural world by humankind: *Time Bomb*, *Last Supper*, *The Gardener of Hope* and *Self-Immolation*. The latter is a lone figure that appears to be burning – a reference to a form of non-violent resistance whereby the protester sets his or her own body on fire. Made from a particularly resilient cement compound this sculpture is covered in stainless-steel spines. Soon after it was installed on the seabed, glowing yellow corals started to grow on it. For *Man on Fire* (2009) Taylor took broken pieces of fire coral and glued them to the body of the figure with a special adhesive. His aim here is to encourage the growth of new coral and, in so doing, to support this process in more general terms. "I want the generations after us to experience all sorts of different corals," he says. As a rule it takes just under two years for the figures to be overgrown with sea grass and for nature to conceal their contours. Art becomes nature and vice versa.

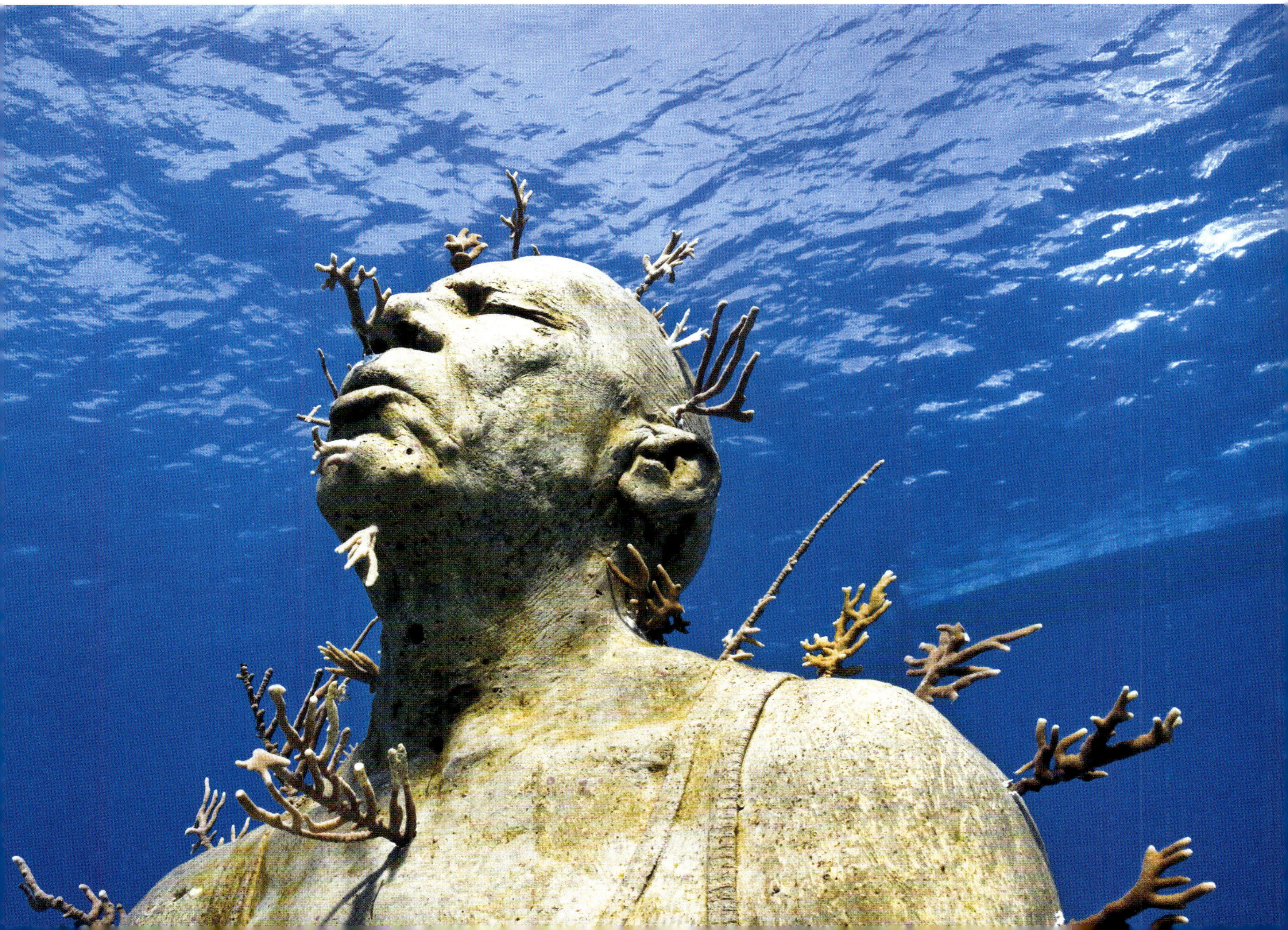

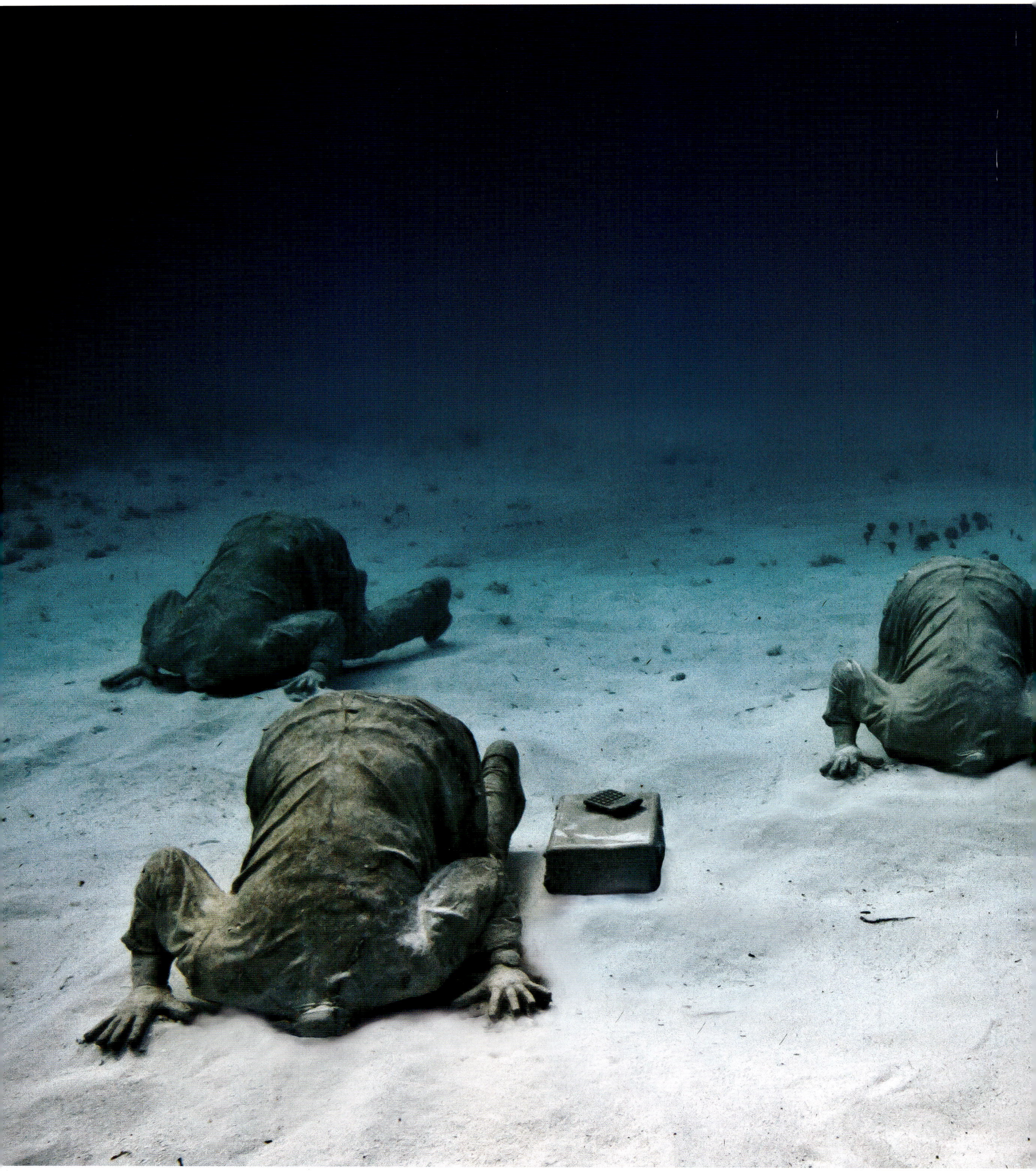

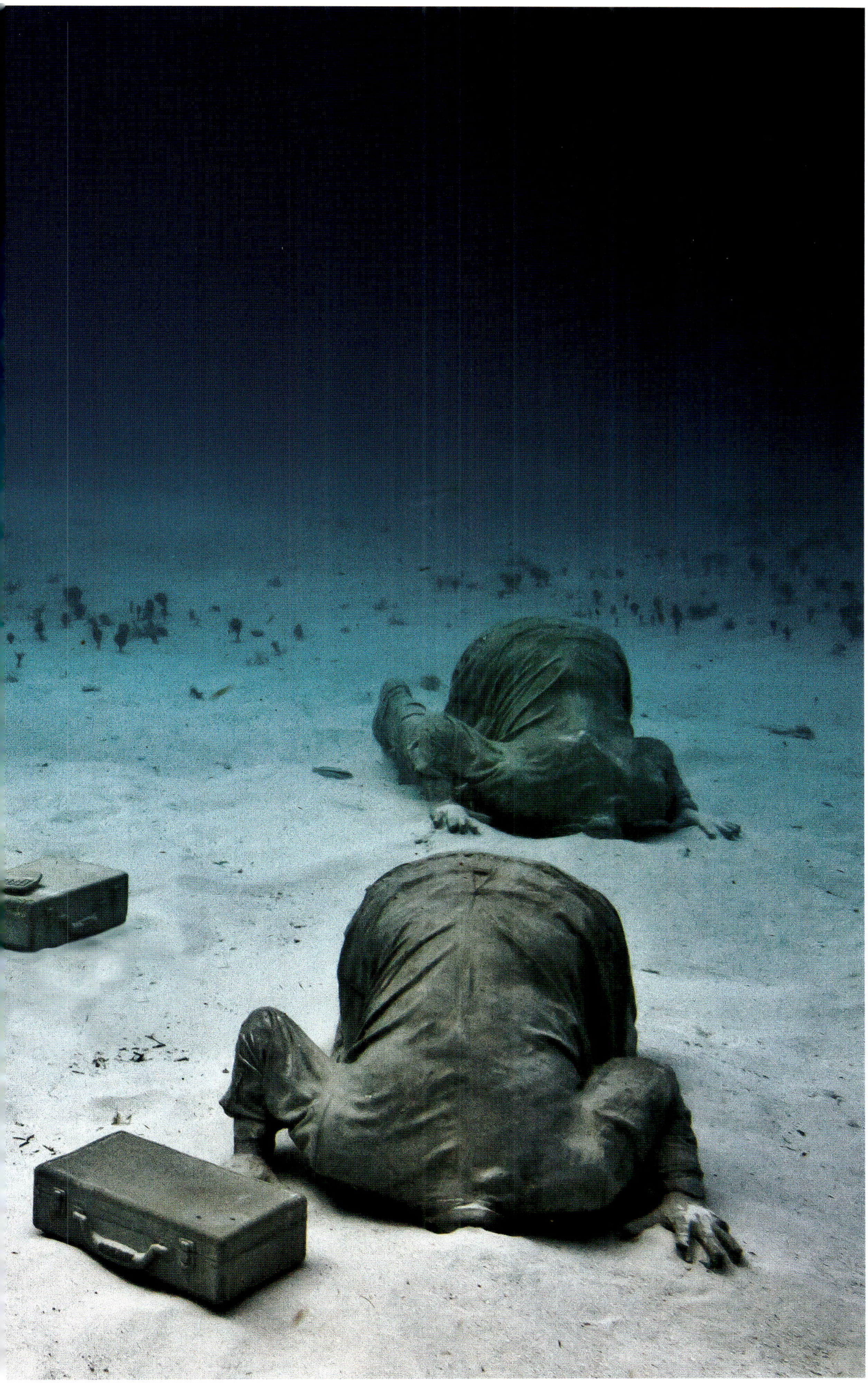

Bankers with their heads in the sand: resigned to the economic consequences of their financial policies or humbly bowing down to nature?

Museo Subacuático de Arte, Mexico

TO ENTER A MEMORY BANK
LA RIBAUTE, BARJAC, FRANCE

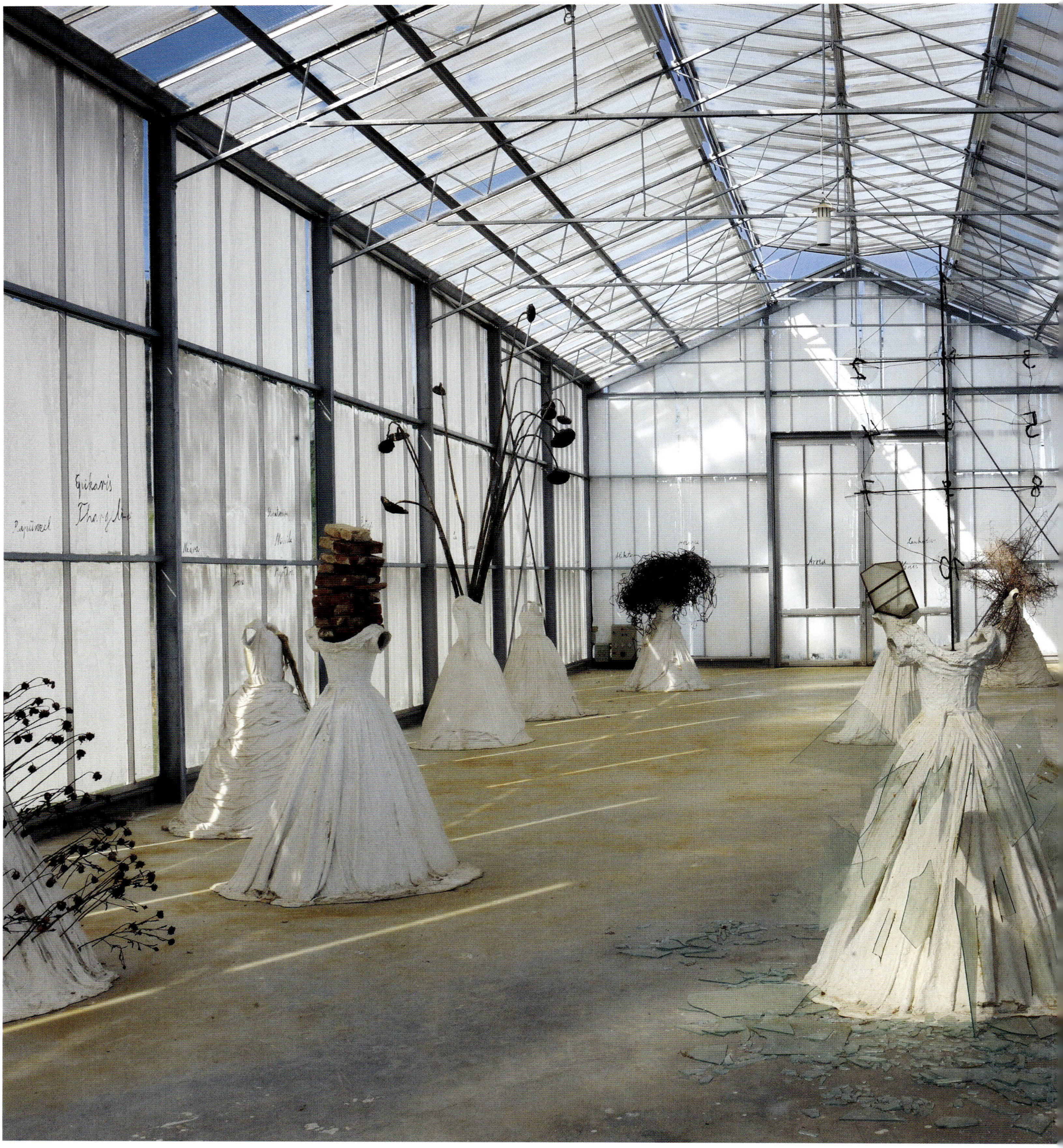

Long white dresses and sunflowers or leaden folios instead of heads – works from Kiefer's cycle *Women of Antiquity*.

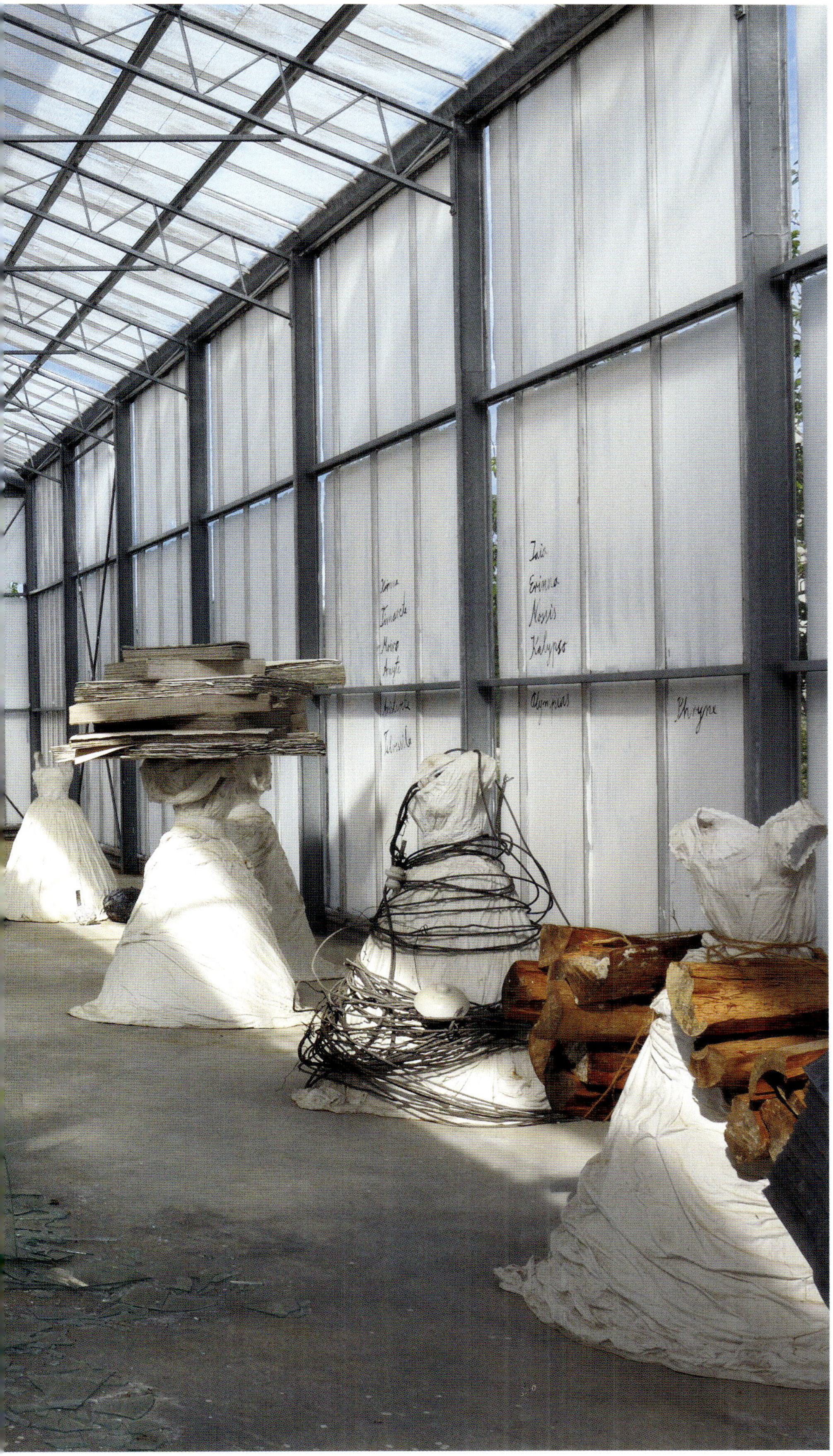

Artists' studios rarely look like this. With its towers and miles of underground passages La Ribaute – once the site of a silk factory near the small town of Barjac in southern France – seems more like a mine. This is not only the place where one of Germany's leading artists, Anselm Kiefer (b. 1945), worked for fifteen years (1993–2008), it also became the centre of his life – a retreat, a source of inspiration, a repository for materials and a studio. In the midst of the hilly landscape of the Cévennes Kiefer constructed a private universe of his own, which embraces all the various aspects of his art: architecture, painting, installations and the natural world all connect here. A site that is laid out as a *Gesamtkunstwerk* with numerous distinct areas above and below ground that reflects Kiefer's approach to his work.

The road to Barjac climbs upwards in long serpentines and seems not to be made for crowds of visitors. And it is all too easy to miss the little sign marked "La Ribaute". This fenced-in, eighty-five-acre site lies at the top of a wooded hill. As the visitor approaches the locked gate, towers suddenly rise up between the trees. Beyond the gate is Kiefer's mystical world: tall pavilions, lining the path, house monumental paintings and installations. With their open doors they seem like shrines. Each bears the name of figures or motifs from Kiefer's fund of ideas: *Sternenfall, Palmsonntag, Für Paul Celan – Geheimnis der Farne, Shevirat Ha-Kelim, Die Sieben HimmelsPaläste, Velimir Khlebnikov.* In this vast site Kiefer's paintings and installations at last have the aura that he had always wished for in exhibitions: "I always found it depressing to see my paintings in museums, crammed together with other objects by uncaring curators or in private collections, next to a potted palm or up above a sofa." Where silk was once spun, Kiefer now created his art. But not only that. The whole site became his studio, a work of art in its own right. Kiefer's utensils are not just paintbrush and spatula: "I use all sorts of machinery – cranes, trucks, diggers.... Art can refer to all kinds of things and the artist can make use of every imaginable tool," he once said, explaining his love of experimentation. Over time he created more than fifty buildings at La Ribaute, some of which are interconnected by means of a complex system of tunnels.

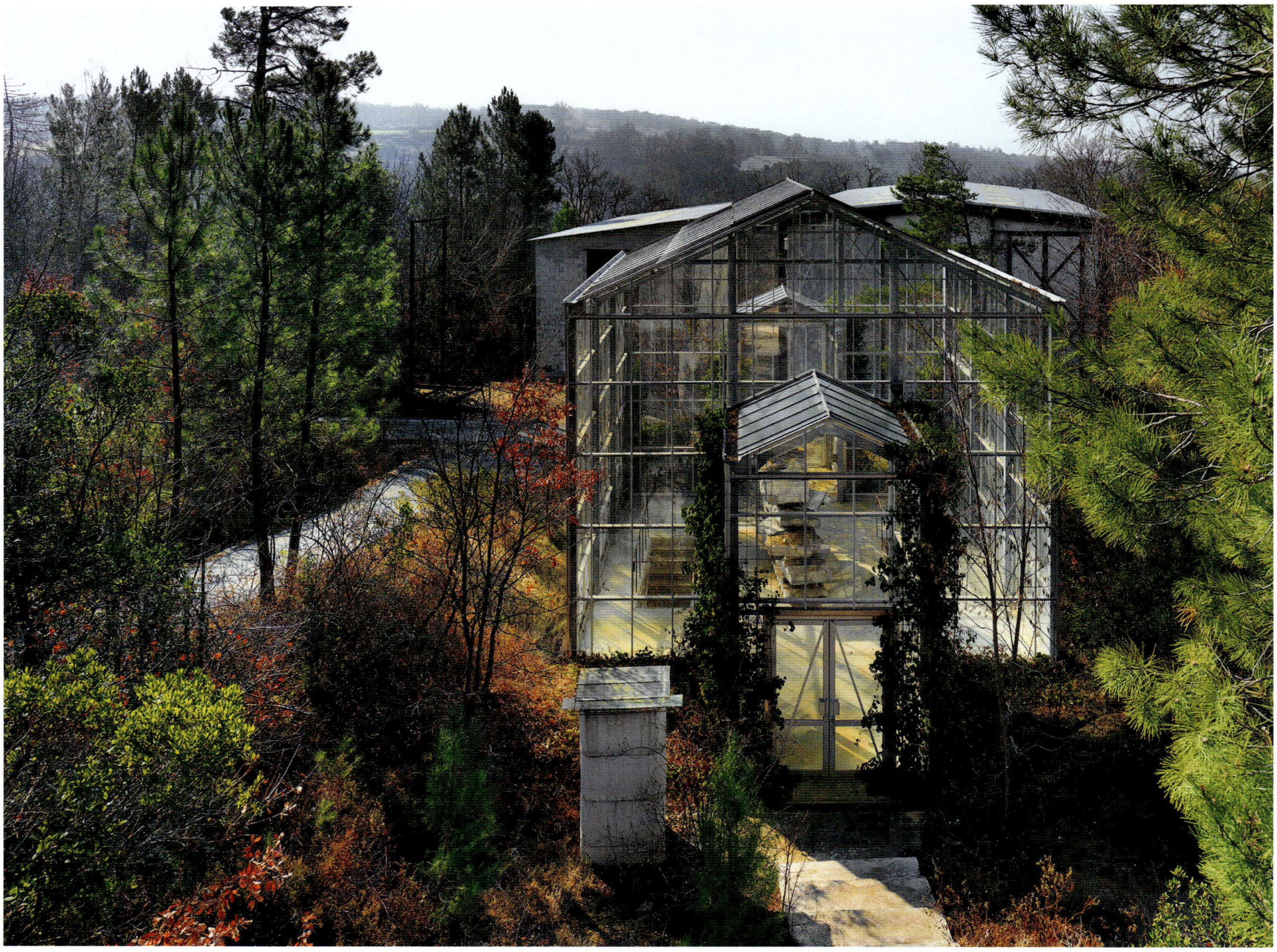

It was in 1993 that the German artist came to Barjac: "After I settled here, everything I made was born from the things I had brought with me from Germany: photographs, books, unfinished paintings and materials, including lead from the roof of Cologne Cathedral." Although France now became the fulcrum of his life, his mindset remained rooted in German history. His biography is the biography of Germany and his works invariably revolve around the same themes – the apocalypse of the Second World War, German culture and history in general and their relationship to the wider world, the Kabbalah, Egyptian and Greek ideas, alchemy.

In the works he made in La Ribaute Kiefer continued to address taboos, exploring the different strata of his own memories and revisiting the poetry of Paul Celan and Ingeborg Bachmann, who – as the literary historian Holger Pausch has put it – examined "the foundations of existence ... freedom and time and the human behaviours that arise from these," particularly in relation to the persecution of the Jews by the National Socialist regime. Kiefer often stores literary fragments away in his mind for a long time before he connects them with a particular work – be it a painting, comprising layers of different materials, or a large-scale installation or mise en scène.

Behind the main building Kiefer created a kind of ruined landscape, with towers of stacked concrete casts of empty containers. These structures appear fragile; they create the impression that they could collapse at any moment, like the Tower of Babel. But what may fill the viewer with trepidation was originally only a game with materials and ideas for Kiefer. It is only subsequently

Anselm Kiefer regards La Ribaute in its entirety as a work of art, including the thirty buildings and more that he has added to it.

Right: One of the passages leads into a huge amphitheatre made from shipping containers.

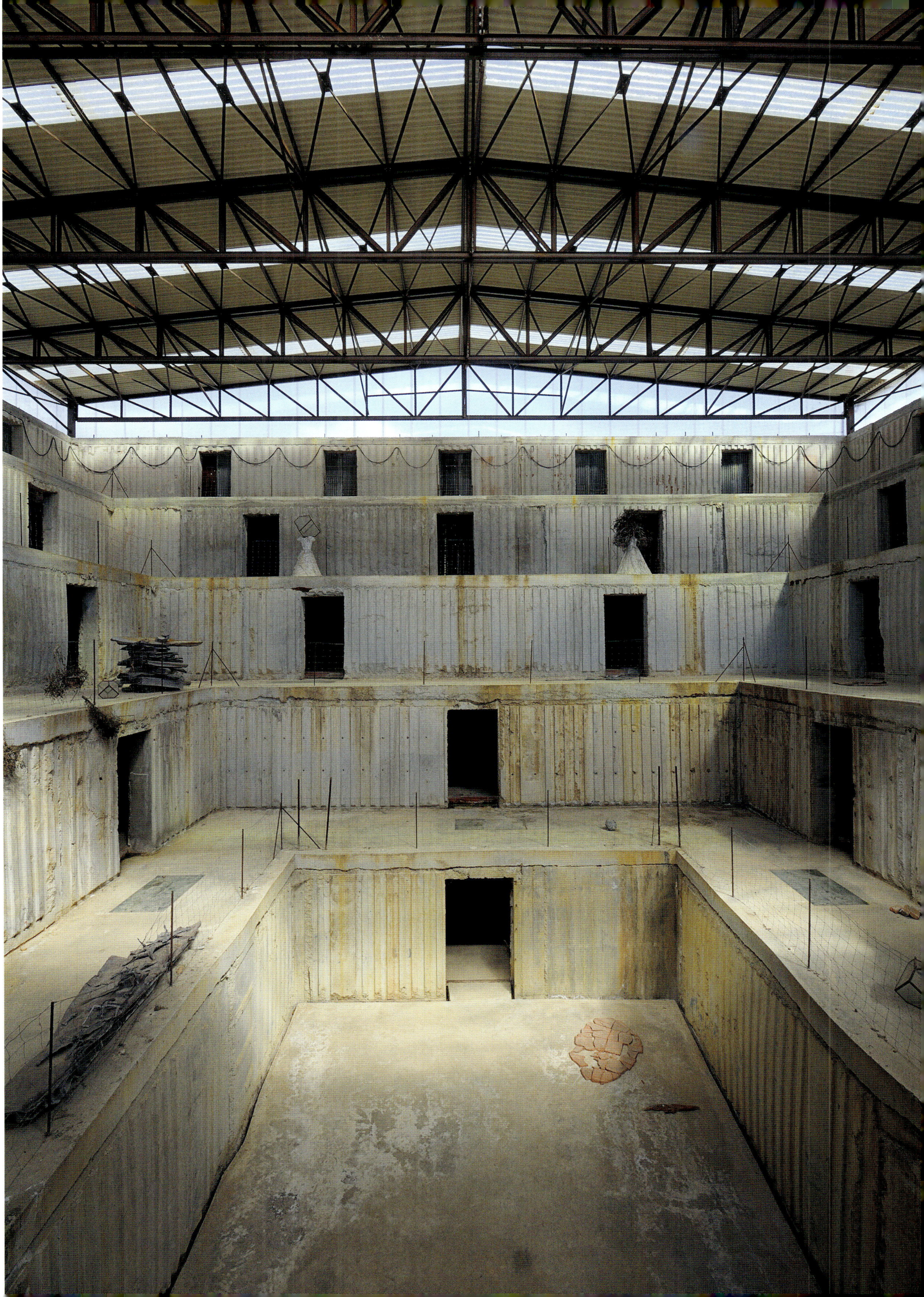

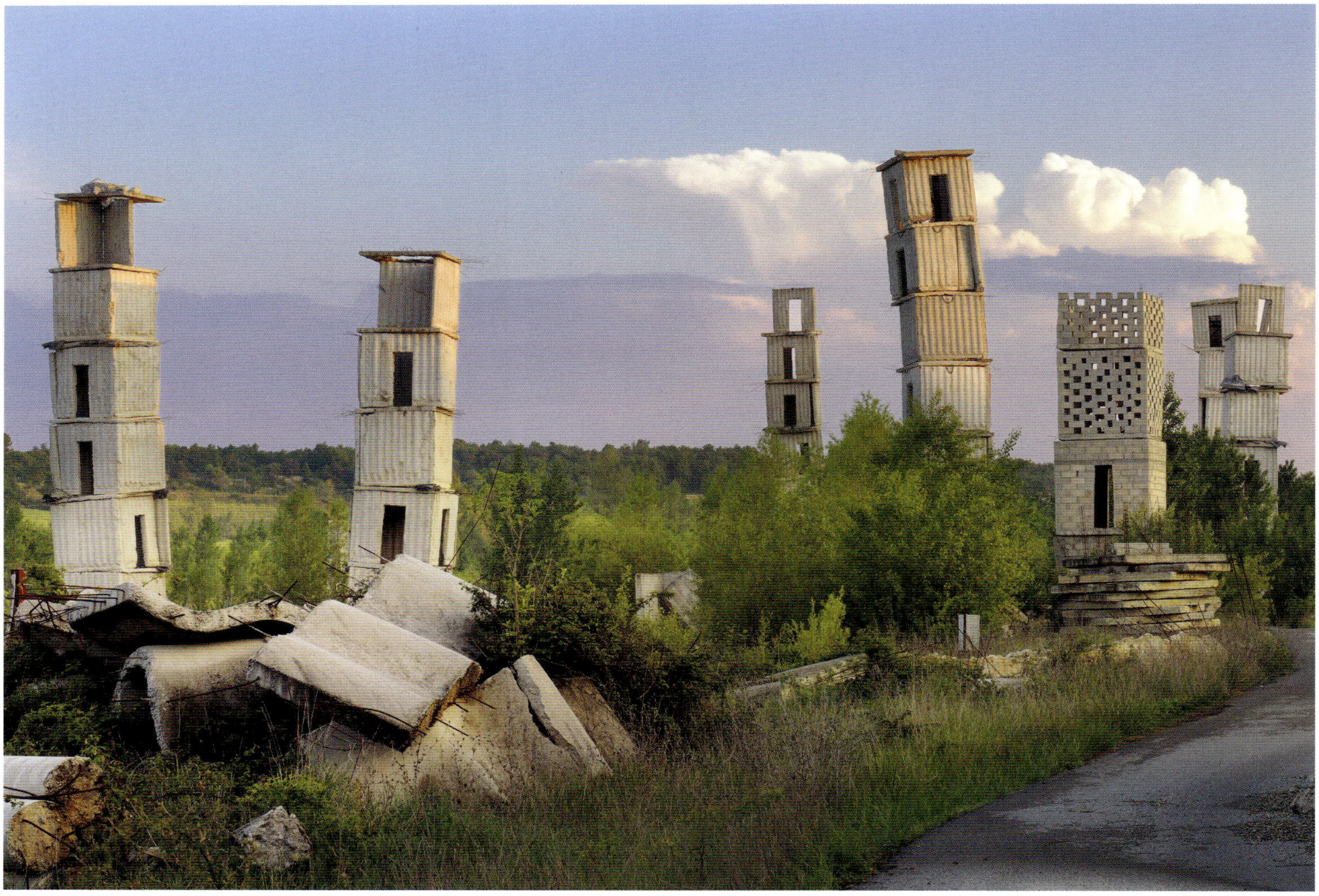

that he charges installations of this kind with meaning. He is particularly drawn to the notion of multiple interpretations, which spur him on to constantly rework pieces and devise new variants. His works – these containers are in fact representative of La Ribaute in its entirety – thus become memory banks where Kiefer deposits the past. But the past has to be faced, because only those who reflect on their own history have any chance of starting afresh. Kiefer underlines this when he says, "I don't at all regard these ruins as ominous; on the contrary, they mark the beginning of a new cycle of time, which advances in circles." These ruins are like the props of our collective memory, which have to be activated for us to progress into the future.

One day Anselm Kiefer went underground and started to construct a subterranean labyrinth as a counterpart to the overground structures. "It wasn't an idea, as such, more of a reflex," as he himself said. Tunnels and shafts now penetrate the hills in all directions and it is not easy to retain one's sense of orientation. The muffled silence, the darkness and the cold create the impression that one is both locked in and locked out. In the long passages it is hard to have any sense of where one is going. But there are also always unexpected escape routes and exits and surprises in this labyrinth – an amphitheatre made from containers, a grand hall with columns, a leaden chamber and a room that seems more like a funerary chapel, with a somewhat smaller version of the installation *Les Femmes de la Révolution* (1992) consisting of rows of bedsteads with lead coverlets. On the facing wall there is a large-format photograph by Kiefer, mounted on a lead panel. Written on the wall are the names of well-known heroines of the French revolution, including Madame de Staël.

These spaces not only increase the size of Kiefer's studio under the ground, they also link the outside world with a subterranean world – one area that is up above and another down below. It is an image of the universe with all its interconnections. It

The towers made from stacked casts of empty containers call to mind devastated landscapes.

Kiefer's universe also includes an underground labyrinth with art spaces, such as this grotto with a chapel-like space for the *Women of the Revolution*.

establishes a relationship between the material and the spiritual, the Earth and the heavens, history and mysticism, darkness and light. At La Ribaute Kiefer melded all of these into a single entity. And every new space adds yet more to this web of interconnections.

Although Anselm Kiefer transferred his main sphere of operations to Paris in 2008, La Ribaute has continued to develop. Kiefer decided that now it was time for other artists to engage with this place and leave their mark there. The first of his friends whom he invited to La Ribaute was the German artist Wolfgang Laib: Kiefer and Laib have both developed a unique language of materials. Laib creates minimalist installations made from natural materials, such as pollen he has collected himself, grains of rice or milk, with which he makes reference to much wider contexts. At La Ribaute he worked on an underground space measuring forty metres in length. The walls, five metres high, are coated with a centimetre-thick layer of beeswax. Now this golden-yellow, intensely aromatic realm of stillness has become yet another destination in Kiefer's universe of art and ideas.

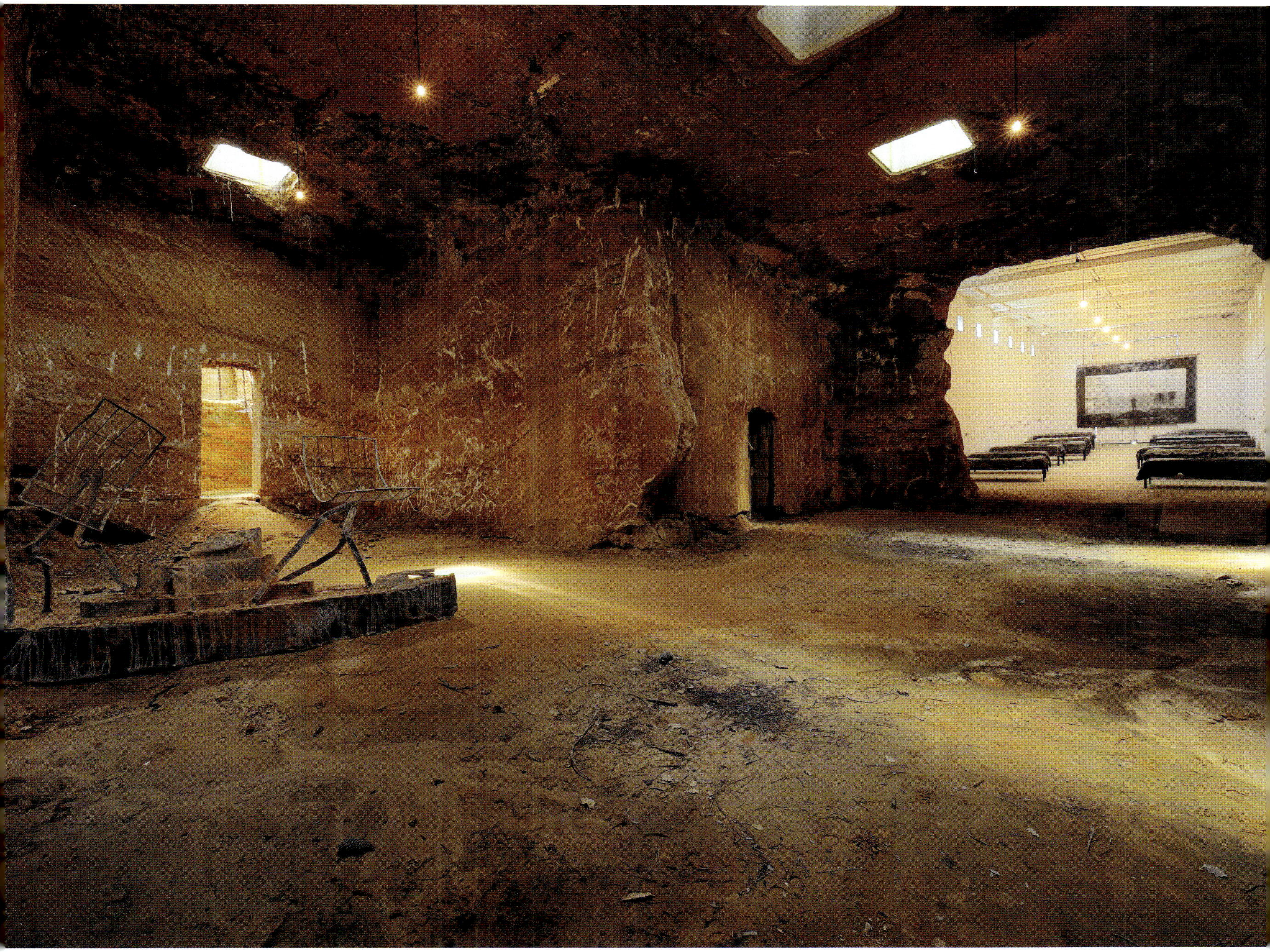

MONUMENTAL NATURE AND ART
GIBBS FARM, MAKARAU, NEW ZEALAND

Intact nature. For artists who create large-scale sculptures and installations for external spaces, New Zealand's landscape with its vast expanses, untouched beaches and forests is a true El Dorado. Here they can experiment and think big. The dimensions of the art and the landscape at Gibbs Farm near Kaukapakapa on North Island, an hour's drive north of Auckland, make it a global sensation. Huge, bright green grassy hillsides with palm groves and numerous artificial pools stretch out towards Kaipara Harbour, the largest harbour in the southern hemisphere. The reflections in the shallow bay make the one thousand acres of former farmland appear to go on forever. The thirty sculptures and installations that international star artists have created for Gibbs Farm seem at first sight like huge toys on a gigantic, grassy playground – a bright red horn in a cleft in a ridge, *Dismemberment, Site 1* (2009) by Anish Kapoor; Neil Dawson's *Horizons* (1994) in the form of a huge steel outline of a piece of cloth on the brow of a hill, which seems about to be blown away by the wind; multicoloured, extra-large building blocks by Leon van den Eijkel, set out on a sloping site as a square *Red Cloud Confrontation in Landscape* (1996). Not far away is *The Mermaid* (1999) by the Dutch artist Marijke de Goey – a series of filigree, interlocking cubes leaping across a lake. Richard Serra's immense steel wall, *Te Tuhirangi Contour* (1999–2001), gracefully snakes across the hillside like a ribbon blown there by the breeze. And in amongst them – one can hardly believe one's eyes – giraffes, zebras, bison, emus and thirty more species of animals.

"Serious fun," is how Alan Gibbs (b. 1939) describes his life's work. This successful engineer, entrepreneur and diplomat, with steel-blue eyes, is one of New Zealand's most important patrons of the arts. Long before he purchased this spectacular stretch of land in 1991 he was already collecting international contemporary art. "Serious fun" would also be a good description of his eccentric ideas and the delight he takes in unusual challenges. He collects tanks and has flown almost right round the world in a helicopter with his daughter and son-in-law, who is a helicopter pilot. At weekends he meets up with his grandchildren and friends in his own specially constructed Wild West town, where they enact shoot-outs in cowboy costumes.

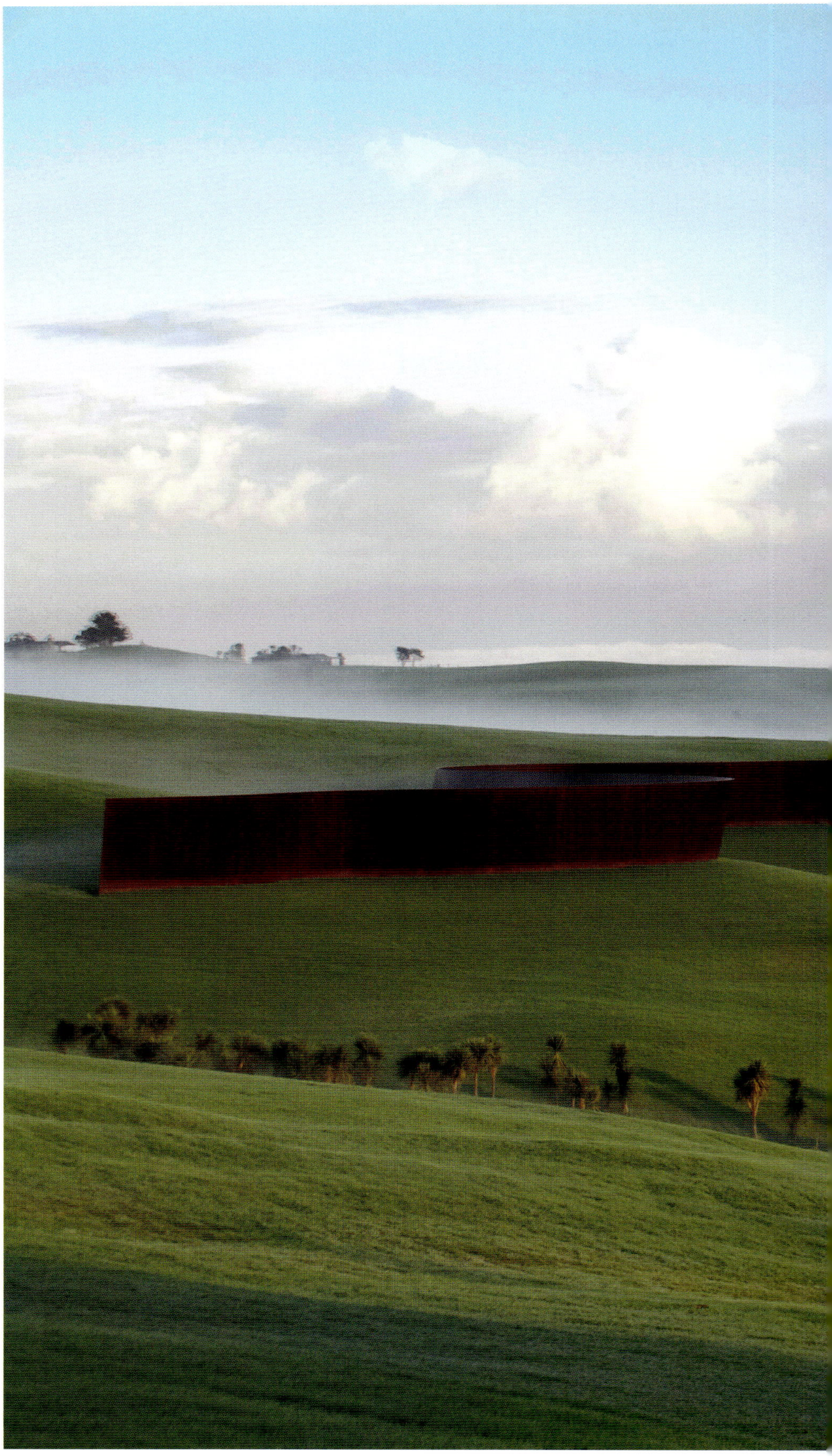

Te Tuhirangi Contour – at 252 metres long and 6 metres high this is Richard Serra's largest work of art and perfect for this vast landscape.

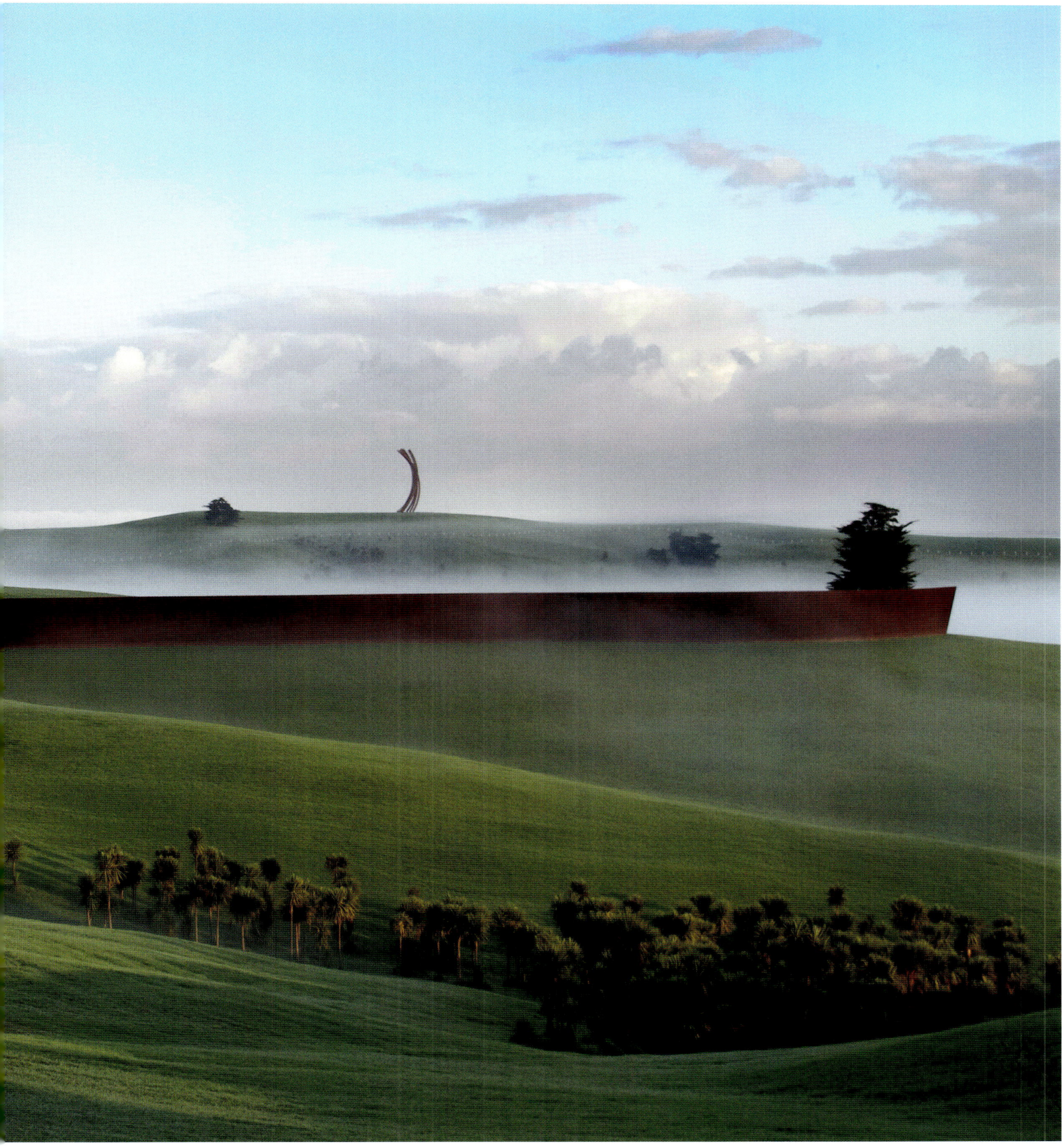

Gibbs Farm, New Zealand

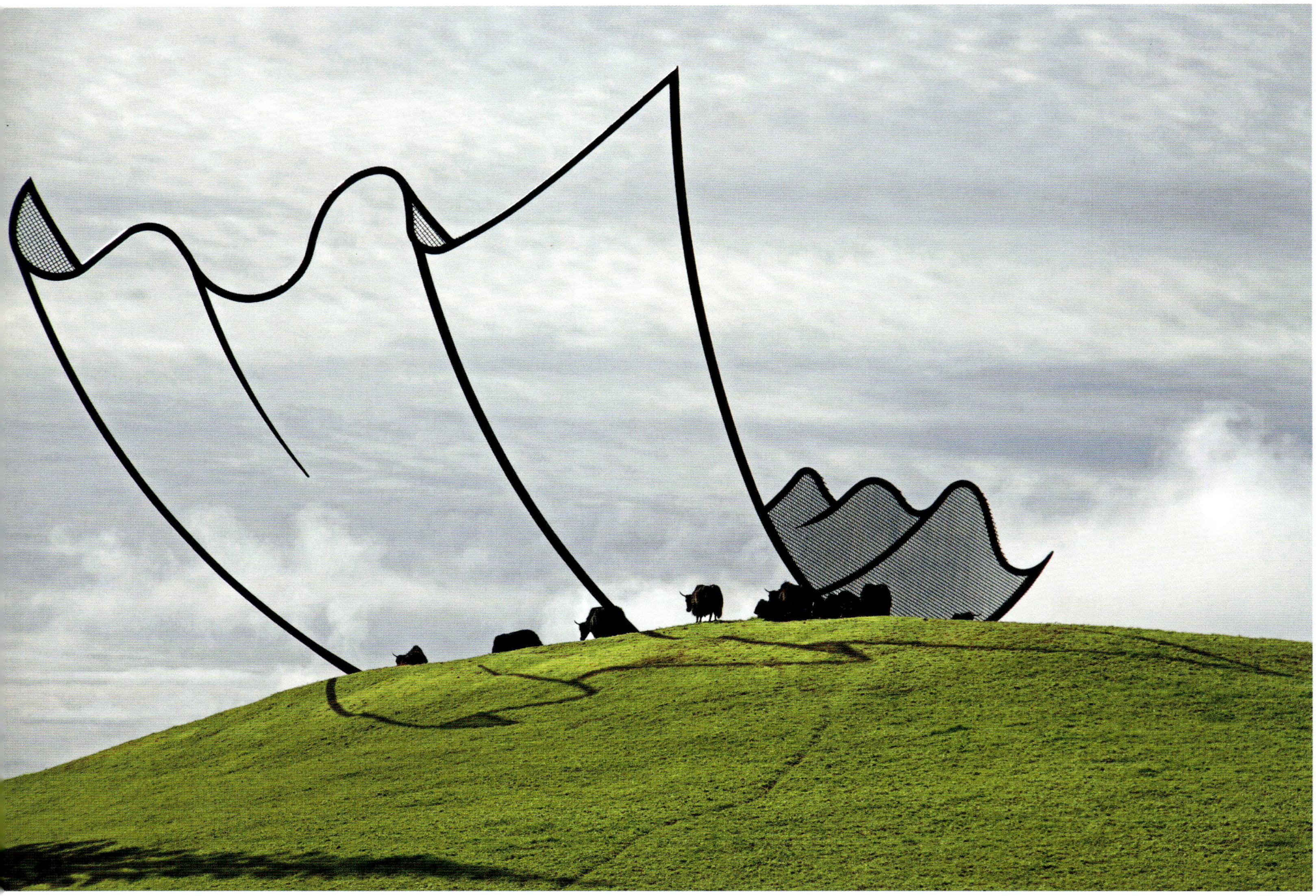

The 'town', which is part of a work of art, is hidden in woodland in the midst of the sculpture park. At the push of a button Gibbs can set it alight with *Saddleblaze* (2011), a light installation by Peter Roche.

In keeping with the demands he makes of himself, Alan Gibbs expects his artists to go to similar extremes. "The landscape here needs that. My artists have to go to the limits of what is doable, even if some are initially shocked when they get here," he says resolutely. As a result almost all the works are on a scale that their makers had previously never even contemplated. Bernar Venet's *88.5° ARC × 8* (2012) comprises a group of eight steles that rise up to a height of twenty-seven metres and look exactly right at the top of this vast ridge, with the open sky as a backdrop. Gibbs had taken an interest in Venet's art for many years before he commissioned a work from him. "In addition to the difficulty of creating a work that can hold its own in this powerful landscape, we also have extremely challenging weather conditions with wind speeds of up to 100 miles an hour." The artists therefore have to take particular care when they are selecting materials and have to ensure that the finished work is stable. It goes without saying that works of this kind require lengthy planning processes and elaborate preparations. But this is precisely the type of challenge that Gibbs loves, not only as a client but also as a passionate engineer and economist. "I help them to realise the maximum that is possible," he comments with a smile. Generally he works closely with the artists from the outset and helps to devise solutions with his architects

No more than a giant steel outline – yet Neil Dawson's 'giant handkerchief' on the horizon looks astonishingly real.

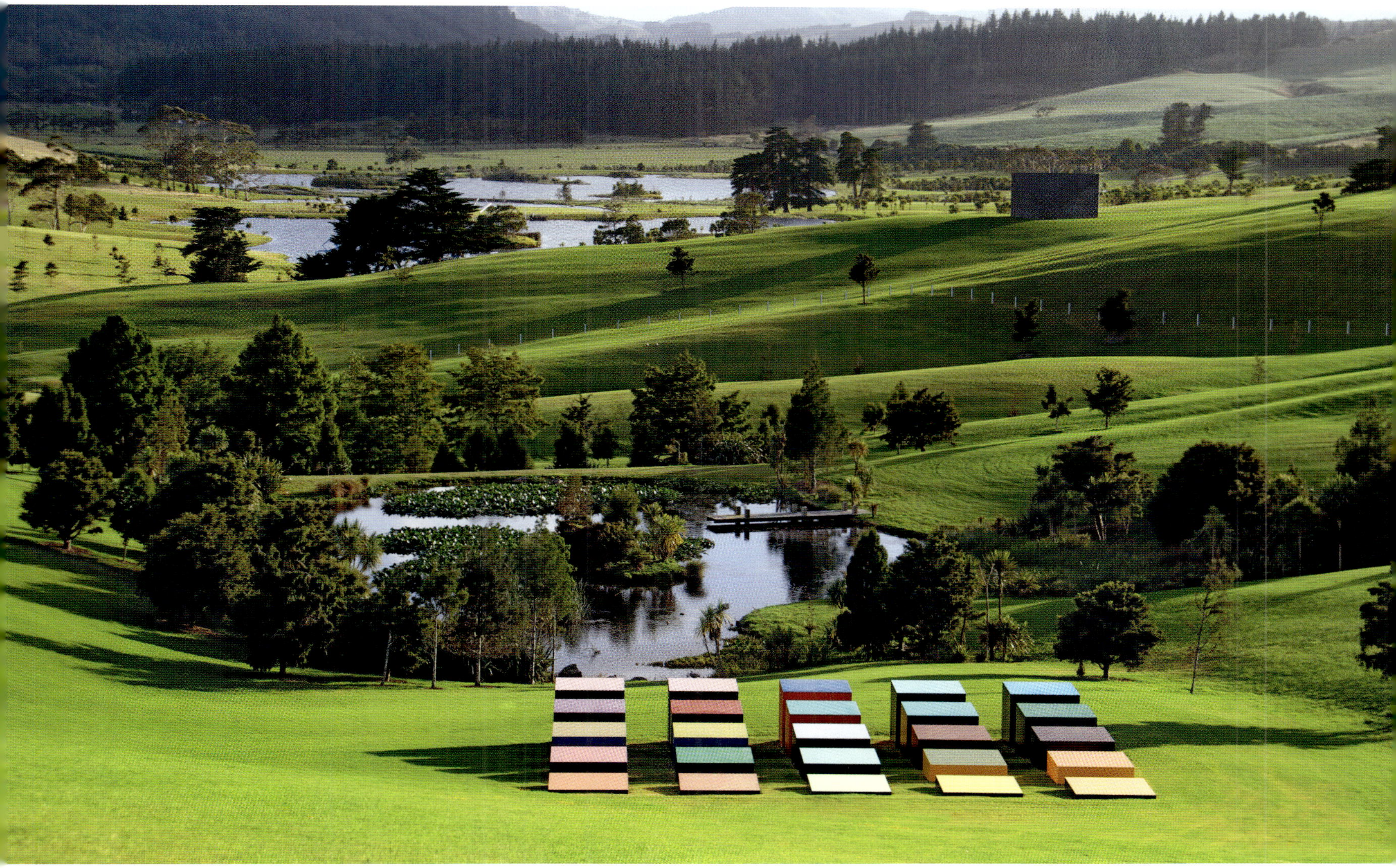

This expansive landscape invites experimentation: Leon van den Eijkel created a contrast to the hilly landscape with his brightly coloured blocks.

and engineers. His motto is that there is "no such thing as can't do." After all, he has already demonstrated this with his amphibian vehicles, which he developed for crossing the extremely shallow harbour and which are now sold worldwide. When Anish Kapoor devised his *Dismemberment, Site 1*, which consists of a blood-red PVC membrane stretched between two huge steel rings, Gibbs immediately had the landscape of the proposed site remodelled. Hilltops were removed, the slope was changed and a cleft was cut into the ridgeline. The gigantic, eighty-five-metre horn is now poised in this cleft, as though someone had just left it there. There are spectacular views of the sea from one opening and of the hills from the other. The connection between two entirely different landscapes is made possible here by art. The wind blows through the work's narrow gullet, and it is almost as though the sculpture were breathing.

In view of high transportation costs the works generally have to be fabricated in New Zealand. "Over the years we have built up a team of local experts, whom the artists can always turn to," says Gibbs. For all the closeness of these collaborations, there can also be strong discussions. Anish Kapoor had initially proposed to create a tunnel structure for Gibbs Farm and in the case of Richard Serra's meandering steel wall, *Te Tuhirangi Contour*, it took two years before he and Gibbs could agree on how the immensely heavy steel plates were to be fixed in the ground in a way that would allow the wall to run at the true perpendicular to the slope of the land, creating the impression that it is nimbly snaking across the ground. "It is very lovely being here in the morning or the evening light," says Gibbs. "The steel positively glows and the wall seems to float in the air." In order to make way for the wall (252 metres long and 6 metres high) a whole row of trees was felled. This major work was not to be concealed in any way. Because of the wind and the angle of the wall it was necessary to create a massive substructure. "We had to dig down nearly ten metres," explains Gibbs. "Serra had never made a work of this size from steel, so he couldn't know how much the fifty-six single steel plates would expand and contract overall." Here Gibbs could again draw on the help of a New Zealand expert. And then the steel plates fell over in the ship before leaving Germany and were damaged. The plates had not been secured carefully enough. It took a whole year before the replacements arrived. "But all these challenges, the discussions with the artists, their visits here and our shared search for solutions accounts for at least 50 per cent of the pleasure this art project gives me." He grins broadly and shoots off in his amphibian to the next lake.

Marijke de Goey's skeleton cubes form a bridge crossing one of the artificial lakes in an almost playful manner.

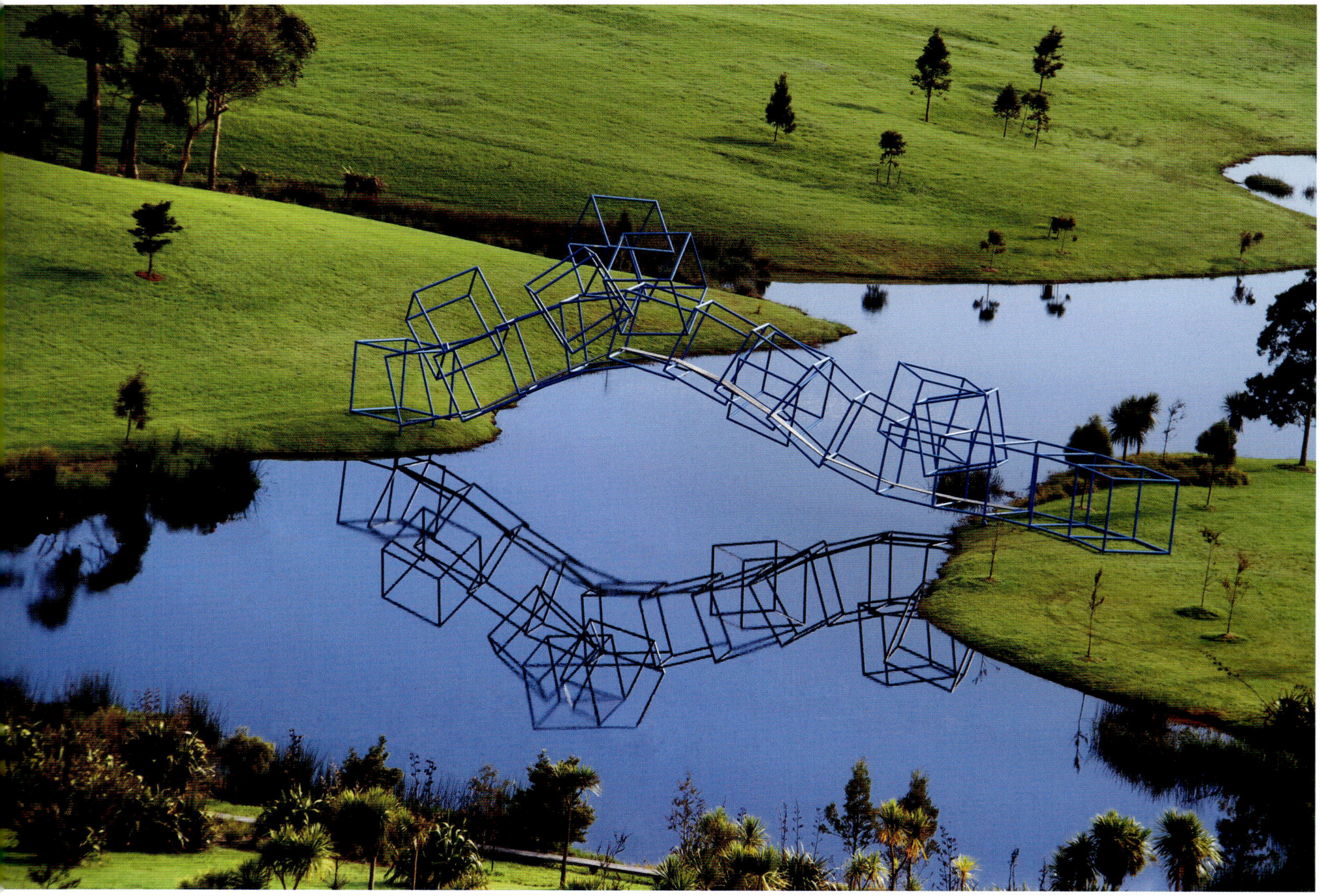

Right: Andy Goldsworthy's *Arches* recall rounded Roman arches. In a play on the notion of transience they are more or less visible, depending on the tide.

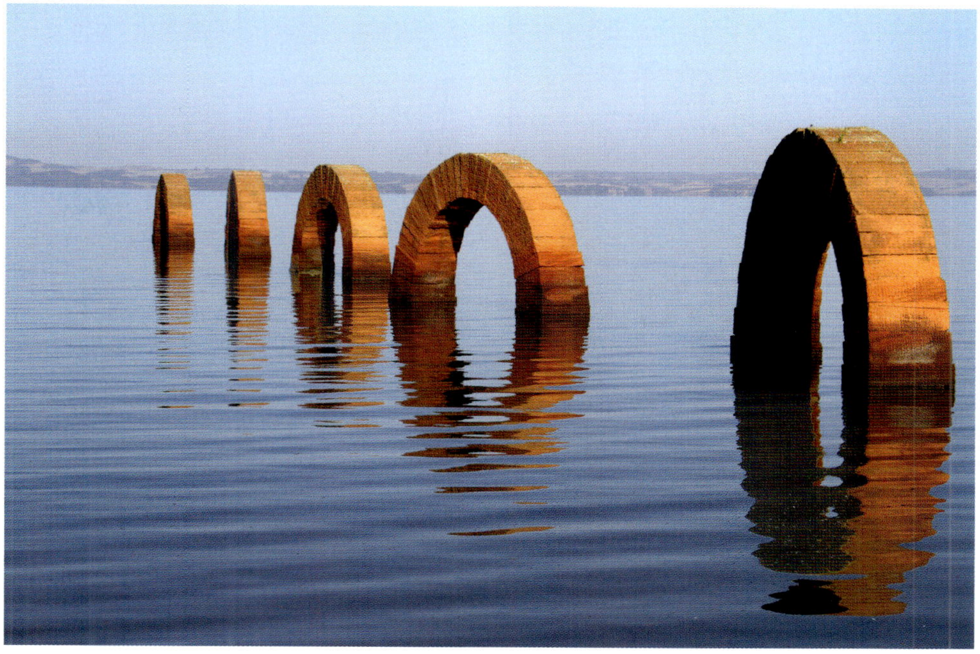

Bernar Venet's 27-metre-tall curves of steel are supported by massive substructures so that they can withstand even the strongest of winds.

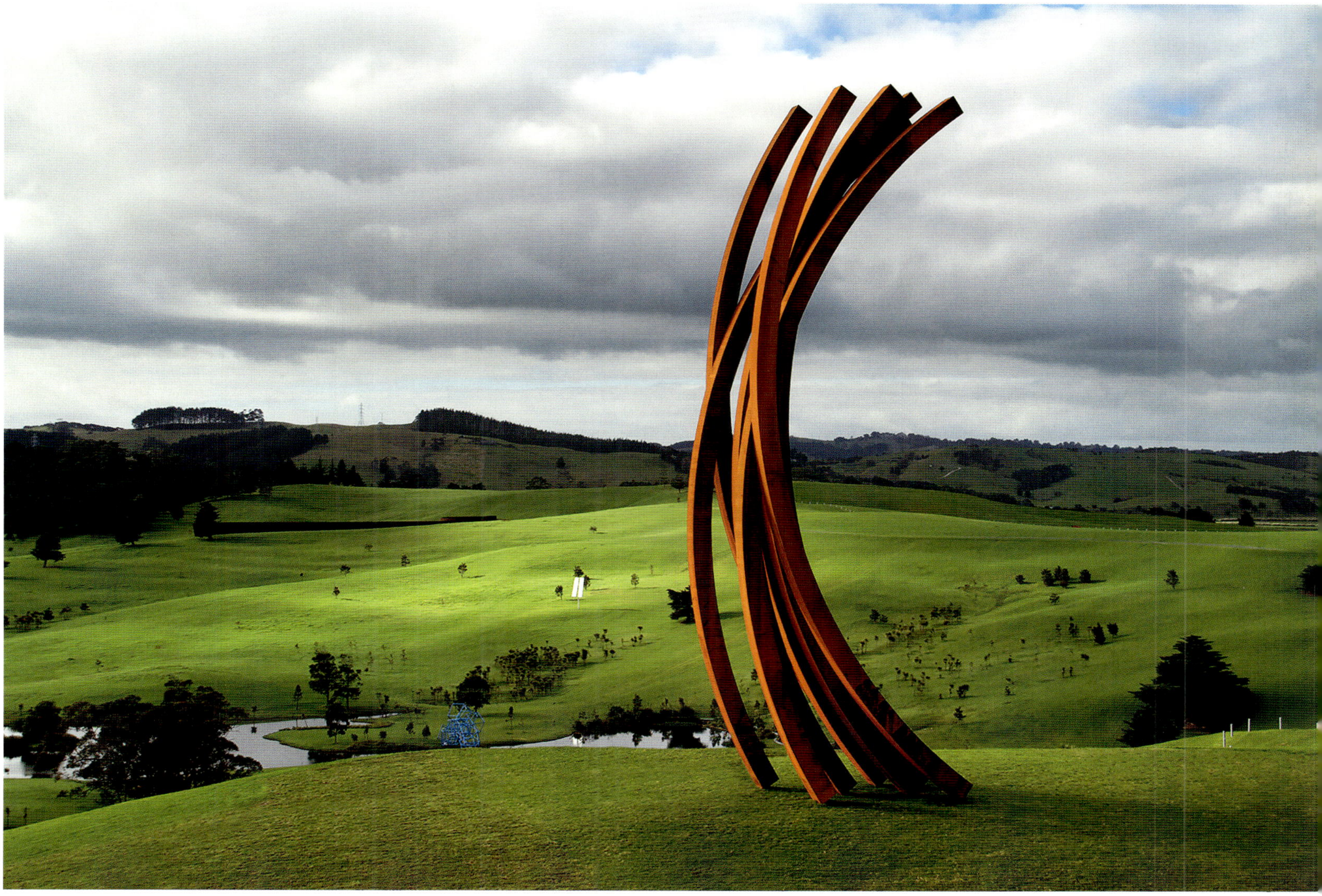

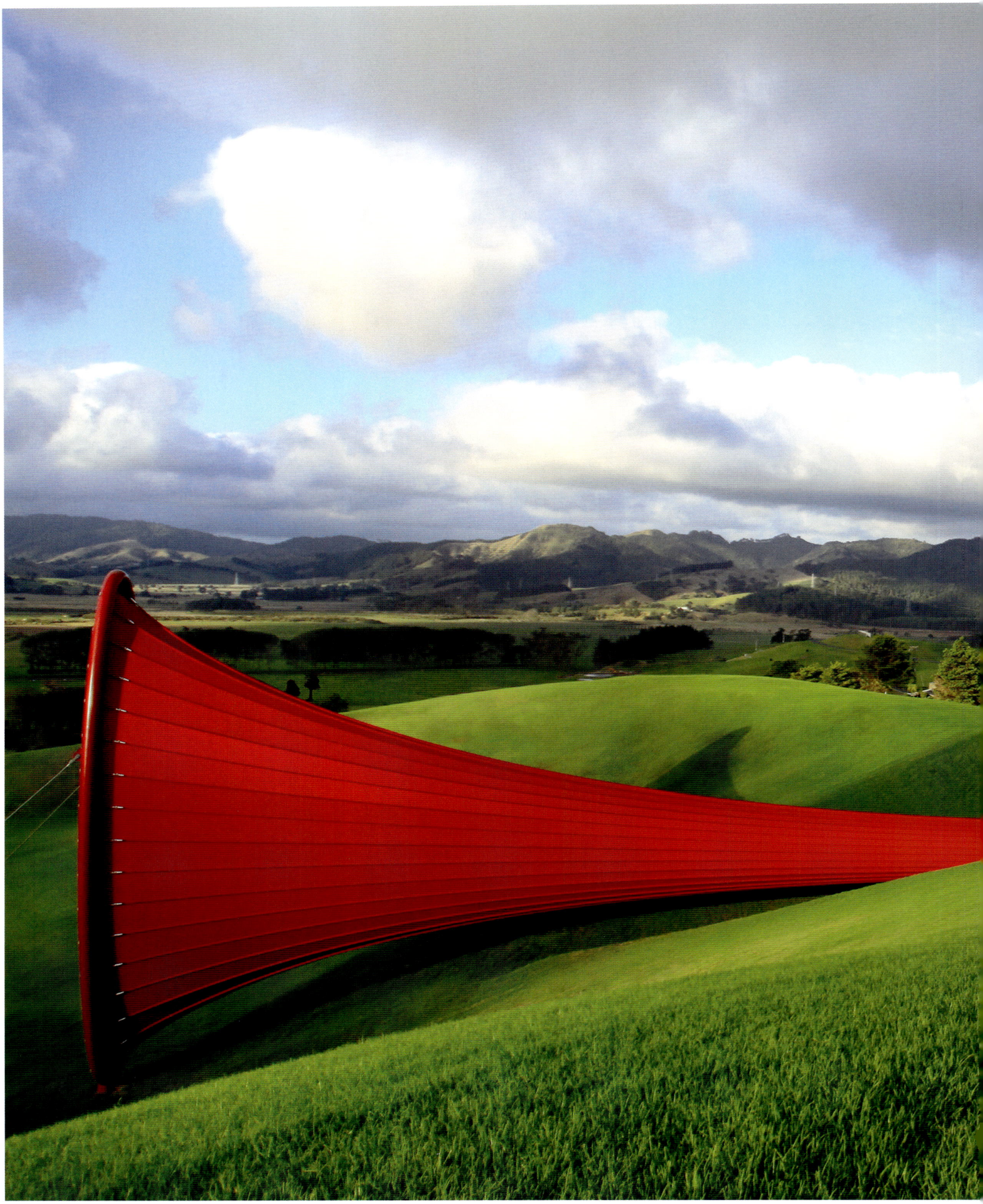

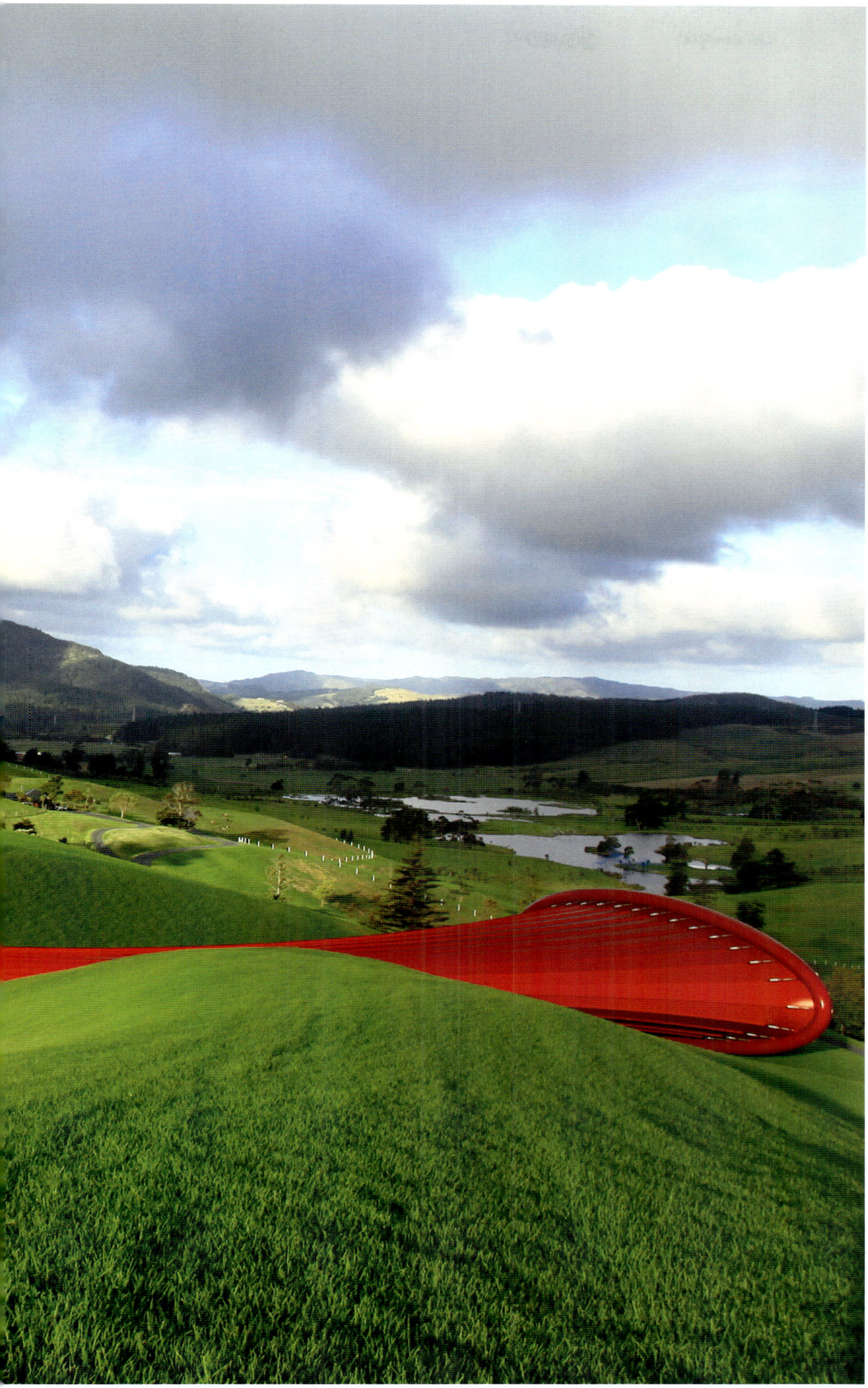

Think big: Alan Gibbs did not hesitate when it came to reconfiguring the landscape for *Anish Kapoor's Dismemberment Site 1*.

ON THE TRAIL OF HUMANITY
TIME AND SPACE, CAPPADOCIA, TURKEY

Like ancient route markers eight basalt steles stand on the brow of a hill high up above the rugged landscape of Cappadocia in central Anatolia: these *Sentinels* are one of thirteen monumental installations created by the Australian artist Andrew Rogers (b. 1947) between 2007 and 2011 in this lonely, high valley that extends from Avanos to Nevşehir. "Time and Space" is the name he has given to this art landscape which covers a distance of 2.5 kilometres. It is recognised as the largest Land Art park in the world and is also part of Rogers' global project *Rhythm of Life*, which he started in 1998 and has already seen him leave impressive marks on the landscapes of all the continents: stone-built structures, archetypal symbols of the civilisations in those regions, which he has placed in very different topographies – from the Gobi Desert in China to the Atacama Desert in Chile to the Chyulu Mountains in Kenya. So far Rogers has installed art works in fourteen countries around the world. It is his answer – as an artist – to globalisation and the march of technology, which are blurring political and cultural boundaries and thus threatening the identities of different cultures. As he himself says, "We define our existences from the interplay of space and time. Nowadays we live in a world where technology is constantly advancing but people are staying where they were. That is why the old values from the past are so important for us today. Our roots are in ancient civilisations and cultures whose legacy we still carry around with us today. That is why I want to connect the old and the new."

The sculptures at Time and Space can be divided chronologically into two groups. During the first phase (2007–09) Rogers used stone walls to create pictures, which he has called geoglyphs, thereby alluding to the Nazca Lines in the foothills of the Andes in Peru: huge images that were scraped into the surface of the ground (by means of sharpened wooden sticks) around 800 BC. Archaeologists have interpreted these images as the remains of a prehistoric civilisation that was rich in mythologies and rituals. They could be sacred sites along pilgrim routes. Rogers also deliberately places his own marks in untouched landscapes, in order to connect with prehistoric civilisations that regarded the Earth as the primal goddess, as Mother Earth, the creator of everything that is alive. Unlike the artists who made the Nazca

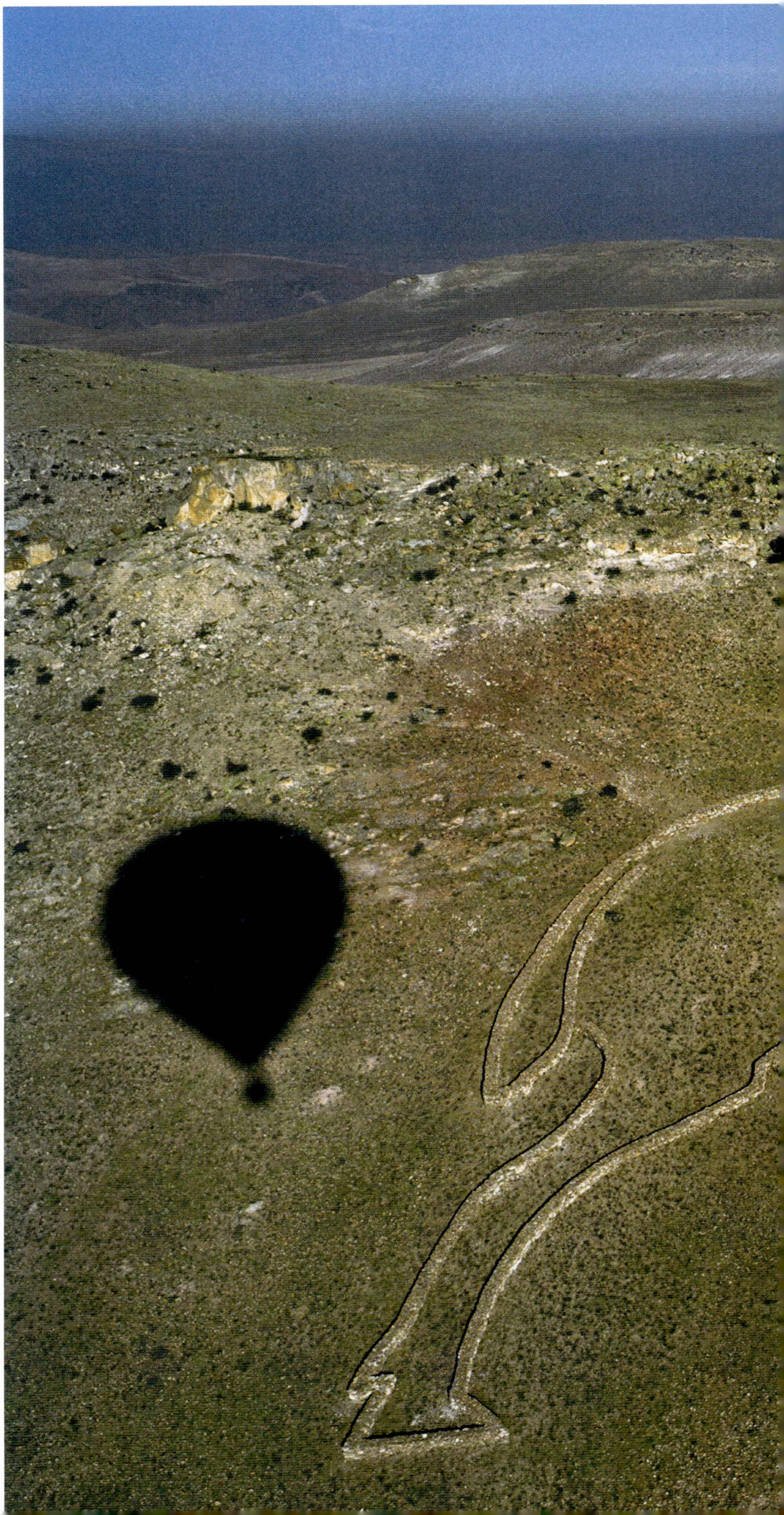

Cappadocia – once the "land of beautiful horses". Rogers replicated the 6,000-year-old rock drawing in the form of a stone wall on the plateau.

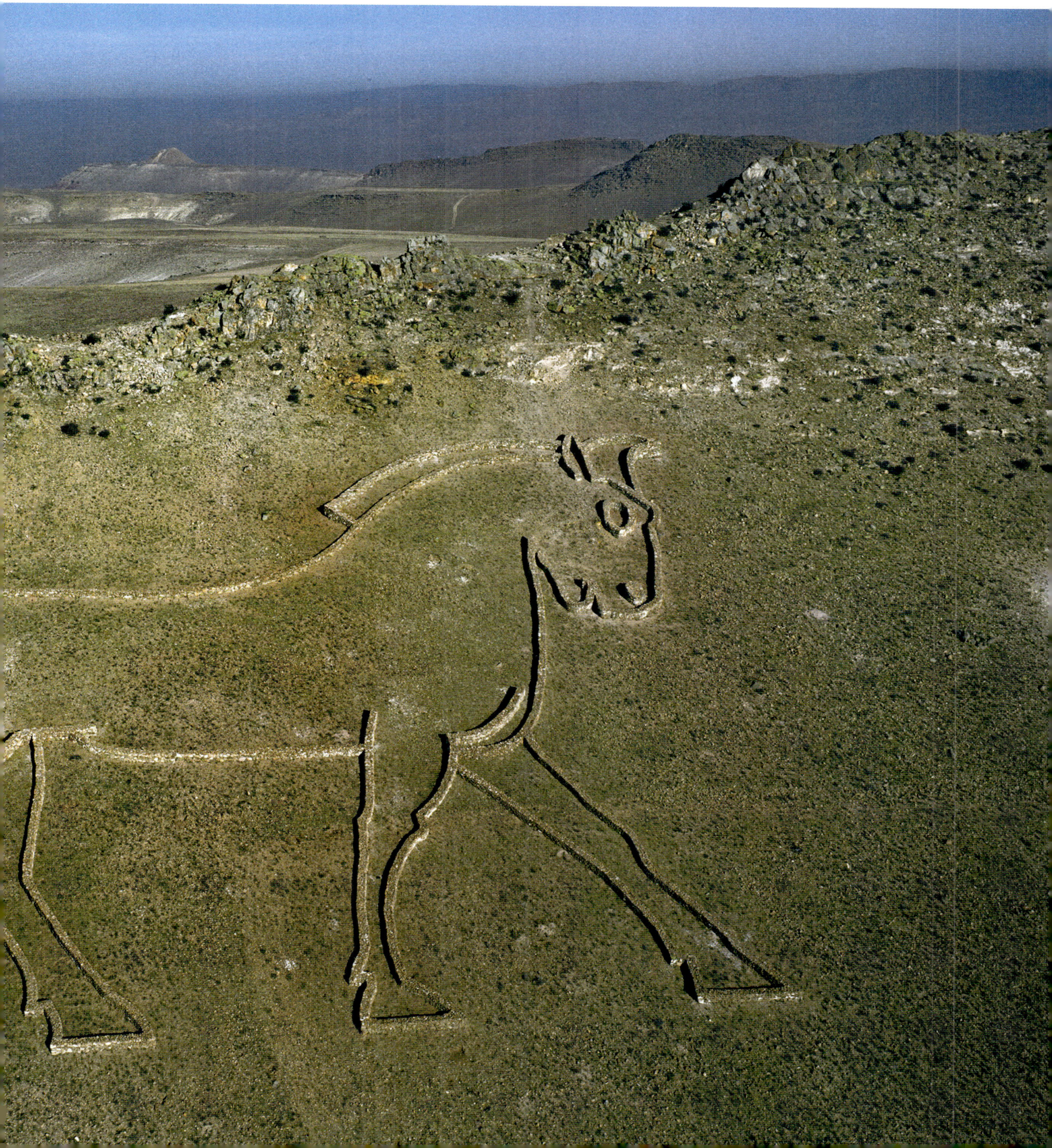

Rhythms of Life: a dynamic structure that symbolises the many different rhythms of life in Rogers' Land Art projects.

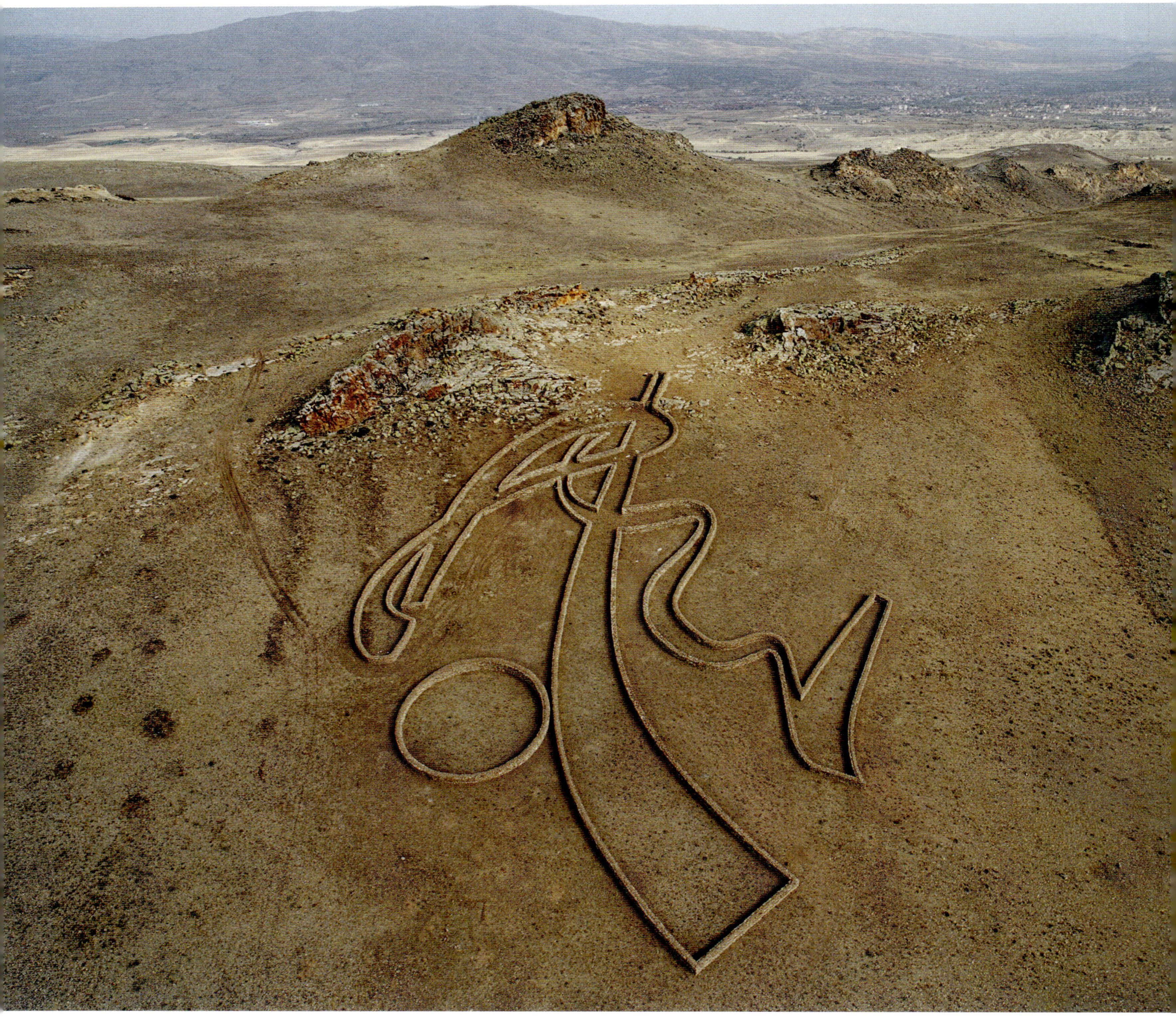

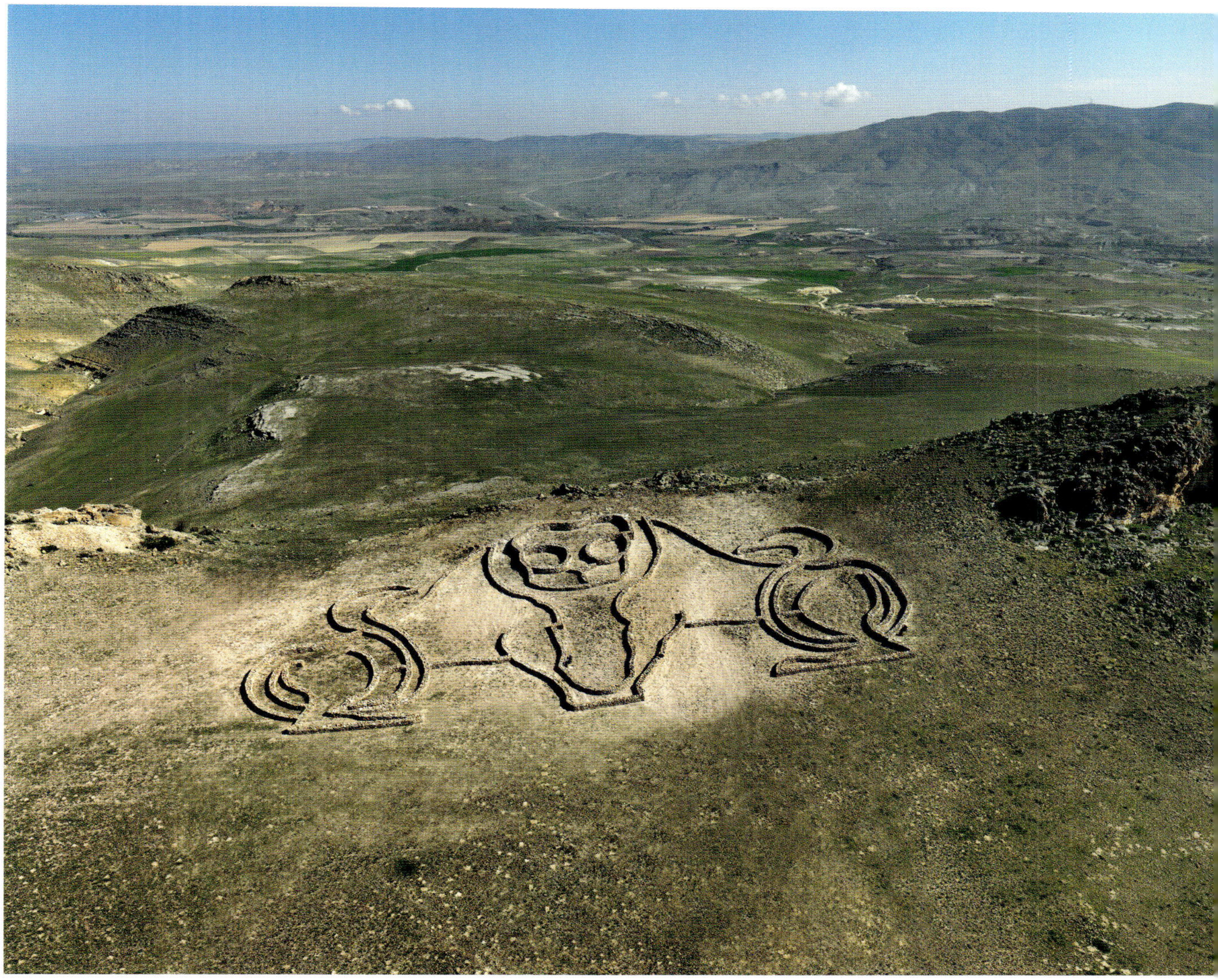

The double-bodied lion is best seen from a hot-air balloon.

Lines, Rogers does not carve his symbolic motifs into the ground but constructs them from hip-high stone walls: a large horse, which gave Cappadocia its name; a millstone, which represents the material basis of life in the village; the mythological figure of a siren as a symbol of temptation; a palm as a tree of life; and a double-bodied lion as a metaphor for strength. All of these motifs are universal archetypes that can be understood the world over. Like a personal tag, Rogers also includes his own sign, *Rhythms of Life*, which is present at all of his projects: a dynamic structure that represents the arbitrary nature of human life. Each of these images, rendered as sculptures, covers an area of up to 100 by 100 metres. As a result they can only be seen in full from raised viewpoints – such as the amphitheatre in Cappadocia, which was carved out of a rock face at the end of a path. "But the best place to see them from is a hot-air balloon," says Rogers.

This is also true of the six installations created during the second phase (2009–11), which Rogers prefers to call "structures": vertical basalt steles, with the tallest measuring fifteen metres. Sometimes they are in rows, sometimes in groups, as gateways and colonnades in an imaginary, ancient temple complex. Archaic-looking remains of lost civilisations are structured according to formulas that are still valid today – the golden section and the Fibonacci sequence It is important to the smart Australian with the cowboy hat that people interact with his works of art. "I want people to touch the walls, to run around in among them, to climb on them. Our sense of touch can teach us a lot about the way our bodies relate to space and objects." Unlike the first exponents of Land Art, Michael Heizer and Robert Smithson, Rogers takes it for granted that he will document the entire process and the finished works by means of videos, photographs and even satellite images. But above all he wants the locals to identify with his projects and with the unusual sculptures in their region. He has often reiterated his belief "that history and our cultural legacy are essential to us as human beings." This is why the social, collaborative aspect of Time and Space was crucial to Rogers. And that was also why he chose Cappadocia as the site for his work, since this area has always marked the juncture between Asia and Europe. As long ago as 4000 BC people were already creating habitable caves in the white stone of this volcanic landscape. Later on the Assyrians, the Hittites, the Mongols and the Persians, Greeks, Romans and the people of the Ottoman Empire all left their marks on the landscape. Entire underground towns and monasteries show the level of threat that was posed by ever-new invaders. "That is why I always start by going to the village elders and asking them what is important to them, what they want to have preserved for posterity. I want them to think about these things, to remember. Memory is the most important thing of all." The response from the villagers was wonderful. "They were immediately on board and told me about the symbols that mattered most to them," he recalls with enthusiasm. Having reviewed their suggestions Rogers then sought out relevant historical, mythological or archaeological remains in their culture, often with the help of anthropologists or archaeologists. That was how he found a 6,000-year-old rock drawing of a horse in Nevşehir Museum. This shows the important role of horses in that area, which is also reflected in the name Cappadocia. The original Old Persian name was "Katpatuka", which means "land of beautiful horses".

Now it was time to realise the concept. Men and women, old people and young people, whole extended families volunteered to help, keen to be part of this immense project. Two leading Turkish businesses covered a large part of the costs. The multitudes of helpers collected tons of boulders that were passed from hand to hand along endless human chains. On their arrival at the site the boulders and rocks were measured and finally used to create walls using the traditional dry-stone technique, which requires no mortar. Finally the women in their brightly coloured dresses danced as the men watched and everyone celebrated a work of art that they had all had a hand in creating – something that has no other function other than to radiate beauty and to prompt those who see it to contemplate human existence.

Andrew Rogers is often asked if his installations – which are entirely without protection – are ever damaged in any way. "No!" he replies emphatically, "the locals are so proud of these works that they take care of them. They reposition stones if they fall out and they keep the whole area clean." Rogers

The 14.5-metre gateway leads to a small amphitheatre hewn into the rocky hillside.

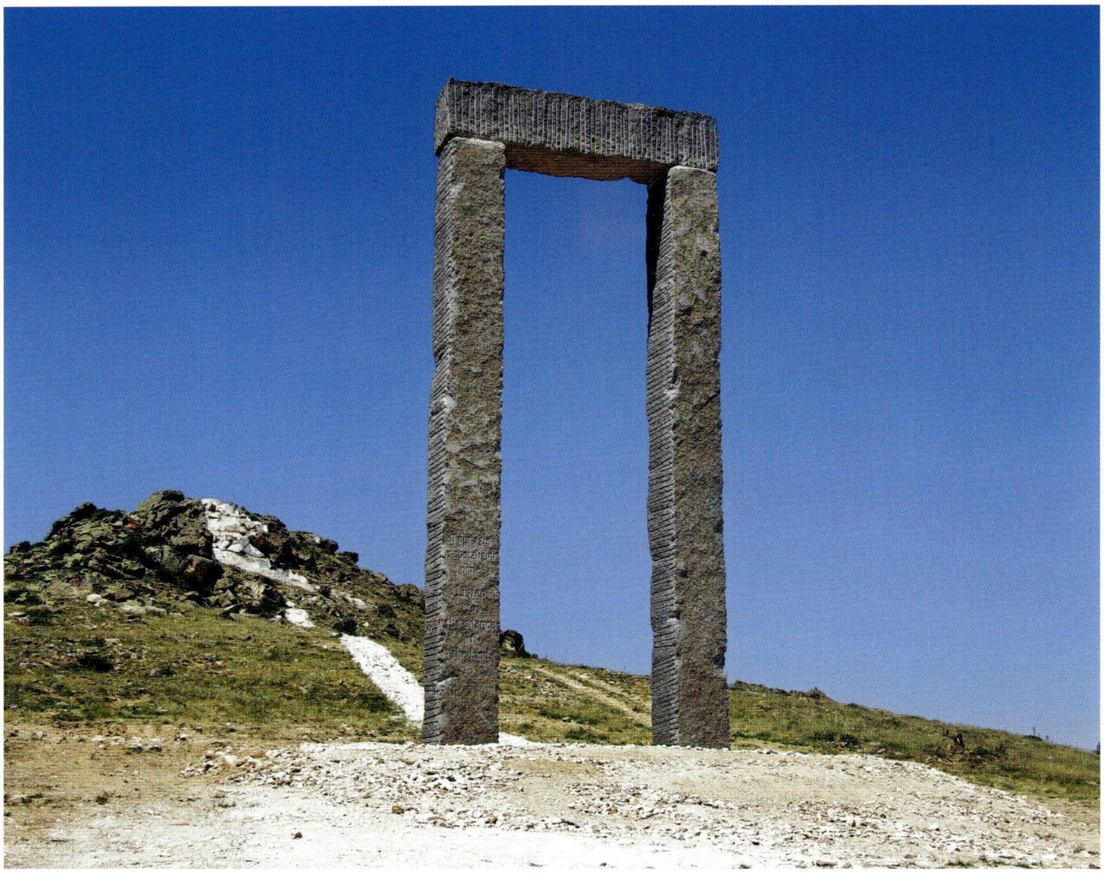

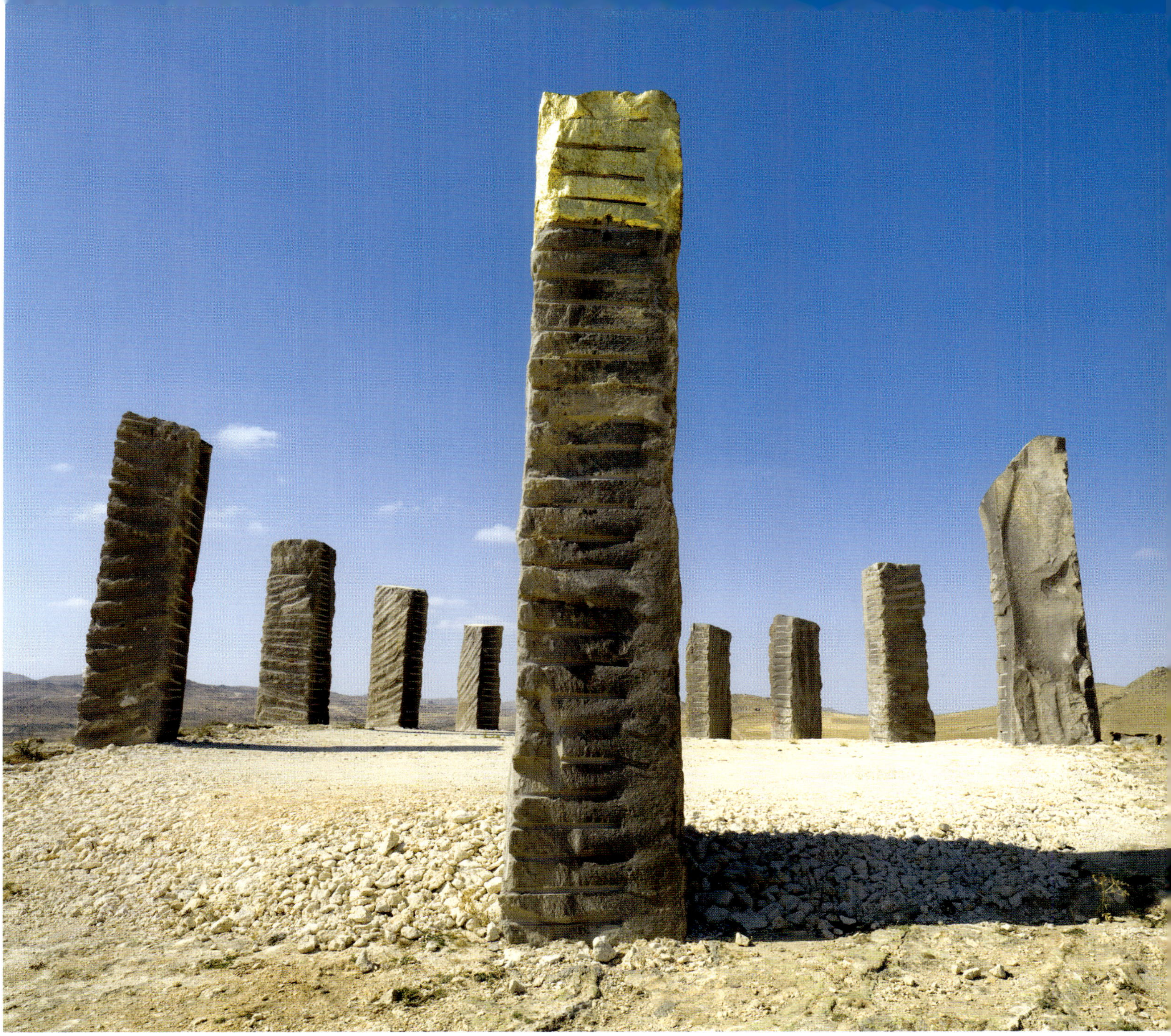

is happy about the appreciation people show for these works, but he is also happy in the knowledge that over the years nature will reclaim what he has appropriated in the name of art. The gradual reincorporation of his works into the natural landscape is an intentional component of his art. All the construction materials – the boulders and the basalt steles – were found in that area or carved out of the rocks there. Stones are Rogers' materials, regardless of where he is in the world: "They attest to the present day, to our existences now. They connect me with the Earth and yet they are also part of the Earth. They are the components that trigger our ideas" – ideas that Rogers enriches with concepts such as liberty, justice, integrity, truth, respect, peace, quiet, hope, optimism, history, tolerance and beauty – values and principles that are embodied in his art as hope for future generations. These concepts are chiselled in Turkish and English into columns recalling a ruin of an ancient temple in *A Day on Earth* – reminders of the past that point the way into the future.

An ellipsoid Fibonacci sequence with twelve basalt steles. The tallest, embellished with gold leaf, marks the course of the Earth around the Sun.

Designed in keeping with the golden section like a classical temple, this installation replicates an ideal of aesthetic proportions.

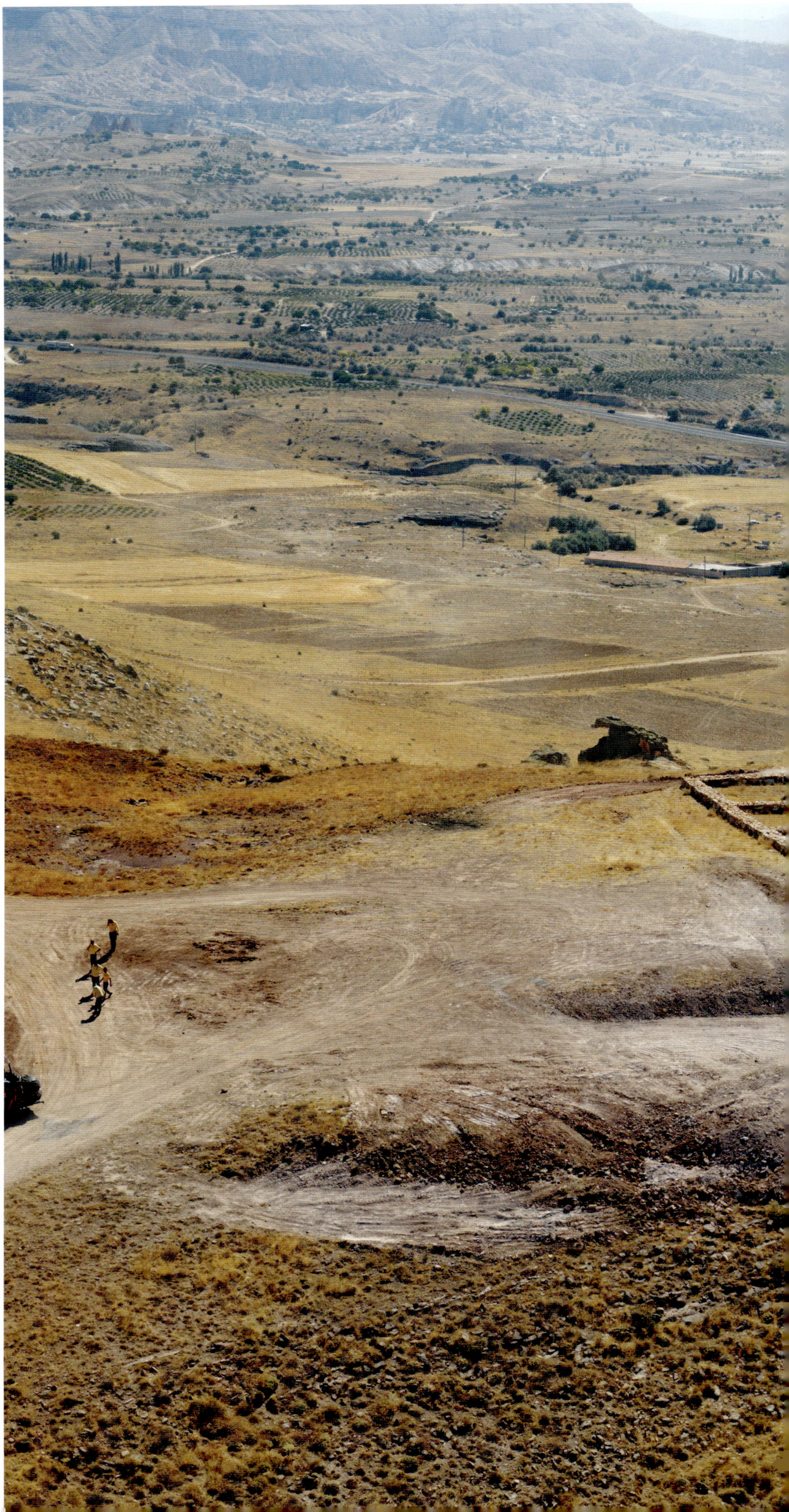

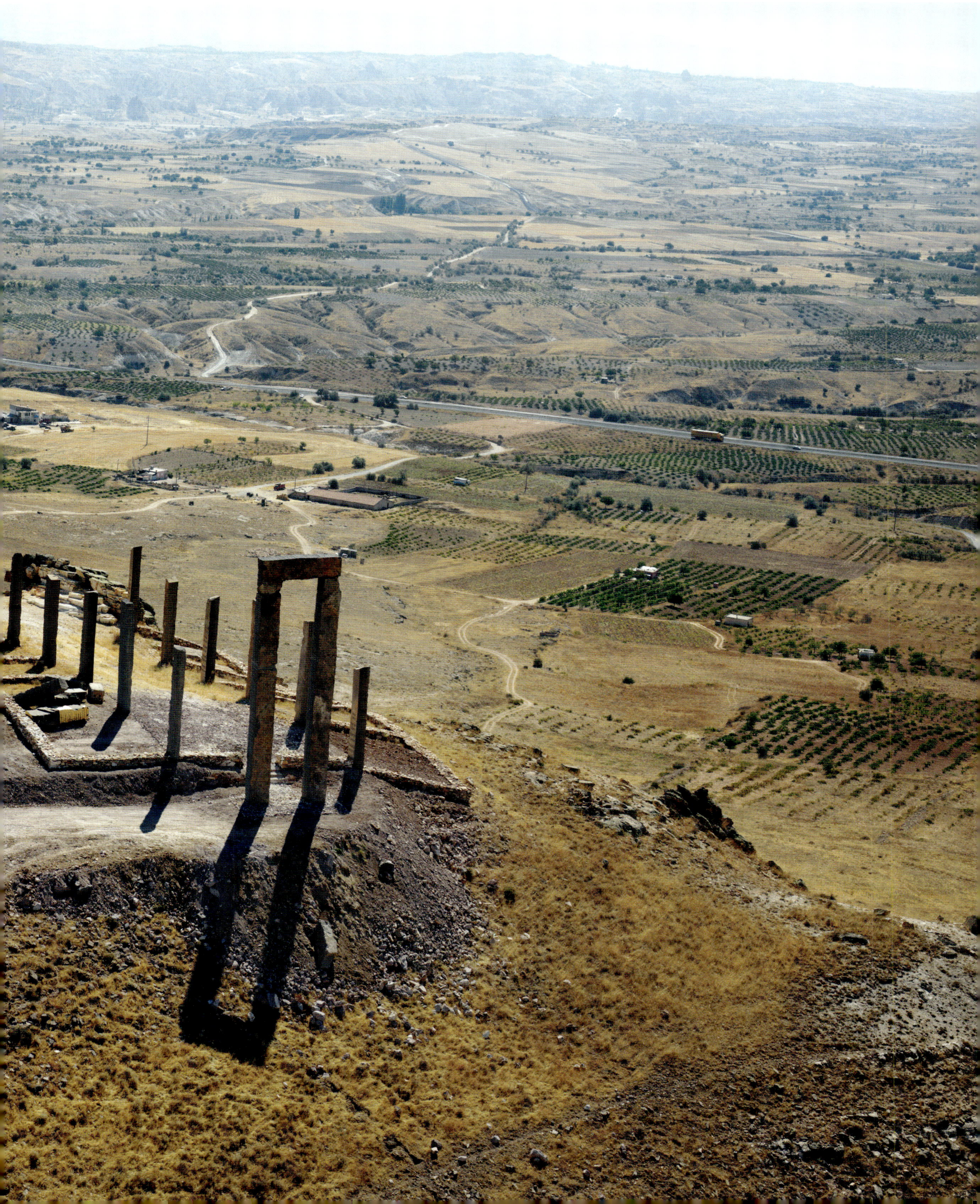

WAR IN ARCADIA
LITTLE SPARTA, DUNSYRE, UK

Little Sparta – the very name of this garden at the edge of the rugged Pentland Hills south of Edinburgh already conveys a sense of the rebellious spirit of Scotland's most famous contemporary artist, Ian Hamilton Finlay (1925–2006). For a long time he was very much at odds with the establishment and felt challenged or misunderstood by national institutions – be it the Scottish Arts Council, the tax authorities or art critics, whom he constantly took to task. As a young shepherd in Perthshire he had come to appreciate solitude and resolved to settle somewhere untouched by civilisation – away from the city, away from commerce. In 1966, not far from the village of Dunsyre, around twenty-five miles south-west of Edinburgh, he and his family moved into a run-down hill farm at the end of a farm track, surrounded by windswept moorland – with the telling name of Stonypath. Ian Hamilton Finlay withdrew to this inhospitable place and spent the next forty years there, day after day working on his poetry and sculpture, reading philosophy and literature.

Little by little Ian Hamilton Finlay wrought a paradise garden from the rough moorland around the house. With almost obsessive determination, he took every penny he earned with his art and invested it in his garden, while he and his family lived very simply. His wife Sue created flower beds and planted trees in the damp ground; Finlay dug out ponds and streams and formed separate sections in the garden with distinctly different characters and themes: the Roman Garden, Julie's Garden, the Temple Pool Garden and the Wild Garden. Little benches invite the visitor to tarry awhile. There are currant bushes within easy reach, planted by Finlay – ever the pragmatic countryman. The garden became the centre of his life and work, and he very rarely left it. By the time of his death in 2006 Ian Hamilton Finlay had laid out a five-acre garden that is composed down to the last detail and contains over 275 of his own works of art: stone pyramids, columns and inscriptions with quotes of his own and from antiquity. Little Sparta is a unique *Gesamtkunstwerk*: the legacy of an artist whose work above all revolves around the written word.

In his garden Finlay tapped into the tradition of poets' gardens in eighteenth-century England. He particularly drew

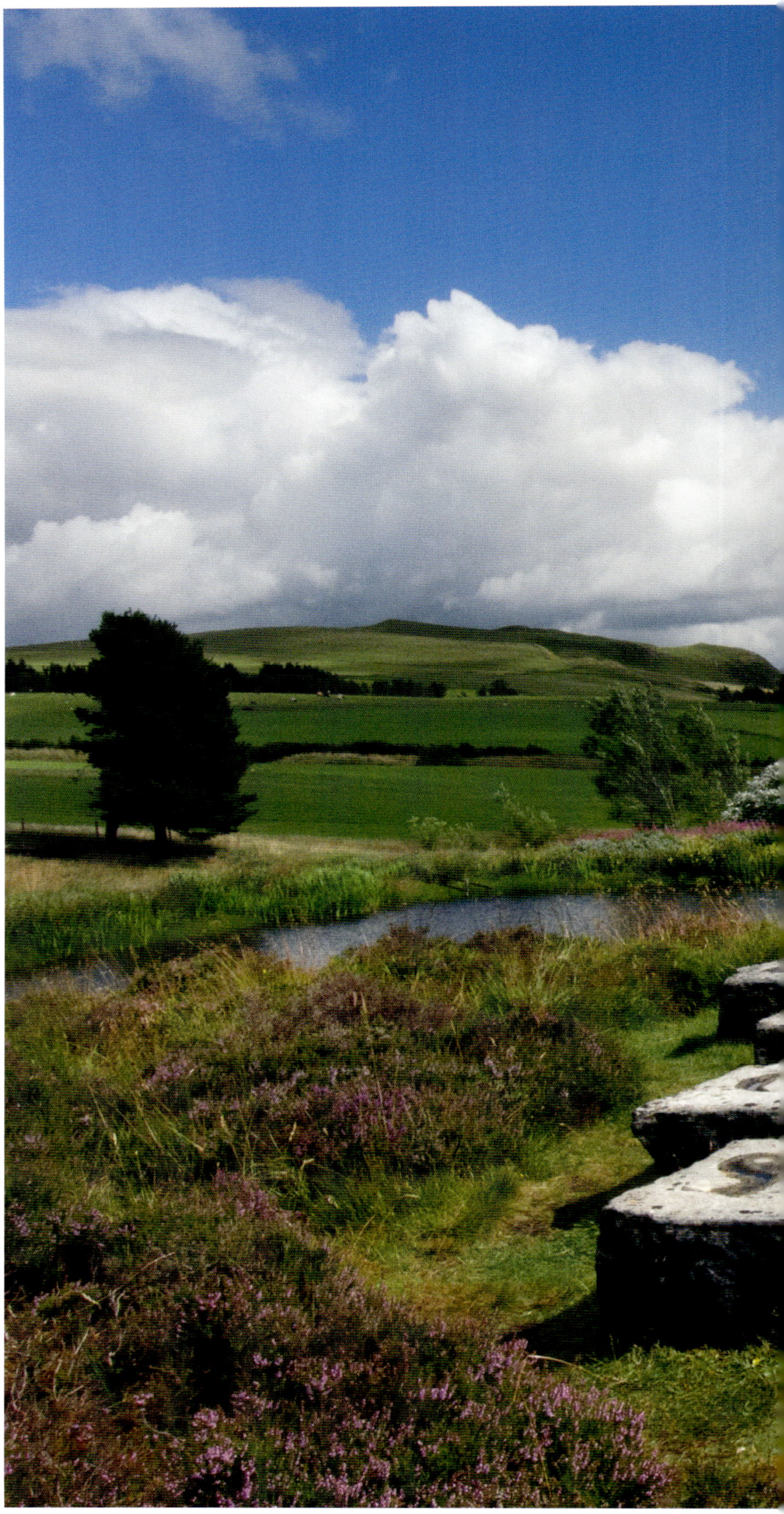

At the edge of his garden Finlay paid homage to the words of the French revolutionary Louis Antoine de Saint-Just: *The Present Order is the Disorder of the Future*.

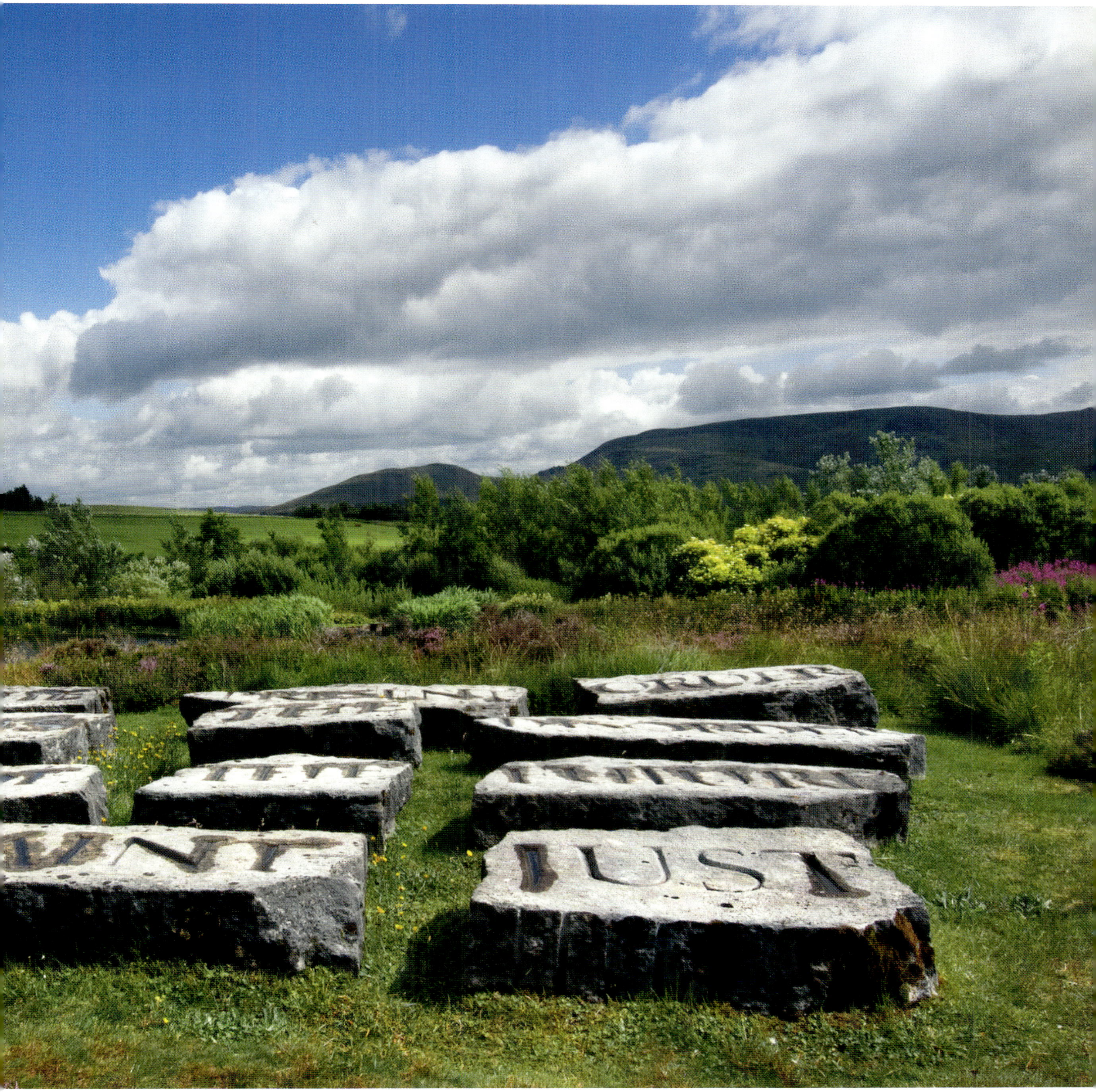

Right: A submarine takes cover in amongst hostas in plant pots.

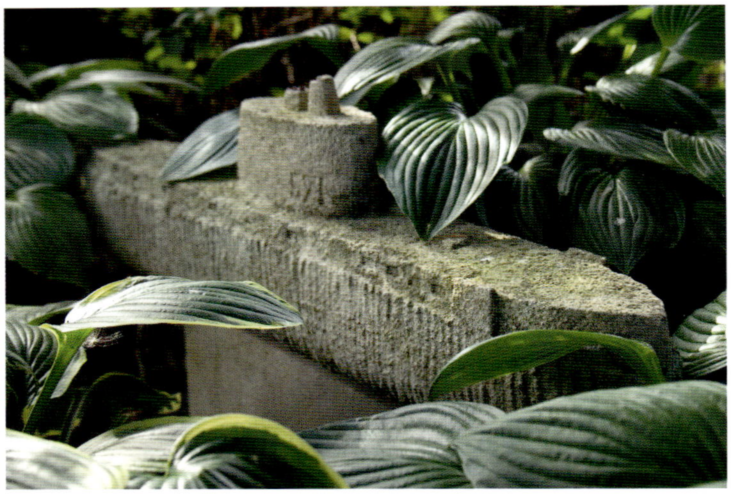

Not an untroubled Arcadia: stone hand grenades on two gate posts.

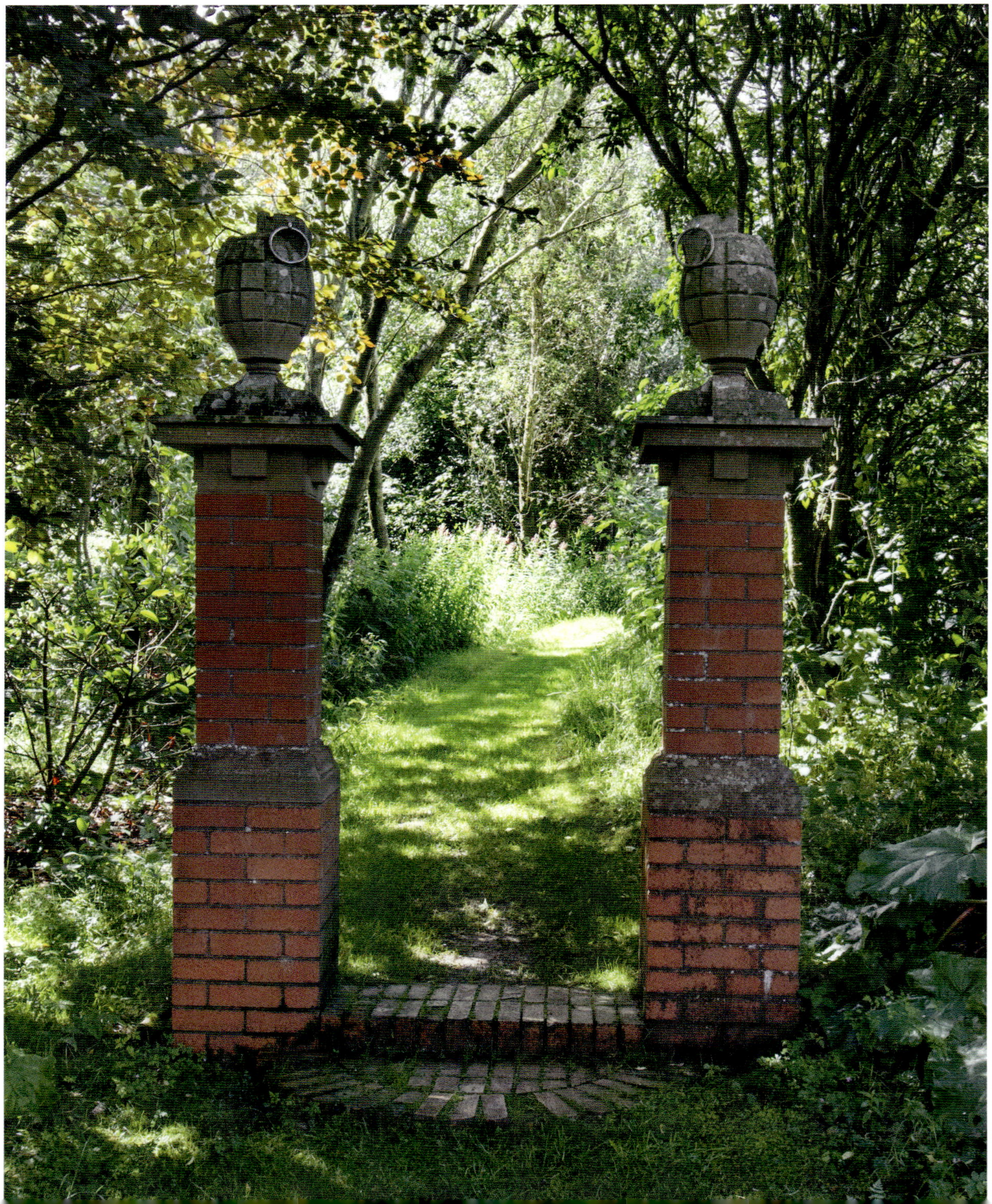

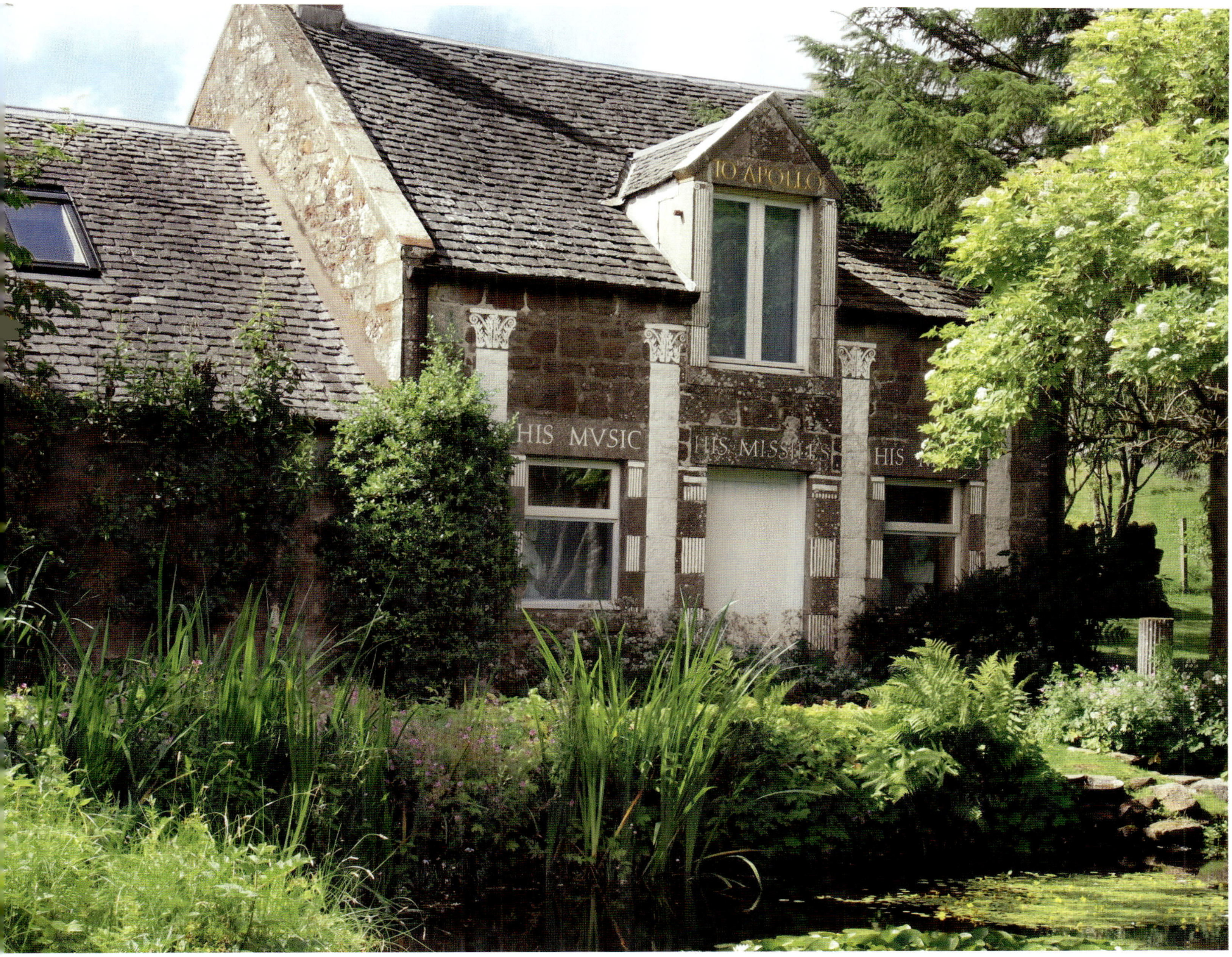

A neoclassical garden: a simple garden house is elevated to become a temple to Apollo.

inspiration from the garden of the writer Alexander Pope (1688–1744) in Twickenham near London, which embodied the classical notion of Arcadia as an image of a better society. But Finlay took this concept a stage further in order to address society's decreasing appreciation of art and culture. His replication of classical forms – pyramids and columns – was only a superficial ploy. Anyone who looks more closely will see that the apparently idyllic nature of Little Sparta is deceptive and filled with symbols of conflict. As in his poetry and art, Finlay also wanted his garden to reflect the eternal struggle between nature and culture, good and evil, war and peace, life and death. He confronts the visitor with slogans from the French Revolution, references to the Second World War, terror and annihilation. Sometimes this is done with a twinkle in his eye, sometimes with open sarcasm – as a coded message, or with ruthless directness. Suddenly this vision of Arcadia turns into a political arena: under the flowers there is a *Panzer Leader* in the shape of a fibreglass tortoise, while a stone submarine, the *USS Nautilus*, surfaces in amongst hostas. Finlay

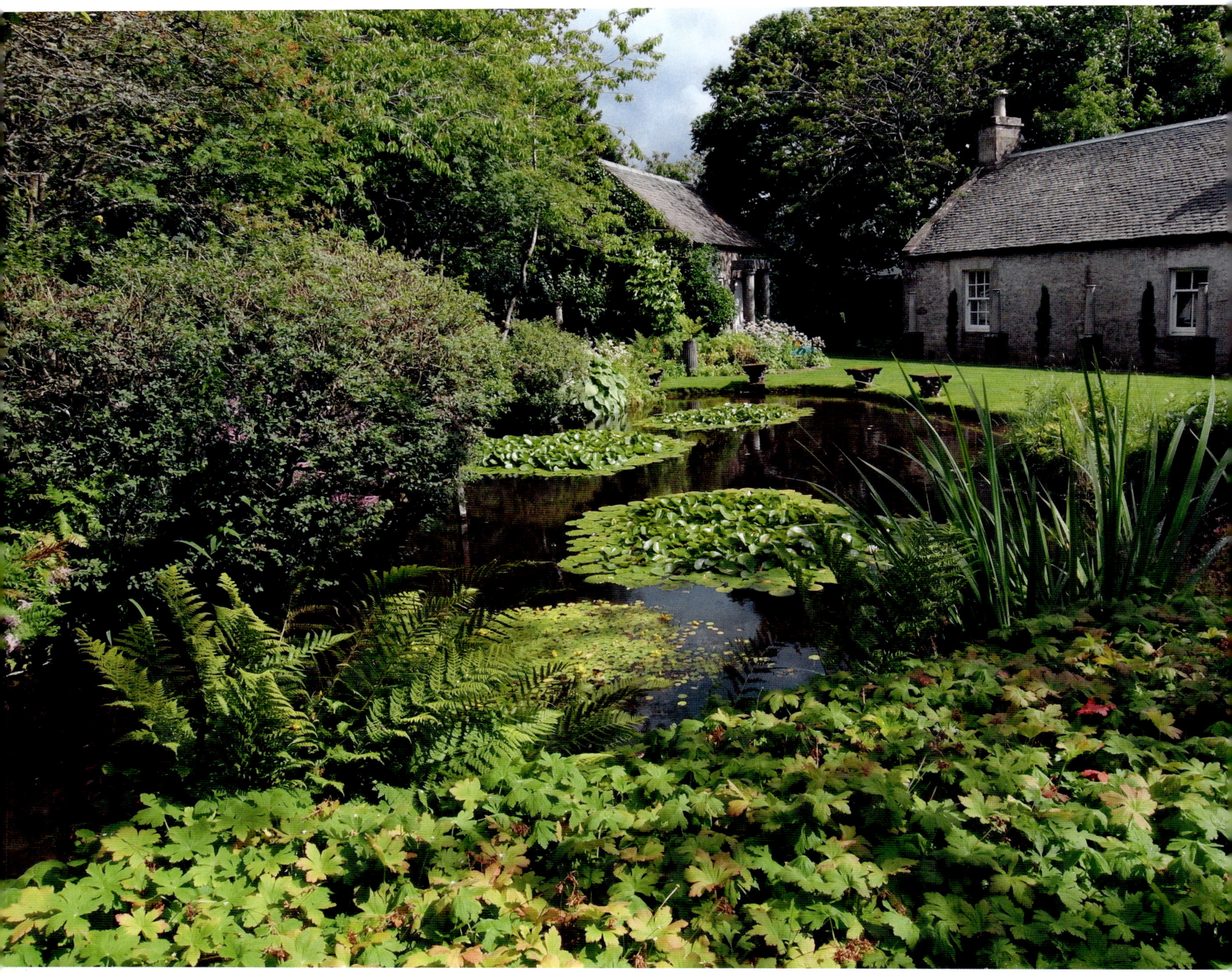

placed little aircraft carriers and warships on plinths and added stone hand grenades to a gateway, reminding the visitor that there is always a potential for violence under the surface of aesthetic beauty or tranquillity. Ian Hamilton Finlay's works of art in this perfectly formed landscape are metaphors for issues that now determine our social structures and actions more than ever. He exhorts the visitor to return to earlier morals and virtues.

In 1983, thanks to his resolve and the help of his supporters, Ian Hamilton Finlay won the First Battle of Little Sparta against Strathclyde Regional Council. The dispute had arisen when the authorities refused to recognise Finlay's Apollo Temple (previously a gallery) as a sacred building, which would make it eligible for rates relief. When the sheriff officer attempted to seize works of art, Finlay's supporters, the Saint-Just Vigilantes, barred his way. They had named themselves after one of the leading figures of the French Revolution, Louis Antoine de Saint-Just (1767–1794). The success of that action led to a far-reaching debate on the definition of religious buildings. Little Sparta thus came to symbolise civil disobedience against

The garden outside Finlay's home. The starting point for Finlay's desire for a better society.

government institutions and the establishment. Ian Hamilton Finlay regarded the French Revolution as a prime example of the dialectics of culture and nature, reason and terror.

For the large-scale installation *The Present Order Is the Disorder of the Future Saint Just*, at the far end of the garden, Ian Hamilton Finlay had this statement by Saint-Just carved, word by word, into eleven separate blocks of stone by the sculptor Nicholas Sloan. If the order of the stones were changed, the meaning of the statement would also change. Finlay thus gives viewers the opportunity to readjust their own perspectives – discovering new meanings and possibly fundamentally doubting their own standpoint.

But, for all the forcefulness of his views, in the end Ian Hamilton Finlay also sought reconciliation. This is seen above all in his last work: an old stone barn (opposite the house), which has had its roof removed. Solid stone walls enclose the barn's interior space; the iron gates are locked. In this quiet internal area suddenly there are no metaphors for war, battles or death. On the contrary – the visitor may be taken aback to discover a formal monastery garden with box hedges and thornless roses: a *hortus conclusus*, a biblical metaphor for paradise.

Omnipresent: poems and wordplays are inscribed into benches, bridges, columns, steles and paving stones.

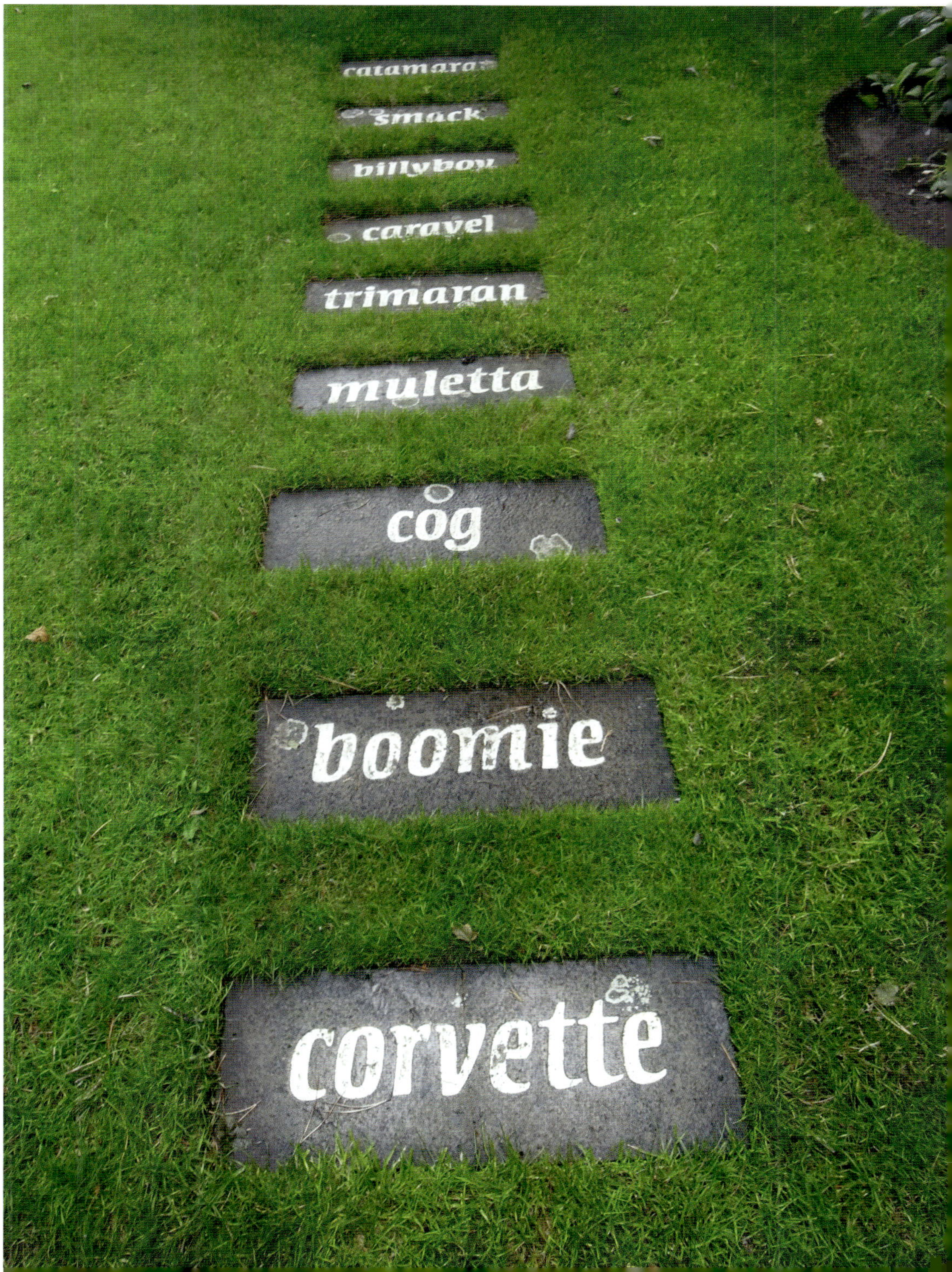

A VISIONARY COUNTERWORLD OF FOUND MATERIALS
THE ROCK GARDEN, CHANDIGARH, INDIA

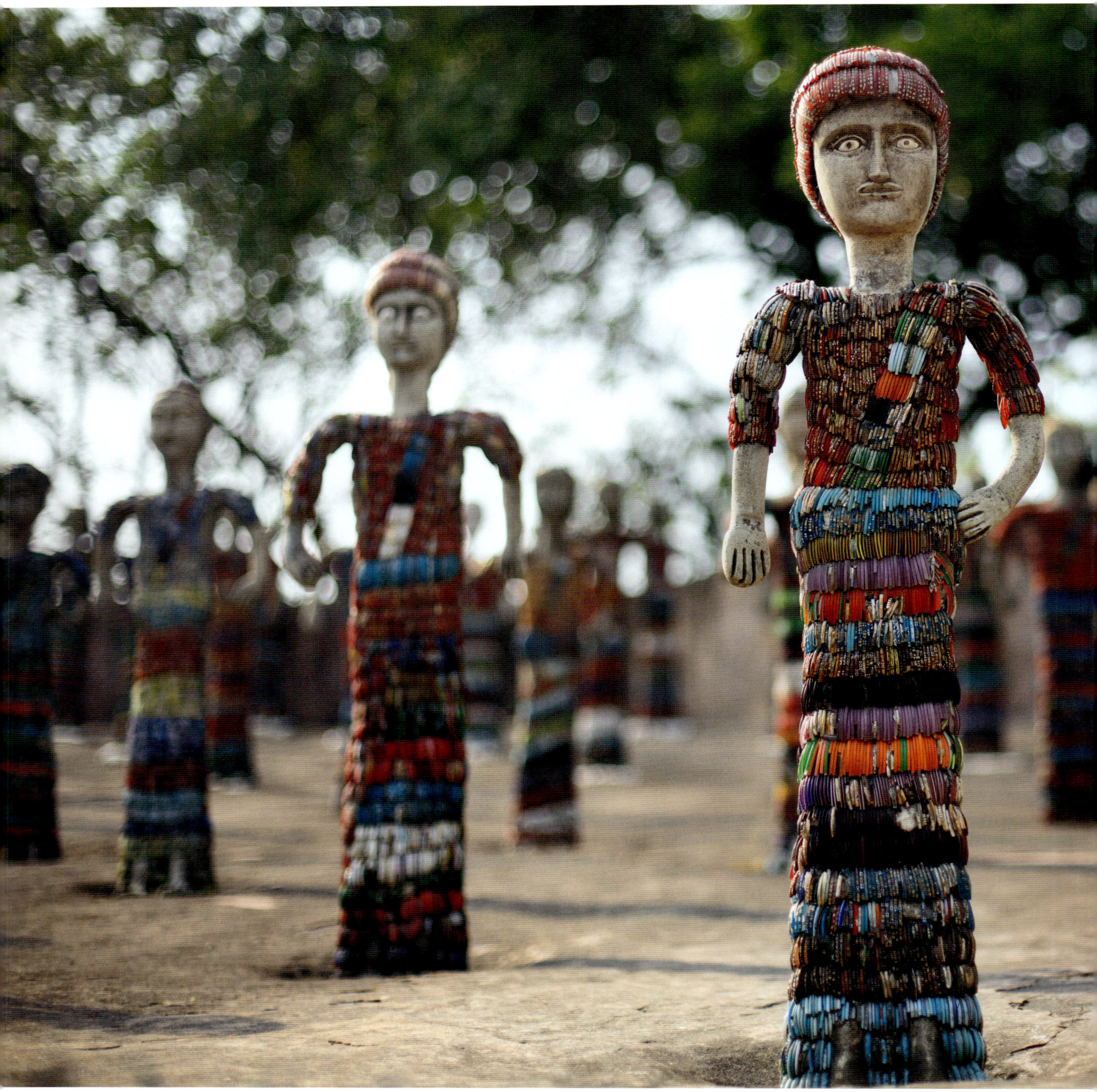

Art from detritus: the colourful gowns worn by the queens are made from broken plastic bangles, of the kind worn by women all over India.

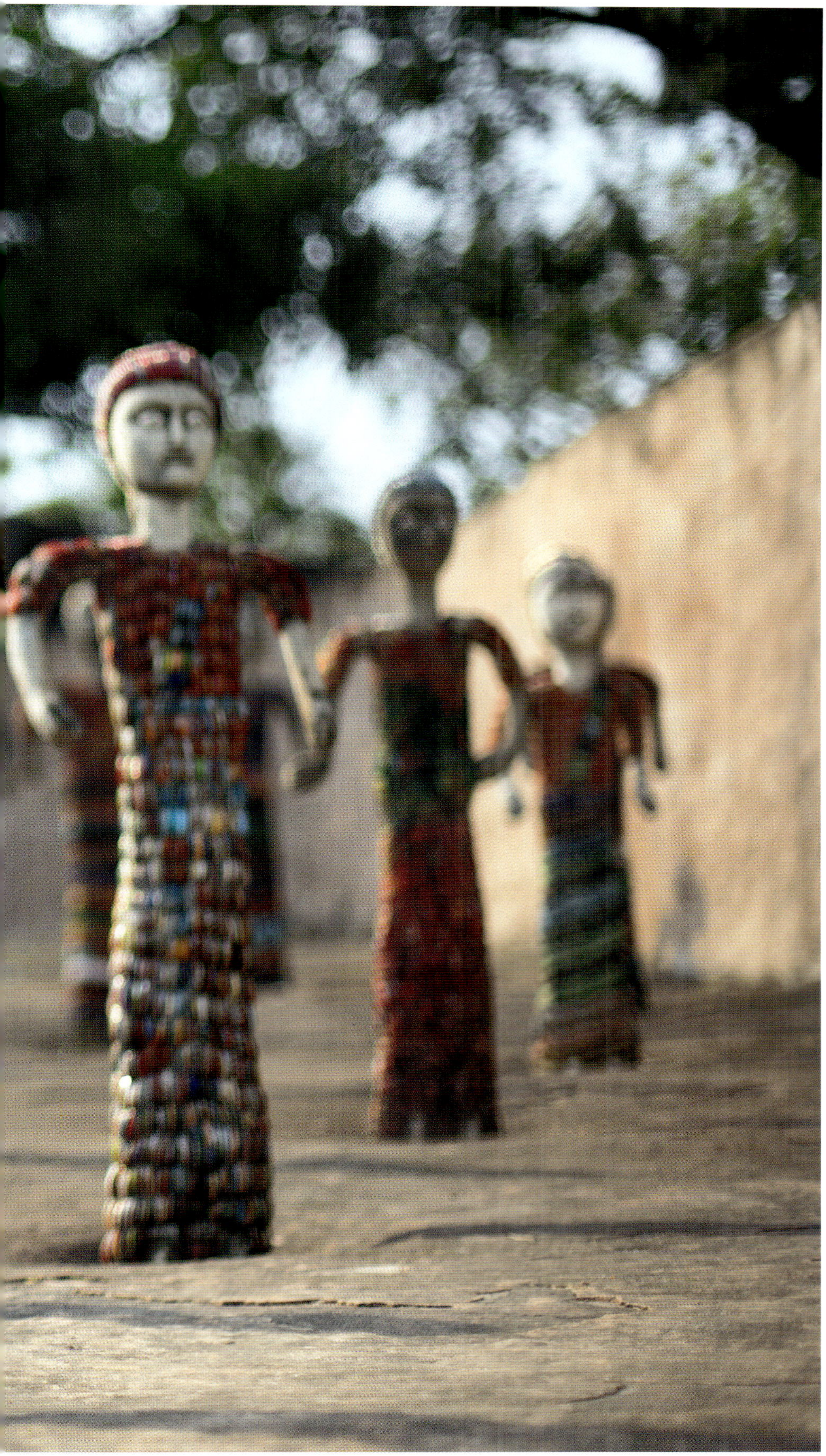

Chandigarh – "the city beautiful" – lies at the foot of the Himalayas in northern India. It presents the visitor with two 'alien worlds', for it was the first city in India to be designed according to Western urban ideals, with a radical grid structure, designated areas of greenery and long, straight boulevards, between which there are low, cuboid concrete buildings – the work of no less an architect than Le Corbusier (1887–1965). Just a few kilometres outside the city is The Rock Garden, a fantasy world constructed by a lowly road inspector, with thousands of sculptures in amongst artificial waterfalls, gorges and a labyrinth of large and small courtyards. Figures, animals and the landscape conjure up an imaginary, spiritual world that the visionary, self-taught artist Nek Chand Saini has created from found and recycled materials.

This garden is closely interwoven with the life story of its maker. Born in 1924 in Barian Kalan, a small town west of the present-day border with Pakistan, in 1947 the young Nek Chand, as a Hindu, had to flee his native town following the partition of India. More than ten million Muslims, Sikhs and Hindus were displaced following the establishment of the new Muslim state of Pakistan. Amongst them were Nek Chand's parents and their seven children. "We left everything we had behind and fled at night, on foot, for the Hindu part of the Punjab." The memory of this trauma – the loss of his homeland, the end of his sheltered upbringing in the country where different ethnic groups had always lived together – has never left Nek Chand. It is therefore not surprising that it later played a crucial part in his concept of a garden. Lahore, the former capital of the Punjab region, was now in Pakistan, so India's first prime minister, Jawaharlal Nehru (1889–1964), decided to build a new administrative capital for the Indian federal state –Chandigarh. This city, with a modern, Western appearance, was to become synonymous with the new independent state of India – a city planned by Le Corbusier who posited his design on the right angle and created a grid structure with uniform sectors. Nek Chand Saini, who had by now moved to Chandigarh with his wife, was employed there as an inspector of roads. He watched as countless old villages were demolished to make way for the new administrative centre. He felt a sense of alienation as a city was constructed on the basis of purely rational precepts, taking no account of the Indian mentality. As a way of compensating for his day job, which he found both senseless and frustrating, each evening after work he would cycle twenty kilometres out into the Shivalik Hills. There he would go to the river and collect stones with bizarre, even anthropomorphic forms, just as he had done as a child. "For me all stones have souls. They are like gods. They are alive," explains the small, quiet man. "When I look at them, they touch my heart." Collecting stones was a way of coping with the trauma of being uprooted and displaced. Outside the city, in a forestry reserve, he found the perfect place to keep his finds.

It was here that he had the idea of creating an imaginary anti-world to the artificially created city of Chandigarh: it would be a "kingdom of gods and goddesses", a fantasy world, filled with memories of his rural homeland. Of course he knew that it was illegal to construct anything in this forest, but he had seen in the plans for the new city that nothing would be built in this jungle area, which had been designated as a green belt area. And as an uncultivated wilderness with thickets, mosquitoes and snakes it was hardly likely to attract day trippers. But where could he find the construction materials he needed for his fantasy world? A nearby dump with detritus from demolished villages provided the solution and became a positive treasure trove for Nek Chand. The idea of turning 'waste materials' into something valuable and noble was very much in the spirit of his concept of a fantasy world. As a child he had already shown a talent for turning supposedly worthless items into something beautiful. For seven years he patiently and painstakingly sorted things he found at the dump: broken pottery and glass, chipped tiles, bottles, electronic waste, rusty pots, bits of bicycles, wash-hand basins and so on. Little by little he took these items, along with building rubble and stones of all sizes, to his chosen site. In 1965 he started to create his fantasy realm of sculpture, architecture and nature (by now covering forty acres), day after day, when his work was done. At night he would continue by the light of burning tires.

Surrounded by an almost three-metre wall of rough stones, with twenty-five life-sized sculptures of birds perched on it, the site is reminiscent of a huge fort. There is no external vantage point where the visitor might have an overview of the labyrinth of courtyards. Nek Chand Saini very deliberately created a counterpart to the easily grasped grid layout of the city of Chandigarh. More than that – anyone who wants to see this magical world has to enter each section by bending down to pass through a small, unremarkable doorway. Nek Chand has thus ensured that visitors have to stoop in the same humble way as the faithful in India when they enter a temple. In addition, this bowed posture increases the impact of the surprise awaiting the visitor on the other side of the wall. Drawing on an inexhaustible repertoire of ideas, Nek Chand gives each of these separate realms its own colours, size and theme. He wants visitors to the garden to be constantly surprised and entranced anew. The different sections include the "King's Court", the "Queens' Bathing Complex", a "Dance Forum for Musicians" and "Scenes of Rural Life". In contrast to Le Corbusier's sectors, Nek Chand talks in terms of the three phases of his garden, reflecting the chronology of their construction.

Phase I contains mainly sculptures made from stones and rocks presented on different stages. Soon these were joined by throngs of musicians, dancers and animals. These bizarre figures are made from cement and enhanced with scraps

Nek Chand Saini celebrates the diversity of creation with different animal species.

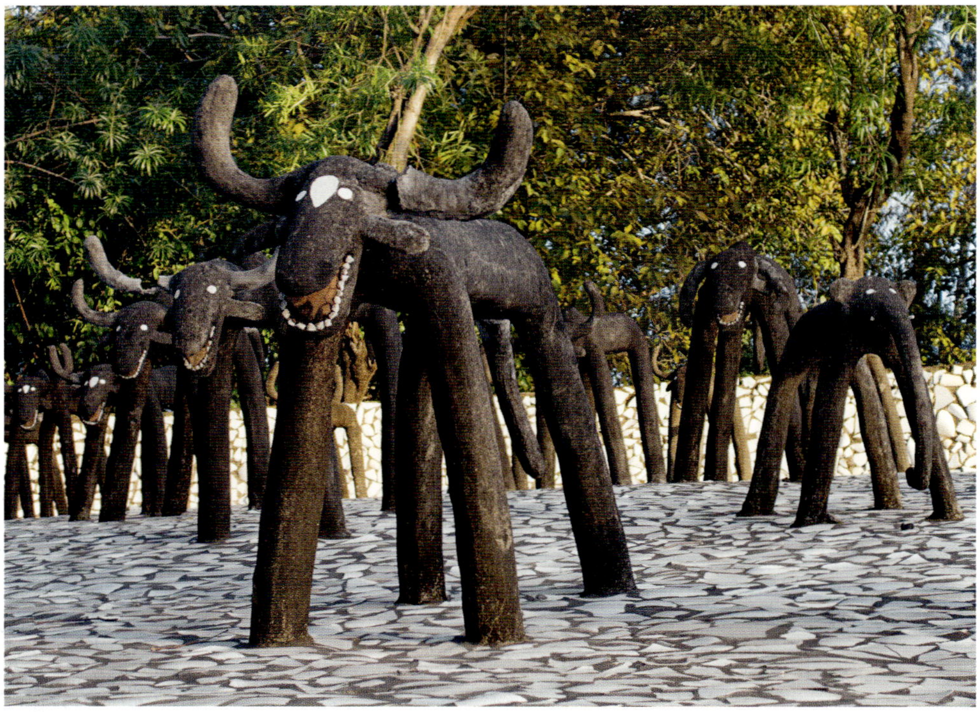

Right: Barely credible – what looks like a cliff face has been built from sacks of cement. Even the waterfall and the temple buildings were constructed by the artist.

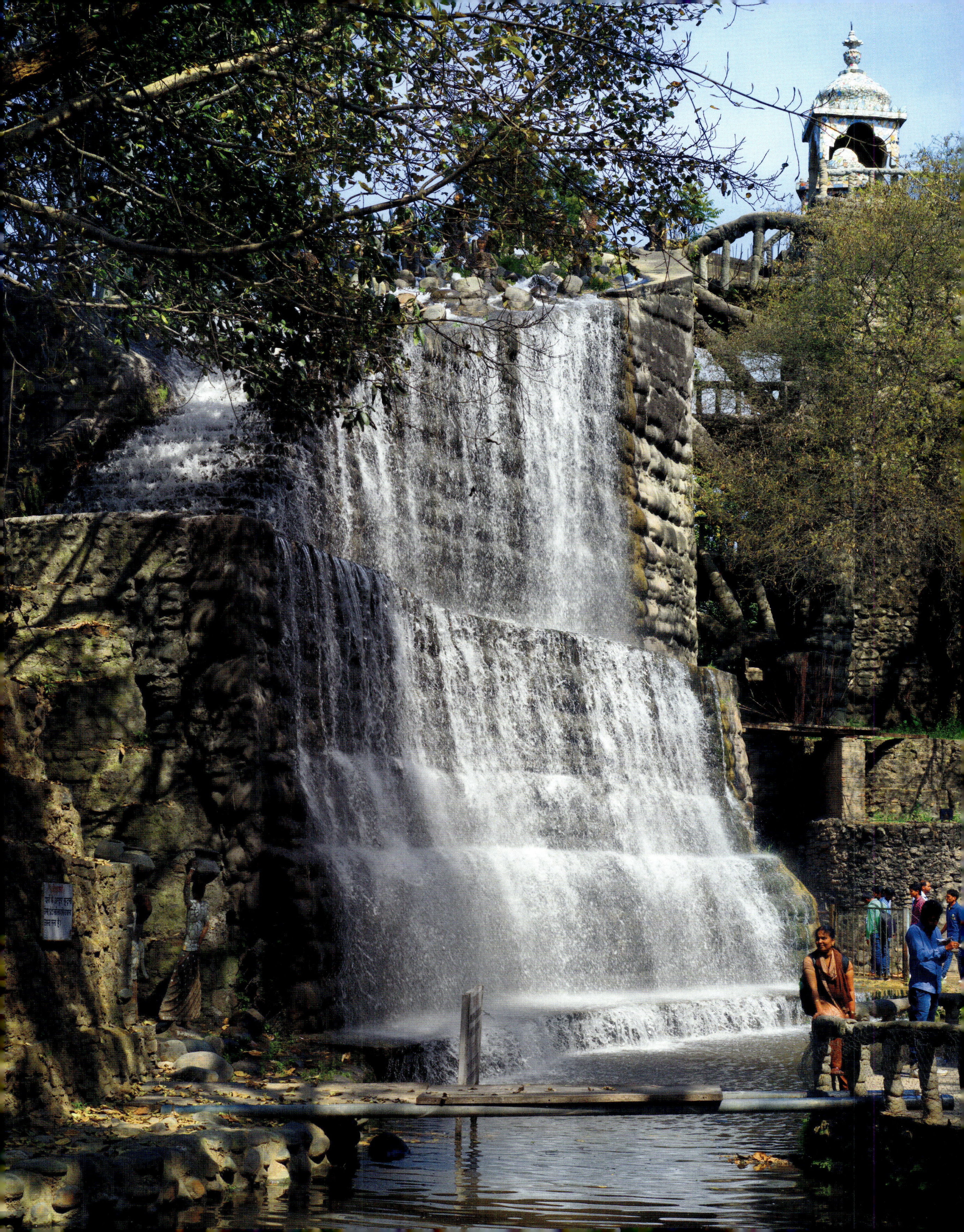

of fabric, bits of pottery, glass and other materials from Nek Chand's repository. "In the first phase of the Rock Garden I wanted to recreate my homeland, which I miss so much," he explained. And his native village, *en miniature*, with small clay houses and temples, now stands at the top of an artificial hill. In order to give the figures different skin colours, Nek Chand Saini mixed powdered tiles, chalk or pigments into the wet cement. He used cowrie shells for the eyes, which are particularly important to him, because all the figures look directly at the visitor. "When we look at them, they look back at us," says Nek Chand Saini. Visitors should feel drawn into the lives of the figures, which is one of the reasons why he has often created large groups of very similar figures, arranged as though they are in an amphitheatre. The figures in his "Group of Queens" are clad in close-fitting garments and decorated with fragments of coloured glass bangles, of the kind worn by ordinary women all over India. These sculptures also line narrow, meandering paths that lead the way between high walls of rock with other groups of figures. Next to the cliffs and in the courtyards Nek Chand has planted cacti, bougainvillea and papyrus plants as points of contrast.

Nek Chand Saini was able to keep his magical realm secret for seven years, until 1972, when a task force from the city stumbled across it and suddenly came face to face with a brightly coloured tribe of around two thousand sculptures. The authorities were outraged. But thanks to persistent protests by the locals in Chandigarh, in the end Nek Chand Saini was not only officially granted permission to retain his garden, he was even given an official position that allowed him to continue to develop it. In return, the garden, now known as The Rock Garden, was opened to the public in 1976. With a budget, fifty workers, building equipment and a connection to the electricity grid, Nek Chand Saini was able to embark on the next level of his vision.

Now his aim was "that his park should serve humankind as a personal symbol of tolerance and peace." In Phase 2 things became more colourful and expansive. The stages became larger, the mood more animated and celebratory, the landscape more distinct. The figures – wild musicians, drunkards, outsiders, snake charmers – range from very small to over two metres in height. Delicate figures on the periphery execute ritual dances. A multitude of laughing, waving figures in brightly coloured garments is accompanied by lively groups of monkeys, deer and water buffalo. In these scenes Nek Chand Saini is celebrating the diversity of creation. He depicts all the elements that play a part in the cycle of life, death and rebirth. There are also juxtapositions with figures from different cultural backgrounds: women in Western clothing encounter other women wearing saris. All the figures have peaceful, untroubled facial expressions; their demeanour is joyful and they are opulently finished with bright colours and patterns. Wide paths lead the visitor along beside a stream to an expansive area with a gigantic waterfall. But there are also other, narrower winding paths that take the visitor along cuttings and hills to a spectacular bridge, deep down into a gorge or through tunnel-like arcades. With masterful skill Nek Chand Saini has transformed this originally flat, sandy wilderness into a constantly changing landscape. What looks

The dancing figures are decorated with crockery shards.

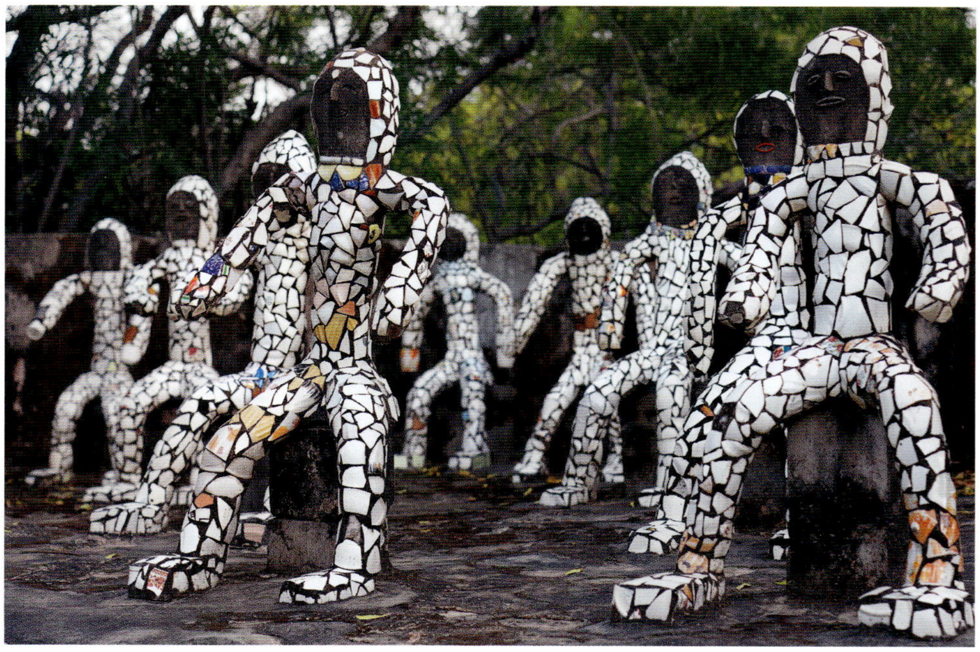

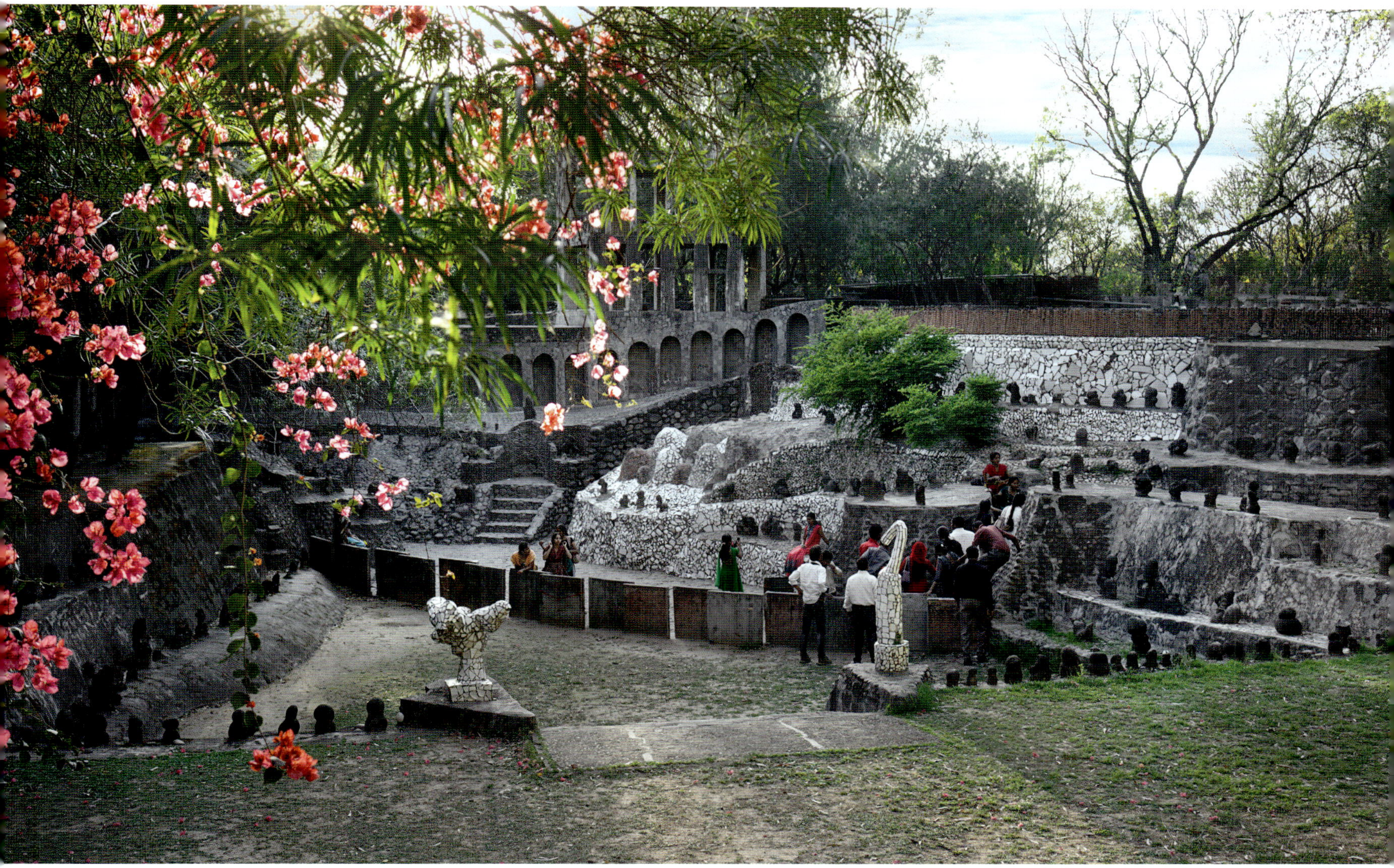

In response to the stereotypical grid layout of the city of Chandigarh, Nek Chand Saini created a realm of welcoming courtyards.

like a solid cliff face is in reality a mixture of concrete and cement, which Nek Chand poured into old, cut-open tea chests. Once it had hardened the resulting shapes were stacked to create walls. The resourceful artist also found another cheap way of creating rocky landscapes by filling simple jute bags with wet cement and using these as building blocks. In the larger courtyards he planted trees that do not grow to any great height, in order not to destroy the proportions of the works of art or otherwise to distract the visitor's attention. One of the main features of Nek Chand Saini's realm is water. It is everywhere – as rivulets and streams, as fountains and waterfalls. By means of a sophisticated system that directs and constantly recycles the water, he is able to deploy precious rainwater for his works of art.

Phase 3 of The Rock Garden has seen an increase in the dimensions of the figures, the animals, the architecture and the landscape. Small, contained courtyards have given way to a plaza with huge sculptures of people and animals. The amphitheatre is decorated with brightly coloured animal motifs on fragments of pale tiles. The high arcades house huge swings that can accommodate several children at a time. And the landscape takes the form of a wide gorge with bridges, long zigzag paths and more spectacular waterfalls, like a vast stage set. The only thing still missing is the end of the circular route leading back to the entrance. "I already have a plan for that," the wiry ninety-year-old tells us. His dark eyes gleam, but then he becomes restless, "I have to go now." He makes his apologies and waves to the workers at his materials store, who are waiting for his instructions.

Nek Chand Saini remodelled a completely flat landscape to create different levels with bridges and valleys.

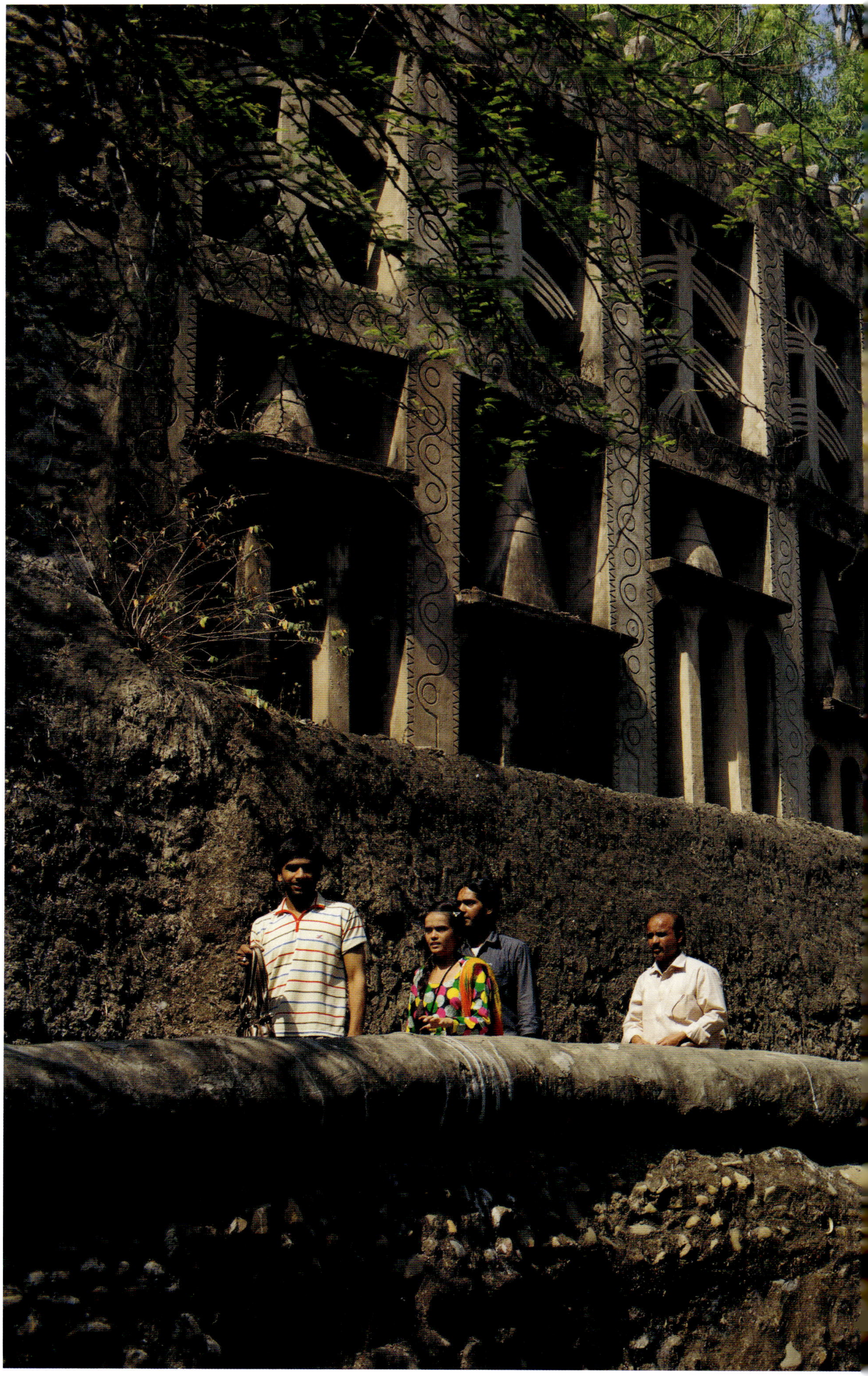

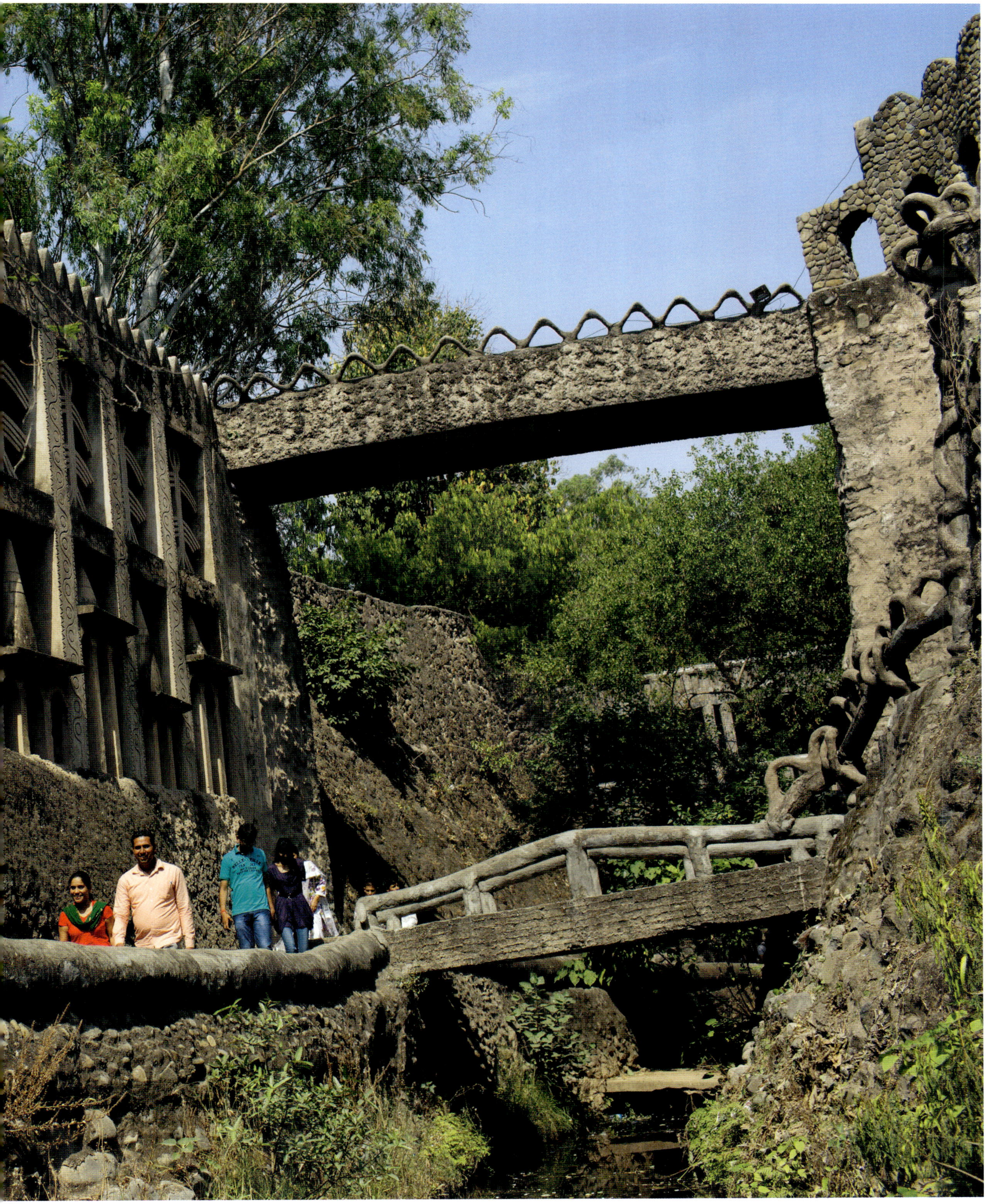

The Rock Garden, India

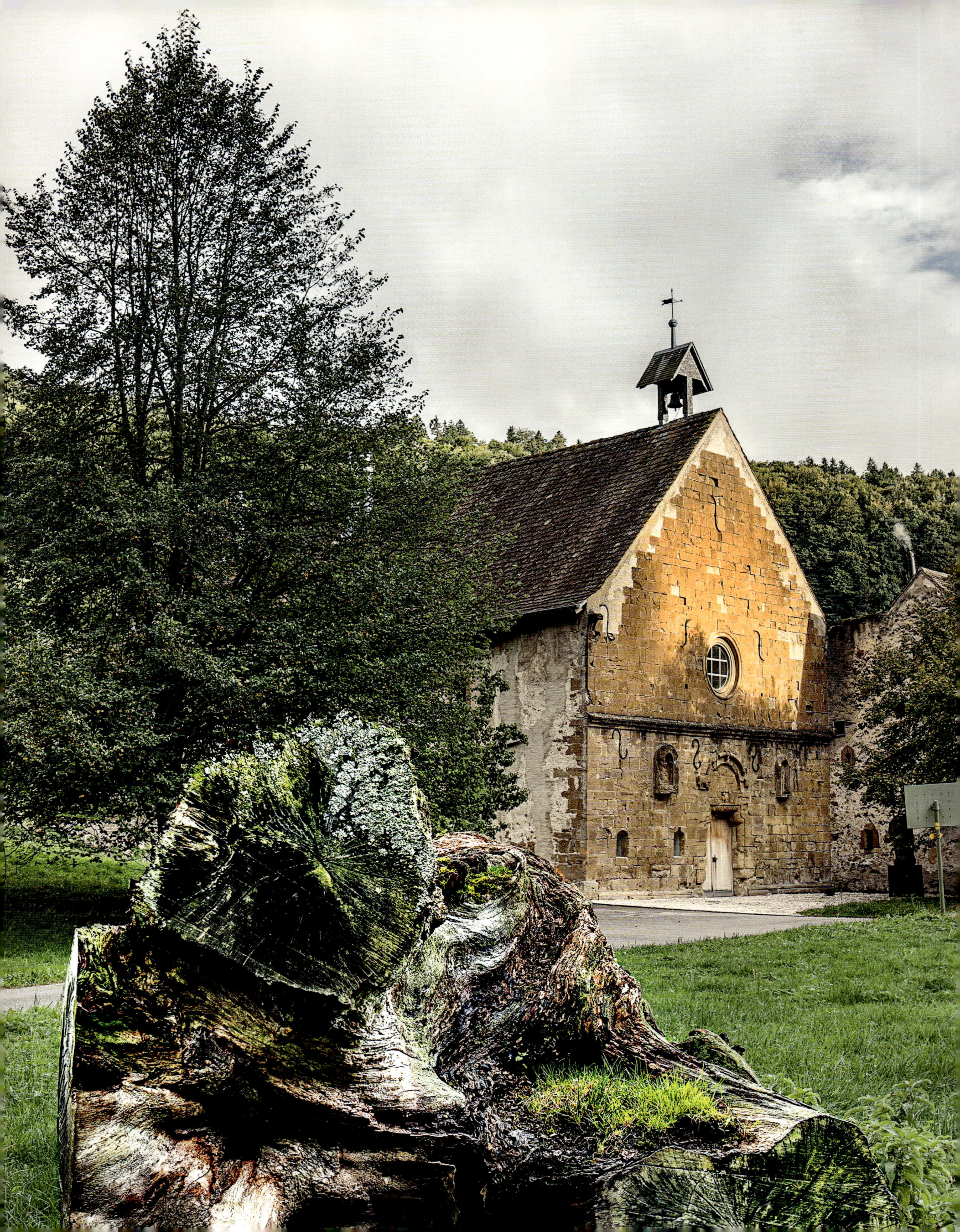

SLOWING DOWN WITH ART IN NATURE
SCHOENTHAL MONASTERY, LANGENBRUCK, SWITZERLAND

The perfect Swiss idyll. Just thirty-five kilometres south of Basel, visitors to Schoenthal Monastery find themselves immersed in an entirely different world, where time seems to stand still. Everything here radiates peace: the rhythmic rise and fall of the foothills of the Jura Mountains, the gentle clink of cowbells in the saturated green meadows, the ancient, picturesque farmhouses with extended roofs and overflowing window boxes. The little hamlet with the former Benedictine monastery, Schoenthal, is situated in a valley that more than lives up to the name of the monastery – "beautiful valley". *Nomen est omen.* Two lime trees face the door of the Romanesque church, whose richly decorated façade is one of Switzerland's art-historical rarities. Dedicated to the Benedictine Order in 1195 through the patronage of Count Adalbero von Frohburg, the monastery was plundered and vandalised during the Reformation. Having even been used as a brickworks for a time, in the late nineteenth century it became a summer retreat for a Swiss family. Today the monastery church is home to a series of art exhibitions; the adjacent buildings are used as seminar and guest rooms. And the church is now also the heart of the remarkable sculpture park founded by John Schmid – a leading advertising consultant from Basel – as a place where he and others can slow down through direct contact with the harmony of nature, art and history.

Sculptures by artists from all over the world are dispersed throughout the meadows and woods of this fifty-acre site. Even a barn and silo are now filled with art. John Schmid has deliberately avoided using signage of any kind. All visitors have as an aid to orientation is a map of the paths. As Schmid himself says, "Things are not managed here," alluding to his former high-octane occupation "with so many clients, so many colleagues, such tight deadlines." He explains his unusually calm demeanour by pointing out that the monastery is a special place – "a location with special energies, which the Benedictines very deliberately chose as the site for their monastery." In fact scientific measurements of energy levels here have shown them to be unusually high. "And everyone who comes here feels that," says Schmid. In the 1980s Schmid was searching for a retreat where he could relax at the weekend. He wanted something with a history. "In advertising, however great it can be, everything you do is ephemeral." However, in 1985, through a friend, he found the former Schoenthal Monastery. "The whole place was a shambles, the church was a ruin," he recalls. "I just thought, I'm here in the nick of time." When he took over the monastery Schmid also became, at a stroke, a landowner with no less than 250 acres of meadows and woods. The sound of the cowbells comes from his ninety cattle. Any thoughts of a retreat were initially put on hold as the restoration work and the business of running the estate took over every waking hour. The idea for a sculpture park came to Schmid, already a passionate art collector, in the early 1990s when he met James Turrell in Skibbereen, Ireland. At the time Turrell was planning his now famous *Irish Sky Garden*. "Earthworks with a crater, from which you can observe the heavens," Schmid says enthusiastically. "Think big. And I realised that that would also be right for Schoenthal." Even if it was ultimately not possible to collaborate with Turrell, the idea

David Nash's *Twisted Oak* and the Romanesque façade of the church – the starting point for the sculpture park.

of a sculpture park had been born. The first artists were invited: David Nash, Nigel Hall and Nicola Hicks. To date twenty-two artists have created twenty-eight works of art for Schoenthal. All the artists complied with the condition that they should visit Schoenthal before developing their works for the site. "I want bold artists who can hold their own with this archaic landscape and work with this triad of history, art and nature. Their works have to have physical strength, resilience, and have to be able to withstand the weather conditions, too, because the climate here at the edge of the Alps is very harsh." In 2000 the monastery was opened as a venue with workshops and guest accommodation for cultural events and meetings. Schmid wanted to share his monastery and its land with people who, like him, are searching for tranquillity and seeking to restore their energy. Anyone coming to contemplate the works of art in this natural environment should allow plenty of time.

The site is hilly and extensive and the sculptures are not always easy to find. Rubber boots for tramping through damp meadows are hung on hooks outside the church – like an installation. John Schmid wants visitors to discover the works of art for themselves, even if that involves detours. There is no prescribed route. "Schoenthal is not an exhibition space where you can already see the next work from the one you are at. You have to find the art by walking – that is part of the concept," he explains. And he is convinced that only by these means will visitors' perception be sensitised to both elements – art and nature. "The real voyage of discovery consists not in seeking new landscapes but in having new eyes": Marcel Proust's words are quoted on

Ian Hamilton Finlay's epitaph with a sarcastic allusion to protected flowers.

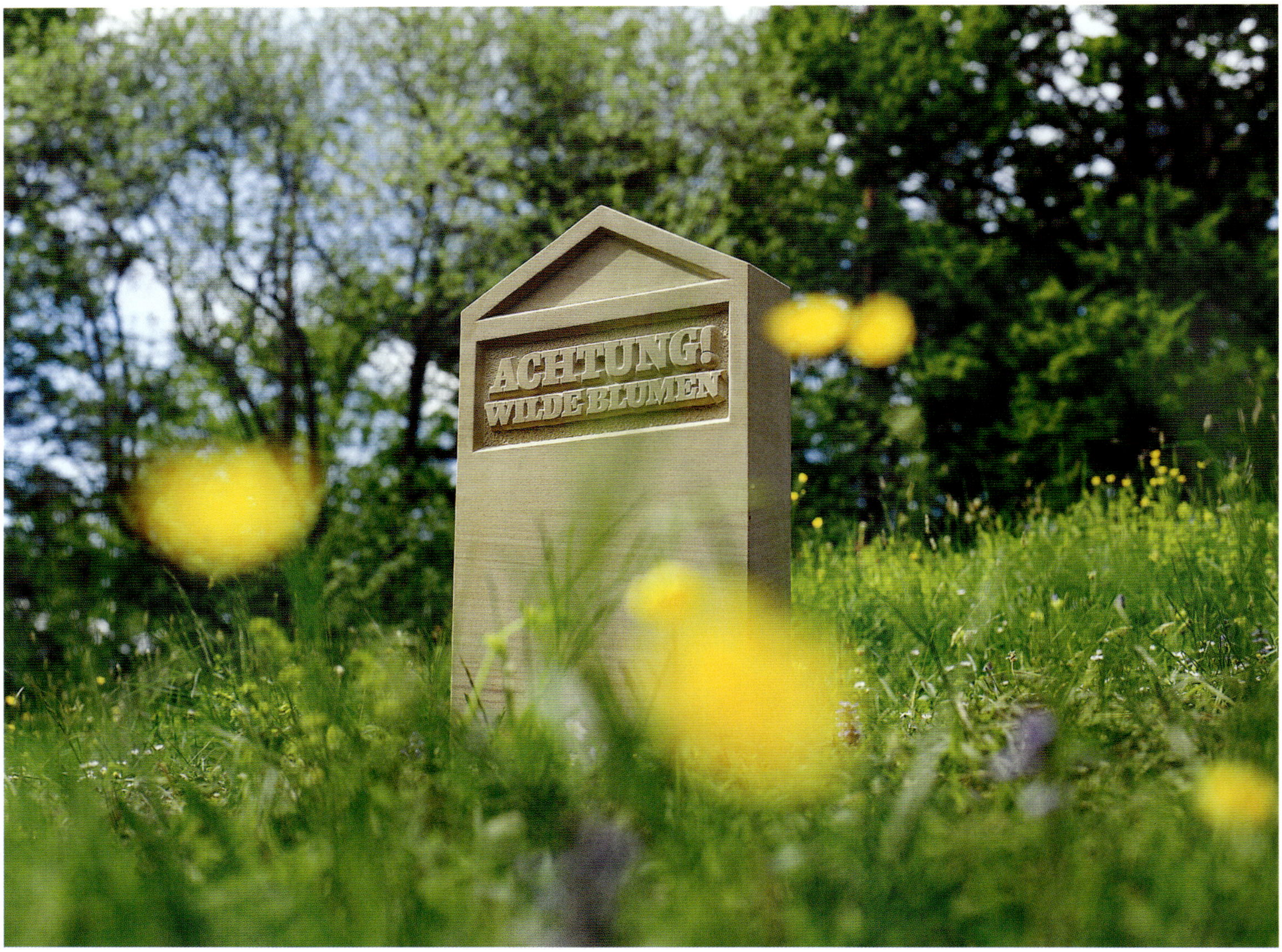

Right: An opened book, softened by use, was Hamish Black's inspiration for *YP 1*.

Nigel Hall's *Soglio* focuses the viewer's gaze on different views of the landscape.

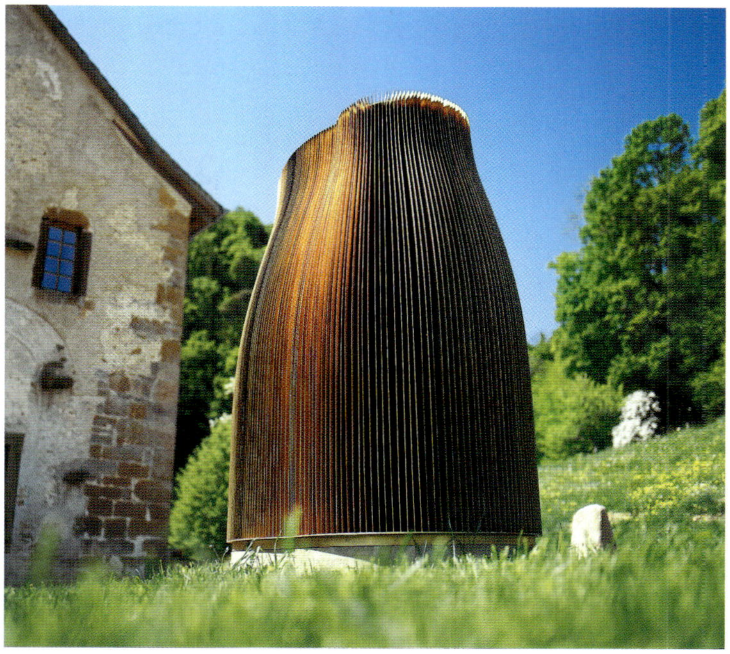

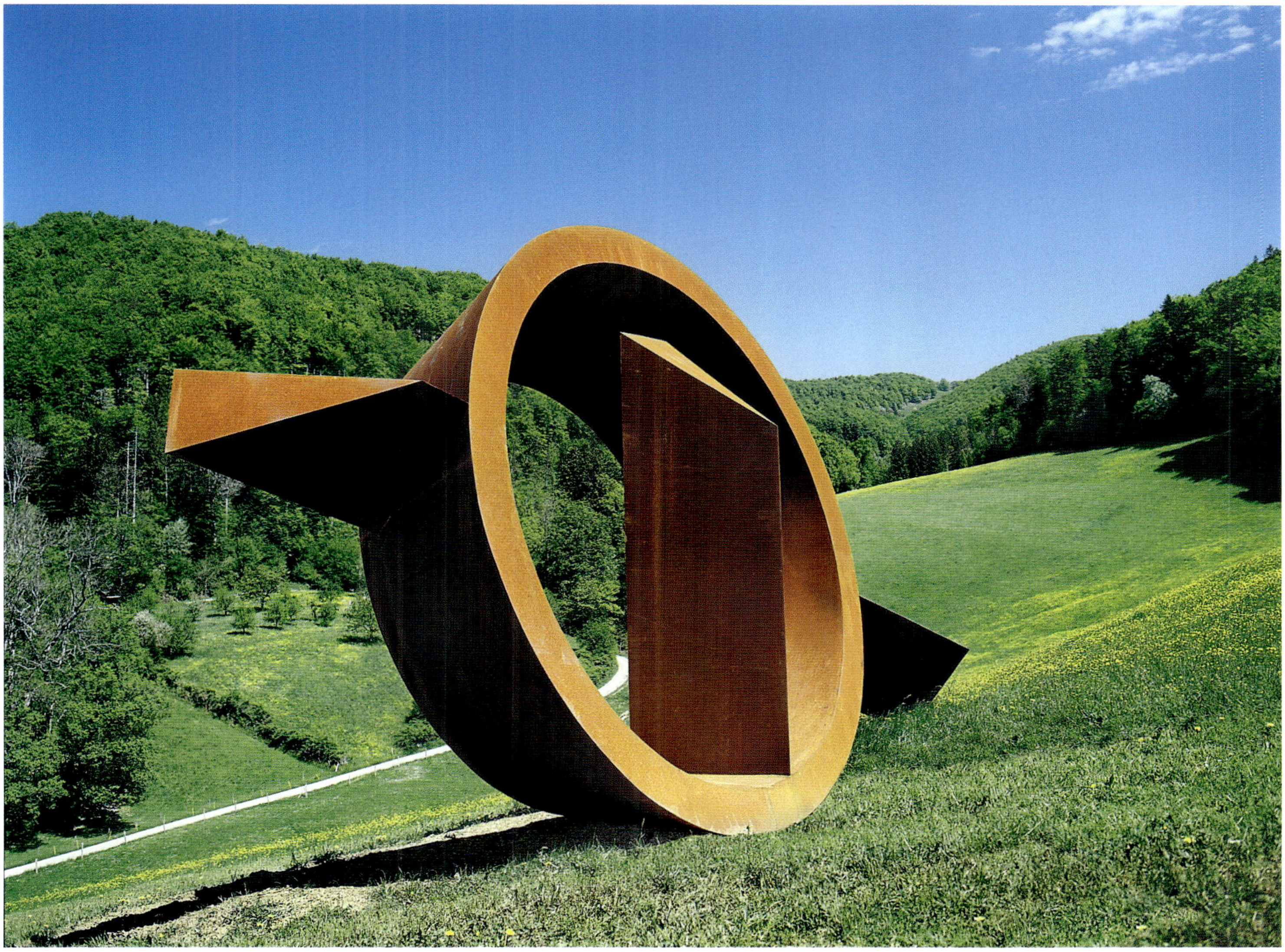

Schoenthal Monastery, Switzerland

the sculpture park's website next to the map of the site. And the works of art here demand close observation. The climb into the beech woods takes the visitor up David Nash's *46 Charred Steps* (2000), a stairway made of solid, charred oak beams. Ian Hamilton Finlay invites visitors to clamber over an archetypal stile, *Stile 1 and Stile 2* (2000). Inscriptions on the stile allude to the fauns and nymphs that used to live in these woods. And those who then proceed across the meadow higher up beyond the stile may find themselves smiling at the cryptic warning "Achtung! Wilde Blumen" (Caution! Wild flowers) on the Scot's marker stone. On the way to Ulrich Rückriem's mighty monolith, *Tempel* (1987), which stands majestically on the brow of the hill, visitors have a magnificent view of the expansive landscape. Looking through the eight-metre-high metal ring, *Soglio* (1994), by Nigel Hall, which seems to be fixed to the hillside, everyone pictures the scene in his or her own way: nature in art, art in nature. By contrast, down below in the valley Peter Kamm placed his meditative installation *Five Stones* (2000) in between the trees at the edge of a stream. While this location is pervaded by an almost religious atmosphere, not far away there is a lively scene with Martin Disler's scrawny, strangely deformed bronze figures executing some kind of wild dance. This is perfectly matched by the humming and flickering of *Kakashi* (2012–13) opposite them on the meadow. This newest arrival from New York is by the Lithuanian artist Žilvinas Kempinas, who spanned a circle of red-and-yellow-striped snow poles with countless brightly coloured ribbons. The wind and the sun turn this installation into a wondrously shimmering, transparent disc that seems to float above the grass in certain light conditions. Visitors seeking out

Anyone who wants to see Ilan Averbuch's *Silent Seas* has to venture into a field of cows.

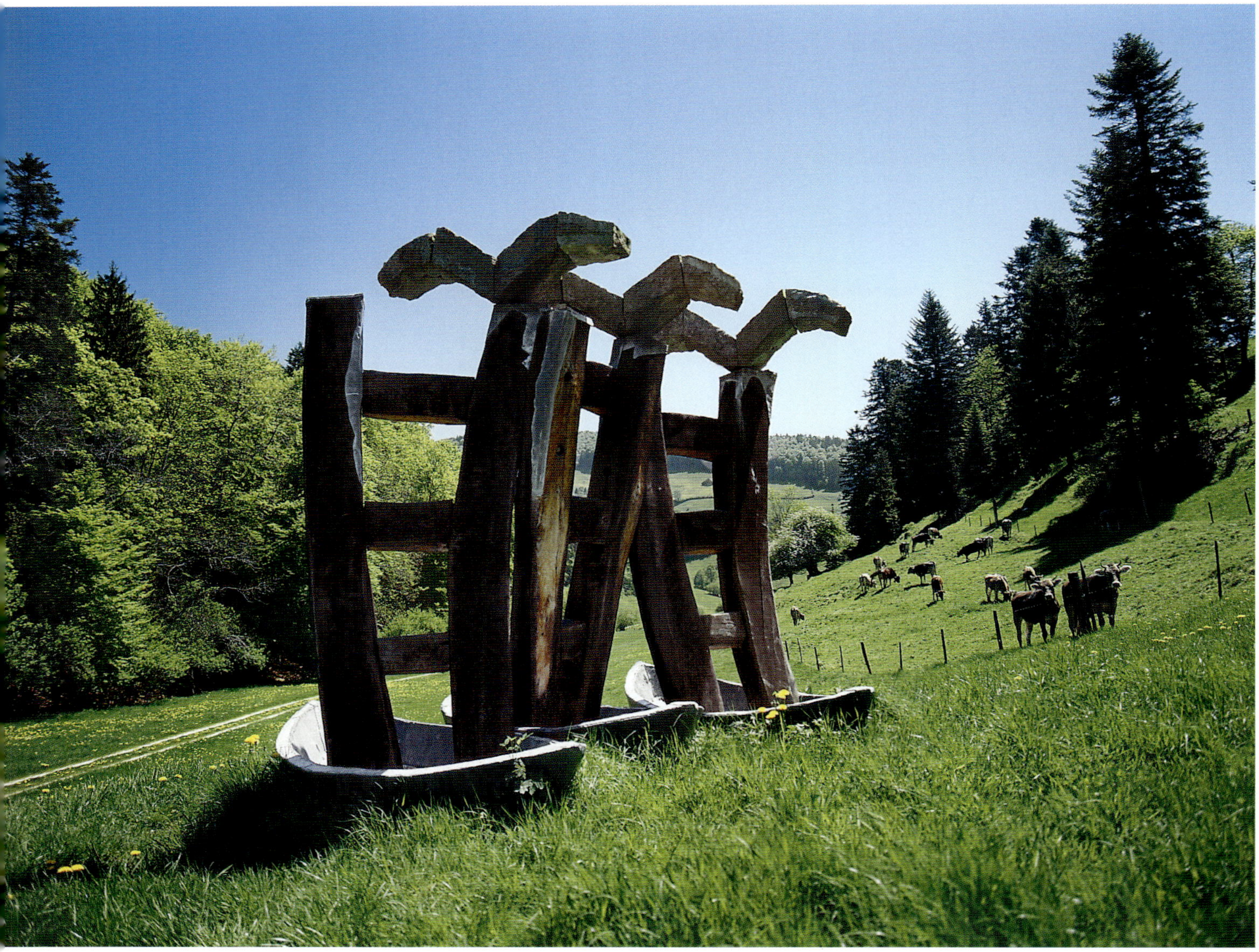

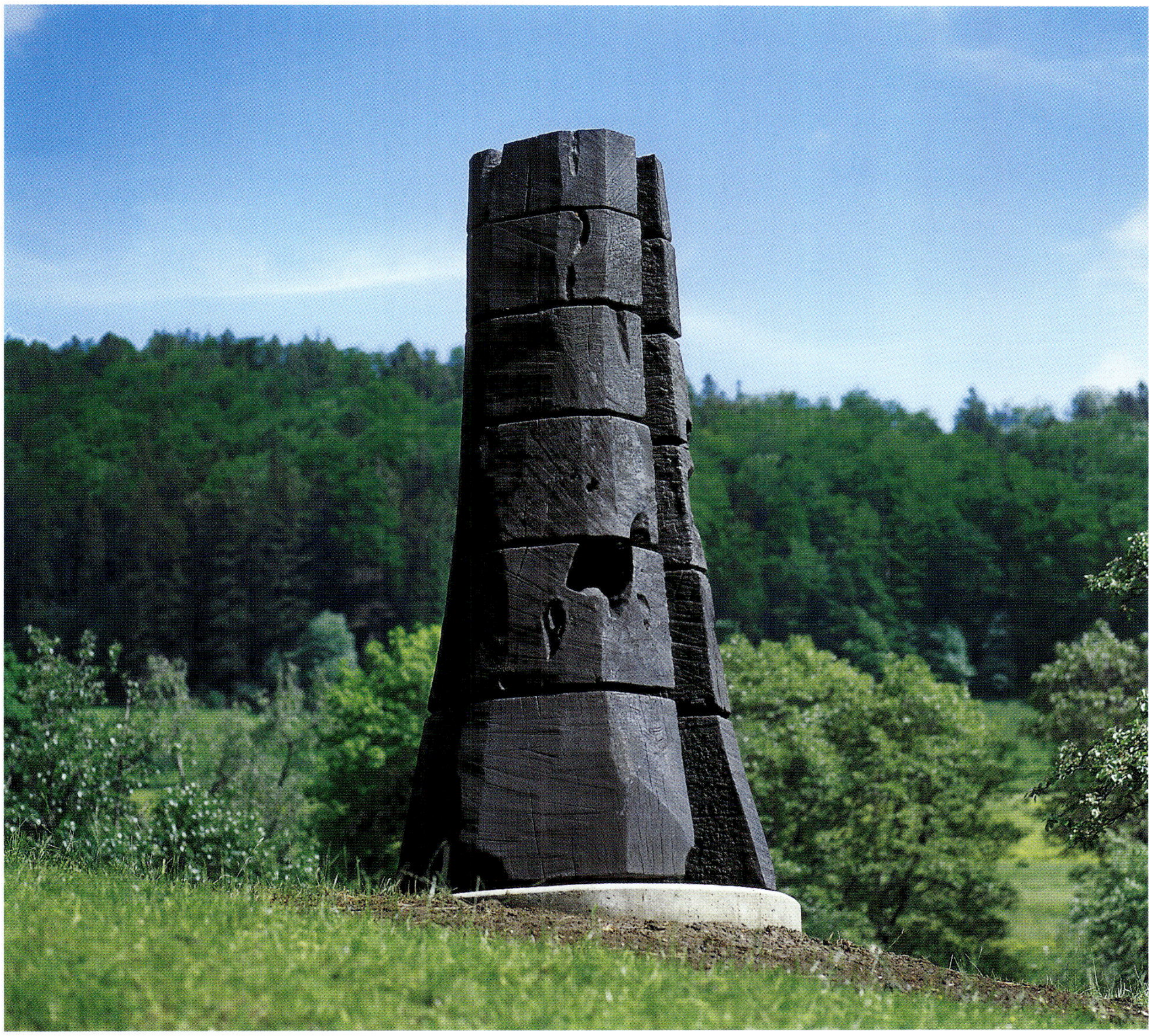

David Nash's preferred medium is discarded wood: the process of charring the wood both preserves it and achieves an aesthetic effect.

these works of art in nature also have to jump over flowing water and open gates. And in the case of Ilan Averbuch's *Silent Sea* (1992) they have to creep up on a group of cows who just happen to be scratching their necks on the work of art. Schmid calls it "awkward communication".

The artistic climax of the collection comes in the two works by Richard Long: *Cowshed Ellipse* (2008) in an old barn – a stone ellipse on the floor of the barn made from pale stones – and *Yellow Mud on Wall* (2008), a large wall drawing made from glowing, yellow clay. "It's a fantastic work, so sacred," says Schmid. And lastly, in the converted silo, a strange sight awaits the visitor: below the Plexiglas cover over the silo's open top the bones and skulls of wild boar are suspended in air. Some of the teeth have even been gilded by the artist duo Steiner & Lenzlinger – in a mocking reinterpretation of the title of the work, *Eldorado* (2011). Originally John Schmid had felt that the silo (without its Plexiglas roof) would have been the ideal site for a Skyspace by James Turrell – the artist whose work he would still very much like to see in Schoenthal. But twilight also has a wonderful feel under the three majestic lime trees on the Schönthalköpfli, where a fifteen-minute sound installation, *Music for Twilight* (2000), by the Swiss composer Walter Fähndrich, enhances the evening atmosphere with minimalist sound sequences. "The perfect end to the day for me," says Schmid, with a contented smile.

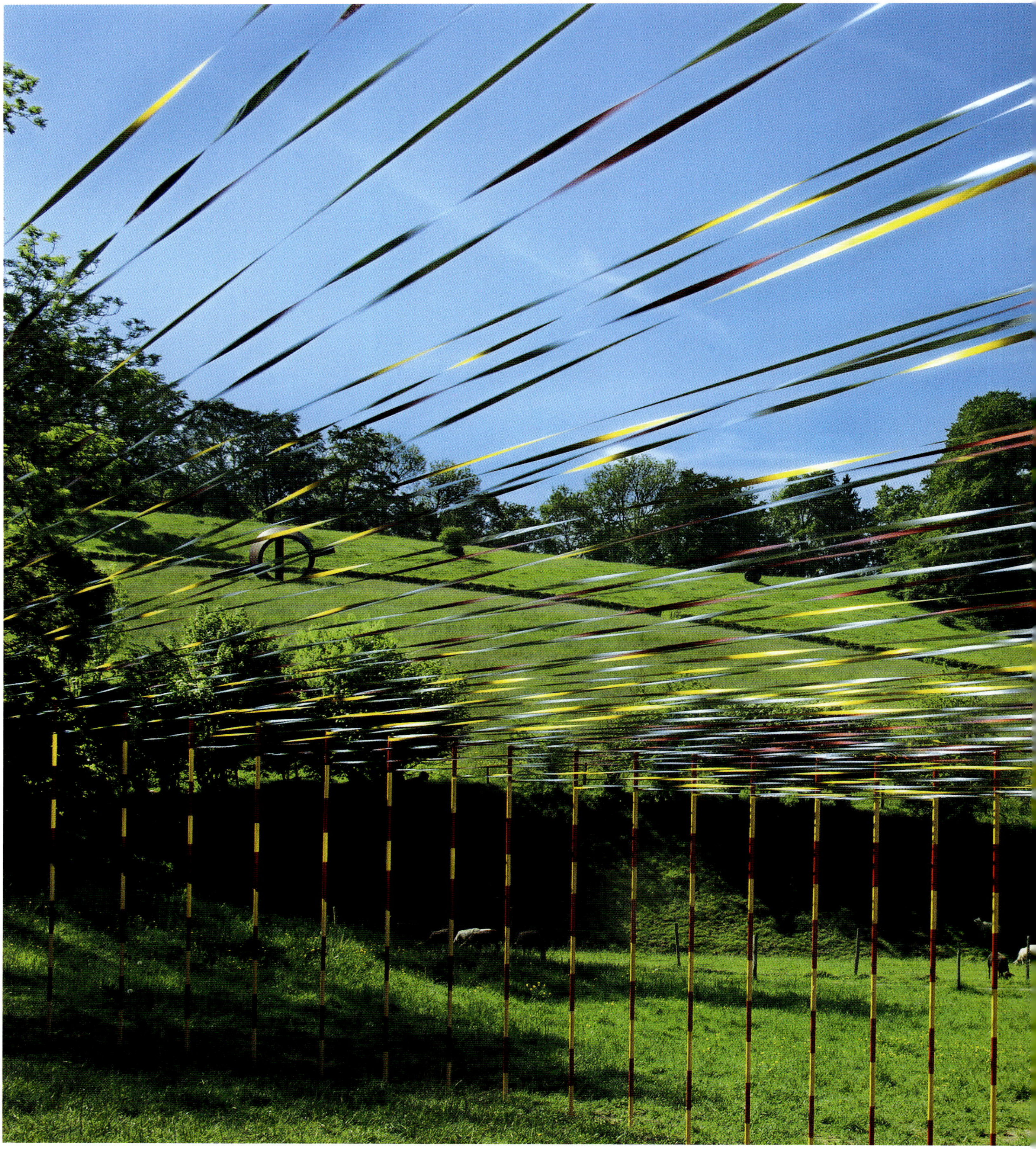

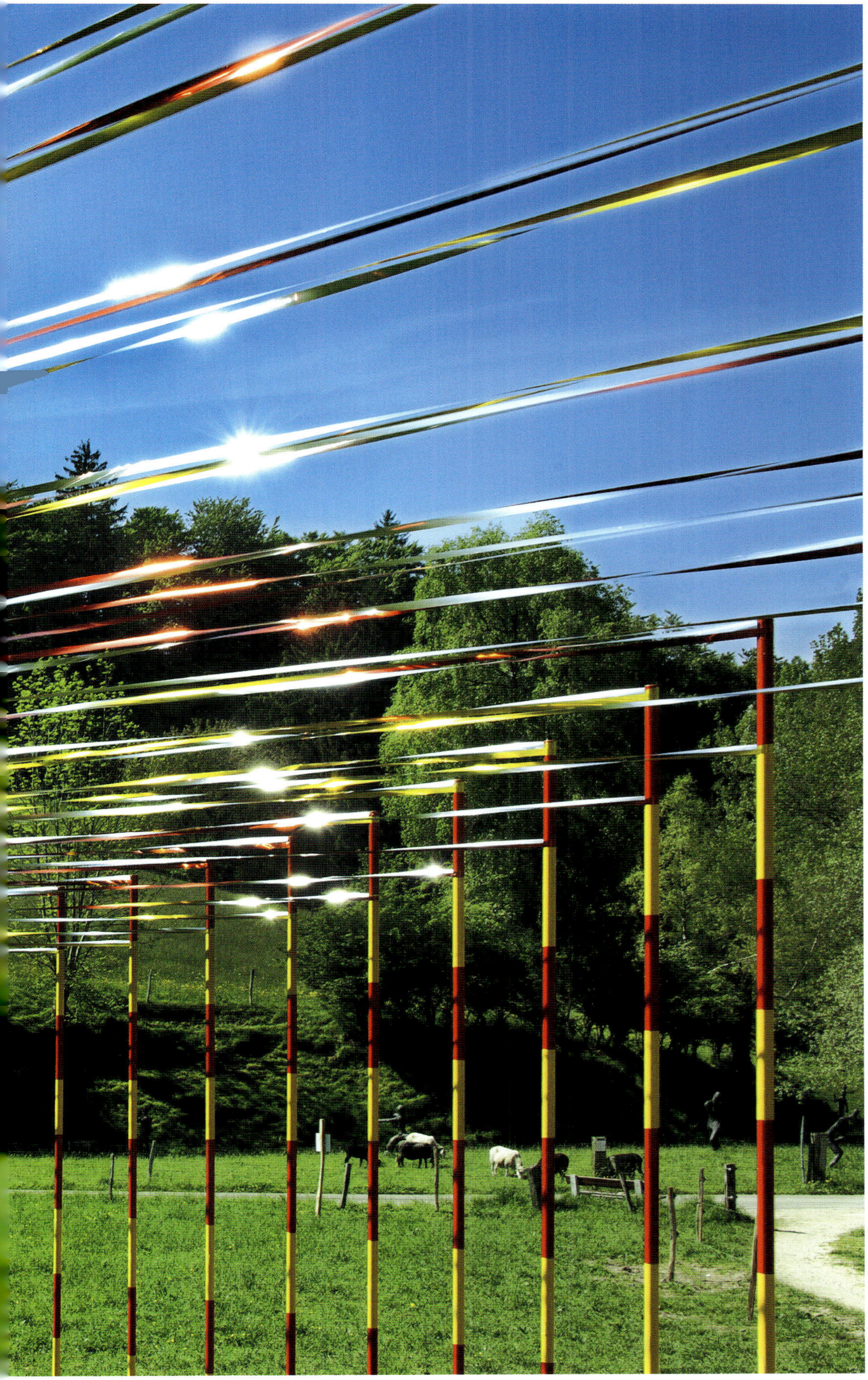

Žilvinas Kempinas's circle of snow poles with countless reflective ribbons becomes a flickering, transparent disc in the sunlight.

Schoenthal Monastery, Switzerland

BOTANY AND ART AGAINST DRUGS
JARDÍN BOTÁNICO CULIACÁN, CULIACÁN, MEXICO

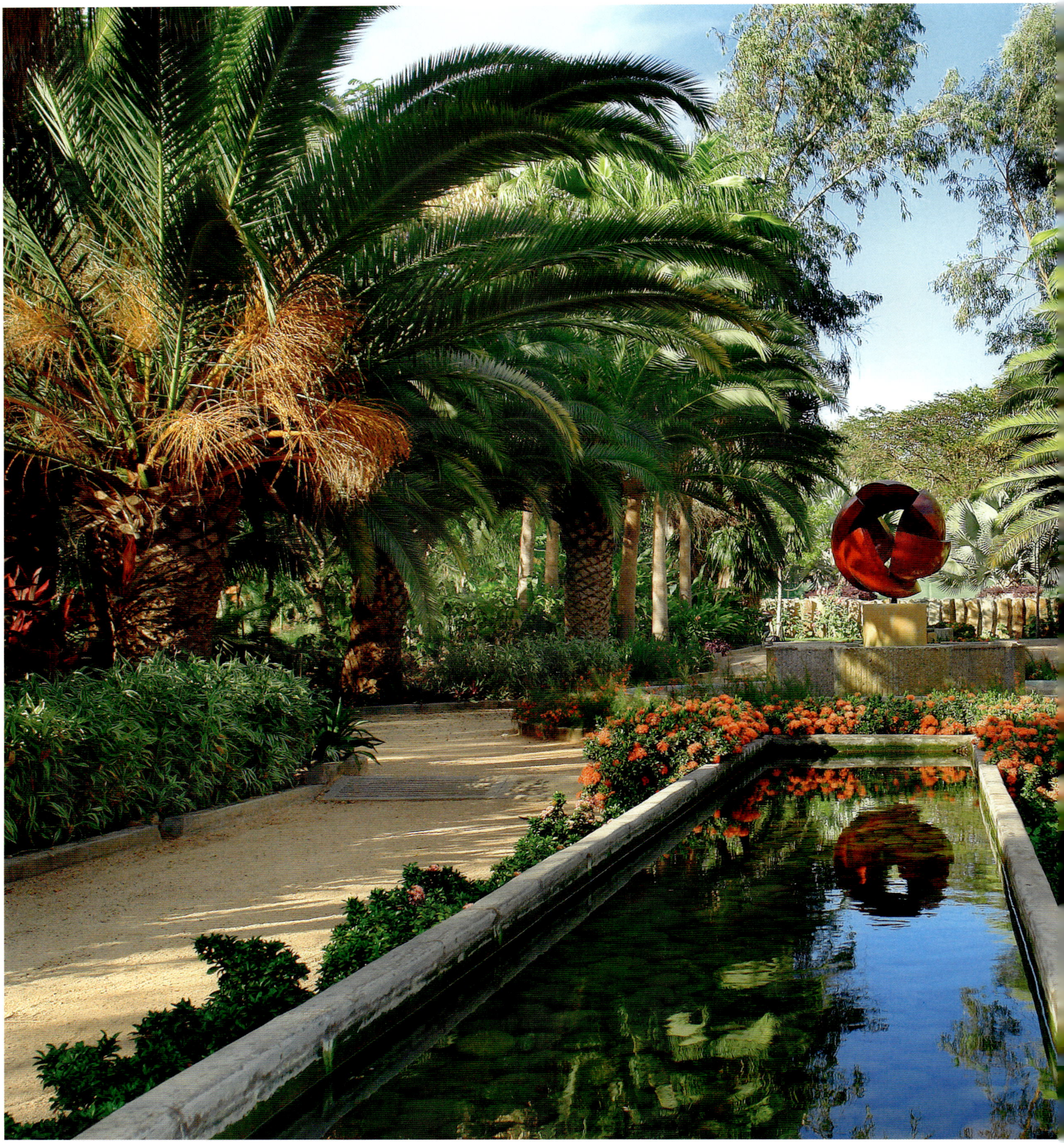

A different world with collections of exotic plants and extraordinary art.

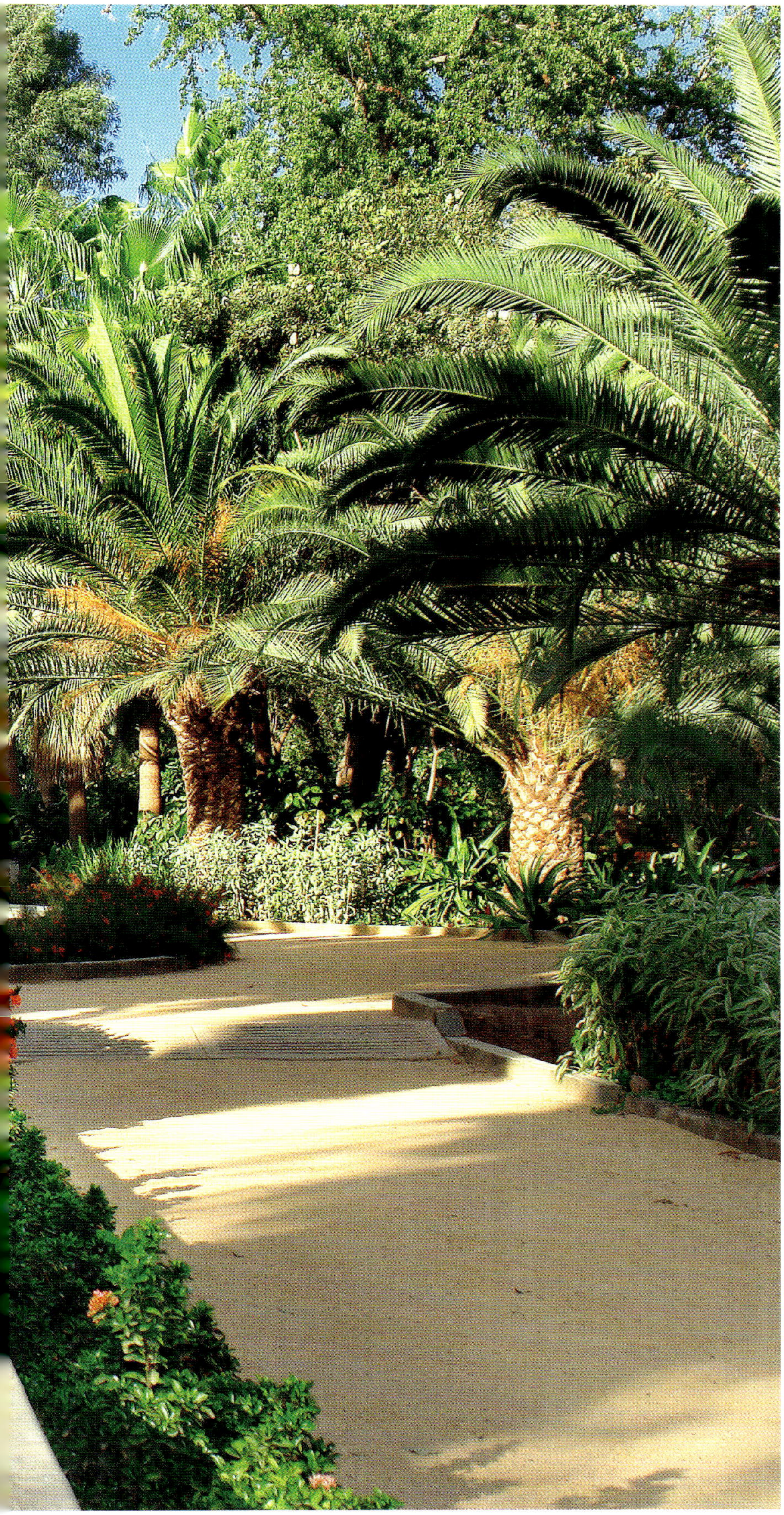

Culiacán – at the mention of the name of the capital of the State of Sinaloa on the western coast of Mexico many people will recall one of the most powerful drug barons in Central America: Joaquín Guzmán, also known as "El Chapo". Up until his arrest in February 2014 he was one of the richest and most wanted men in the world. His Sinaloa drug cartel controls drug trafficking along the Pacific coast as far as the US. Guzmán is held responsible for thousands of deaths. And yet many Mexicans admire him as a folk hero because he created jobs and put money into the construction of roads and hospitals. In their eyes he is not just a gangster and a murderer, he is also an employer and benefactor – a Robin Hood figure who takes from the rich and gives to the poor, who was clever enough to evade the police for years.

Carlos Murillo Depraect and Agustín Coppel – one a successful engineer and an amateur botanist, the other a wealthy entrepreneur and art collector – developed an unusual concept against this backdrop of crime. They combined their skills and passions and, in 1986, created a botanic garden with contemporary art as a tangible anti-world. The starting point for this symbiosis of art and nature was initially the twenty-five-acre park in the centre of the city that Carlos Murillo had created through his obsession with collecting plants. Carlos Murillo junior, who is now the director of the park, explains that "even on their honeymoon in Acapulco all my parents did was go from tree nursery to tree nursery." And whenever his father was on business trips at home or abroad he would systematically seek out the seeds and seedlings of indigenous or threatened plants – often hiding them in his pockets and smuggling them back to his home town of Culiacán. He would then plant them out in an unused plot of land owned by the city. Between the 1960s and the 1990s this site in the heart of the city grew into a botanic garden with around 1,200 plant species, which now urgently needed retrospective planning permission. The opportunity to achieve this arose when Murillo, on a visit to a sauna, happened to meet a leading local government official and was able to persuade him of the need for a public park in the city. In return Murillo offered to open his extraordinary collection to the public. The site now became officially known as the Jardín Botánico Culiacán. No other garden in Mexico boasts such a variety of native and foreign plants or plants threatened with extinction. The palm collection alone comprises 120 species – including the rare Madagascar palm and the talipot palm from Sri Lanka. But the maintenance of the twenty-five-acre park was no easy matter and it was difficult to manage with the limited municipal funding.

It was at this point that Murillo's friend Agustín Coppel offered to participate in the venture. The park now became part of the Agustín and Isabel Coppel Foundation. Coppel shared Murillo's love of plants, beautiful gardens, nature. But as an art collector there was also another aspect of the Jardín Botánico Culiacán that interested him, namely as a freely accessible location where he could create encounters between people and art in places where they did not expect it. He had a vision of top-quality art for everyone – joggers, mothers and toddlers, but also the homeless or lovers – the park's usual visitors. "Most people who go to the park have never been to a museum and have no intention of going to one," says Mireya Escalante, director of Agustín Coppel's art collection. "They can enjoy the park not only as a green refuge and learn about the diversity of nature as they do so, they also have the chance to be inspired by art." And Patrick Charpenel, curator of the park and director of the Museo Jumex in Mexico City, adds, "Everyone who spends any time in the park can see that there are other ways of finding fulfilment in difficult surroundings – as a scientist, as an artist, as a gardener."

For that reason, Coppel decided only to show art that had some connection with the place. All the commissioned sculptures, architectural structures and installations were specifically conceived for this park. Coppel's determination to pursue his vision is apparent even in the gardening tools used here: they have all been made from melted-down guns seized from drug traffickers – on the inspiration of the Mexican artist Pedro Reyes. The artists were jointly selected by Agustín Coppel and Patrick Charpenel. With his global connections and status as a key figure in the Mexican art scene, Charpenel drew up a long list of outstanding artists. As he explains, "the artists had to come to Culiacán and visit the park before they could submit their proposals. They had a free choice of location for their works." Thirty-seven artists in total received commissions – including many leading figures such as Dan Graham, Francis Alÿs, James Turrell and Anri Sala, but most importantly their number also includes South American stars such as Gabriel Orozco, Jorge Pardo, Valeska Soares and Adrián Villar Rojas. Twenty works have already been realised and installed in the park. The others are following one by one. The master plan for the extended concept of art in the midst of the botanic collection was drawn up by the young Mexican Tatiana Bilbao, a rising international architect. Bilbao is known for developing her architectural structures from their location. "When I first went to Culiacán," she recalls, "I was filled with some trepidation. I knew nothing about botany." However, inspired by the

Pablo Vargas Lugo's burst-open reinforced-concrete star as a brutal alien body in amongst delicate bamboo leaves.

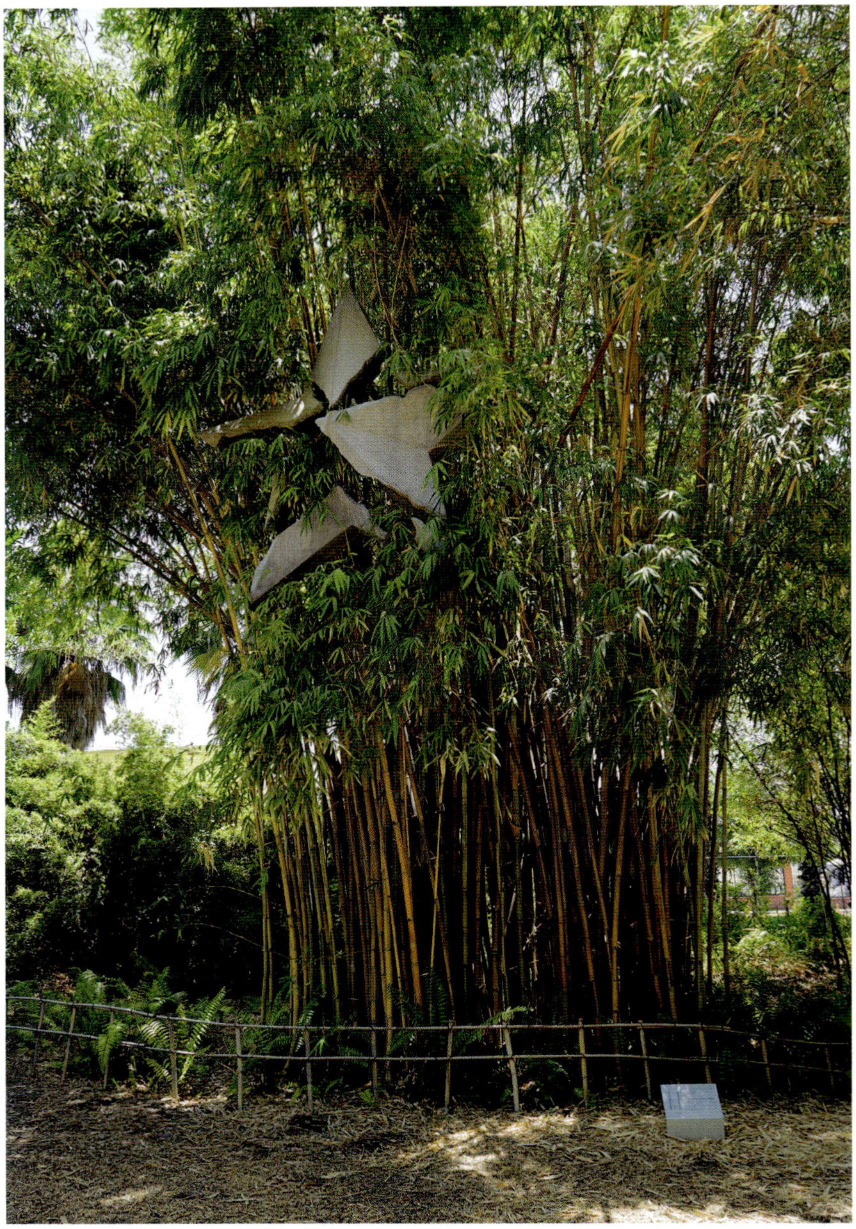

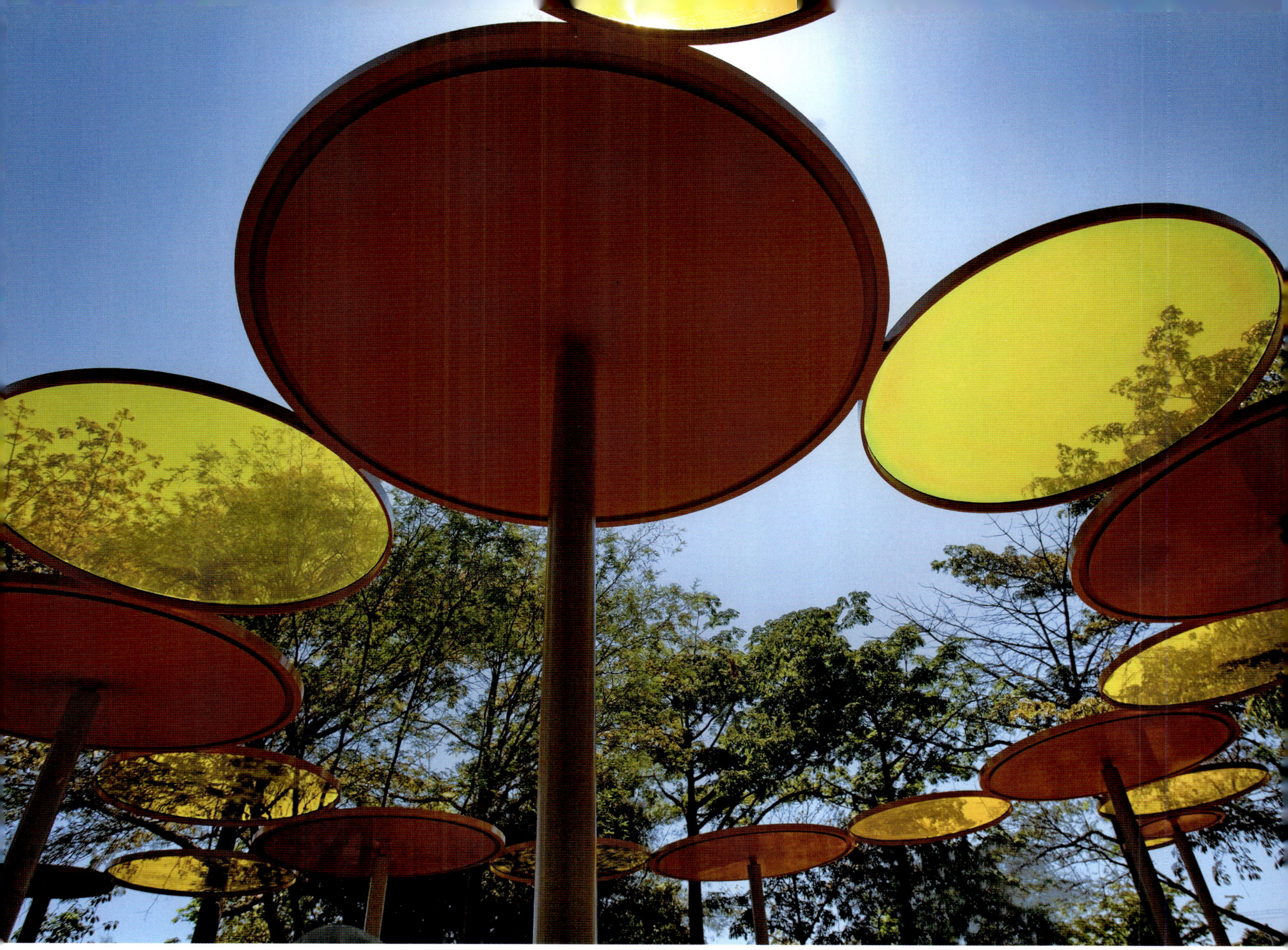

Sofía Táboas's installation of discs around a rare mesquite tree conveys a sense of poetic melancholy.

sheer variety of trees, she came up with the idea of creating a futuristic route map by laying a branch across a ground plan of the park. The natural bifurcations of the branch created separate zones for different parts of the collection: landscapes for palms and bamboo, desert plants, a tropical garden, a sensory garden and future projects such as a coffee forest and a small rainforest, where artificial rain will maintain the necessary level of humidity. Unlike the customary, clearly marked routes in other parks, this unorthodox system allows visitors to explore the park as the whim takes them. Bilbao explicitly wanted "people to be surprised, to delight in investigating the many facets of the garden and its works of art." There are parallel paths, zigzags, dead ends and paths that terminate in small plazas. Everywhere there is art, often appearing quite unexpectedly – like the VW Beetle that Francis Alÿs drove from Mexico City to Culiacán, where (to the horror of some visitors) he drove it into a tree in the botanic garden. With ambiguous irony he titled his installation *Game Over* (2008). And there is also a disturbingly gruesome aspect to the small, secluded plaza with 'loungers' by Teresa Margolles, inviting visitors to rest for a while. If they look more closely and read the inscription on the back of the concrete loungers, they will be shocked to discover that the water used to mix the concrete had previously been used to wash the corpses of victims shot in the war against drugs. But there are also moments of laughter, for instance when the visitor spots not a branch but a leg growing out of a tree, by the artist duo Allora & Calzadilla.

In order to inform visitors to the park about both the art and its plants, when

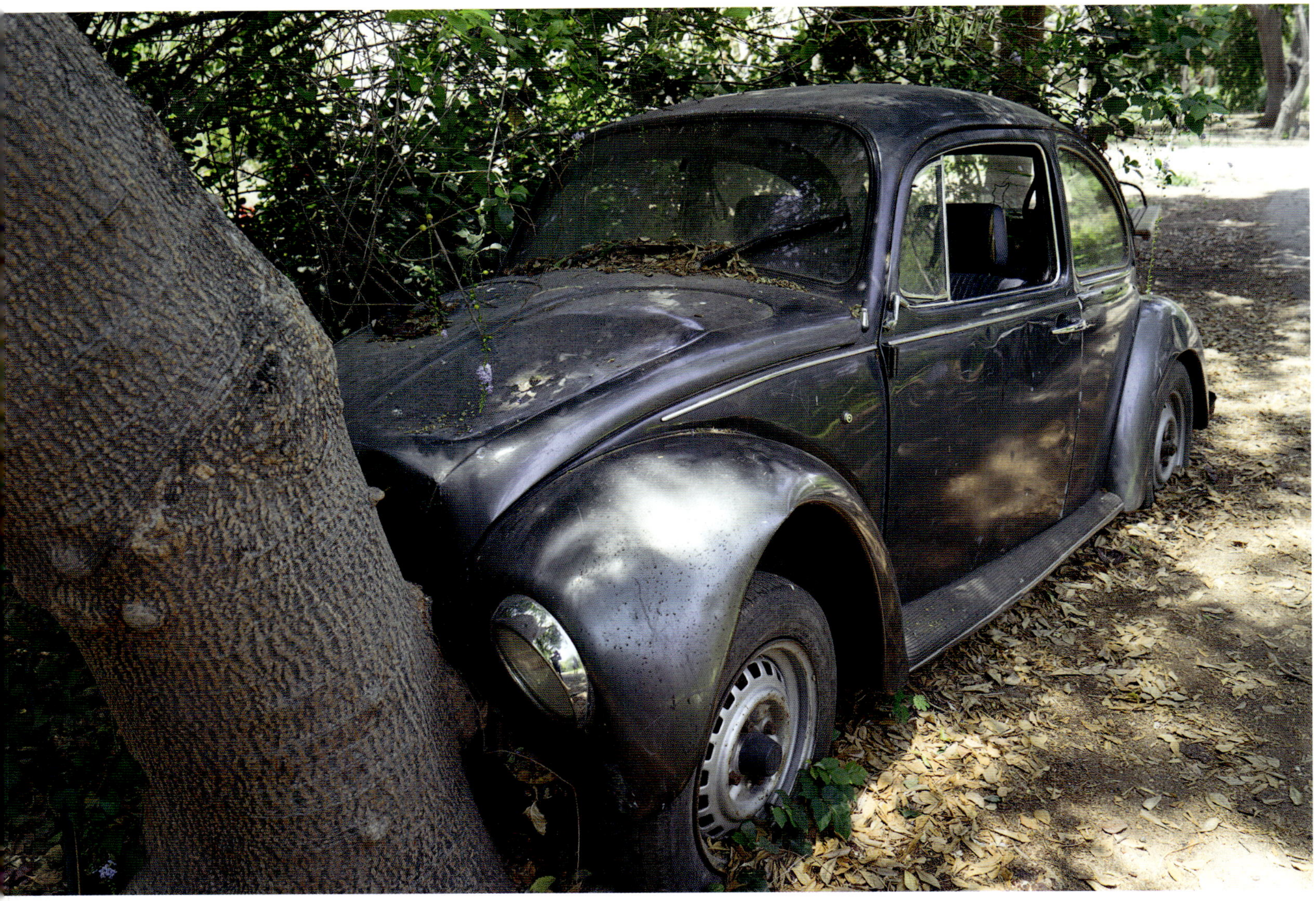

A constant source of discomfort to visitors: Francis Alÿs's VW Beetle, which he deliberately ran into a tree in the middle of the park.

Murillo and Coppel set up their joint project they placed particular importance on a professionally run education programme. And this has continued unabated since Murillo's death in 2006, with botanists, biologists, ornithologists, architects and art historians working closely together. There are signs with information relating to the plants and the works of art. Tatiana Bilbao's master plan also includes venues for lectures and film screenings, a plaza for reading and discussion, a library and dedicated spaces for the extensive children's programme: small buildings with just one room and just one function. "It's more concentrated, and the forms echo natural forms, for instance the shape of a rock. That makes them easier to integrate into the landscape," Bilbao explains, with reference to her asymmetric concrete structures with large windows. The artist collective Tercerunquinto, for example, used rubble from Murillo's earlier, temporary structures to create undulating lawns where children can play and run around.

Some of the projects required a lengthy period of preparation. In the case of Valeska Soares's installation *Caprichos* (2004), it took years for a seven-and-a-half-metre fence to be overgrown with jasmine until, finally, in 2014 the pool enclosed by the fence could be filled with water. By contrast, James Turrell's Skyspace *Encounter* (2007–14) was preceded by seven years of discussions between the artist and the client (concerning costs and technical issues), until Turrell devised a new concept. After just six months his Skyspace was inaugurated in November 2014: an oval, grassy hill with a roof seemingly floating above it. Despite its size it is as hard to spot the Skyspace in the dense palm groves as it is to realise one is looking at Tacita Dean's *Untitled (Bed of Clovers)* (2010): a meadow planted with lucky four-leaf clovers, with which the artist represents the symbol of the drug mafia in Culiacán.

This park is all about the immediacy of the experience, which is why there are no fences or signs preventing visitors from this or that. The intention is that visitors can explore the park and the art as they wish, and they are welcome to touch any of the plants or trees. The paths are edged with small pots planted with herbs, inviting visitors to stop and take in their aroma. There are experts on hand to answer horticultural questions and visitors can buy plants at the exit. And the artists also hope that people will engage with their sculptures, clambering over them or entering them. To this end Gabriel Orozco devised his own version of the game Go – *Go 4 no borders* (2006) – using brightly coloured natural stones. Marco Rountree installed a swing in his sculpture, *Sin título* (2011), which has since become a favourite site in Culiacán for photographs marking traditional *quinceañera* celebrations – the day when girls reach their fifteenth birthday and celebrate their transition into the adult world. Agustín Coppel is happy about the locals' easy interaction with the art and the park. "Every day on average five hundred people from the city come to visit the park. They take in the art and the nature and see the connection between the two – and maybe they then also incorporate them into their own lives."

Art as a playground: the collective Tercerunquinto used building rubble to create an undulating lawn.

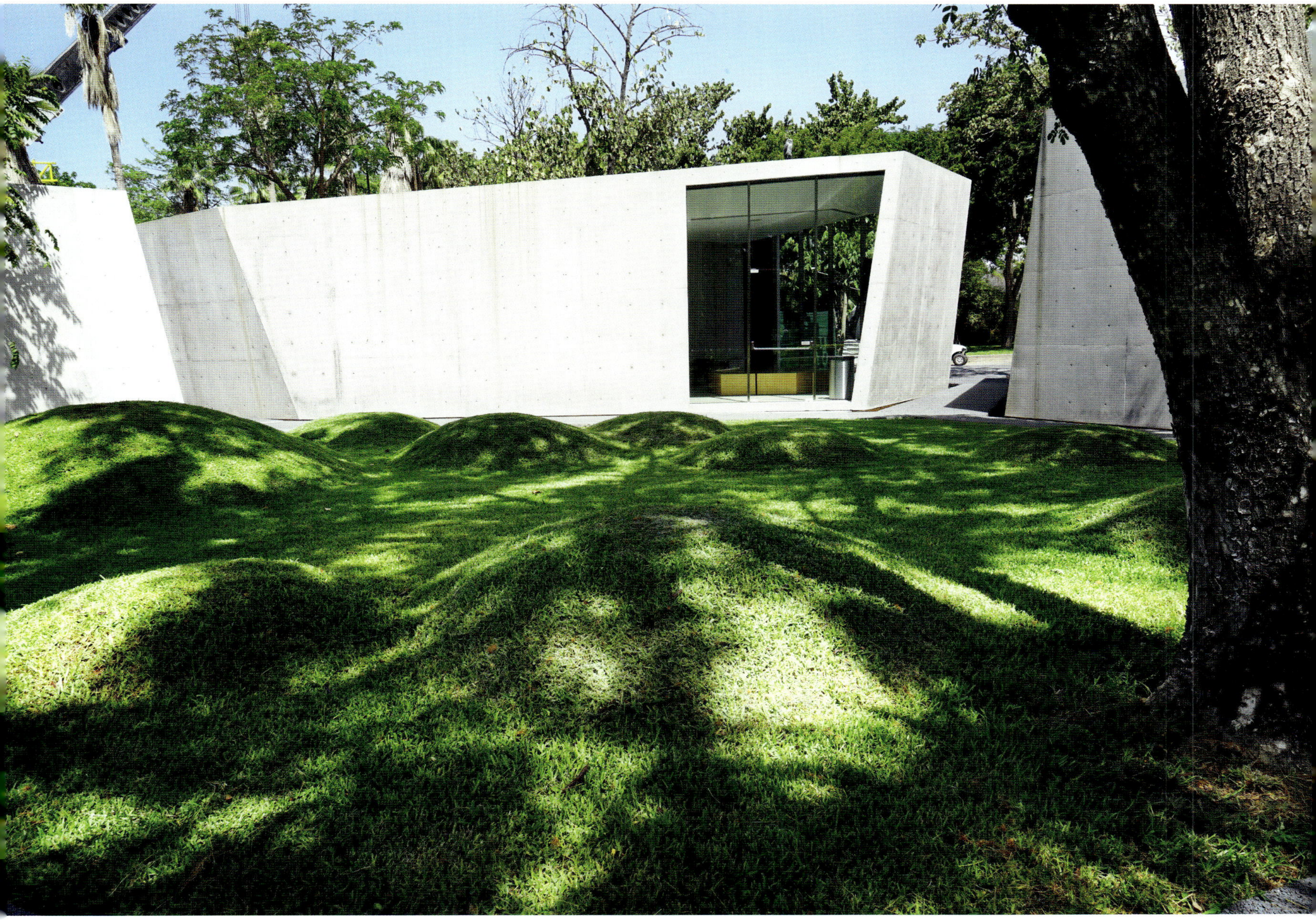

A game with light and shade: Olafur Eliasson's *Flower Archway* with aromatic climbers spans a junction of different paths.

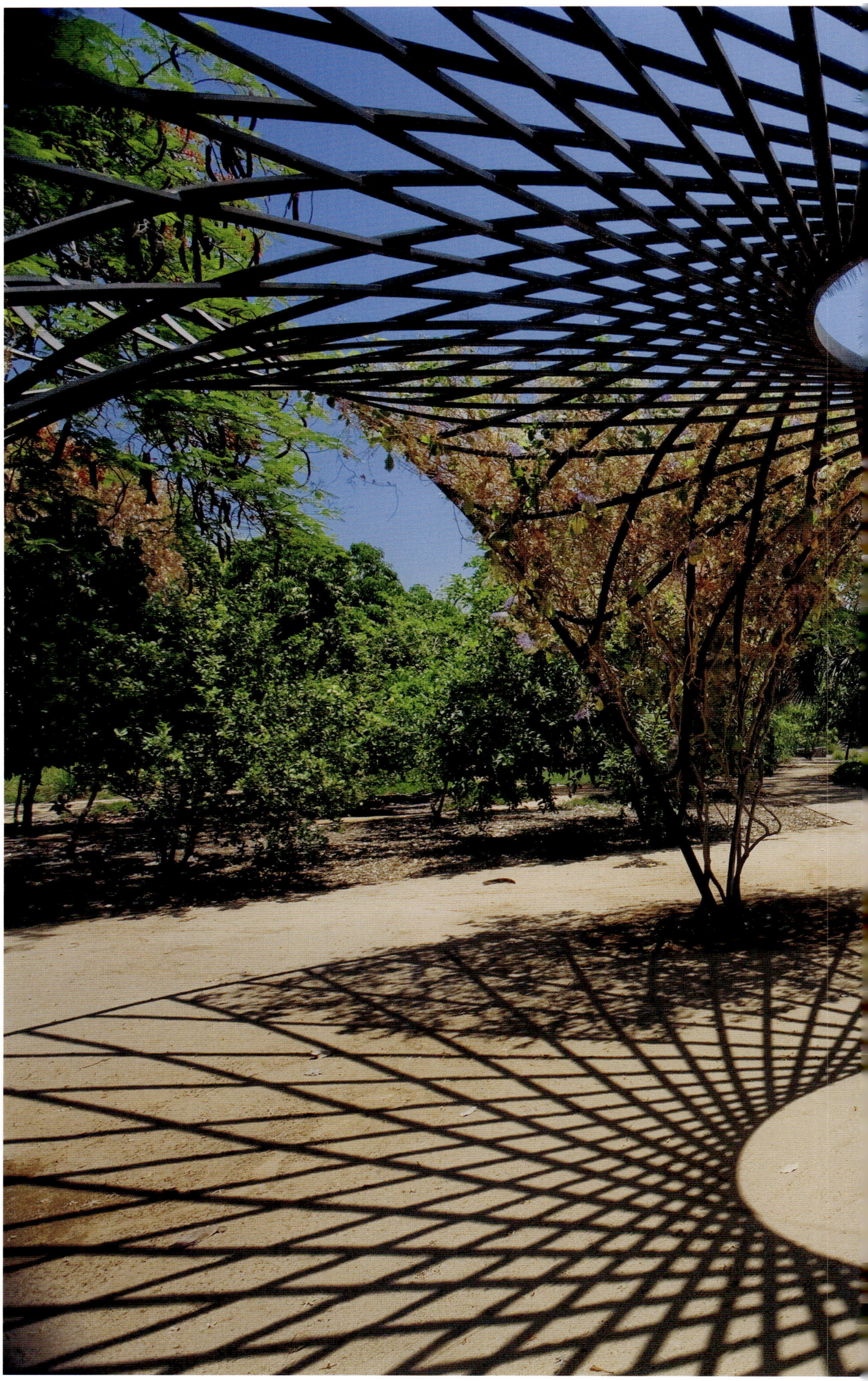

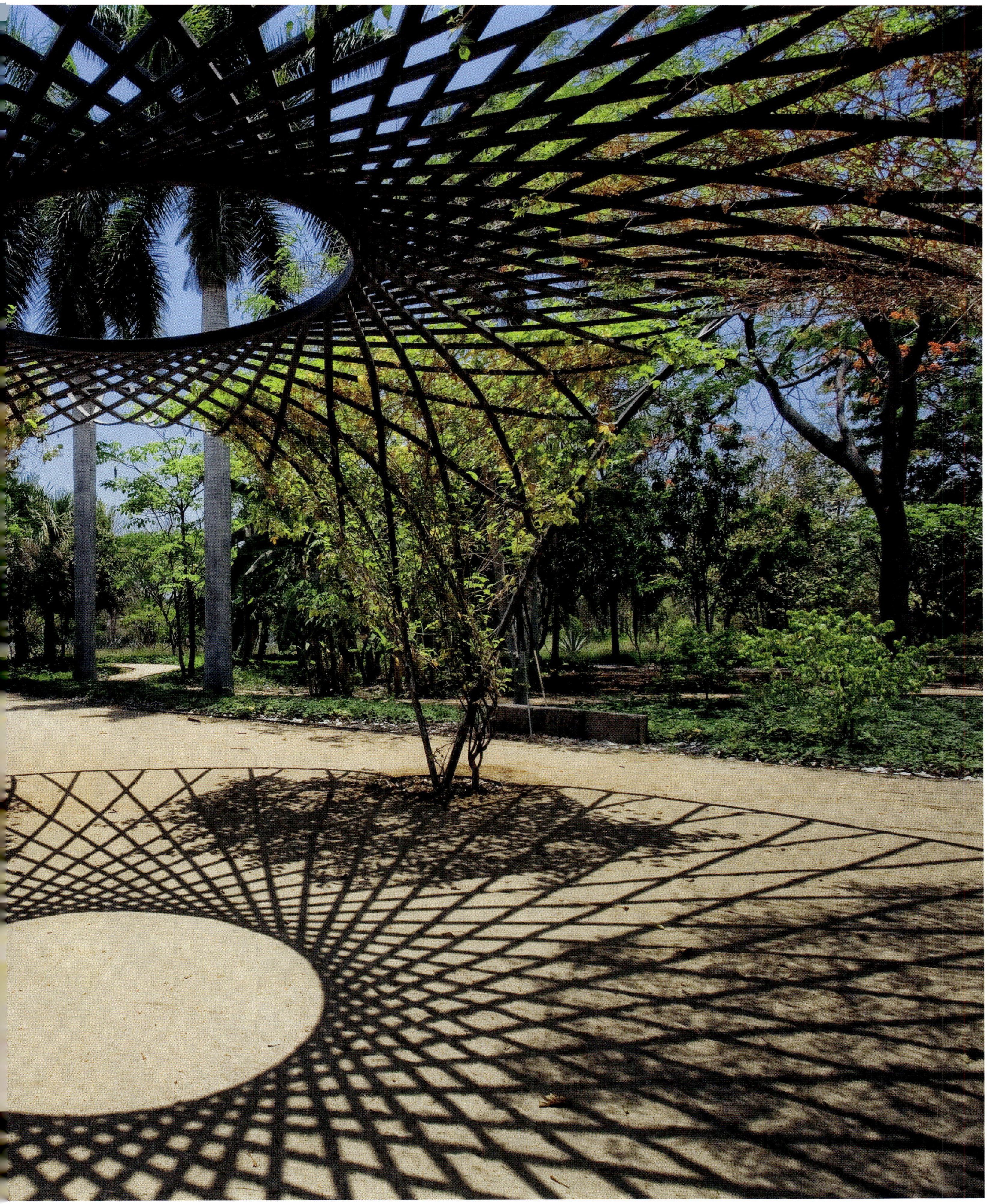

Jardín Botánico Culiacán, Mexico

A VOLCANO AS LIGHT ART
RODEN CRATER, FLAGSTAFF, USA

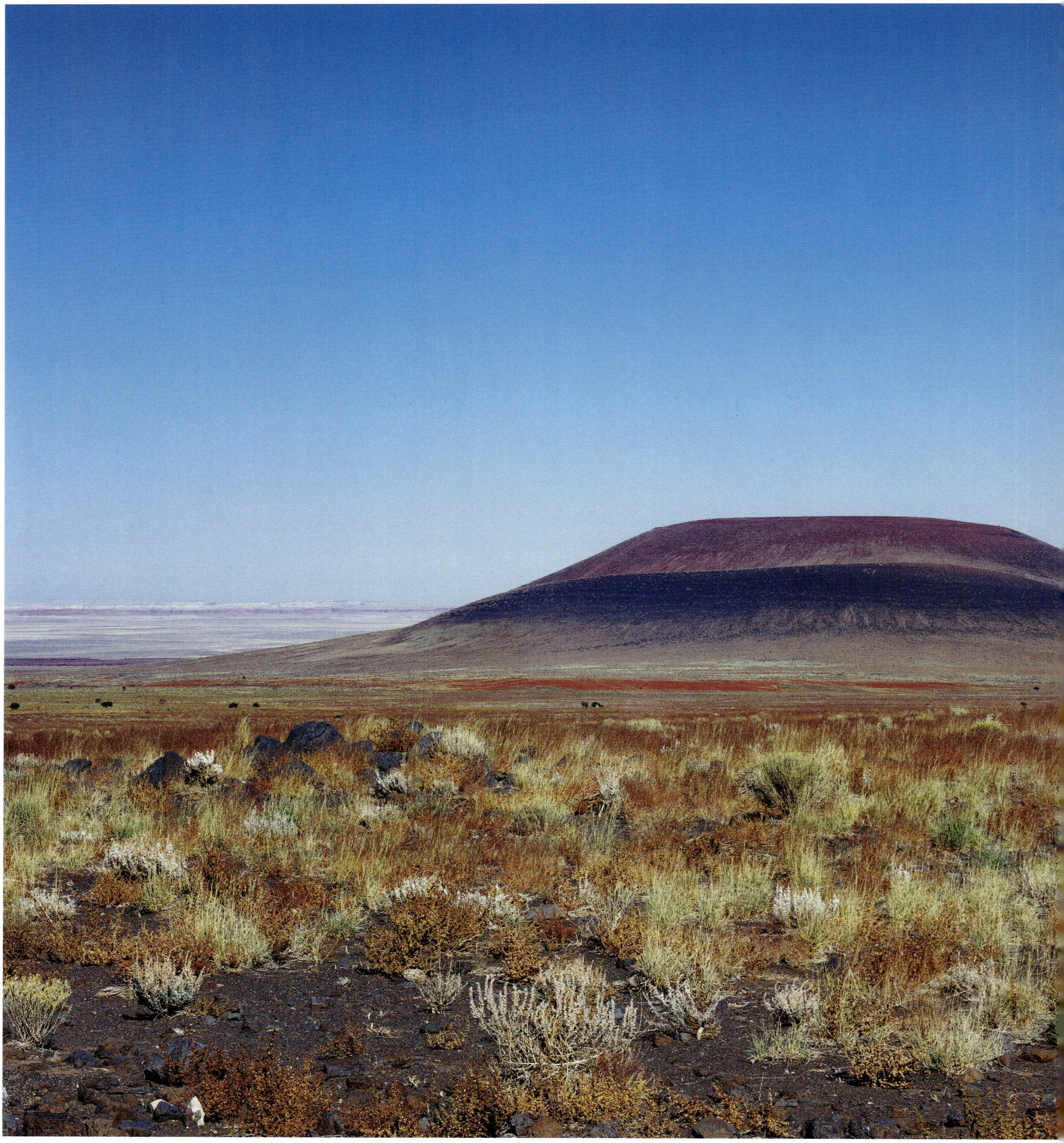

The Roden Crater: a 400,000-year-old volcanic crater in the Arizona desert as a light sculpture.

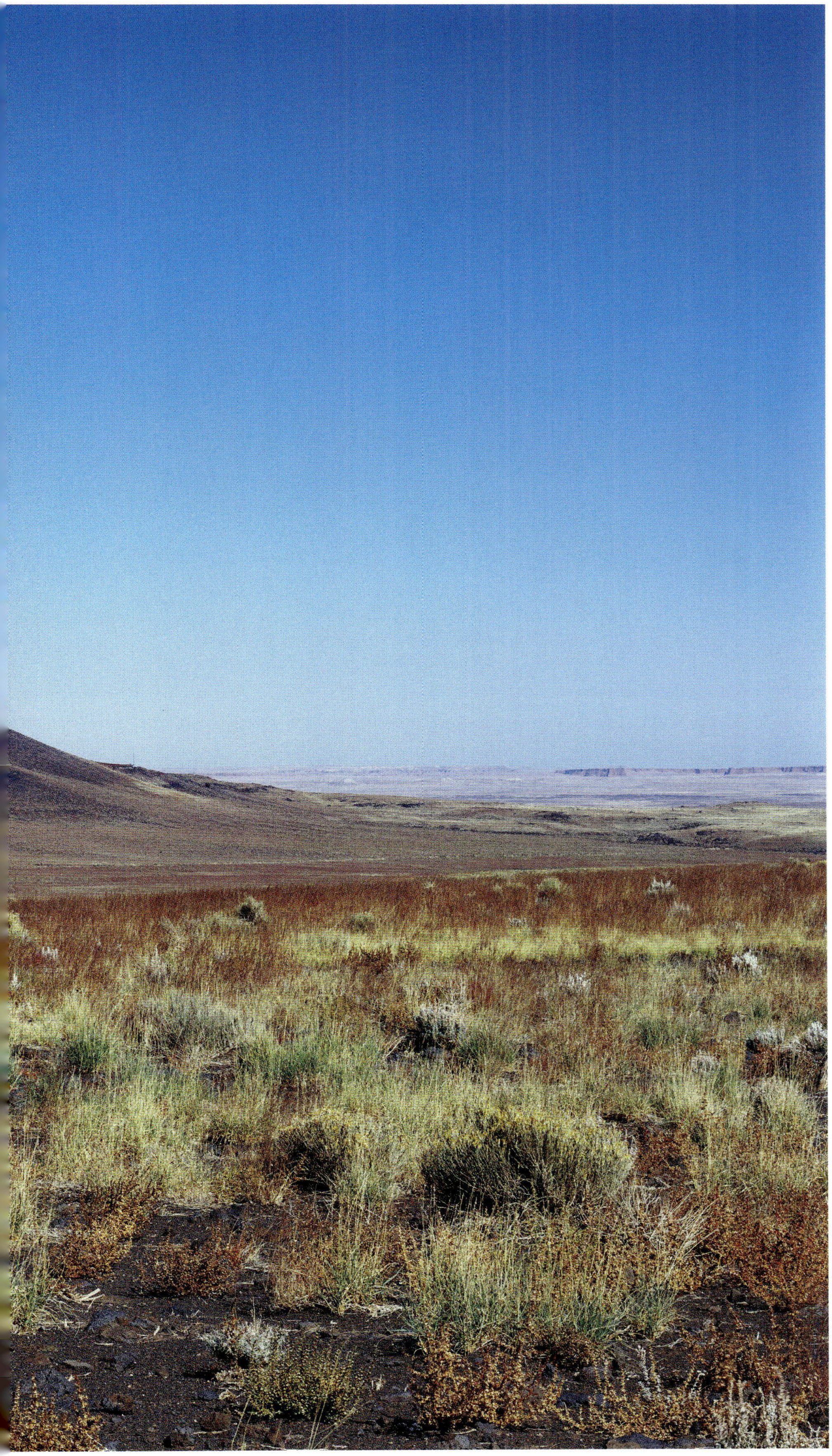

For seven months James Turrell (b. 1943) criss-crossed the American West in his little one-engine plane looking for a suitable crater for his life's work: the biggest work of art on the planet. With his knowledge of geological processes, Turrell wanted to create a space where celestial events can be registered as light. The crater was to become a huge observatory that would allow the viewer to experience the light from the heavens, the sun, the moon and the stars with different degrees of intensity, with constantly changing colours and levels of brightness. In 1974 he found Roden Crater – a 400,000-year-old, extinct volcano around 600 feet in height – some sixty kilometres north of Flagstaff, Arizona. He still recalls every detail of his first impressions: "I saw it coming from the west, so the crater was bathed in the light of the afternoon. It was standing out there beautiful by itself. I also liked it because of the colour of the desert, the Painted Desert, where you can literally feel geological time." American Indians had settled there in the past specifically so that they could observe the stars, because the unusually clear air on this high plateau is perfect. There is neither humidity nor dust to obscure one's view. For Turrell the shape of the crater was also important for his celestial observations. He could "form it in such a way that changes occur in one's perception of the size and shape of the sky."

Roden Crater is the key work in James Turrell's oeuvre. Here, more than in any of his other works, we see his personal relationship with the sky – the source of his artistic inspiration. Turrell is not only an artist, he is also a keen pilot. His plane was also always his studio, where he could explore the nature of light and space. When he flies through cloud formations these become a Ganzfeld for him – a space where one no longer has any sense of distances and colours, light and movement. And it is these conditions, which are not found in that form anywhere on Earth, that have always fascinated him and led to his light installations. While other artists paint light or use light to shape different parts of a painting, Turrell turns light into art: its transparency, volume and colours.

Turrell is interested in the physical aspect of art. Since human beings have a primal relationship with light, he wants to make this physically palpable and give it a

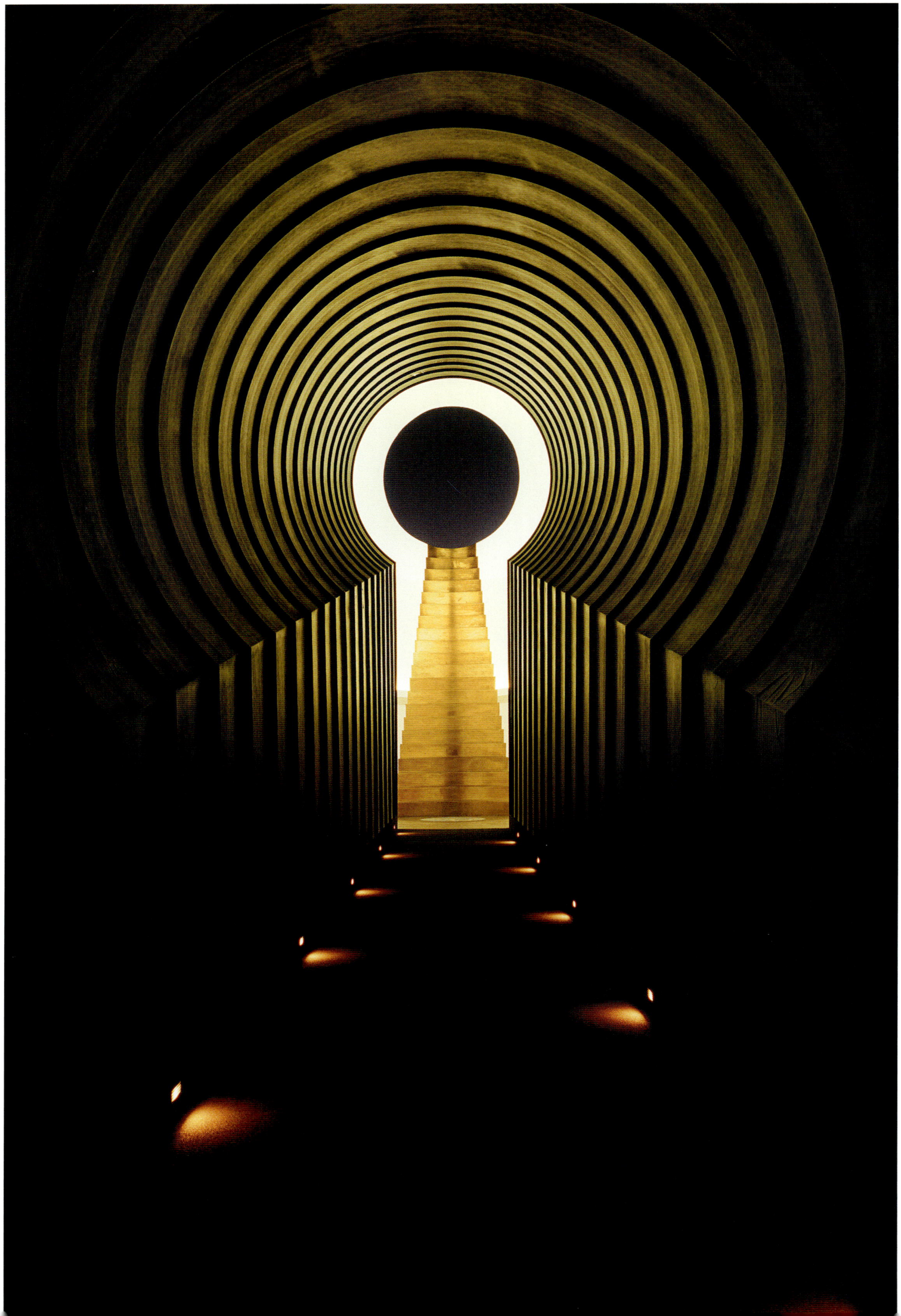

corresponding presence. So he has created light spaces all over the world, where he toys with people's perceptions. These works are about the reaction of people's eyes and brain to what they see, or rather, to what they think they are seeing. Projections create illusions of floating geometric bodies; hidden light sources surround the viewer with a nebulous glow or create Ganzfeld theatrical realms of sensation before our very eyes. And in his Skyspaces Turrell draws the sky downwards to the same height as the ceiling. In his experiments he detaches light from its spatial perspective: light-filled depth becomes tangible proximity. All these complex light spaces relate to Roden Crater.

For the last thirty-five years Turrell has been transforming this extinct volcano into a gigantic Land Art sculpture. Here, too, he is exploring the physicality of light. With the idea of a volcano as a light sculpture he is now taking the light, which he has materialised in his light spaces, back into a natural, light-intensive environment – into the Arizona desert. Initially Turrell was only able to purchase the volcano and the land around it on condition that he farmed the land. So the artist also became a cattle rancher and built up a huge herd, which is now run by his daughter. Having purchased the site, in the late 1970s Turrell started work on the crater, constantly having to struggle for funding and permissions. In the first construction phase between 1997 and 2000 at least 345,000 cubic yards of earth had to be moved. By now this number has almost tripled. The porous volcanic rock was far from ideal for Turrell's vast construction projects. In addition, there was no infrastructure to support the logistics of an undertaking of this size. "There was nothing here. No water, no electricity, no radio connection. We're very far away from everything here and first had to build a road through the desert to the crater. The early construction phases were really hard," he recalls, and strokes his dense white beard pensively. He grins and adds, "and we were certainly eighteen miles from a cold beer."

Architects, construction engineers and astronomers have assisted him in his efforts to transform his meticulous plans into complex, predominantly subterranean structures. First he had to ensure that the entire rim of the crater was at the same level in order to reinforce the impression of a celestial dome. Next came the internal structuring of the crater: tunnels were dug, light shafts and chambers were created so that the visitor experiences the sky, the sun and the light in all sorts of different ways – a 'school of seeing' that requires the deepest contemplation from the viewer. But Turrell is not only an artist, he is also a scientist. Before embarking on an art degree, he had already studied perceptual psychology, mathematics and astronomy at Pomona College, California. His later analyses of the construction of renowned ancient sites – Machu Picchu, Borobudur and the temples of Angkor Wat, which were even then used as observatories by their makers – crucially informed the plans he developed for Roden Crater.

But then Turrell himself still decides who is allowed to visit Roden Crater, his most important work of art. It is not open to the public. So far only friends, collectors and patrons of the arts have seen it. At any rate, Turrell is very generous with his time on these occasions. He collects visitors from Flagstaff and drives them for a good hour along the dirt track through the desert to South Lodge. This guest house sits halfway up the southern flank of the crater; inside it there is an open-plan space with a kitchen area. On the side towards the volcano there is sleeping accommodation for eight people. Looking out from the large window terrace the visitor has a breathtaking view of the endless expanses of this primal, volcanic landscape, which almost looks like a moonscape. The artist explains his complex thinking to his guests, describing the existing constructions and his plans for the crater and for more spaces for celestial observations yet to be realised – these include the Fumarole

Observing the movements of the planets: the *Sun / Moon Chamber* with a monolith as a projection surface for the light from the Sun and the Moon.

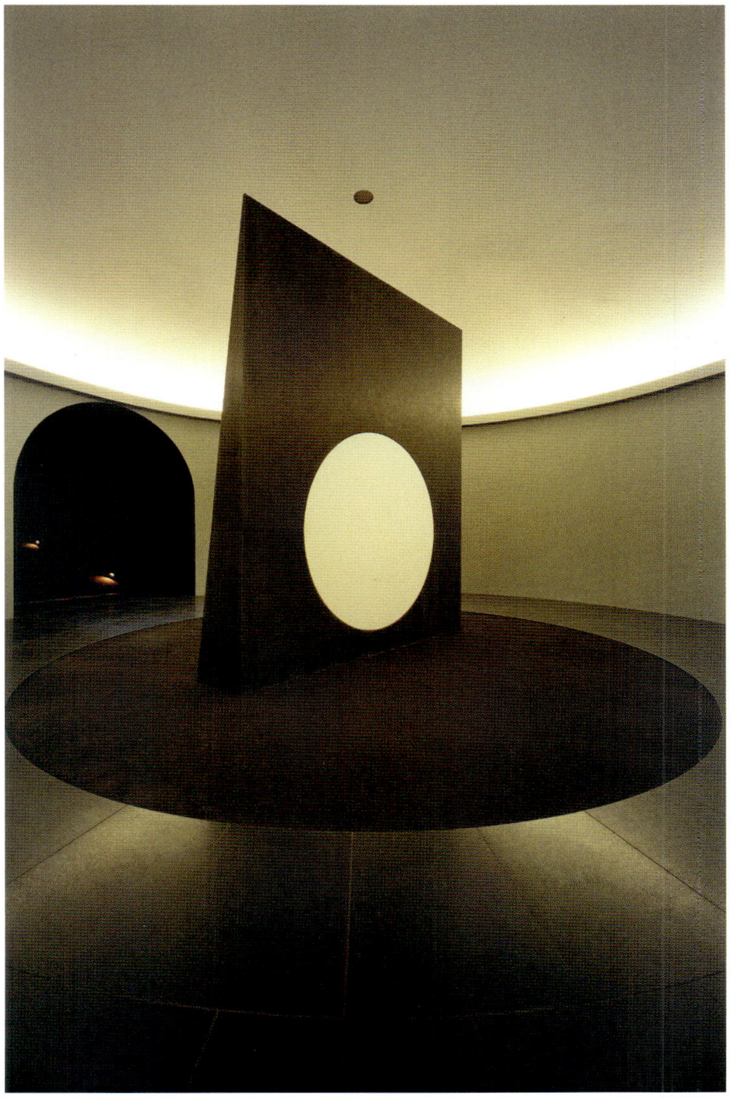

Left: The Alpha Tunnel extends for 200 metres through the volcano – towards the light.

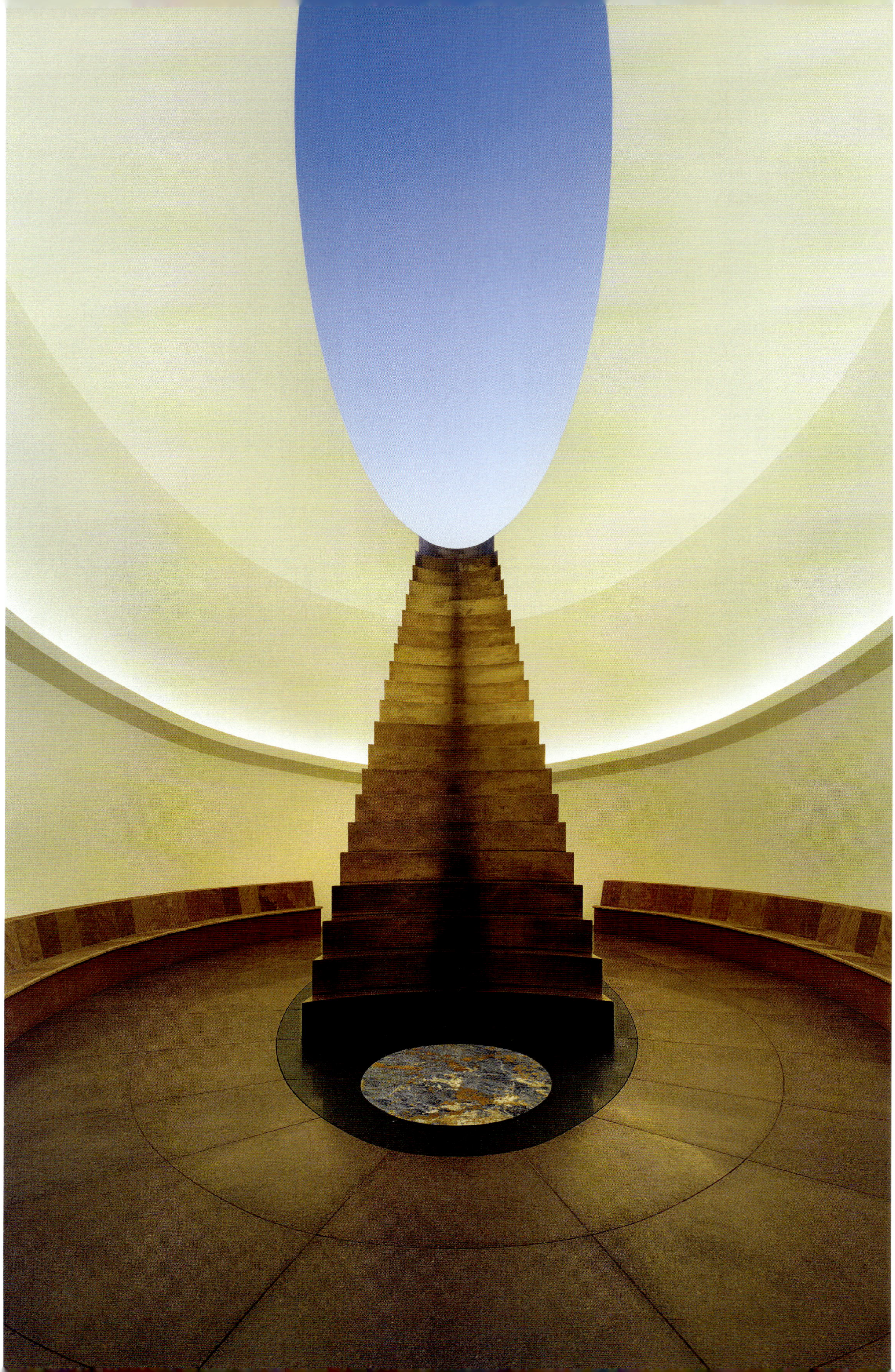

The *East Portal* – a space that leads up to the edge of the crater.

Space, the South Space and the North Moon Space, the Beta Tunnel and even an amphitheatre. Turrell knows he will not see the final completion of his gigantic project, but this does not bother him: "What matters to me is that all the plans are finished. Then other people can carry them out."

Gradually dusk descends. For Turrell this is the ideal time to experience his light experiments in the crater, because "we're not made for the day ... we squint and we put dark glasses on. So we're made for twilight, we're made for the light of the cave," he explains, with a reference to Plato's parable of the cave, which inspired Turrell's earliest projections of external and internal light. And he continues, "When you reduce the level of light and the pupil opens, then a feeling like touch comes out of the eye and you can feel colour."

Turrell takes his guests further up the wall of the crater to the fumarole in the south-east side of the volcano: a second, smaller mound with an opening which emitted steam when the volcano was still active. Turrell used this hole as an entrance into his subterranean world. A mighty bronze door opens. A short passage leads into the interior, first to the Sun | Moon Chamber (1997) – one of the dome-like chambers in the interior of the crater that allows the viewer to experience celestial events. In this case the events are sunrise and sunset each day, and the twice-yearly solstice. In the centre of the chamber, placed in a circle of volcanic ash, there is a black wedge of stone, with a white marble moon set into it. This serves as a projection surface for the images of the sun and the moon that travel into the interior along two long light tunnels (large enough for people to walk along): the Alpha Tunnel and the Beta Tunnel. A huge lens at the midpoint of the tunnel enlarges the projections accordingly. At present only the Alpha Tunnel is finished, which means that images only appear on the west side of the projection stone. No doubt the Beta Tunnel will be finished by the time there can be a simultaneous projection of both the Sun and the Moon, because this phenomenon only takes place every 18.61 years, when the moon reaches its declination. The next occurrence is not until the year 2025.

Beyond the Sun | Moon Chamber the visitor walks along the ten-foot-high rounded black interior of the Alpha Tunnel, travelling over 1,000 feet upwards towards the light at the end of the tunnel. At first it looks like a blueish-black egg, but ultimately it proves to be an elongated, elliptical opening in the ceiling. A steep flight of steps leads upwards to the East Portal. When the moon sets in its southernmost declination, it becomes a huge disc, which precisely fills the opening in this ceiling at the edge of the crater.

The East Portal is part of a Skyspace, a room with an opening in the ceiling revealing the sky. When dusk falls the space is subtly lit with artificial light and the visible section of sky appears to become an almost tangible, coloured light field. Simple architectural strategies thus allow the viewer to experience the universe as a different, extended space. The room becomes an observatory for each individual. The steep flight of narrow bronze steps leads up into the flank of the bowl of the crater. However, if one looks through the ceiling opening, the East Portal, back into the tunnel exit, it looks like an oversized keyhole. Turrell drew his inspiration for the bronze stairway from the Pueblo Indians who used to ascend to the light from their underground *kivas*, cave-like rooms for gatherings and rituals – a metaphor for the path that people take from the underworld into the human world.

Besides light, Turrell also includes sound in his perceptual experiments. Any human cries in the tunnel resonate depending on the size of the space and the distance, and the sound waves penetrate one's body. Thus sounds become physically palpable, like light. Directly beyond the staircase the tunnel leads into an area with more light chambers, which ultimately lead to the centre point of the crater, the Crater's Eye (1997): a circular meditation dome with a diameter of over forty feet and curved benches around the wall. The ceiling with an opening in the centre coincides with the floor of the crater. The visitor is now sitting inside the crucial mechanism for seeing – the eye itself. The Crater's Eye is a naked-eye observatory. At night the opening frames the glittering multitudes of stars in the night sky like a picture. It is as though Turrell has reconstructed the prototype for all his Skyspaces, which he first devised as an entirely new type of work in the early 1970s. Turrell regards them as "an artistic intervention, but consistent with nature."

Outside, at the Crater's Eye Plaza, stone benches invite visitors to lie down on their backs, with their heads tipped back. Looking around from this position the visitor sees the extraordinary, extreme curvature of the sky that results from the height of the rim of the crater. By contrast the sky beyond the rim of the crater appears to go on forever. Associations with ancient cult sites, temples and holy mountains come to mind – places where light was revered as a deity.

Turrell's fascination with light is closely connected to his own personal quest to identify mankind's place within the universe. Born into a Quaker family he very early on developed a sense of the sublime and of the notion of meditation or silent contemplation. "My grandmother always told us we had to 'greet the light in us'. Quakers believe in the divine light within us. They search for it in silent meditation. Later on I felt a desire to draw external light closer to the internal light within us." In his many and various perceptual experiments Turrell's aim is to trigger the same emotional responses that

In the bowl of the crater: at the *Crater's Eye Plaza* the levelled edge of the crater makes the horizon appear to curve upwards – the sky as a dome.

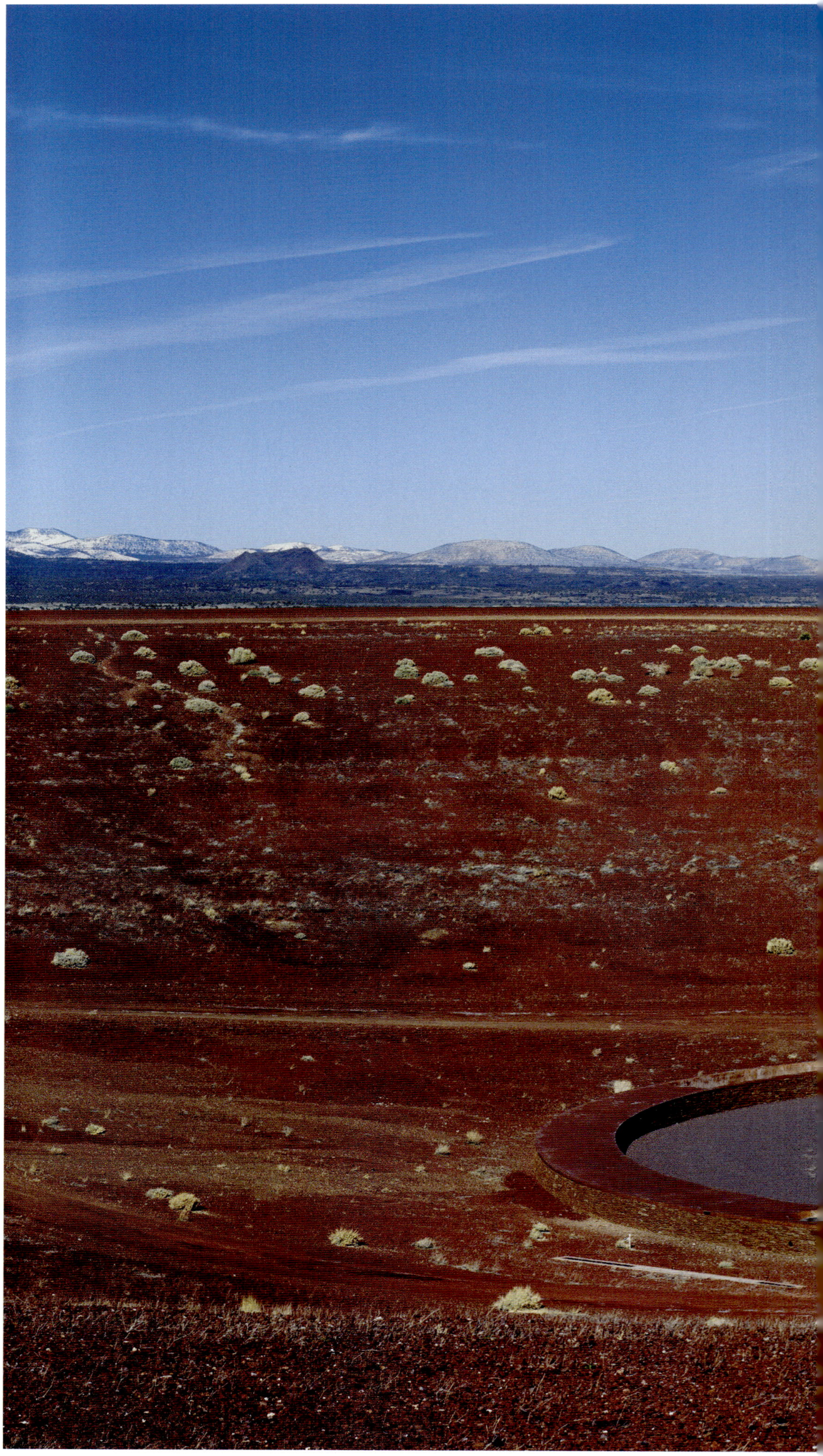

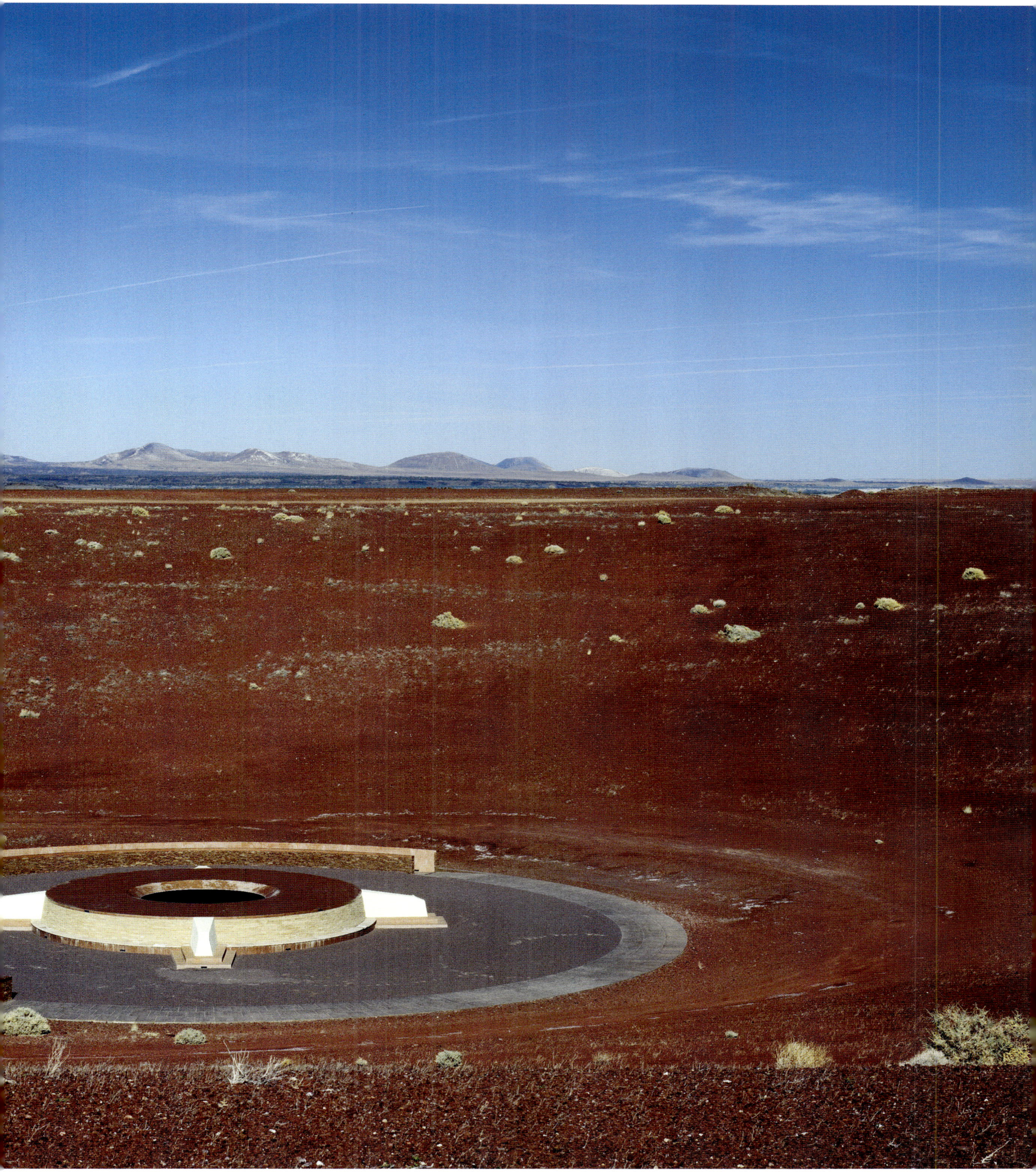

ART MEADOWS WITH MINIMAL ART
ART PARK, VERZEGNIS, ITALY

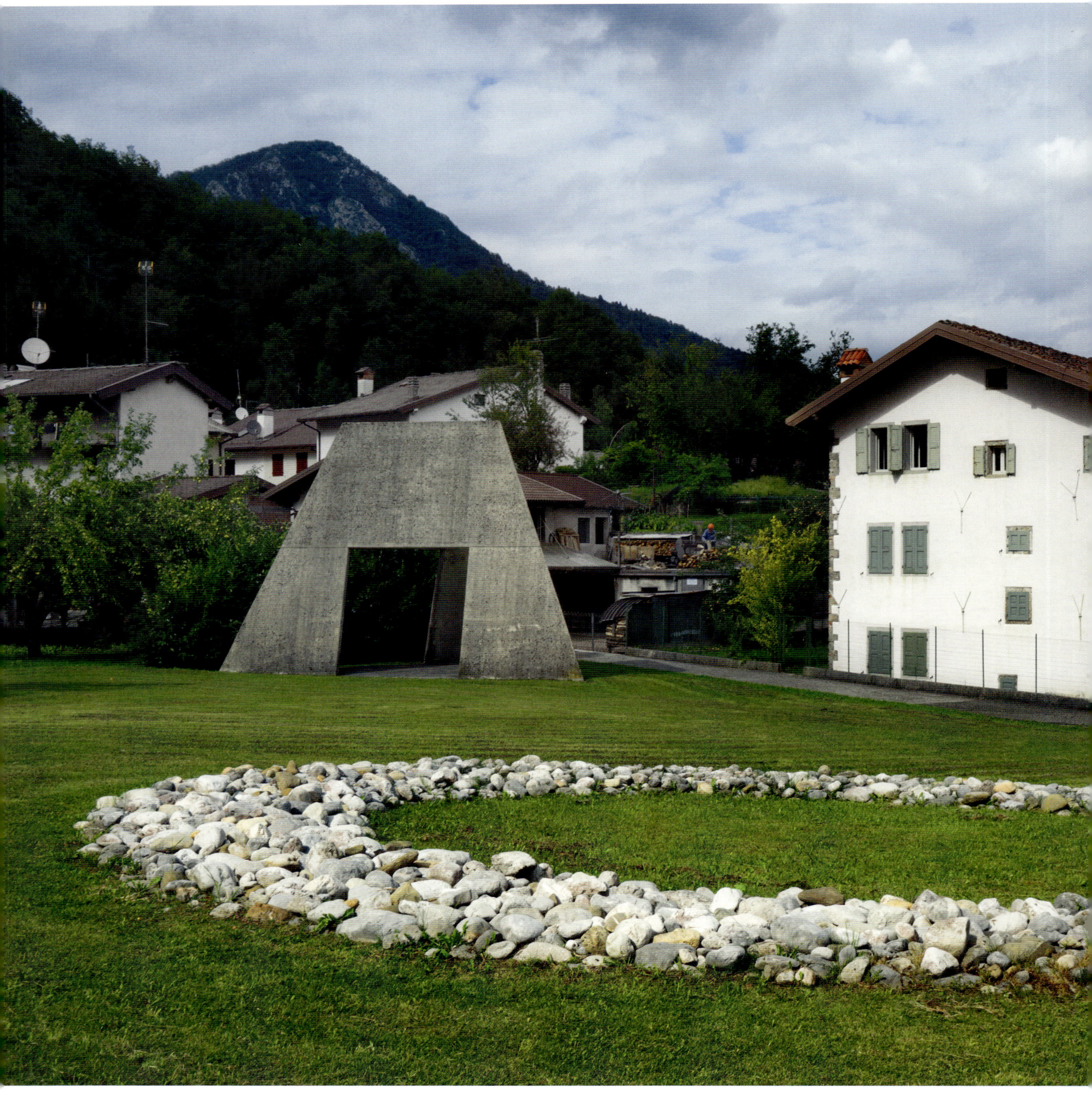

Icons of Minimal Art on a village green: a stone circle by Richard Long and a pyramid room by Bruce Nauman.

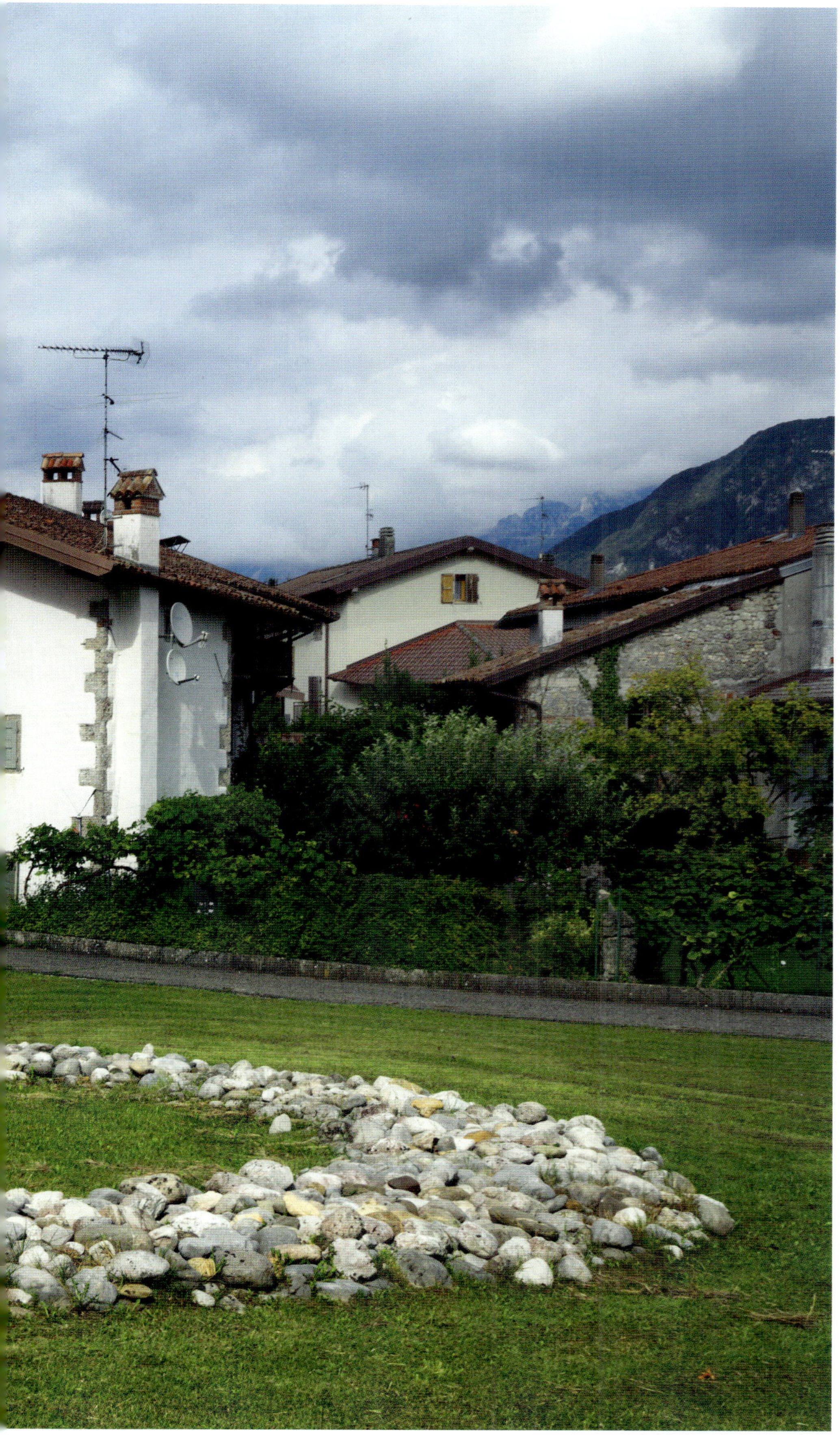

The art in the little mountain village of Verzegnis in Friuli, Italy, dates back to 1989, just after the publisher and art collector Egidio Marzona (b. 1944) had acquired properties and land that had previously been owned by his Friulian ancestors. His best friend and adviser, the Düsseldorf gallerist Konrad Fischer, immediately had an idea: "Egidio, now that you've got so much land, you'll have to do something with artists." – "And then he just called Bruce Nauman," says Marzona with a laugh. The American conceptual artist, who was also a friend of Marzona, was immediately taken by the idea. Just three months later his *Truncated Pyramid Room* (1987–90) was in place on a grassy area in the middle of Verzegnis. At six by six metres, this is the largest poured-concrete sculpture that Nauman has ever made. With this triangular form the artist both referred and responded to the surrounding mountains. Large openings in the side walls of the pyramid catch the light, and the appearance of the space is constantly changing throughout the day. At the same time, it provides unusual views of the mountains and the village. It reflects Bruce Nauman's interest in optical perception, which is shared by Dan Graham, whose glass-and-steel *Bisected Two-Way Mirror Triangle* (1998) stands at the foot of the mountain slope. Reflected images, including that of the viewer, seem to float endlessly in the landscape like a Fata Morgana. Fictive, transparent spaces arise. Other leading artists whose work is represented in Verzegnis – including Carl Andre, Richard Serra, Lawrence Weiner and Richard Long – are similarly interested in space and shapes.

Many of the artists who have created sculptures for Verzegnis have long been friends of Egidio Marzona. In their various ways they are exponents of Minimal Art and have featured in Marzona's extensive art collection since the outset. In the summer months they were frequent visitors to the sleepy little village in the far north-east of Italy, just forty kilometres north of Udine. Above all it was the unspectacular character of the place, its isolation and the simplicity of life in the midst of this grandiose setting with its backdrop of mountains that suited their artistic creativity and inspired them to make works in situ. The large area of pastureland at the foot of the sublime mountain scenery was very much in keeping with their mindset, which was also shared by Egidio Marzona, that is to say, a desire to concentrate fully on the essence of things, a deep sense of connection with the natural world and a disdain for the commercialism of the art business. This is the perfect setting for art that is guided by the simplicity of forms and materials such as stone, wood, glass and metal. There is nothing garish here, there are no opulent shapes – just rigorous stereometric forms: lines, circles, cubes. And yet, even when Nauman's sculpture had been installed, Marzona still had no thought of a large-scale project with external sculptures. "It really came about of its own accord," he says modestly. For instance, he had acquired a drawing by Sol LeWitt for a wall painting with a striped cube, but was uncertain which wall in his house would be most suitable for it – "so I invited Sol LeWitt to Verzegnis," as he recalls. LeWitt arrived with his family and stayed for two weeks. "We didn't once talk about the wall painting," says Marzona. However, shortly after leaving Italy, LeWitt called Marzona with new ideas for Verzegnis: an extension of the cube theme in a large triptych for the wall above the fireplace in the *salone* and five wall paintings on the long window wall. Marzona remembers that moment: "I took a deep breath at the thought of cost, but then I agreed." In the end it came to the point where Sol LeWitt said, "Listen Egidio, we should also talk about something outside. Two models are already on their way to you by courier." A gentle smile passes across Marzona's face and he draws deeply on his pipe: "So of course I couldn't resist." The sculpture *HRZL 1* (1990), an eight-section geometric staircase sculpture, was created to suit the dimensions of the site next to a wall in Marzona's garden. And more works came into being, in a similar manner, by Carl Andre, Lawrence Weiner, Stephen Kaltenbach, Dan Graham and Richard Nonas. Richard Long's gigantic stone circle *Tagliamento River Stone Ring* (1996) has an almost primal sense of the sacred about it. This installation by the Land Art specialist goes well with the weighty appearance of Nauman's monumental pyramid, as does the immensely long line of adjoining wooden blocks by Carl Andre, which runs right across the property until it disappears into bushes on the horizon. As Marzona says, "Here in Verzegnis, in

Dan Graham challenges human perceptions with his hybrid glass pavilion *Bisected Two-Way Mirror Triangle*. To the left is an installation by Carl Andre.

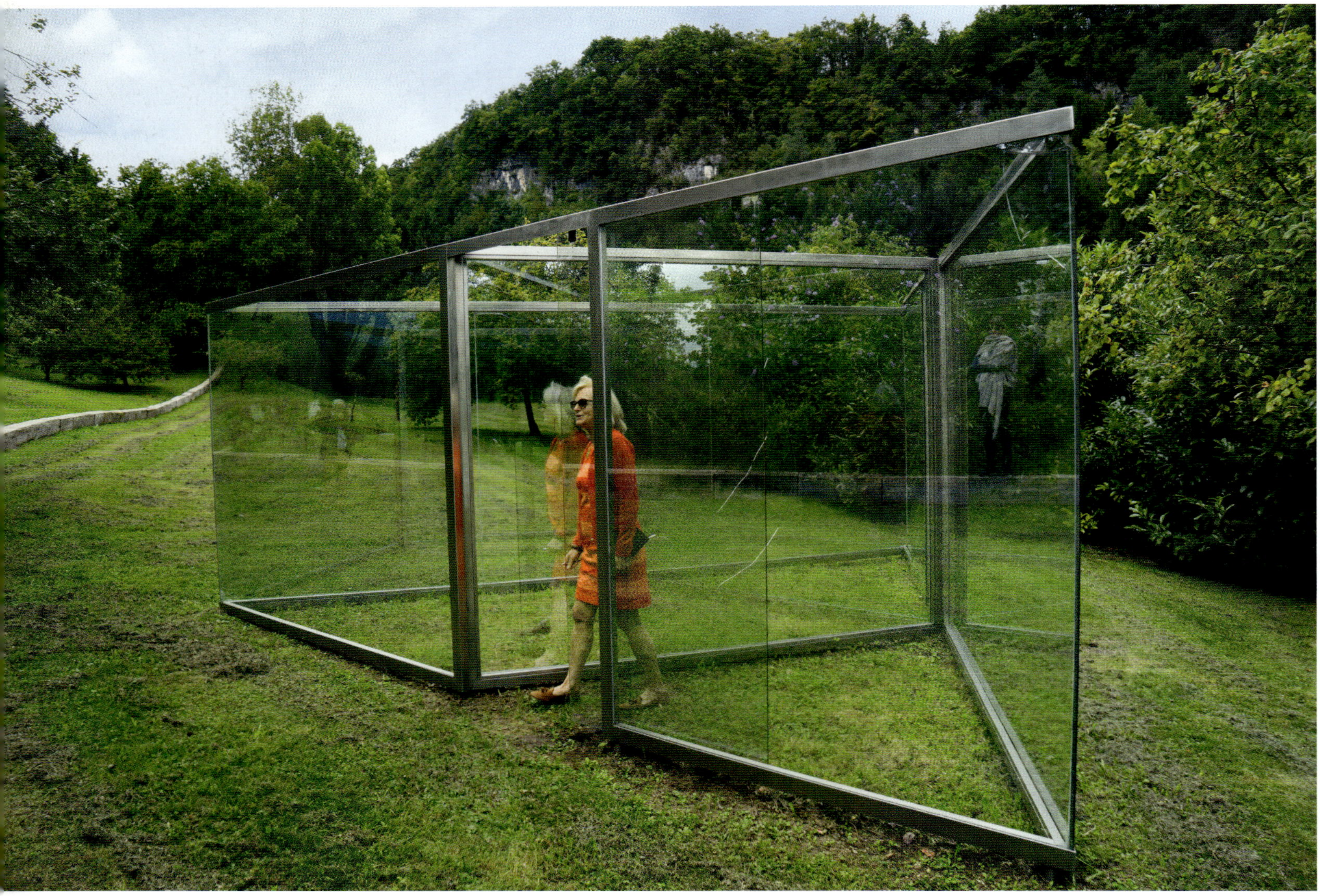

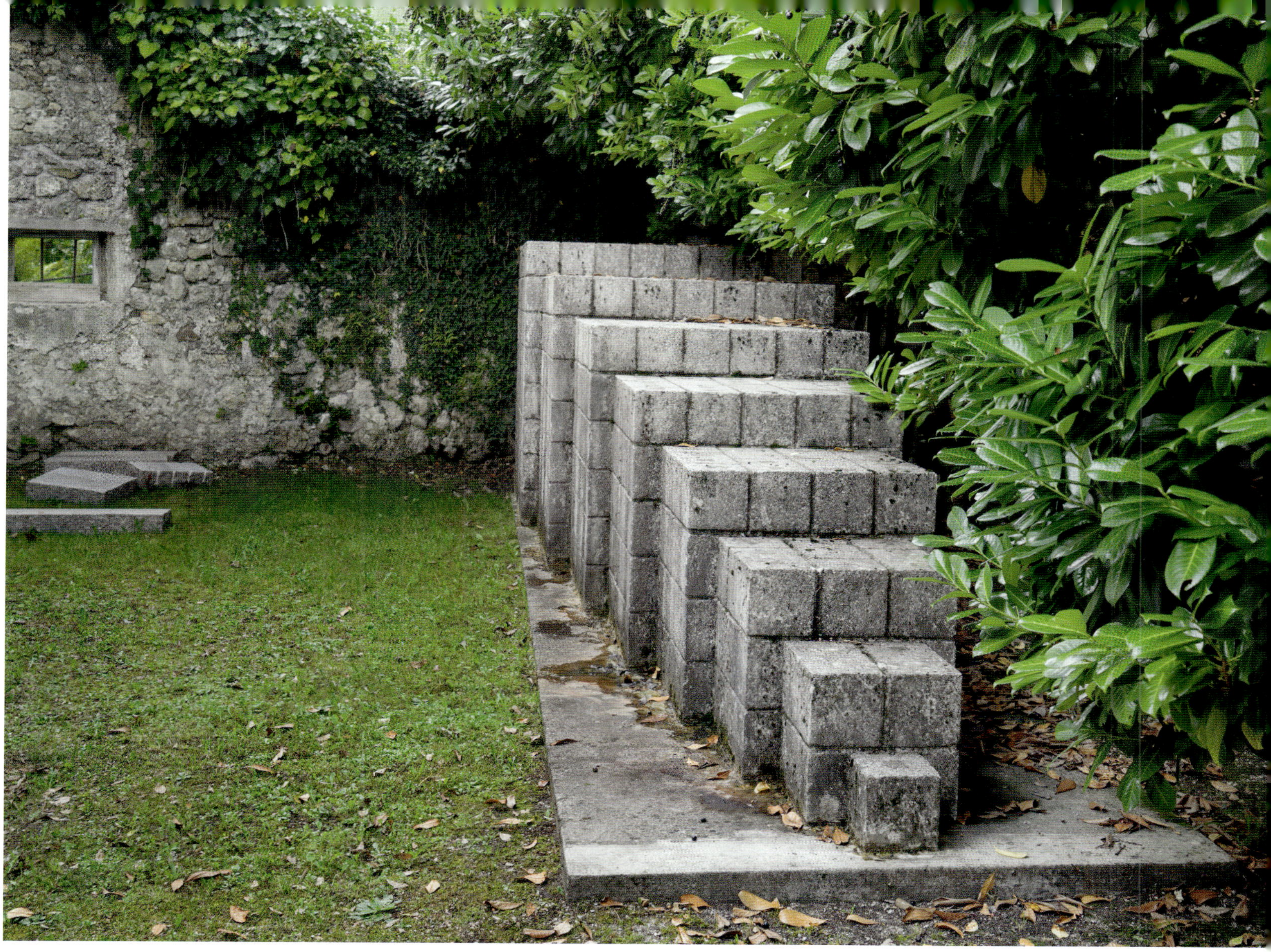

Sol LeWitt is one of the many Minimalists who complemented their wall paintings in the house with an additional outdoor sculpture.

this monumental natural setting, you can understand the significance of Minimal Art as an exploration of space and materials."

The history of the Marzona family in Verzegnis goes back to the seventeenth century. The main street was named after them, as was the local school. And although Egidio Marzona grew up in Germany, in Bielefeld, he very much feels that his roots are here. "Most of my ancestors worked here as teachers or builders," he says. In the late nineteenth century his grandfather emigrated to Germany, "but the women of the family, including my mother, always came back to Verzegnis to give birth," he adds, not without some pride. His father was an engineer who had created a successful business in Bielefeld manufacturing prefabricated concrete building materials. As the only son, Egidio was expected to take over the business, but he was much more drawn to the art scene in nearby Düsseldorf. "When I bought a painting by Robert Ryman – at the age of twenty – for 300 marks, my parents were aghast: '300 marks for a white canvas!'" Having initially set up an art gallery in Düsseldorf, he then founded his own publishing company, Edition Marzona. Not least benefiting from good advice from Konrad Fischer, the renowned avant-garde gallerist, Marzona started to collect art early on. Going against the current trend, he concentrated on Conceptual Art, Land Art, Minimal Art and Arte Povera – "art that you could still acquire in those days for a few hundred marks," as he himself says. He has since built up one of the most important collections worldwide. A few years ago he gifted a large part of his collection, around 800 works, to the Nationalgalerie in Berlin.

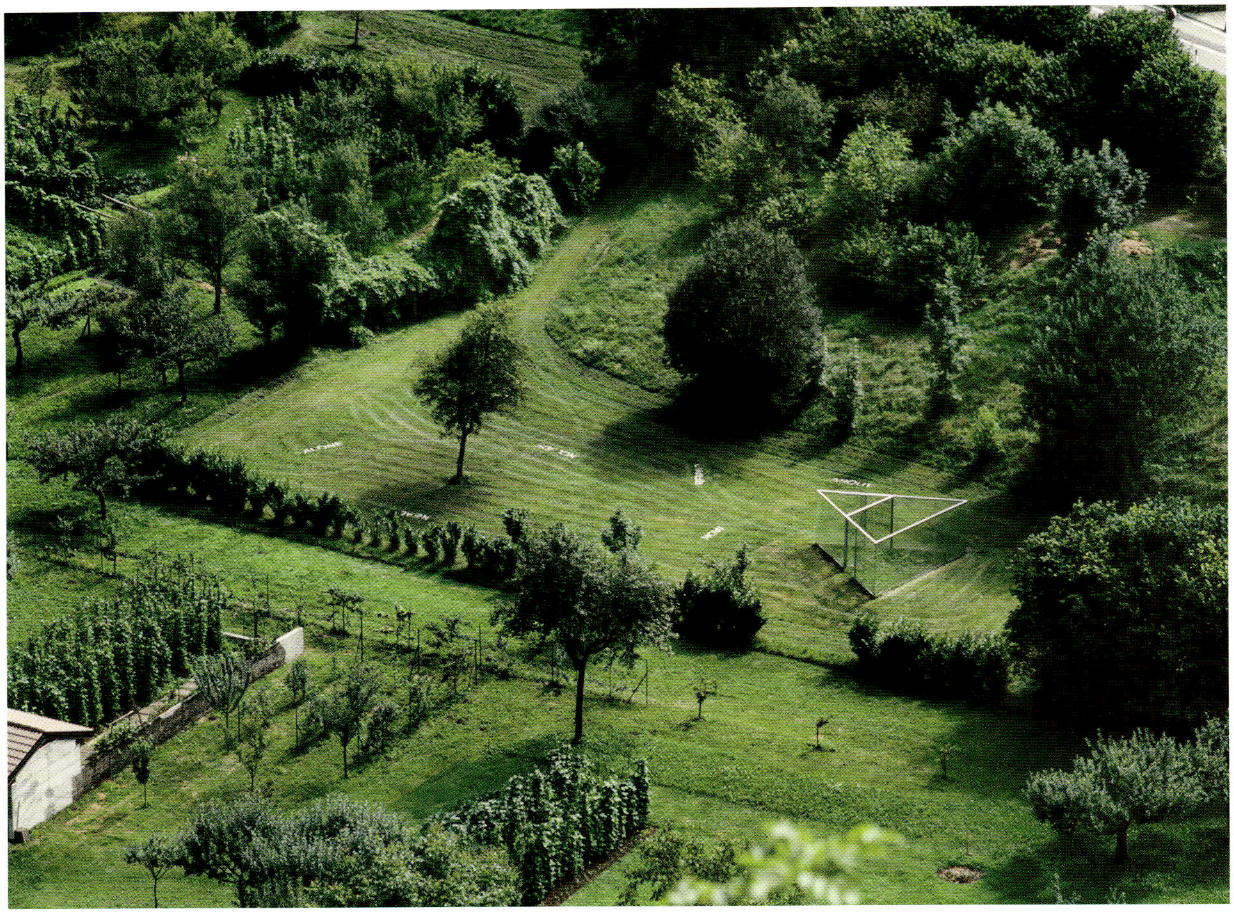

Rural gardens and art: inscribed wordplays by Robert Barry and Dan Graham's glass pavilion.

Egidio Marzona is not someone who wants to contemplate his collection in splendid isolation. This highly cultured man, with an ever-alert gaze, is constantly engaged in debate and discussion, researching, travelling across the world, meeting intellectuals and other art collectors. His work as a publisher often involved intense research, for instance in connection with his comprehensive publication on Bauhaus photography. It was through these activities that Marzona started to collect 'bits and pieces' – postcards, notes, letters –, all those things that document an artist's life. This then became the basis of a huge archive relating to twentieth-century art. Like Verzegnis and the works of art in museums in Berlin, the plan is that, as soon as possible, this archive should provide all those who are interested with a new, interactive, multifaceted means of accessing modern art.

As it happens, almost all the artists whose work is seen in Verzegnis are represented there with two works: one outside in the "art meadow" or in the garden and one inside the house. This house, which is notable for its spartan furnishings, is nevertheless filled with wall paintings: artists such as Daniel Buren, Richard Long, Robert Barry and Sol LeWitt have created minimalist wall paintings in the entrance, the stairwell and the large salon. These works relate to the sculptures outside. "Verzegnis should be seen as a *Gesamtkunstwerk* comprising the garden, the meadow and the house," as Marzona says. And he continues, "Sometimes there's a real rivalry between the artists." When Richard Long was painting the dark surface of the wall behind the dining table in the salon with pale mud, he kept looking at Bruce Nauman's mighty pyramid outside. "When he saw the grandiose effect of the rigorous shape of the pyramid in the monumental landscape, he was determined to do something outside, too."

Egidio Marzona's unusual art project was not initially welcomed by all the inhabitants of Verzegnis. There was trouble with the authorities when artists started to install their works outside. Charges were brought against Marzona because building permission could not be granted for agricultural land. "I hadn't asked anyone, I'd just gone ahead – after all, it was my land," says Marzona in his own defence. It was only thanks to the friendship of the local mayor and an astute architect friend that Marzona was able to formulate his application in such a way that retrospective planning permission was granted for the works of art in this rural setting. "But each time it was unbelievably laborious and wearing," recalls Marzona. In the end, a friend – the renowned architect Pietro Valle – had an inspired idea. In 1999 there were widespread discussions in the region of Udine concerning the need for new land-use plans. In view of this, Valle and Marzona decided to organise an international conference in Verzegnis for architects, town planners and representatives from the relevant local authorities. Marzona managed to arrange for the conference to take place in the historic school building at the edge of the village which his own great-grandfather had endowed. And it was in the context of this conference that the meadow in Verzegnis was presented as an exemplary cultural use of land in a rural setting. Everyone was taken by this unusual idea. And immediately Marzona's land was officially designated an "art meadow" – "The only legally certificated art meadow in Europe," adds Marzona, not without some satisfaction.

The village has by now taken the works of art to heart. The locals soon became proud of their "Art Park", as they call Egidio Marzona's project. In the tourist information leaflet and at the car park next to the meadow, this is the name that is used for this special attraction. By chance the collector discovered that there is even an audio guide with descriptions of the works, which people can borrow, free of charge, in a local pub. But Marzona does not like terms such as "sculpture park" or "art park". As he says, "I keep hearing that. But the sculptures are not in a park. It's a perfectly normal meadow. That's why I prefer to describe it as an 'art meadow'. There's no fence around it, people can go there whenever they want." And that is what they do. Sometimes the priest comes and shows the pyramid to the altar boys, sometimes young people have parties there at night with garish lighting, sometimes there are jazz concerts in amongst the sculptures. When Marzona installed Stephen Kaltenbach's ice sculpture *Fire on Ice* (2007), spectators came from all over the region. "I have no idea how the word spread so quickly." He shrugs his shoulders and looks around questioningly. The long slabs of ice for the temporary sculpture had to be specially brought from Naples on a lorry and stored in the mountains at a height of 6,000 feet until all the preparations had been made. When the massive block of ice was at last standing in the meadow without its cladding, images of flames were projected onto its surface. "It was wonderful – people stayed until late into the night." It took all of five days until the whole block of ice had melted away.

In art circles the art meadow has long been known to insiders. Students and art historians from Udine and Trieste regularly come to Verzegnis and discuss art in the midst of the sculptures. "Everyone uses the art in their own way," says Egidio Marzona, who takes great pleasure in the high degree of acceptance for contemporary art in this area: "In twenty-five years I have never once had any trouble with vandalism. The art is treated with respect. It has become part of the village – in the same way that Verzegnis is part of my life."

In Peter Kogler's labyrinth the visitor passes through a hip-high replica of the structure of the human brain.

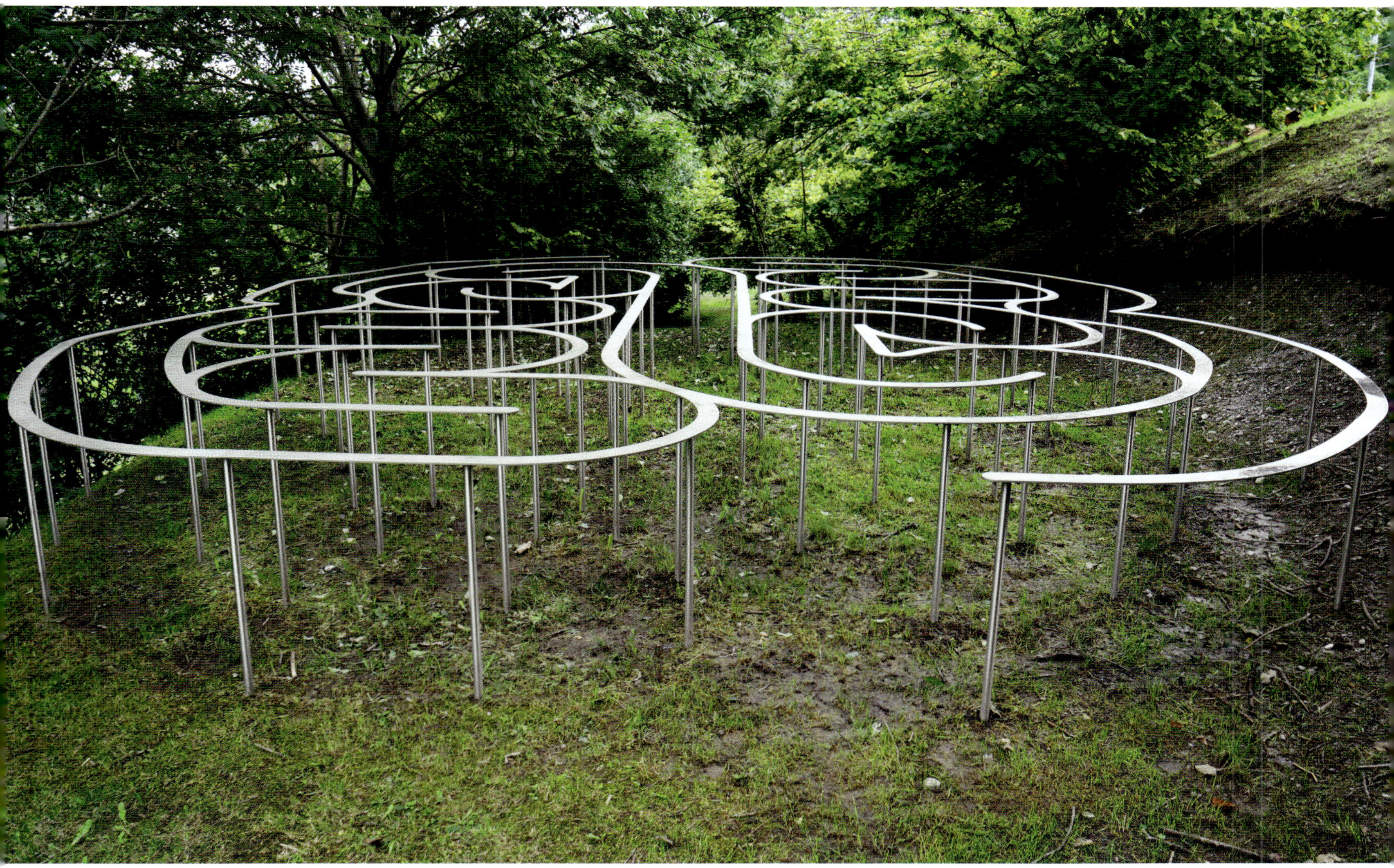

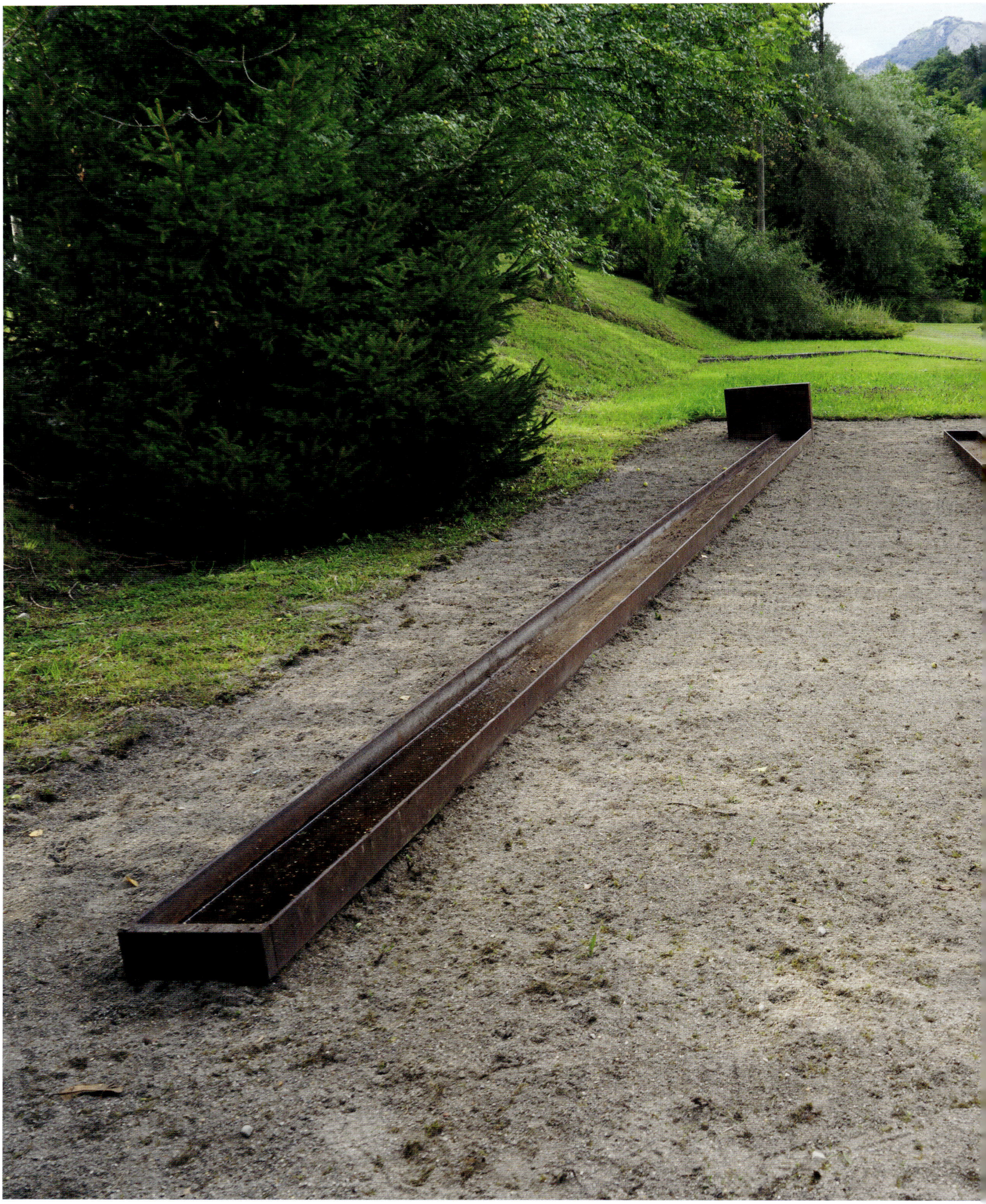

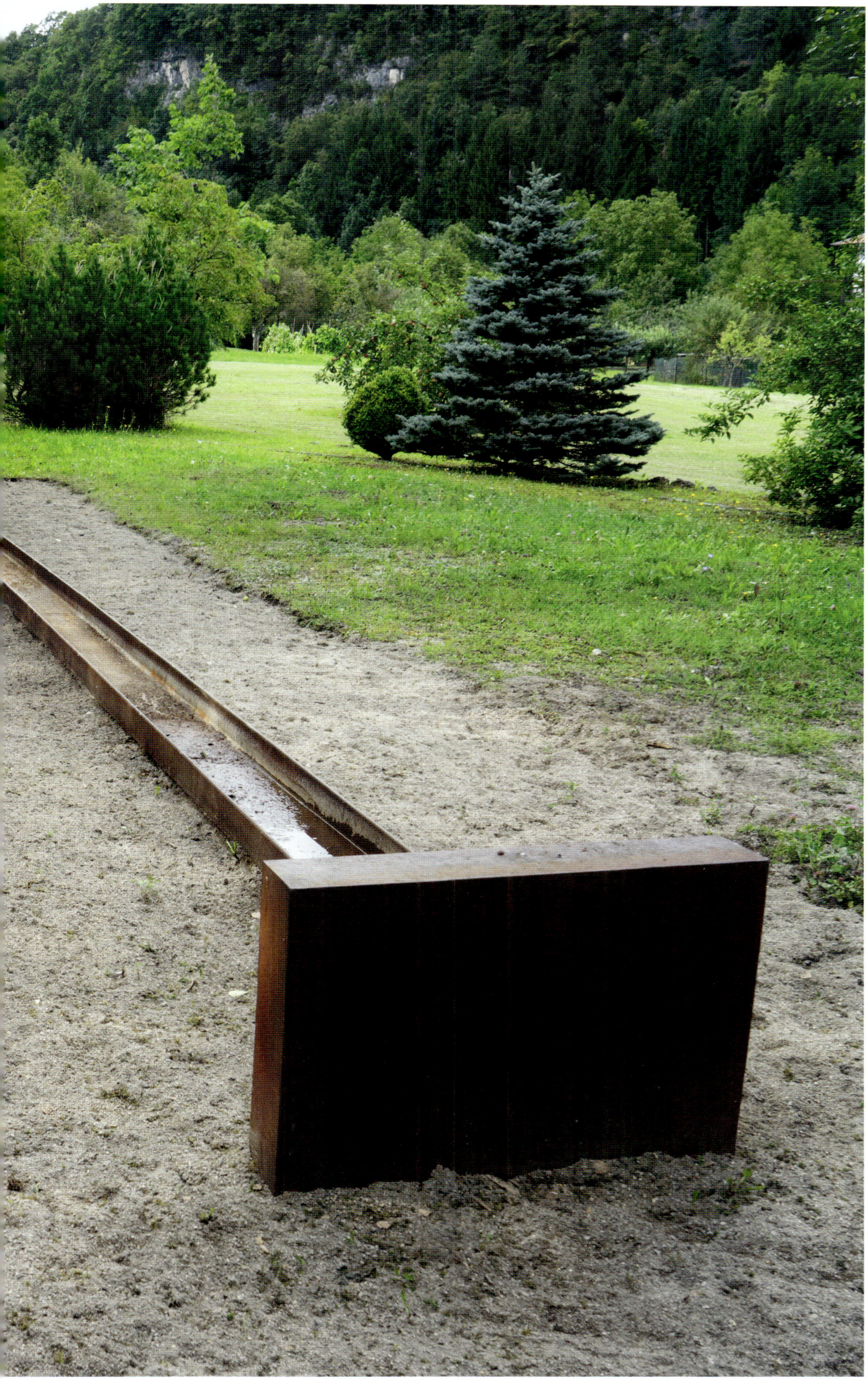

Depending on the visitor's standpoint, Richard Nonas's steel beams either appear to be parallel to each other or, as in this case, to be angled away from each other.

HUMOUR AGAINST NATURE'S PRIMAL FORCES

ART BY THE SEA, ZEALAND, DENMARK

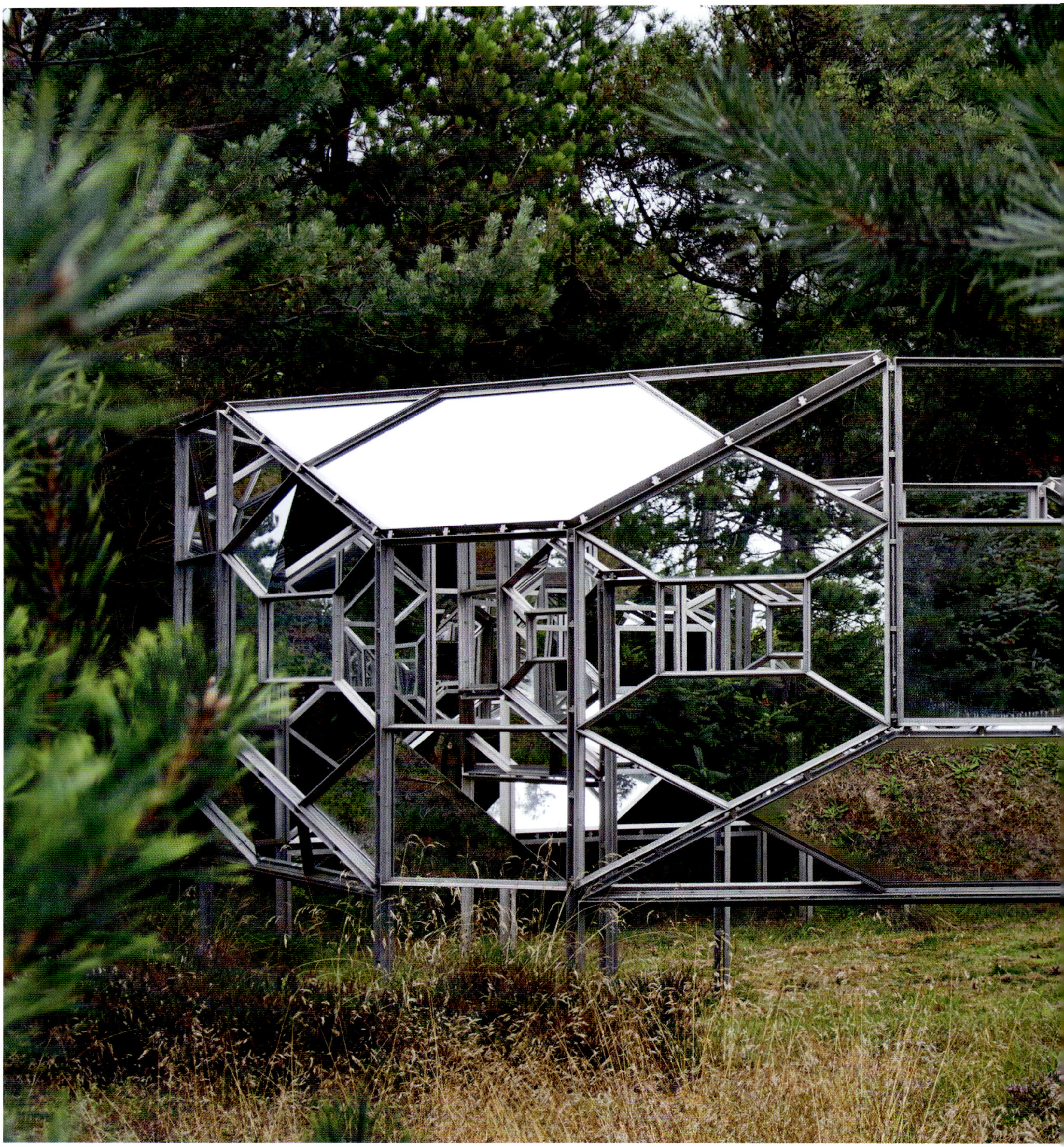

Olafur Eliasson's ***Your invisible house*****, a steel pavilion with panes of mirror glass disappears in amongst the pine trees.**

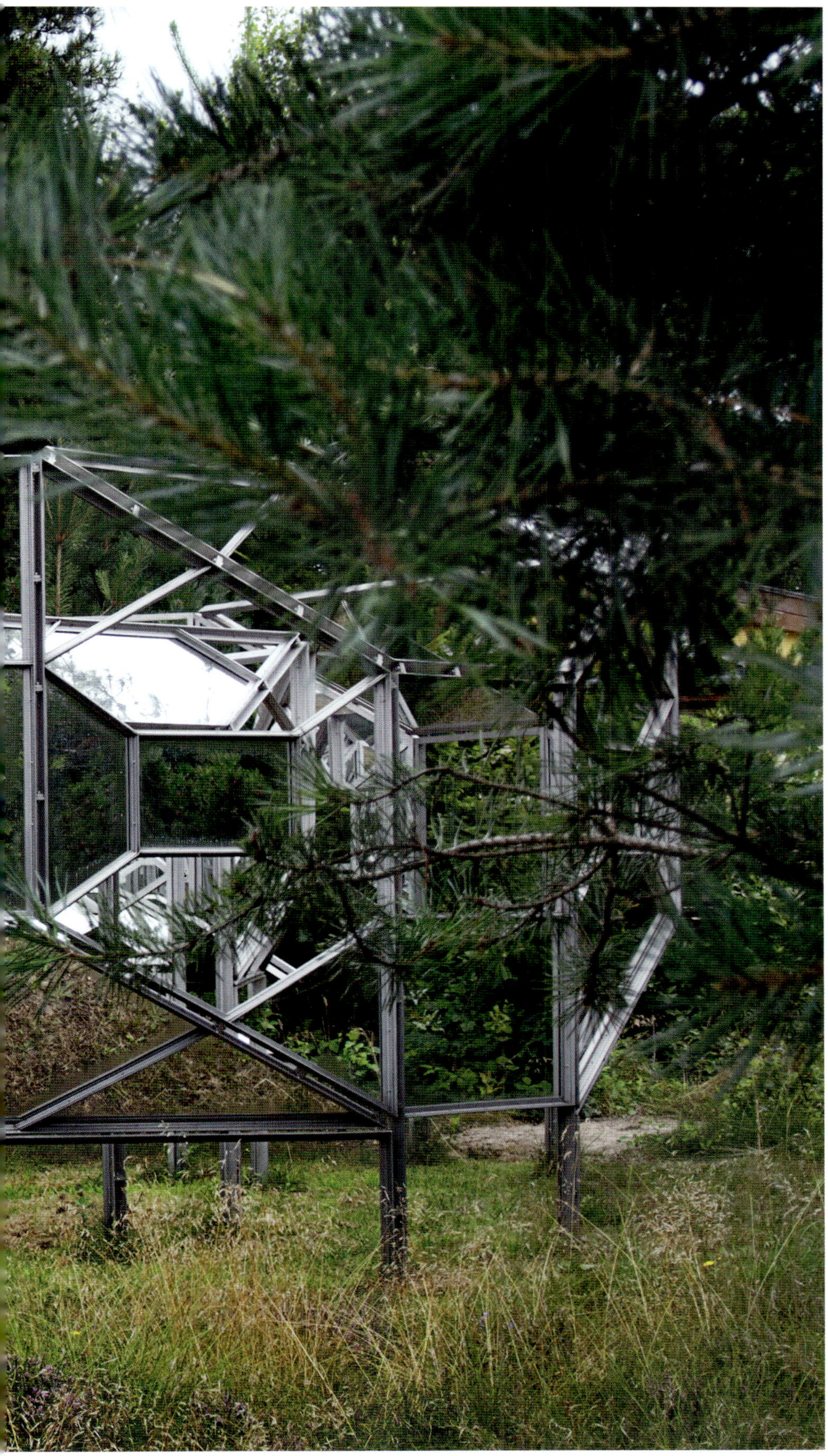

Carl Christian and Janne Ægidius epitomise the Scandinavian phenotype: tall, blond, direct. They are passionate sailors; they love the sea, the salty air, the wind. "Our sculpture garden could only exist in Denmark – where you can really feel the force of nature, where the landscape is so powerful," as Carl Christian says with conviction. They also like laughing – and that is reflected in the art in their grounds. A man-sized gorilla, bursting with energy, suddenly stretches his head towards visitors as they come up the otherwise unremarkable drive. *I Promise I Will Not Do It Again* (2004) is the macabre title of this sculpture by Angus Fairhurst. Barely have visitors passed this one-gorilla welcoming party than they find themselves parking next to *Mobili* (2001), a racing car (of sorts) by Miquel Barceló, with a chassis in the shape of a bird's skull and four flat tyres. Mockery also exudes from the gruesome monster, lurking in the bushes, by Andreas Golder, with the rather unsettling title, *In Memory of the Last Guest* (2008) – and then there is the human face by Fang Lijun, which appears to be ebbing away on a low wall. One thing is clear: this is the home of people who not only love bizarre things but who can also laugh about themselves. "There are so many art collectors who pursue their passion with positively deadly zeal. We're not like that. For us, art must above all be a source of joy; there has to be something in our works of art to make you smile," says Janne with a grin. Sharp humour, a tendency towards the bizarre or at least the capacity to somewhat unnerve the viewer is evident in almost all of the thirty or so sculptures that occupy this extensive site by the shore of Zealand. Many of the works are deliberately hidden: glancing into the shrubbery, the visitor suddenly spies a strange creature with chicken legs, which Bas de Witt has put into gumboots. The title, *Errors and Omissions Accepted* (2008), is a perfect fit for this sexless being. Only visible from behind, it appears to be relieving itself against one of the trees. And then there is bewilderment at the sight of *The Mad Glad Tree* (2005) by Kenny Scharf, which stops the visitor cold: a tree, grimacing wildly, bearing fruit on its branches in the shape of laughing sperm. In the lower part of the grounds there is Olafur Eliasson's *Your invisible house* (2005) – a spectacular mirror installation, mysteriously shimmering through the dark pines. This pavilion with mirror-glass facets consists of two steel structures, one within the other. Its geometric shapes create multiple perspectives that appear to cause the work to dematerialise. Eliasson toys wonderfully with the viewer's perceptions, constantly unsettling them. Standing inside the artwork with its many window-like openings, it is hard to decide whether one is looking at the real heathland or reflections of it. These multiple reflections make it appear as though the pavilion is merging into its surroundings, with the visitor caught up in the midst of it.

Another weird creature confronting the visitor is the oversized, painted bronze eagle by Jonathan Meese, *TOTALADLER, Baby-CHEF der Kunst (das Ei des Columbussy)* (2007), which stands in open ground. Its feathers are laden with grotesque allusions – from the Dionysian egg to lunch boxes, from egg boxes and bottle tops to a Viking-style headdress. And what is that dark figure by Yue Minjun doing at the sandy area at the furthest edge of the grounds? A Chinese man, grinning for all he is worth and wielding a metal detector, has just come across a tractor. *3009* (2008) is the title, making a mockery of what we are leaving for posterity: the archaeologists of the future – naturally all of them Chinese – will only find industrial waste in the Western world. But at the same time Yue Minjun also casts doubt on the superiority of his compatriots. The Chinese peasant's grin is exaggerated and his expression is more of an artificial grimace, of the kind seen on so many of the painted and sculpted faces by the artist; it is the smile of a population trained to grin and bear whatever life (and politics) throws at them. After all, who believes everything they see? Carl Christian takes the view that "it's good to be challenged in such a fun way to take a second look at things."

The idea of creating a sculpture garden in the wild grounds around their striking thatched home directly by the sea "was never a clearly defined intention, it just happened over the years," as Carl Christian's wife Janne explains, recalling their initial forays into collecting, in 2002. However, they were very clear about one thing: they did not want to have a garden where the works of art are simply added as embellishments. "There are too many gardens like that. For us the idea of nature as the right frame for art was as important as the works of art," she explains. Before any purchases, the couple discuss where any new works would best be placed. And it is only when both are sure they have reached the right conclusion that they start making the necessary preparations in the garden, which can be very complex. Not only

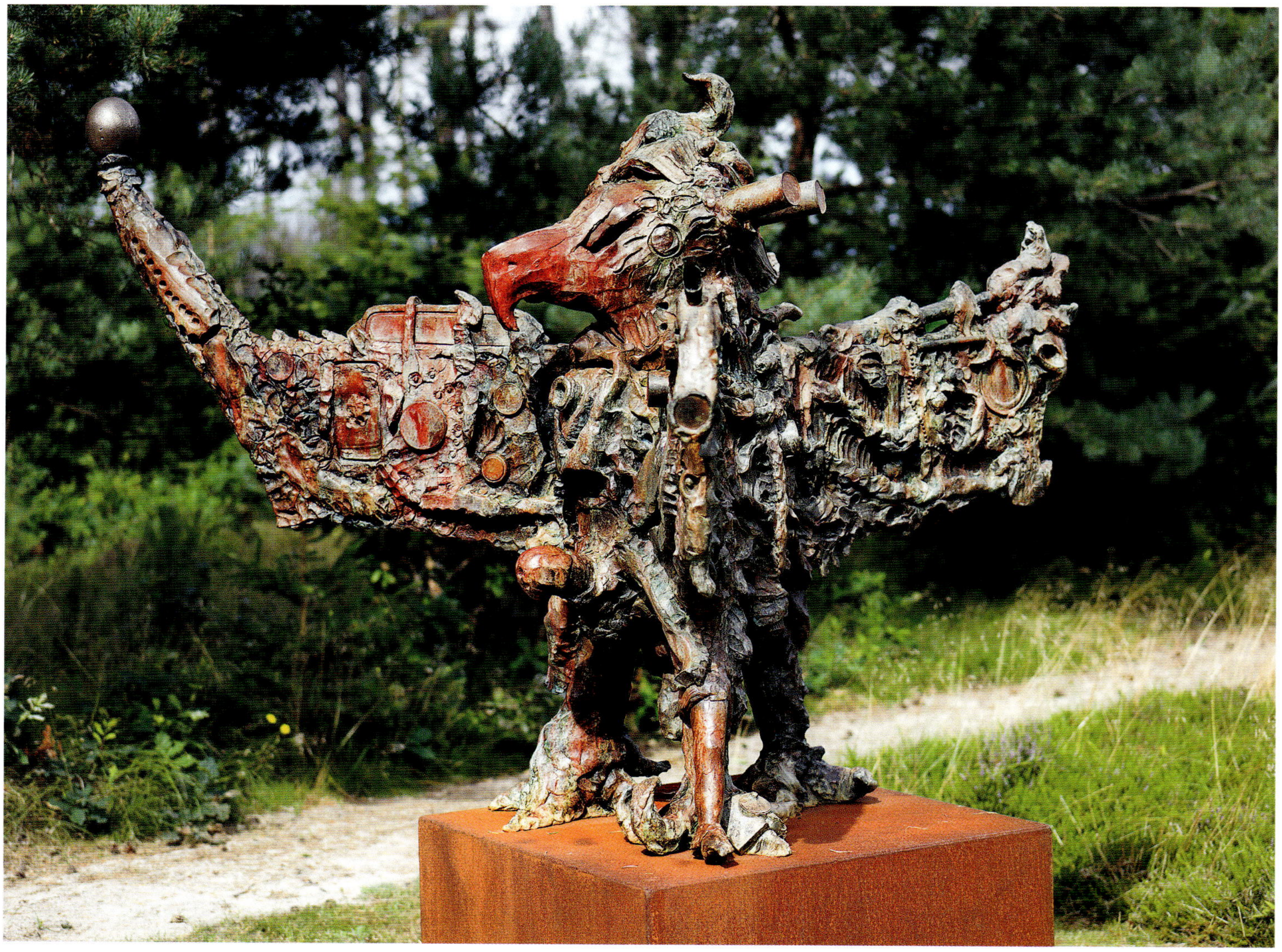

Left: Jonathan Meese pokes fun at the German Federal eagle with casts made from scraps and rubbish.

have trees been felled, rhododendrons moved, terraces created and stable plinths anchored in the ground, the existing vegetation has at times been 'helped along' with plants that are native to the area, such as heathers, gorse and dog roses, as Janne describes the work they undertake in the garden. "In our garden every sculpture has the space it needs, but it also blends harmoniously with the natural setting. Our overriding aim is to make any interventions into nature as imperceptible as possible. The work of art should, as far as possible, be so embedded in its natural surroundings that you would think it had always been there." The best example of this is Jonathan Meese's *TOTALADLER*. It occupies a prominent position in a flowering heathland. The colours on its feathers seem to have been taken from its own natural setting: lilac, brown, blue, green. In reality, before the eagle arrived Carl Christian and Janne Ægidius painstakingly planted the heathers in this barren, sandy soil. Day after day they watered and weeded. "People always think this sculpture was specifically made for this spot, but we bought it as it is. Jonathan was thrilled when the helicopter lowered the bird into our heathland. The colours, the structures – in any other situation they would never make the same impact as in these surroundings," explains Carl Christian.

Many of the sculptures here, above all the more recent ones, were made in situ in close collaboration with the two collectors. When, for instance, it was time to choose the colour for the sculpture *On Top of One Another* (2009) by Thomas Kiesewetter, the artist was in favour of white. "But white was out of the question, as far as we were concerned," recalls Janne. "There are no whites here, if anything there are blues, like

A sarcastic greeting to guests coming up the drive: Angus Fairhurst's gorilla detaches his own head.

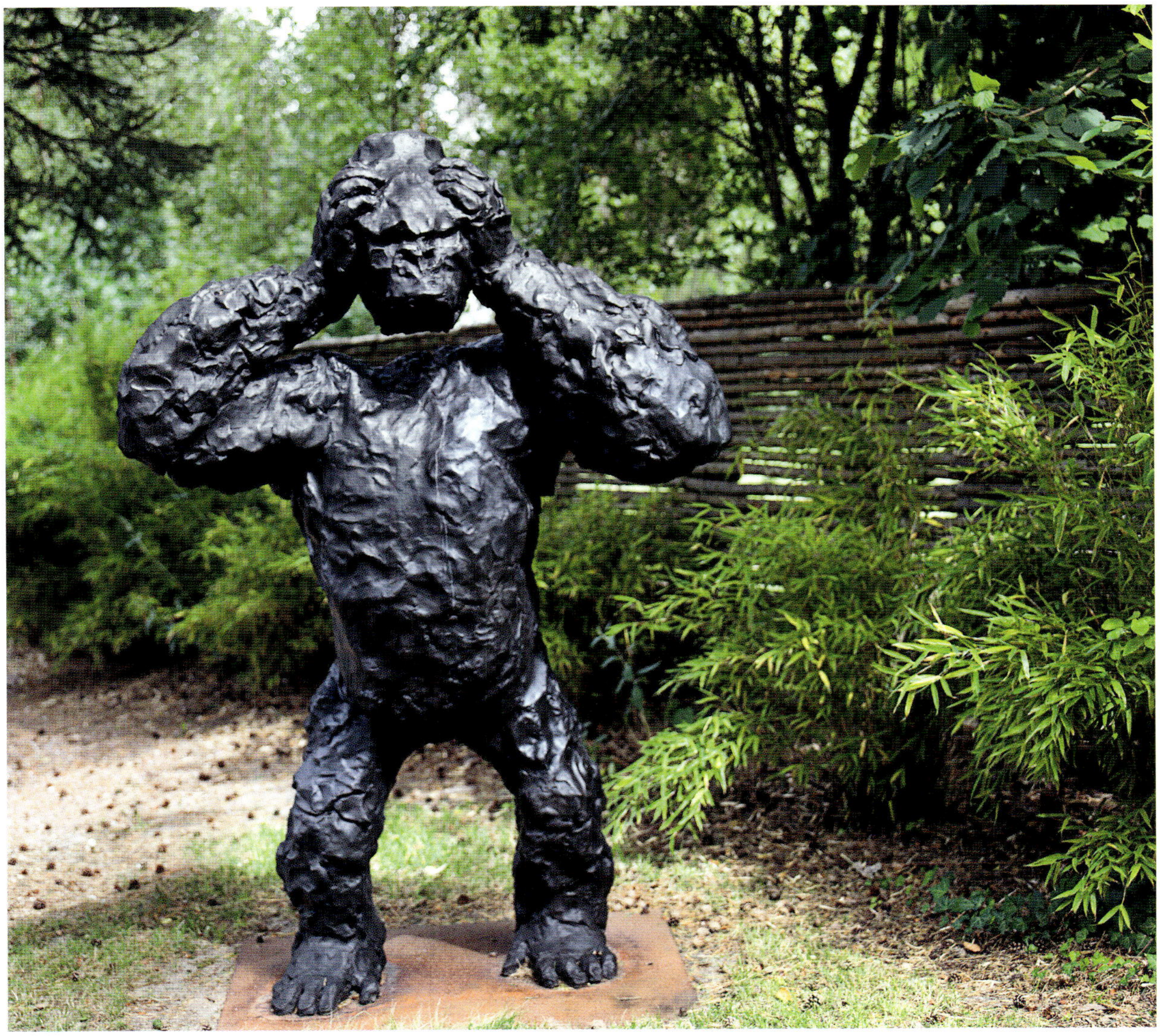

the sky and the water. But it couldn't be a pure blue – anyone who knows the sea also knows that the colours of the sea are always changing; it had to be a matt blue, with a lot of grey in it. And he agreed with us." Colour is also under discussion in the case of a relatively new commission, *Who Is There* (2011), which the Berlin artist Katharina Grosse returned to work on – a brightly coloured volcano that extends from one side of the garden into the terraced central section and onto a bench. "Our bonsai volcano," as the collectors and the artist affectionately call it, because although it is tiny compared to a real volcano it exudes the majestic presence of a huge mountain as one walks round it or sits down on the bench and feels the 'mountain' at one's back. The effort required for this installation was immense. The site had to be cleared and re-terraced and a steel foundation had to be anchored in the ground under the artificial mountain in order to support the covering of earth and paint. The artist raises another cause for concern: "Our main worry, however, is the climate here, and the very high salinity of the air." In light of this, she has come back to apply another coat of varnish before winter sets in. But this is also a visit to friends, because while Janne and Carl Christian live for and with their works of art, they also feel as though the artists are "part of the family ... they all like coming here, they love the place, the peace, the expansiveness of the natural setting." For the collectors there is nothing better than sitting with their friends at the long dining room table. Apart from that they live very quietly and would rather that strangers did not come to visit their garden. Only one is always welcome: in the middle of the vast terrace, there is a stranger (*Der Fremde*, 2010) sitting on the ground – a dark-skinned youth, with a naked upper body, by Stella Hamberg – gazing with a melancholy air out over the garden to the horizon beyond the sea's vast expanse.

Miquel Barceló's racing car *Mobili* in the car park by the house.

Right: Yue Minjun's image of metal-detecting in the year 3009 envisages the future's amusement at finds from present-day Europe.

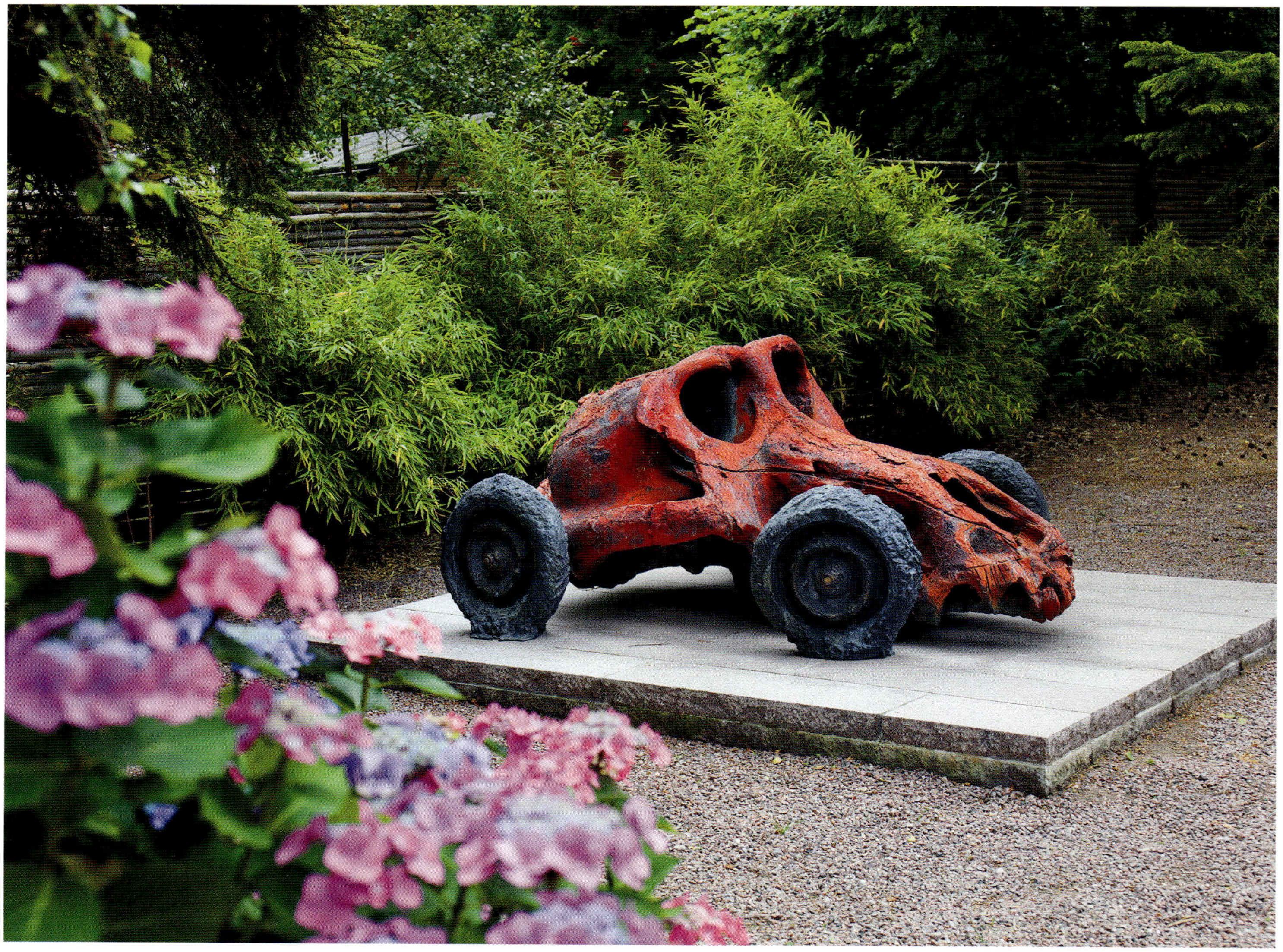

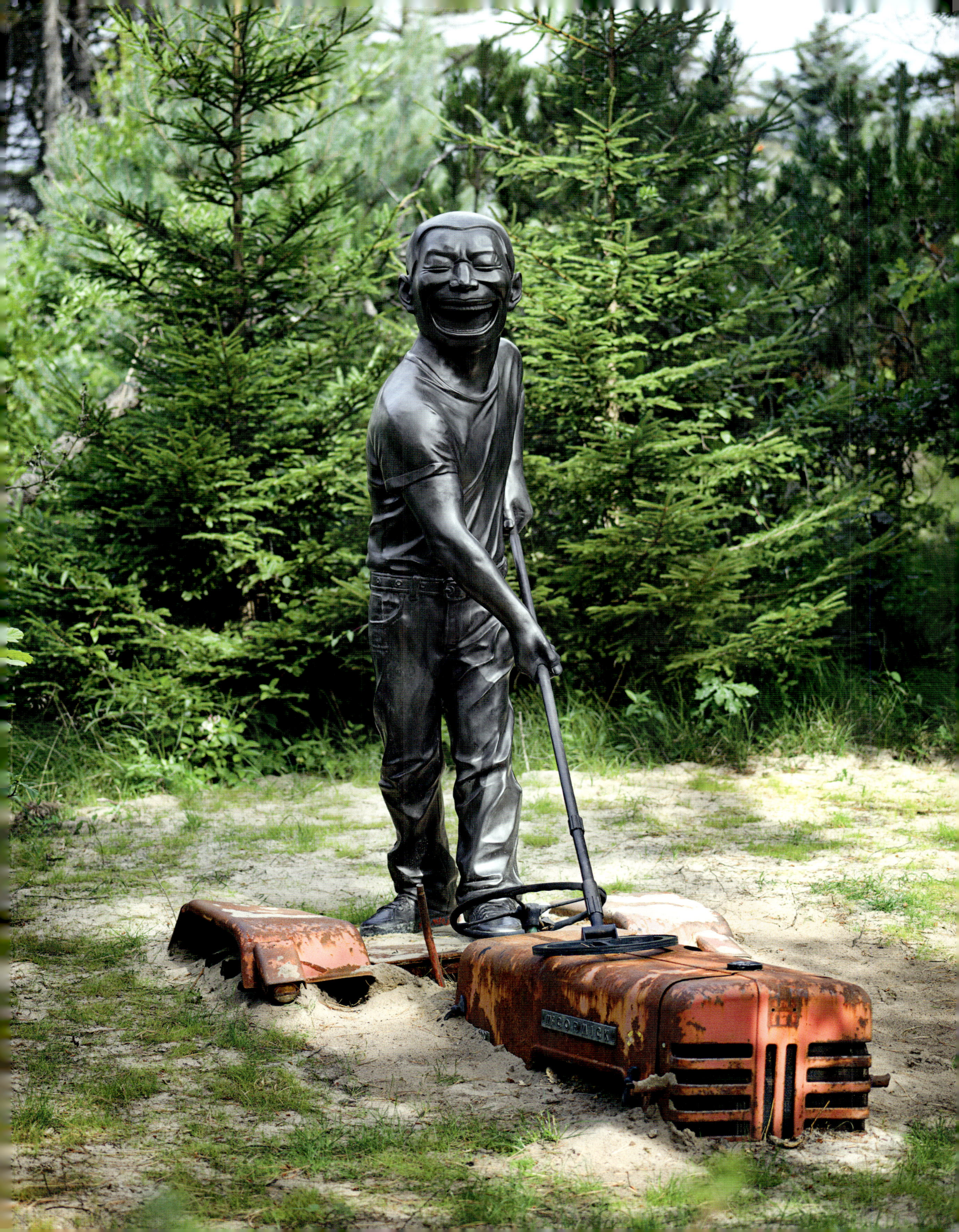
McCORMICK

ARTISTIC DIALOGUE AT A CROSSROADS OF HISTORY
ST. MARGARETHEN SCULPTURE PARK, ST. MARGARETHEN, AUSTRIA

St. Margarethen Sculpture Park in northern Burgenland is situated in a special part of Austria. On one side of this striking hill in the easternmost region of Austria the visitor can gaze across the misty Neusiedler Lake to the endless Hungarian Puszta; on the other side the vast Austrian plain is interrupted by the Leitha Mountains, beyond which lies Vienna, with its long and complex history. The sculpture park is on the cusp between Western and Eastern Europe. Throughout history this region has been highly contested and an ancient point of contact for different cultures. These lands, once ruled by the mighty Hungarian princes from the Esterházy family, marked the end of the caravan routes used by peoples from the Steppes, and it was here that Turkish warriors gathered before launching their attack on Vienna. For forty years after the Second World War, up until 1989, the Iron Curtain ran past the foot of the hill, dividing Europe into a democratic West and a communist East and symbolising the Cold War being waged by hostile super powers. Now that same hill is part of the UNESCO World Cultural Heritage Site because of its history and special fauna.

One person who witnessed that division and found it insufferable was the stone sculptor Karl Prantl (1923–2010) from nearby Pöttsching. In 1958, when the provincial government in Burgenland commissioned him to create a sculpture for the border crossing between Nickelsdorf in Austria and Hegyeshalom in Hungary, he named his work *Grenzstein* (Boundary Stone) – as a political statement and as a plea for peace and the abolition of all borders. Prantl wanted to galvanise the public. And he and a number of other sculptors repeated this statement in 1961 in Berlin not far from the Reichstag, in protest at the construction of the Berlin Wall. Both actions created a considerable stir in the media. But the work Prantl had done on his *Grenzstein* in the St. Margarethen quarry in 1958 also came to mean more to him, giving rise to his idea of creating a forum for international dialogue by setting up a series of sculptors' symposiums. His plan was to work with sculptors from abroad – above all from the Eastern Bloc – throughout the summer months, exchanging ideas and ultimately blazing an artistic trail with the works they had created, unconstrained by national borders and political systems.

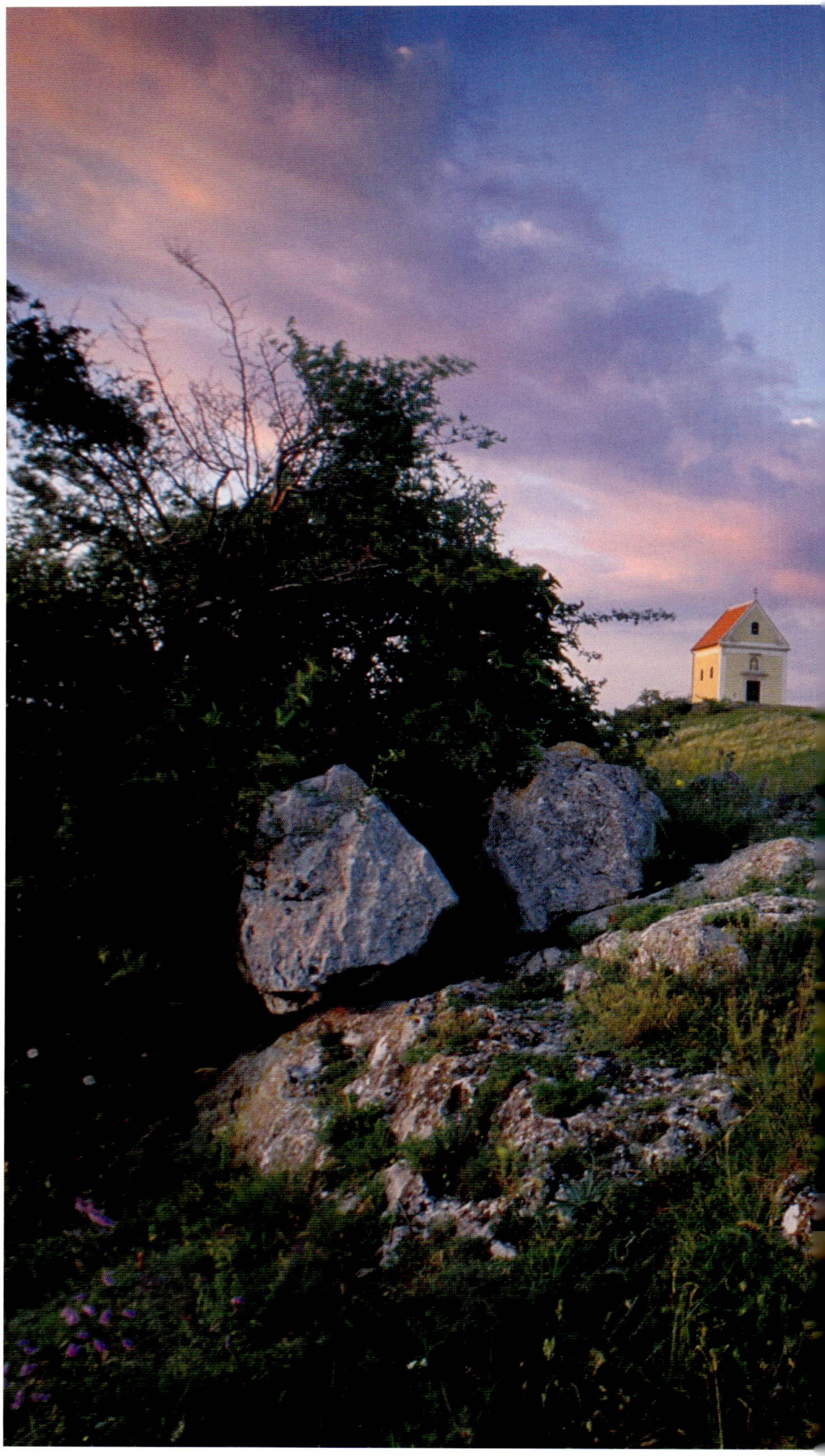

Minoru Niizuma's imposing sculpture balances on a rocky perch within sight of the chapel on the hill at St. Margarethen.

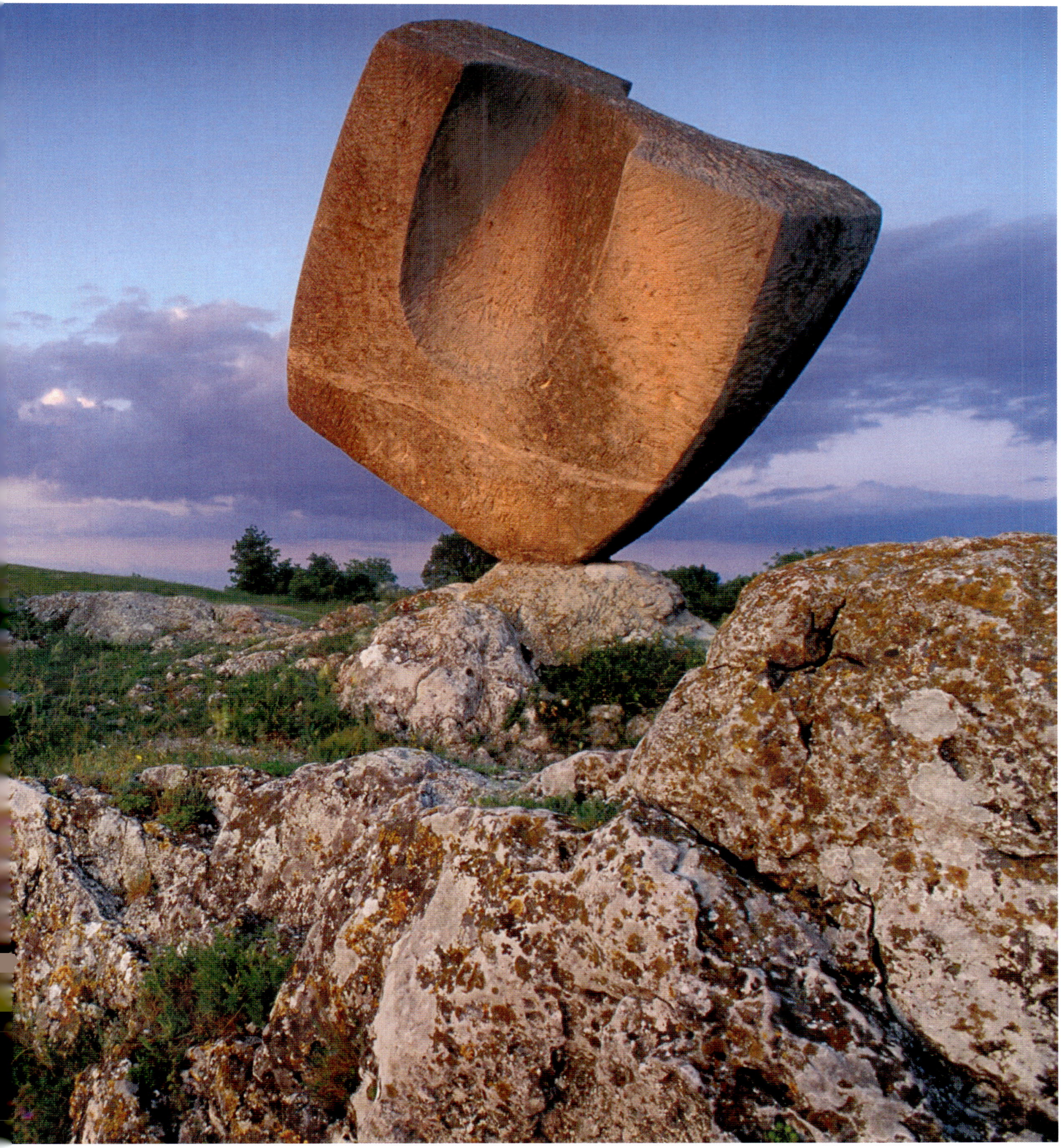

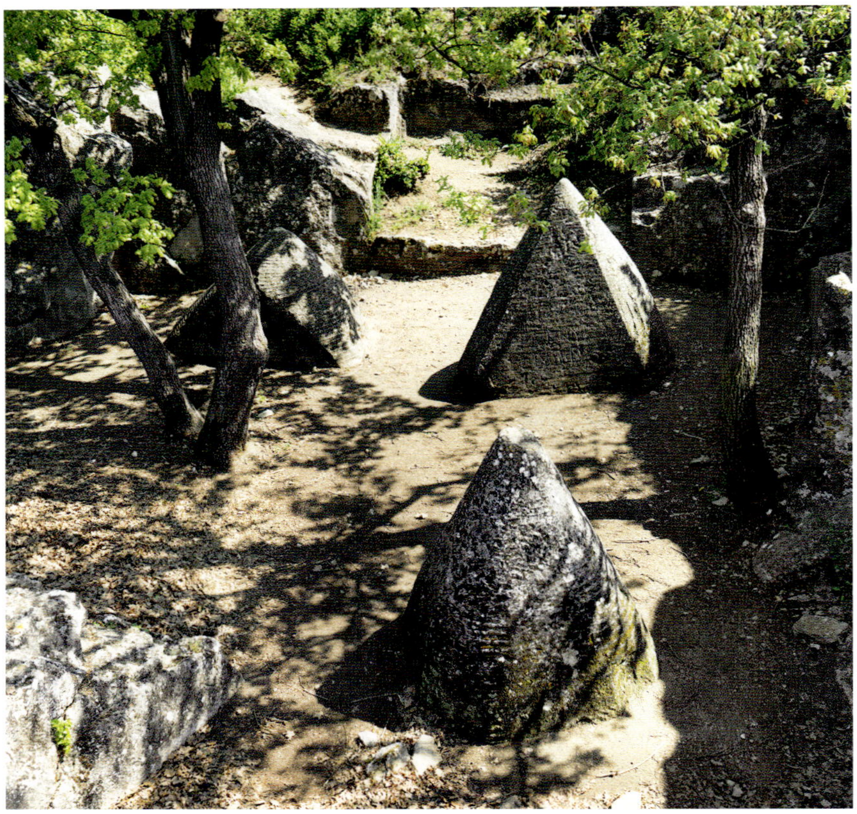

A gift from one culture to another: Kengiro Azuma has hidden his Land Art installation between cliffs.

And so it was that the first St. Margarethen Sculptors' Symposium, in 1959, instigated an international movement. Participants at that first symposium subsequently set up similar events in their home countries – initially across Europe and ultimately throughout the world.

The St. Margarethen quarry became an international art mecca. Each year Karl Prantl invited up to sixteen artists from abroad to spend the summer in St. Margarethen. They lived and worked side by side in the open air, engaging in conversation and debate. By the 1970s the artists had created over a hundred works, distributed across the hillside where the St. Margarethen quarry is located. Little by little, one of the earliest and most impressive sculpture parks in Europe came into being, with a wide variety of abstract works made from the local, pale sandy limestone – some in the form of steles or blocks, others with perforations or constructed from several parts. The broad saddle of the hill was now home to sculptures – some as tall as their makers – that could be seen from afar in this otherwise flat landscape. And anyone climbing the hill today will also find works that seem to be hiding in their natural surroundings, or have become part of nature, like the four-part installation *Untitled* (1971) by Kengiro Azuma in a deep hollow or the *Japanische Linie* (1970), a piece of Land Art jointly created by five Japanese artists – Makoto Fujiwara, Makio Yamaguchi, Tetsuzo Yamamoto, Takao Hirose and Satoru Shoji – which runs, in the form of a incision, from the innermost depths of the quarry up through the rocks to the brow of the hill.

The artists only worked where they found their materials – in the quarry and, later on, on the hillside. After all, it was down in the quarry that the idea of the sculptors' symposium had been born. It had been here, in 1958, working on his *Grenzstein*, that Prantl experienced and re-evaluated the essence of stone sculpture from the point of view of the sculptor. The forms he created arose not from preparatory drawings but from his dialogue with nature, from his intense, direct engagement with the stone itself. Before laying bare the stone's 'veins', he would touch and listen to the rock. As he explained, "The stones talk to me." His approach to his material placed him firmly in the tradition of the Romanian sculptor Constantin Brancusi (1876–1957). Karl Prantl wanted other artists to share with him the intensity of this dialogue between a sculptor and his materials in the midst of nature – in the very place where the rocks were extracted from the ground, in one of the largest and oldest quarries in Europe. The Romans had already quarried sandy limestone in St. Margarethen. The quarry had provided the stone used for such notable buildings as the medieval Stephansdom (St Stephen's Cathedral) and the Baroque Karlskirche (St Charles' Church) in Vienna. The participating artists in the symposium showed their respect for this ancient material by pledging to only work with hammer and chisel – and thus to return to the methods used by the very first sculptors – slowly working the massive blocks of limestone with those principles in mind. That had in fact been the main consideration for Prantl when he first came up with his idea: to share an intense dialogue on the way that the sculptor engages with his or her material, wrestling with the hard stone, experiencing that physical and mental effort and making the results – the works of art – visible to others in the landscape, and challenging others to engage in their own international dialogue and ultimately to take things forwards together.

However, the organisation of that first symposium in 1959 proved to be more complicated than Prantl had imagined. While he took care of the logistics in St. Margarethen, his two co-organisers – the Viennese sculptor Heinrich Deutsch (1925–2004) and the psychologist and art critic Friedrich Czagan (b. 1927) – searched Europe for artists who represented the new zeitgeist, whose work was exclusively abstract and who were interested in working with other artists rather than competing with them. Although the quarry's leaseholder, Gustave Hummel, provided the sculptors with head-high blocks of stone free of charge, it was still a major challenge to raise the funds needed for this ambitious project – which included free board and lodging for the artists throughout their

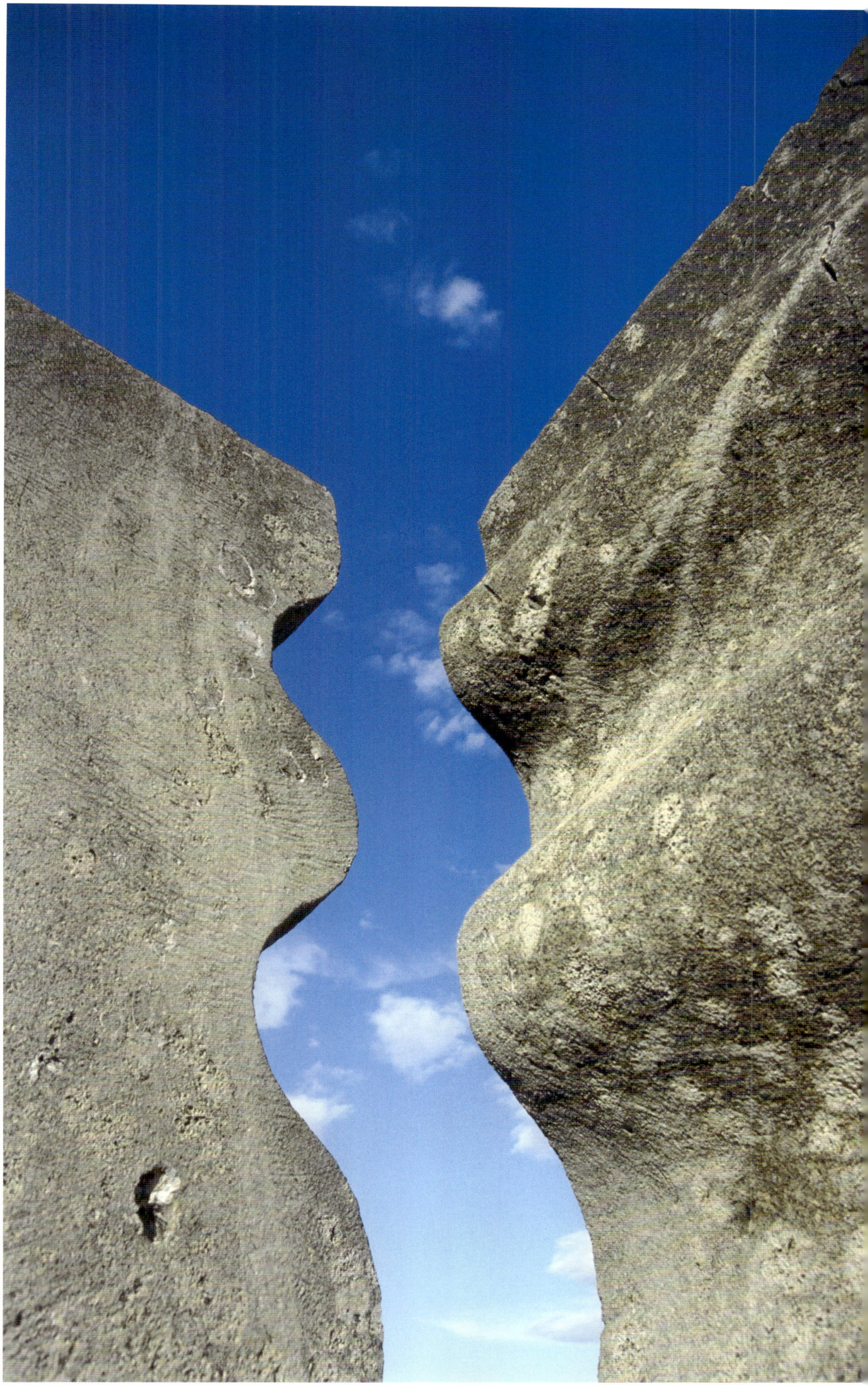

A detail of Peter Holowka's sculpture. He was only allowed to work with hammer and chisel – out of respect for the ancient material.

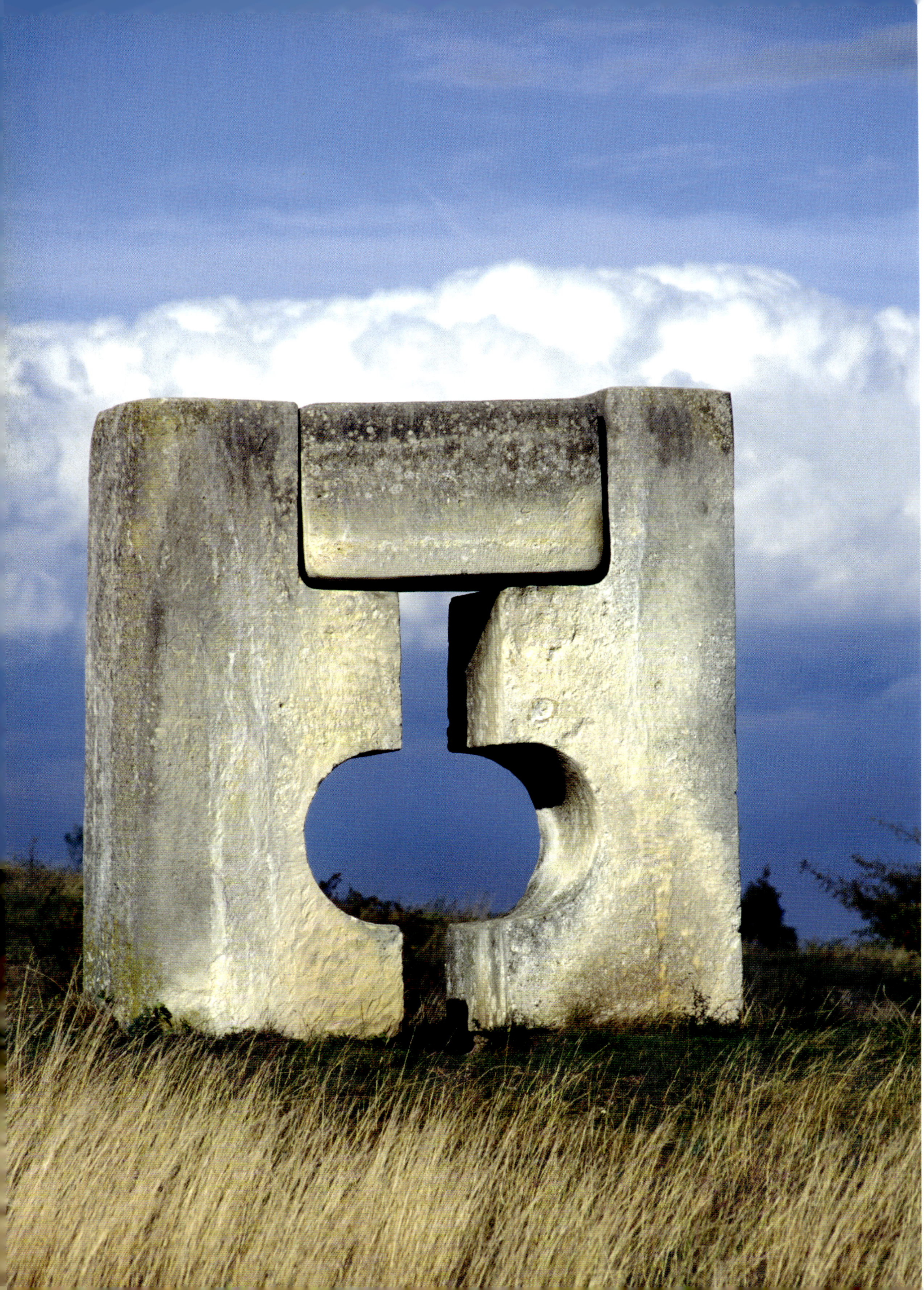

Left: Like all the artists who worked here, Barna von Sartory created an abstract piece.

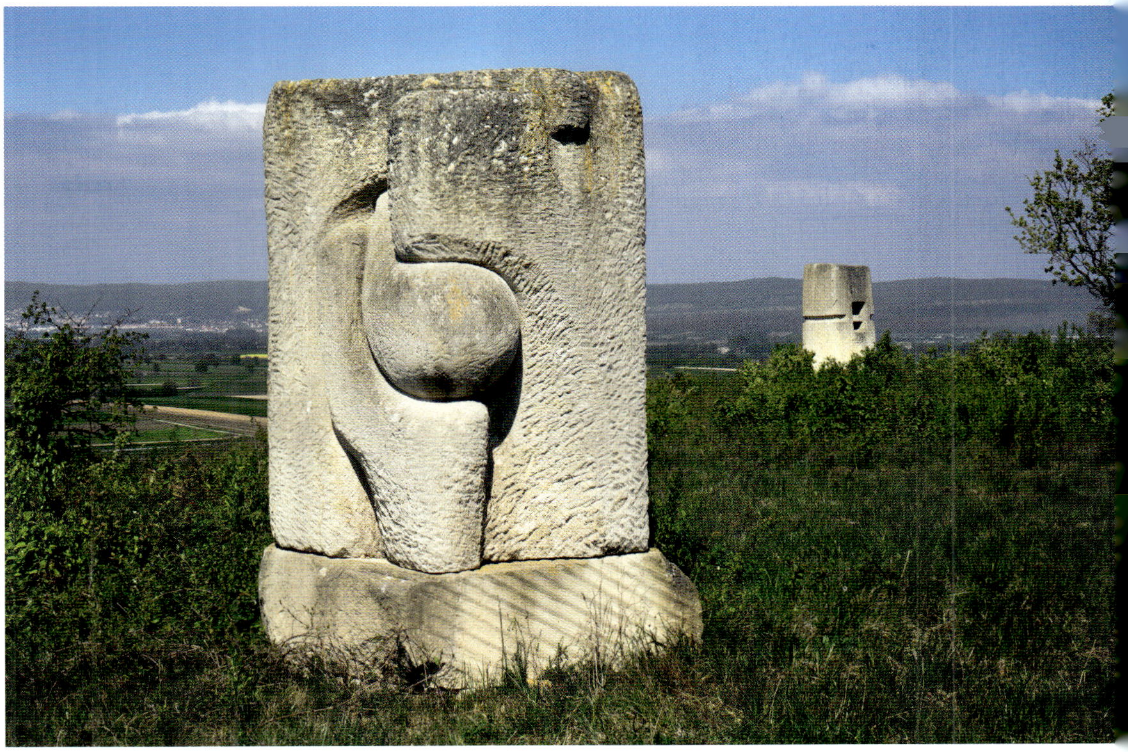

The artists often worked within sight of each other – the hill was workshop and exhibition space in one.

three-month stay. The first eleven artists came from eight countries: Karl Prantl (Austria), Dino Paolino (Italy), Peter Meister (Switzerland), Eugène Dodeigne (Belgium), Jacques Moeschal (Belgium), Hans Verhulst (Holland), Gerson Fehrenbach (Federal Republic of Germany), Erich Reischke (German Democratic Republic), André Willequet (Belgium), Josef Wyss (Switzerland) and Janez Lenassi (Slovenia). Looking back, Prantl's wife, Uta Prantl-Peyrer, commented that they had "so little money, they could only give the artists a watery bowl of soup once a day." They ate in a little shed out in the quarry. The artists slept in tents or stayed in simple lodgings in the surrounding area. It was only later that those first participants founded an association that would allow them to receive public funding and thus to ensure, as far as possible, the financial viability of future symposiums. In 1967 it also allowed them to construct their own sculptors' house, designed by the avant-garde architect Johann Georg Gsteu (1927–2013), on the western side of the hill where the quarry was situated. Here, too, the spartan sleeping quarters with bunk beds and the large common room reflected Prantl's vision of the sculptors living and working together.

When the sculptures made during that summer of 1959 were exhibited at the end of the first symposium, the undertaking's success was immediately obvious. Reviewers made particular mention of the spirit of "international rapprochement and of the bonds forged between different peoples in this coming together of young Europeans," and in 1960 the renowned art critic Alfred Schmeller was openly enthusiastic: "This symposium of European sculptors in the most beautiful quarry has to be the most interesting artistic experiment of our own time – workshop and exhibition in one." In the 1960s and 1970s the symposium became synonymous with artistic freedom for all the artists, but especially for those from the Eastern Bloc. By the second year of its existence Prantl was already receiving enquiries from artists outside Europe – in Japan, Israel and India – wishing to participate. On their return home many founded similar symposiums. Prantl's idea had made a global impact.

Although each year saw a new group of participants arriving in St. Margarethen, the works of art they placed in the landscape remained – as a record and as a symbol of the artistic and spiritual dialogue surrounding their making. Moving monumental blocks of stone from the quarry into position by means of winches and rollers – operated by human power alone – was always an arduous task. Little by little an art landscape came into being, with highly diverse artistic positions. And even though, following the death of her husband Karl in 2010, Uta Prantl-Peyrer relocated some important works to his home parish of Pöttsching, St. Margarethen is still regarded as one of the most important sculpture landscapes in Europe. Many founders of new sculpture parks have sought inspiration here.

The symposiums became the life's work of their initiator, Karl Prantl. And to this day the idea of the symposiums is still nurtured by his family, who have adapted it to a contemporary context. Karl Prantl's son Sebastian now uses the sculptures in St. Margarethen as the central focus of his international workshops for dance, photography, botany and drawing.

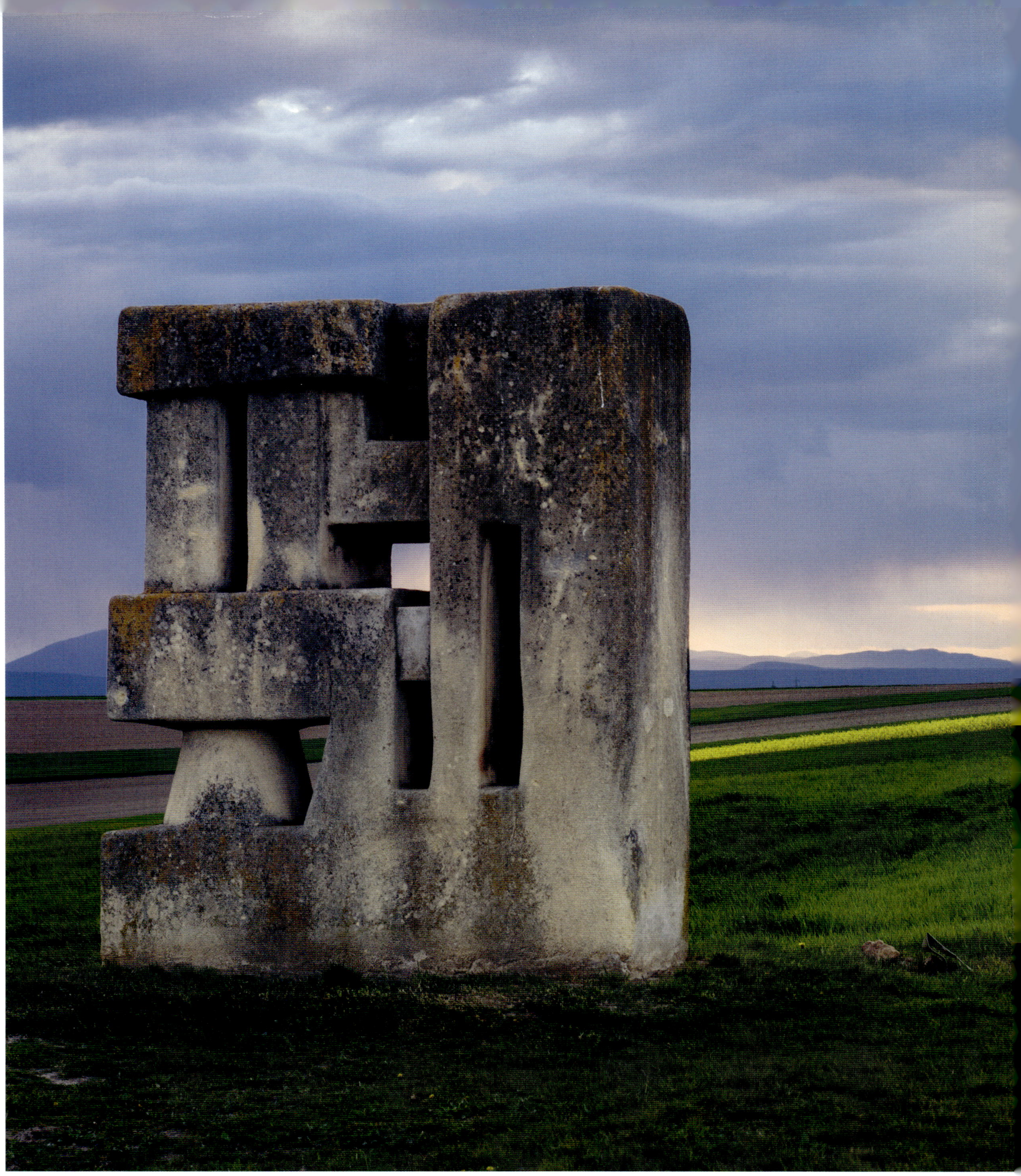

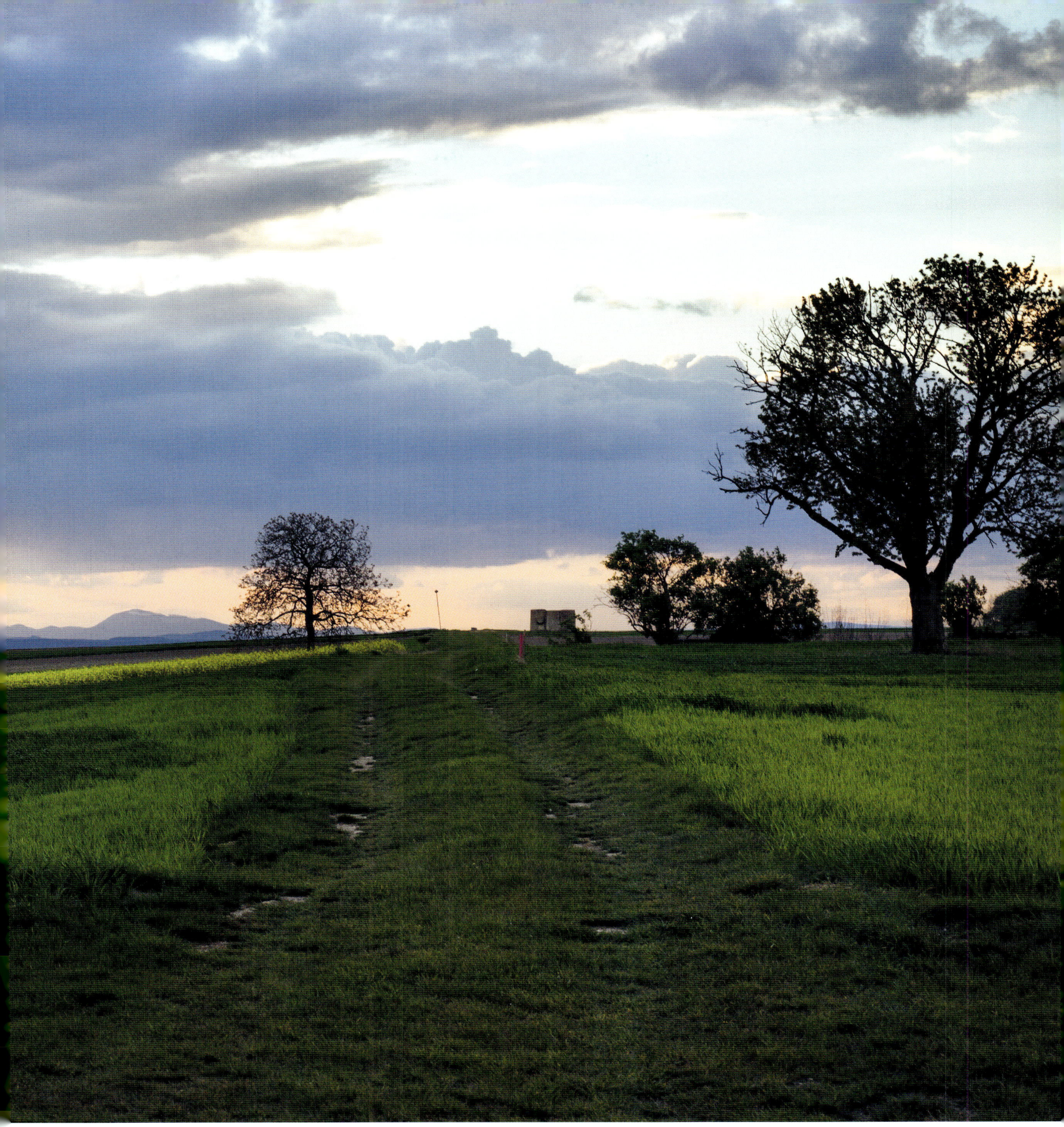

Karl Prantl's *Grenzstein* – a symbol not only of the division of Europe but also of the potential for greater mutual understanding through artists' symposiums.

ADDRESSES AND VISITOR INFORMATION

Architectural Sculptures on the Plaine de Marha
Oasis de Fezna, Erfoud, Errachidia Province
Morocco
www.hannsjoerg-voth.de/10c_englisch.html
Visits must be scheduled with a tour guide in advance.

Art by the Sea
Zealand
Denmark
Not open to the public

Art Park
Villa di Verzegnis
33020 Verzegnis (Udine)
Italy
www.carniamusei.org/museo.html?entityID=435
Guided tours upon request. Open year-round

Benesse Art Site Naoshima
On the islands of
Naoshima, Kagawa 7613110
Teshima, Tonosho-cho, Shozu-gun, Kagawa 7614662
Inujima, Higashi-ku, Okayama 7048153
Japan
www.benesse-artsite.jp/en
Open year-round

Centro de Arte Contemporânea Inhotim
Rua B, 20, Inhotim
Brumadinho, 35460-000 (Minas Gerais)
Brazil
www.inhotim.org.br/en
Open year-round, Tuesday through Sunday

Château la Coste
2750 Route de la Cride
13610 Le Puy-Sainte-Réparade (Bouches-du-Rhône)
France
www.chateau-la-coste.com/home
Visitors must register in advance.

Connells Bay
142 Cowes Bay Road
Waiheke Island
New Zealand
www.connellsbay.co.nz
Guided tours upon prior registration.
Open late October to late April

Ekebergparken
Kongsveien 23
0193 Oslo
Norway
www.ekebergparken.com/en
Guided tours upon prior registration.
Open year-round

Fattoria di Celle
Gori Collection
Via Montalese 7
51030 Santomato (Pistoia)
Italy
www.goricoll.it
Guided tours upon prior registration.
Open May to September

Fundaziun Not Vital
At the western village entrance
7554 Sent
Switzerland
www.notvital.ch/not-dal-mot/en.php
Guided tours upon prior registration.
Fridays from June to October

The Garden of Cosmic Speculation
Portrack House
Dumfries, Dumfries and Galloway, Scotland, DG2 0RA
UK
www.charlesjencks.com/#!the-garden-of-cosmic-speculation
Open on one day each year or upon prior request

Gibbs Farm
2421 Kaipara Coast Highway
Makarau 0984
New Zealand
www.gibbsfarm.org.nz
Visitors must register in advance.

Jardín Botánico Culiacán
Avenida de las Américas 2131, Col. Burócrata
Culiacán, Sinaloa 80030
Mexico
www.botanicoculiacan.org
Open year-round

Judd and Chinati Foundation
Judd Foundation
104 Highland Avenue South
Marfa, Texas 79843
USA
www.juddfoundation.org
Visitors must register in advance.
Open year-round

The Chinati Foundation
1 Cavalry Row
Marfa, Texas 79843
USA
www.chinati.org
Guided tours upon prior registration.
Open year-round, Wednesday through Sunday

La Ribaute
Near
30430 Barjac (Gard)
France
Not open to the public

Las Pozas
20 de Noviembre
Xilitla, San Luis Potosí 79900
Mexico
www.xilitla.org
Open year-round

Little Sparta
Stonypath
Dunsyre, Lanark, South Lanarkshire, Scotland, ML11 8NG
UK
www.littlesparta.org.uk
Open June to September, Friday through Sunday

Museo Subacuático de Arte
Between Punta Nizuc and Isla Mujeres
Cancún, Quintana Roo 77500
Mexico
www.musacancun.org/english
Diving tours permitted only when accompanied by an authorised guide.

Oliver Ranch
22205 River Rd
Geyserville, California 95441
USA
www.oliverranchfoundation.org
Guided tours only upon prior registration and donation. Open mid-April to early June and mid-September to early November

The Rock Garden
Sector No.1
Chandigarh (U.T.), 160010
India
www.nekchand.com/about-the-garden
Open year-round

Roden Crater
North-east of Flagstaff, Arizona 86004
USA
www.jamesturrell.com/roden-crater/roden-crater
Not open to the public

St. Margarethen Sculpture Park
Römersteinbruch St. Margarethen
7062 St. Margarethen in Burgenland
Austria
www.bildhauersymposion.wordpress.com
Visits are only possible with a guided tour. Open May and June, Friday through Sunday and holidays; open daily in July and August, open in September and October, Friday through Sunday and holidays

Schoenthal Monastery
Schönthalstrasse 158
4438 Langenbruck
Switzerland
www.schoenthal.ch/main_en.php
Open year-round

Stiftung Insel Hombroich
Raketenstation Hombroich 4
41472 Neuss
Germany
www.inselhombroich.de/?lang=en

Museum Insel Hombroich
41472 Neuss
Open year-round

Raketenstation Hombroich
Raketenstation Hombroich 4
41472 Neuss
The buildings at Raketenstation Hombroich can be visited during guided tours or during the opening hours of exhibitions.

Kirkeby Field
Berger Weg
41472 Neuss
Feld-Haus is open year-round Saturday and Sunday. Other buildings at Kirkeby Field can be visited during guided tours.

Time and Space
Between Avanos and Nevşehir, near Göreme
Cappadocia
Turkey
www.andrewrogers.org/land-art/turkey
The artworks are best viewed from a hot-air balloon.

BIBLIOGRAPHY AND SOURCES

General

Beardsley, John, *Earthworks and Beyond: Contemporary Art in the Landscape*, New York 1989.

Beitmann, Bert, 'Gartenkunst. I. Einst war sie die bedeutendste unter den Künsten', *Gartenkunst-Beitmann*, n.d. <http://www.gartenkunst-beitmann.de/weiter.php?buch=1&kap=1>, accessed 24 October 2014.

Blázquez Abascal, Jimena, and Valeria Varas, *Sculpture Parks in Europe: A Guide to Art and Nature*, Basel/Berlin/Boston 2006.

BMW Group, Independent Collectors (ed.), *Der zweite BMW Art Guide by Independent Collectors. Der globale Führer zu privaten, doch öffentlich zugänglichen Sammlungen zeitgenössischer Kunst*, Ostfildern 2013.

Cigola, Francesca, *Art Parks: A Tour of America's Sculpture Parks and Gardens*, New York 2013.

Cooper, Guy, and Gordon Rattray Taylor, *Paradise Transformed: The Private Garden for the Twenty-First Century*, New York 1997.

'Das Museum im 21. Jahrhundert. Ikonen und ihre Schöpfung', *Du*, no. 823 (February 2012). Davies, Douglas, *Art and the Future: A History/Prophecy of the Collaboration Between Science, Technology, and Art*, New York 1973.

Dempsey, Amy, *Destination Art*, Berkeley 2006.

Garraud, Colette, *L'artiste contemporain et la nature. Parcs et paysages européens*, Paris 2007.

Heckmüller, Skadi, *Privatzugang. Private Kunstsammlungen in Deutschland, Österreich und der Schweiz*, Berlin 2011.

Kastner, Jeffrey, and Brian Walls, *Land and Environmental Art*, London 1998.

Krauss, Rosaline, 'Sculpture in the Expanded Field', in: Institute for Architecture and Urban Studies (ed.), *October* 8 (Spring 1979), pp. 30–44.

Mosser, Monique, and Georges Teyssot, *Die Gartenkunst des Abendlandes. Von der Renaissance bis zur Gegenwart*, Stuttgart 1993.

Ryan, Raymund, *White Cube, Green Maze: New Art Landscapes*, Pittsburgh/Berkeley/London 2012.

Stace, Alison, *Sculpture Parks and Trails of England*, London 2008.

Voss, Julia, and Niklas Maak, 'Gigantomanie in der Kunst. Groß, größer, am größten', *Frankfurter Allgemeine Zeitung*, 28 August 2014 <http://www.faz.net/aktuell/feuilleton/kunst/gigantomanie-der-kunst-gross-groesser-am-groessten-13118737.html>, accessed 24 October 2014.

Waibl, Elmar, *Ästhetik und Kunst von Pythagoras bis Freud*, Vienna 2009.

Weilacher, Udo, *In Gardens: Profiles of Contemporary European Landscape Architecture*, Basel/Berlin/Boston 2005.

Weilacher, Udo, *Zwischen Landschaftsarchitektur und Land Art*, Basel/Berlin/Boston 1999.

Individual Sculpture Parks and Art Landscapes

***Architectural Sculptures on the Plaine de Marha*, Morocco**

Visit to the Plaine de Marha and interview with Hannsjörg Voth in February 2014.

Institut für Moderne Kunst Nürnberg (ed.), *Hannsjörg Voth. Goldene Spirale*, Nuremberg 1998.

Institut für Moderne Kunst Nürnberg (ed.), *Hannsjörg Voth. Stadt des Orion*, Nuremberg 2005.

Voth, Hannsjörg, *Zeitzeichen – Lebensreisen* (exhib. cat., Siegen, Städtische Galerie Haus Seel et al.), Munich 1994.

Voth, Hannsjörg, and Ingrid Amslinger, *Voth. Hassi Romi – Himmelstreppe*, Frankfurt am Main 1990.

Weilacher, Udo, 'Zeichen der Erinnerung. Hannsjörg Voth', in: *Zwischen Landschaftsarchitektur und Land Art*, Basel/Berlin/Boston 1999, pp. 55–70.

***Art by the Sea*, Zealand, Denmark**

Visit to Zealand and interview with Janne and Carl Christian Ægidius in August 2012.

***Art Park*, Italy**

Visit to Art Park and interview with Egidio Marzona in August 2014.

Comune di Verzegnis and Egidio Marzona (eds.), *Visione Continua. Musei all'aperto: inserimento urbanistico e territoriale. Egidio Marzona e Villa di Verzegnis*, Verzegnis 1999.

***Benesse Art Site Naoshima*, Japan**

Visit to Benesse Art Site Naoshima and interviews with Mr Kaneshiro in June 2012. Interview with Soichiro Fukutake in Auckland, New Zealand, in February 2013.

Fukutake, Soichiro (ed.), *Becoming: Benesse Art Site Naoshima*, Naoshima 2013.

Müller, Lars, and Miki Akiko (eds.), *Insular Insight: Where Art and Architecture Conspire with Nature; Naoshima, Teshima, Inujima*, Baden 2011.

Ryan, Raymund, *White Cube, Green Maze: New Art Landscapes*, Pittsburgh/Berkeley/London 2012, pp. 54–71.

Tadao, Ando, 'A Powerful Message from Naoshima', in: 'Messages from the World', *Naoshima Note*, no. 3 (November 2011).

Yukinori, Yanagi, *Inujima Note*, Tokyo 2010.

***Centro de Arte Contemporânea Inhotim*, Brazil**

Interview with Jochen Volz, curator of Centro de Arte Contemporânea Inhotim, in London in October 2013.

Busch, Alexander, 'Nach zwei Tagen ein anderer Mensch', *Wirtschaftswoche*, 19 August 2012 <http://www.wiwo.de/erfolg/trends/kunst-nach-zwei-tagen-ein-anderer-mensch/6984386.html>, accessed 24 October 2014.

Erne, Eduard, 'Kunst im Dschungel. Der Park Inhotim in Brasilien', *3sat Kulturzeit*, 15 March 2011 <http://www.3sat.de/page/?source=/kulturzeit/themen/152761/index.html>, accessed 24 October 2014.

Moura, Rodrigo, and Adriano Pedrosa (eds.), *Through: Inhotim, Centro de Arte Contemporânea*, Brumadinho 2008.

Perrottet, Tony, 'Mining Magnate Bernardo Paz's Dedication to Inhotim', *Wall Street Journal*, 20 August 2013 <http://online.wsj.com/articles/SB100014241278873243547045786382816634811 50>, accessed 24 October 2014.

Ruiz, Cristina, 'Where Dreams Come True', *Art Newspaper*, no. 218 (November 2010).

Ryan, Raymund, *White Cube, Green Maze: New Art Landscapes*, Pittsburgh/Berkeley/London 2012, pp. 72–87.

Schwerfel, Heinz Peter, 'Paradiesische Zustände', *Art*, no. 1 (2013), pp. 72–81.

***Château la Coste*, France**

Visit to Château la Coste and interview with Daniel Kennedy, director of the sculpture park, in June 2013.

Adam, Georgina, 'Contemporary Vintage: Works by Leading Sculptors Adorn Château La Coste's Vineyard in Provence', *Financial Times*, 23 November 2013 <http://www.ft.com/cms/s/2/c38f3bb6-3335-11e2-aa83-00144feabdc0.html>, accessed 24 October 2014.

Galloway, David, 'Fruits of the Vineyard: An Ancient French Vineyard Is Reborn as a Site for Permanent Art Installations and Modern Architecture', *ARTnews*, 26 December 2012 <http://www.artnews.com/2012/12/26/fruits-of-the-vineyard/>, accessed 24 October 2014.

***Connells Bay*, New Zealand**

Visit to Connells Bay and interview with John and Jo Gow in February 2013.

Fusco, Cassandra, 'In Praise of Sculpture and the Land: Connells Sculpture Park', *World Sculpture News* 12, no. 4 (2006), pp. 32–38.

Woodward, Robin, 'Antipodean Treasure. Connells Bay Sculpture Park', *Sculpture* 31, no. 3 (April 2012), pp. 53–58.

Woodward, Robin, 'To the Island', *ARTnews*, Summer 2009, pp. 112–15.

Woodward, Robin, Lara Strongman and Connells Bay Sculpture Trust (eds.), *Connells Bay Centre for Sculpture*, Waiheke Island 2007.

***Ekebergparken*, Norway**

Visit to Ekebergparken and interview with Christian Ringnes in August 2014.

Mikkelsen, Egil, Magne Malmanger and Margrethe Geelmuyden, *Ekebergparken*, Oslo 2013.

***Fattoria di Celle*, Italy**

Visit to Fattoria di Celle in September 2012 and August 2013 and interview with Giuliano Gori.

Amendola, Aurelio, and Francesca Amendola, *Gori Collection: Site Specific Art at the Fattoria di Celle*, Pistoia 2009.

Barilli, Renato (ed.), *Art in Arcadia: The Gori Collection at Celle; A Tuscan Patron of Contemporary Art at His Country House*, Turin 1994.

Gori, Giuliano (ed.), *Fattoria di Celle: Collezione Gori; Walk Through Site Specific Art*, Pistoia 2007.

Hegyi, Lóránd, Olivier Kaeppelin, Fondation Marguerite and Aimé Maeght, *Arcadia in Celle. L'art pour la nature, la nature pour l'art* (exhib. cat., Saint-Paul de Vence, Fondation Maeght), Saint-Paul de Vence 2012.

Mathis, Catherine, 'Giuliano Gori une Arcadie en Toscane', *Art Press*, no. 394 (November 2012), pp. 51–53.

***Fundaziun Not Vital*, Switzerland**

Visit to Sent and interview with Not Vital in June 2013 and June 2014.

Hönig, Roderick, and Annina Weber, 'Alles oder nichts. Der Künstler Not Vital hat in Sent ein Haus gebaut, das auf Knopfdruck in der Erde verschwindet', *Hochparterre* 22, no. 4 (2009), pp. 42–44.

Website of the community of Sent: www.sent-online.ch/attracziuns/parkin

Website of the artist: www.notvital.com

***The Garden of Cosmic Speculation*, UK**

Visit to the Garden of Cosmic Speculation and interview with Charles Jencks in August 2013.

Cooper, Guy, and Gordon Rattray Taylor, 'Charles Jencks & Maggie Keswick', in: *Paradise Transformed: The Private Garden for the Twenty-First Century*, New York 1997, pp. 66–77.
Jencks, Charles, *The Architecture of the Jumping Universe*, London 1995.
Jencks, Charles, *The Garden of Cosmic Speculation*, London 2003.
Sager, Peter, 'Die Natur des Universums. Im Chaosgarten von Charles Jencks', in: *Englische Gartenlust. Von Cornwall bis Kew Gardens*, Berlin 2012, pp. 155–65.
Schuch, Christoph (dir.), *Neue Gartenkunst. Gärten der Welt: Im Kosmos von Charles Jencks*, Germany: Ilona Grundmann Filmprod./ZDF, ARTE, 2001–05, 26 min.

***Gibbs Farm*, New Zealand**

Visit to Gibbs Farm and Interview with Alan Gibbs in February 2013.
Garrett, Rob, 'The Farm: Alan Gibbs', *Art World UK*, International Edition, no. 12 (August/September 2009), pp. 124–129.
Goldsmith, Paul, *Serious Fun: The Life and Times of Alan Gibbs*, Auckland 2012.
Hartley, David, *Gibbs Farm*, London 2012.

***Jardín Botánico Culiacán*, Mexico**

Interview with Tatiana Bilbao, Mireya Escalante and Patrick Charpenel in Mexico City in May 2014. All of them have been significantly involved in the establishment of the art park. Subsequent visit to the park in Culiacán and interview with Carlos Murillo, the founder's son, and Barbara Apodica, coordinator of the park.
Alonso, Idurre, Susan Golden and Martha Guzmán, *Mexico: Expected/Unexpected* (exhib. cat., Museum of Contemporary Art San Diego et al.), La Jolla 2011, pp. 15–27.
Ryan, Raymund, *White Cube, Green Maze: New Art Landscapes*, Pittsburgh/Berkeley/London 2012, pp. 88–103.
Solares, Martin, Alejandro Hernandez and Ana Elena Mallet Cardenas (eds.), *Una vida en el jardín. Arquitectura de paisaje de Carlos Murillo Depraect*, Coyoacán 2008.

***Judd Foundation and Chinati Foundation*, USA**

Visit to Marfa in October 2013.
Judd, Donald, *Complete Writings, 1959–1975*, Halifax 2005.
Noever, Peter (ed.), *Donald Judd: Architecture*, Ostfildern-Ruit 2003.
Serota, Nicholas (ed.), *Donald Judd*, Cologne 2004.
Stockebrand, Marianne, 'The Making of Two Works: Donald Judd's Installations at the Chinati Foundation', Lecture at the Courtauld Institute of Art London, 26 February 2004.
Stockebrand, Marianne, Donald Judd and Rudi Fuchs (eds.), *Chinati: The Vision of Donald Judd*, Marfa 2010.

***La Ribaute*, France**

Visit to La Ribaute in June 2013; interview with Arne Ehmann, director of the Galerie Thaddaeus Ropac, in Salzburg in August 2014.
Arasse, Daniel, *Anselm Kiefer*, Munich 2007.
Assouline, Pierre, *Sternenfall: Anselm Kiefer au Grand Palais*, Paris 2007.
'Bekommt Südfrankreich eine Anselm Kiefer-Stiftung?', *Monopol. Magazin für Kunst und Leben*, 1 June 2011 <http://www.monopol-magazin.de/artikel/20102853/Bekommt-Suedfrankreich-eine-Anselm-Kiefer-Stiftung-.html>, accessed 24 October 2014.
Cohn, Danièle, 'Barjac, ein Atelier in der Natur', in: Danièle Cohn (ed.), *Anselm Kiefer – Ateliers*, Munich 2013, pp. 35–51.
Kiefer, Anselm, *L'art survivra à ses ruines. Anselm Kiefer au Collège de France*, Paris 2011.
Mengham, Rod, 'Rod Mengham Visits Anselm Kiefer's Studio Complex in Barjac, France', *Saatchi Art*, 5 May 2009 <http://magazine.saatchiart.com/culture/reports-from/romania/rod_mengham_visits_anselm_kief>, accessed 24 October 2014.
Pausch, Holger, *Ingeborg Bachmann*, Berlin 1975.
Ransmayr, Christoph, 'Der Ungeborene oder Die Himmelsareale des Anselm Kiefer', in: Fondation Beyeler (ed.), *Anselm Kiefer. Die sieben HimmelsPaläste 1973–2001*, Ostfildern-Ruit 2001, pp. 11–25.
von Uthmann, Jörg, '"Ich bin ein Impressionist". Anselm Kiefer im Pariser Grand Palais. Der Künstler über seine Hausbauten und die Faszination durch deutsche Mythen', *Die Welt*, 2 June 2007 <http://www.welt.de/welt_print/article914020/Ich-bin-ein-Impressionist.html>, accessed 24 October 2014.

***Las Pozas*, Mexico**

Visit to Las Pozas and interviews with Zaira Linan and Gabriela Gastelum in May 2014.
Coleby, Nicola, *A Surreal Life: Edward James, 1907–1984* (exhib. cat., Brighton Museum and Art Gallery), London 1998.
Danziger, Avery, and Sarah Stein (dir.), *Edward James: Builder of Dreams*, US: Top Drawer Productions, 1995, 58 min.
Hooks, Margaret, *Surreal Eden: Edward James and Las Pozas*, New York 2006.

***Little Sparta*, UK**

Visit to Little Sparta and interview with Pia Simig, director of the park, in August 2013.
Abrioux, Yves, *Ian Hamilton Finlay: A Visual Primer*, London 2001.
Campbell, James, 'The Concrete Poet as Avant Gardener', *The Guardian*, 16 November 2012 <http://www.theguardian.com/books/2012/nov/16/ian-hamilton-finlay-concrete-poetry>, accessed 24 October 2014.
Dixon Hunt, John, *Nature Over Again: The Garden Art of Ian Hamilton Finlay*, London 2009.
Gillanders, Robin, *Little Sparta: A Portrait of a Garden*, with an epilogue by Alec Finlay, Edinburgh 1998.
Sheeler, Jesse, *Little Sparta: The Garden of Ian Hamilton Finlay*, London 2003.
Weilacher, Udo, 'Lyrik in ungebändigter Wildnis. Ian Hamilton Finlay', in: *Zwischen Landschaftsarchitektur und Land Art*, Basel/Berlin/Boston 1999, pp. 87–104.

***Museo Subacuático de Arte*, Mexico**

Interview with Jason deCaires Taylor in July 2014 after a visit to MUSA in June 2014.
deCaires Taylor, Jason, 'News and Press', *Underwatersculpture*, n.d. <http://www.underwatersculpture.com/news.press/features/>, accessed 24 October 2014.
'Ertränkte Kunst – Jason deCaires Taylor', *I-REF. Magazine for Contemporary Culture*, 18 March 2013 <http://www.i-ref.de/2013/03/18/ertrankte-kunst-jason-de-caires-taylor/>, accessed 24 October 2014.

***Oliver Ranch*, USA**

Visit to Oliver Farm and interview with Steve Oliver in June 2014.
Reichert, Rachelle, 'A Conversation with Steven Oliver', *Art-Rated*, 18 October 2013 <http://art-rated.com/?p=1161>, accessed 24 October 2014.
Website of Oliver Ranch Foundation: www.oliverranchfoundation.org

***The Rock Garden*, India**

Visit to The Rock Garden and interview with Nek Chand in March 2014.
Bandyopadhyay, Soumyen, and Iain Jackson, *The Collection, the Ruin and the Theatre: Architecture, Sculpture and Landscape in Nek Chand's Rock Garden*, Liverpool 2007.
Mehta, V. P., and Nek Sand Chaini, *Rock Garden: A Vision of Creativity; Memoirs of Nek Chand*, Chandigarh 2011.

Peiry, Lucienne, John Maizels, Philippe Lespinasse and Nek Chand, *Nek Chand's Outsider Art: The Rock Garden of Chandigarh*, Paris 2006.
Weilacher, Udo, 'Der Zaubergarten von Chandigarh', *Neue Zürcher Zeitung Folio*, March 2000 <http://folio.nzz.ch/2000/marz/der-zaubergarten-von-chandigarh>, accessed 24 October 2014.

***Roden Crater*, USA**

Interview with Max Gölitz, director of the gallery Häusler Contemporary München, in Munich in June 2014.
Ammann, Jean-Christophe, 'Shimmering Deep-Blue Purple. James Turrell 1', in: 'Collaborations James Turrell and Katharina Fritsch', *Parkett*, no. 25 (1990), pp. 78–80.
Flood, Richard, and Carl Stigliano, 'Interview with James Turrell', in: 'Collaborations James Turrell and Katharina Fritsch', *Parkett*, no. 25 (1990), pp. 100–106.
Giménez, Carmen, and Nat Trotman, *James Turrell* (exhib. cat., New York, Solomon R. Guggenheim Museum), New York 2013.
Govan, Michael, and Christine Y. Kim (eds.), *James Turrell: A Retrospective* (exhib. cat., Los Angeles County Museum), New York 2013.
Hess, Ewa, 'James Turrell im Gespräch mit Ewa Hess. 42 Museen zwischen Hotel und Kirche', in: 'Das Museum im 21. Jahrhundert. Ikonen und ihre Schöpfung', *Du*, no. 823 (February 2012).
Hickey, David, 'James Turrell: Living in the Big Light', in: 'Collaborations James Turrell and Katharina Fritsch', *Parkett*, no. 25 (1990), pp. 88–91.
Kratzert, Armin, and Florian Holzherr (dir.), *James Turrell. Den Himmel auf Erden*, Germany: Bayerisches Fernsehen/Lido, 2013, 44 min.
Noever, Peter (ed.), *James Turrell: The Other Horizon* (exhib. cat., Vienna, MAK Wien), Ostfildern-Ruit 1999.

***St. Margarethen Sculpture Park*, Austria**

Visit to St. Margarethen and interview with Uta Prantl-Peyrer, the artist's widow, and his daughter Katharina Prantl in Pöttsching in April 2014.
Hartmann, Wolfgang (ed.), *Karl Prantl. Steine 1969–1979* (exhib. cat., Kiel, Kunsthalle zu Kiel), Kiel 1980.
Hartmann, Wolfgang, and Werner Pokorny (eds.), *Das Bildhauersymposion. Entstehung und Entwicklung einer neuen Form kollektiver und künstlerischer Arbeit*, Stuttgart 1988.
Prantl, Karl, and Urs Lüthi, *Steine 1978–1980* (exhib. cat., St. Gallen, Erker-Galerie), St. Gallen 1980, pp. 3–5.
Prantl, Karl, and Ludmilla Vachtova, *Steine 1964–1976* (exhib. cat., St. Gallen, Erker-Galerie), St. Gallen 1976.
Prantl, Katharina (ed.), *Gehen über den Hügel von St. Margarethen von Stein zu Stein*, Vienna 2004.
Sotriffer, Kristian, *Symposium europäischer Bildhauer St. Margarethen*, St. Margarethen 1966.
Weidinger, Alfred (ed.), *Wir wollen Zeichen setzen. 50 Jahre Bildhauersymposion St. Margarethen*, Weitra 2009.

***Schoenthal Monastery*, Switzerland**

Visit to Kloster Schoenthal and interview with John Schmid in June 2013.
Muscionico, Daniele, 'Landschaft, mit Gegenwartskunst gedüngt', *Neue Zürcher Zeitung*, 3 September 2006 <http://www.nzz.ch/aktuell/startseite/articleEA983-1.57425>, accessed 24 October 2014.
'Museumsportrait. Schatzsuche in Gummistiefeln', *Kunstmarkt*, 10 June 2009 <http://www.kunstmarkt.com/pagesmag/kunst/_id184919-/portraits_detail.html?_q=%20>, accessed 24 October 2014.

***Stiftung Insel Hombroich*, Germany**

Visit to Stiftung Insel Hombroich and interview with Tatjana Kimmel, head of communications and press relations, in August 2014.
Cézanne, Paul, *Über die Kunst. Gespräche mit Gasquet, Briefe*, Hamburg 1957.
Kimmel, Tatjana, 'Lebensräume und Experimentierfelder in den Erft-Auen', *Zeitkunst*, no. 3 (2014), p. 14.
Kling, Thomas, 'Karl-Heinrich Müller', in: Kunststiftung NRW (ed.), *Energien – Synergien* 3, Cologne 2004.
Korte, Bernhard, *Insel Hombroich*, Grevenbroich 1988.
Ryan, Raymund, *White Cube, Green Maze: New Art Landscapes*, Pittsburgh/Berkeley/London 2012, pp. 38–53.
Stiftung Insel Hombroich (ed.), *Stiftung Insel Hombroich. Museum und Raketenstation*, Neuss 2000.

***Time and Space*, Turkey**

Interview with Andrew Rogers in Auckland, New Zealand, in February 2013.
Rogers, Andrew (ed.), *Time and Space: Cappadocia, Turkey, 2007–2011*, Canberra 2013.

PHOTO CREDITS AND COPYRIGHTS

pp. 4–5: Marijke de Goey, *The Mermaid* (1999), Gibbs Farm, see p. 126/photo: David Hartley/Gibbs Farm; pp. 6–7 (l. to r.): Dave McCracken, *Best Laid Plans Go West* (2009), Connells Bay, see pp. 34–35/photo: James Gow/Connells Bay; Edward James, *Bamboo Palace* (n.d.), Las Pozas, see pp. 56–57/photo: © Amanda Holmes. All rights reserved/Las Pozas; Louise Bourgeois, *Crouching Spider 6695* (2003), Château la Coste, see pp. 26–27/photo: Château la Coste/© The Easton Foundation/VG Bild-Kunst, Bonn 2015; Leon van den Eijkel, *Red Cloud Confrontation in Landscape* (1996), Gibbs Farm, see p. 125/photo: David Hartley/Gibbs Farm; p. 8: photo: Ivar Kvaal/Ekebergparken; p. 11: photo: Jerry L. Thompson/Mark di Suvero, *Pyramidian* (1987–98), steel, 65' × 46' × 46' and *Beethoven's Quartet* (2003), steel, stainless steel, 24' 7" × 30' × 23' 3", lent by the artist and Spacetime C.C., New York, *Mon Père, Mon Père* (1973–75), steel, 35' × 40' × 40' 4", and *Mother Peace* (1969–70), painted steel, 41' 8" × 49' 5" × 44' 3". All works gift of the Ralph E. Ogden Foundation, Inc. unless otherwise noted/© Storm King Art Center, 1 Museum Road, New Windsor, NY 12553; pp. 12–13: photo: Bruno Barbier/akg-images/Centro de Arte Contemporânea Inhotim; p. 14: photo: Anita Back/laif/Centro de Arte Contemporânea Inhotim; pp. 15, 16: photos: Malte Jaeger/laif/Centro de Arte Contemporânea Inhotim/Chris Burden, *Beam Drop Inhotim* (1984), approx. 60 Steel I-beams, concrete, 35 square feet and *Beehive Bunker* (2006), concrete, steel rebar, steel wire, cast, iron manhole cover, plastic hoses, 304.8 × 284.5 cm, edition of 3/© Chris Burden. Courtesy Gagosian Gallery; p. 17: photo: Bruno Magalhaes/Nitro Imagens/laif/Centro de Arte Contemporânea Inhotim/© Matthew Barney; pp. 18–19: Luiz Maximiano/laif/Centro de Arte Contemporânea Inhotim/© Doug Aitken; pp. 20–21: photo: Andrew Pattman/Château la Coste/© VG Bild-Kunst, Bonn 2015; p. 22: photo: Château la Coste; p. 23: photo: Andrew Pattman/Château la Coste/© Andy Goldsworthy. Courtesy Galerie Lelong, New York; pp. 24–25: photo: Château la Coste/© Gehry Partners, LLP; pp. 26–27: photo: Château la Coste/© The Easton Foundation/VG Bild-Kunst, Bonn 2015; pp. 28–33: photos: Ingrid Amslinger/Hannsjörg Voth/© VG Bild-Kunst, Bonn 2015; pp. 34–35: photo: James Gow/Connells Bay; p. 36: photo: Gill Hanly/Connells Bay; pp. 37, 38: photos: Hubertus Langen/Connells Bay; p. 39: photo: Rob Suisted/Connells Bay; pp. 40–41: photo: Hubertus Langen/Connells Bay; pp. 42–47: photos: Eric Gregory Powell/Fundaziun Not Vital/© Courtesy Fundaziun Not Vital, Sent, Switzerland; pp. 48–49: photo: Hubertus Langen/Fundaziun Not Vital/© Courtesy Fundaziun Not Vital, Sent, Switzerland; pp. 50–51: photo: Robert Harding/mauritius images/Las Pozas; p. 52: photo: Amanda Holmes. All rights reserved/Las Pozas; p. 53: photo: Hubertus Langen/Las Pozas; p. 54: photo: Amanda Holmes und Greg Passmore. All rights reserved; p. 55: photo: Hubertus Langen/Las Pozas; pp. 56–57: photo: Amanda Holmes. All rights reserved/Las Pozas; pp. 58–59: photo: Berthold Steinhilber/laif/Fattoria di Celle/Courtesy Fattoria di Celle, Collezione Gori; p. 60: photo: Aurelio Amendola/Fattoria di Celle/Robert Morris, *Labyrinth* (1982), Serpentin, Trani, Zement (12 × 12 × 12 × 2 m)/Courtesy Fattoria di Celle, Collezione Gori/© VG Bild-Kunst, Bonn 2015; p. 61: photo: Hubertus Langen/Fattoria di Celle/Courtesy Fattoria di Celle, Collezione Gori; p. 62: photo: Carlo Fei/Fattoria di Celle/Daniel Buren, *Cabane eclatée aux 4 salles* (2005), construction with mirrors, colour, marble (8.75 × 8.75 × 4 m)/Courtesy Fattoria di Celle, Collezione Gori/© VG Bild-Kunst, Bonn 2015; p. 63: photo: Berthold Steinhilber/laif/Fattoria di Celle/Courtesy Fattoria di Celle, Collezione Gori/© VG Bild-Kunst, Bonn 2015; p. 64–69: photos: Charles Jencks/The Garden of the Cosmic Speculation; pp. 70–71: photo: Murdo Macleod/Polaris/laif/The Garden of the Cosmic Speculation; pp. 72–73: photo: Douglas Tuck, courtesy of the Chinati Foundation/© Judd Foundation. Licensed by VAGA, NY/VG Bild-Kunst, Bonn 2015; p. 74: photo: Florian Holzherr, courtesy of the Chinati Foundation/© Artists Rights Society (ARS), New York, NY/VG Bild-Kunst, Bonn 2015; pp. 75, 76: photos: Douglas Tuck, courtesy of the Chinati Foundation/© Judd Foundation. Licensed by VAGA, NY/VG Bild-Kunst, Bonn 2015; p. 77: photo: Florian Holzherr, courtesy of the Chinati Foundation/© Judd Foundation. Licensed by VAGA, NY/VG Bild-Kunst, Bonn 2015; pp. 78–79: photo: Florian Holzherr/Ekebergparken/© James Turrell; p. 80: photo: Ivar Kvaal/Ekebergparken/© The Easton Foundation/VG Bild-Kunst, Bonn 2015; pp. 81, 82: photos: Ivar Kvaal/Ekebergparken; p. 83: photo: Florian Holzherr/Ekebergparken/© James Turrell; pp. 84–85: photo: Ivar Kvaal/Ekebergparken/© Dan Graham; p. 86: photo: Tomio Ohashi/Benesse Art Site Naoshima; p. 88: photo: Fujitsuka Mitsumasa/Benesse Art Site Naoshima; p. 89: photo: Hiroshi Sugimoto/Benesse Art Site Naoshima; p. 90: photo: Noboru Morikawa/Benesse Art Site Naoshima; p. 91: photo: Daici Ano/Benesse Art Site Naoshima; pp. 92–93: photo: Mitsue Nagase/Benesse Art Site Naoshima; pp. 94–95: photo: Tomas Riehle/Artur Images/Stiftung Insel Hombroich/© VG Bild-Kunst, Bonn 2015; pp. 96, 97: photos: Tomas Riehle/Artur Images/Stiftung Insel Hombroich; pp. 98, 99: photos: Tomas Riehle/Artur Images/Stiftung Insel Hombroich/© VG Bild-Kunst, Bonn 2015; pp. 100–101: photo: Tomas Riehle/Artur Images/Stiftung Insel Hombroich; pp. 102–103: photo: Hubertus Langen/Oliver Ranch; p. 104: photo: Alex Fradkin/Oliver Ranch; p. 105: photo: Alex Fradkin/Oliver Ranch/© Judith Shea for Oliver Ranch Foundation; pp. 106, 107: photos: Alex Fradkin/Oliver Ranch/© VG Bild-Kunst, Bonn 2015; pp. 108–115: photos: Jason deCaires Taylor/MUSA/© Jason deCaires Taylor. All rights reserved, DACS 2014/VG Bild-Kunst, Bonn 2015; pp. 116–121: photos: Charles Duprat/La Ribaute; pp. 122–123: photo: David Hartley/Gibbs Farm/© VG Bild-Kunst, Bonn 2015; pp. 124–126: photos: David Hartley/Gibbs Farm; p. 127 (above): photo: David Hartley/Gibbs Farm/© Andy Goldsworthy. Courtesy Galerie Lelong, New York; p. 127 (below): photo: David Hartley/Gibbs Farm/© VG Bild-Kunst, Bonn 2015; pp. 128–129: photo: David Hartley/Gibbs Farm/© Anish Kapoor. All rights reserved/VG Bild-Kunst, Bonn 2015; pp. 130–137: photos: Andrew Rogers/Time and Space; pp. 138–139: photo: Hubertus Langen/Little Sparta; p. 140 (above): photo: mauritius images/Alamy/Little Sparta; pp. 140 (below)–143: photos: Hubertus Langen/Little Sparta; pp. 144–145: photo: Brent Lewin/Redux/Redux/laif/The Rock Garden; pp. 146–149: photos: Hubertus Langen/The Rock Garden; pp. 150–151: photo: Brent Lewin/Redux/Redux/laif/The Rock Garden; p. 152: photo: R. Schär, Zürich/Schoenthal Monastery; pp. 154–159: photos: Heiner Grieder/Schoenthal Monastery; pp. 160–161: photo: Javier López Acosta/Jardín Botánico Culiacán; p. 162: photo: Hubertus Langen/Jardín Botánico Culiacán; p. 163: photo: Francisco Kochen/Jardín Botánico Culiacán; pp. 164, 165: photos: Hubertus Langen/Jardín Botánico Culiacán; pp. 166–167: photo: Francisco Kochen/Jardín Botánico Culiacán; pp. 168–175: photos: Florian Holzherr/Roden Crater/© James Turrell/Roden Crater; pp. 176–177: photo: Hubertus Langen/Art Park/© VG Bild-Kunst, Bonn 2015; p. 178: photo: Hubertus Langen/Art Park/© Dan Graham; p. 179: photo: Hubertus Langen/Art Park/© VG Bild-Kunst, Bonn 2015; p. 180: photo: Marcus Schneider/Art Park; p. 181: photo: Hubertus Langen/Art Park; pp. 182–183: photo: Hubertus Langen/Art Park/© Richard Nonas; courtesy of Fergus McCaffrey, New York; pp. 184–185: photo: Hubertus Langen; p. 186: photo: Hubertus Langen/© VG Bild-Kunst, Bonn 2015; p. 187: photo: Hubertus Langen; p. 188: photo: Hubertus Langen/© VG Bild-Kunst, Bonn 2015; p. 189: photo: Hubertus Langen; pp. 190–191: photo: Heeb/laif/St. Margarethen Sculpture Park; p. 192: photo: Hubertus Langen/St. Margarethen Sculpture Park; p. 193: photo: mauritius images/Alamy/St. Margarethen Sculpture Park; p. 194: photo: mauritius images/Alamy/St. Margarethen Sculpture Park/© VG Bild-Kunst, Bonn 2015; p. 195: photo: Hubertus Langen/St. Margarethen Sculpture Park; pp. 196–197: photo: Hubertus Langen/St. Margarethen Sculpture Park/© VG Bild-Kunst, Bonn 2015; pp. 206–207: Olafur Eliasson, *Viewing machine* (2001–08), Centro de Arte Contemporânea Inhotim, see p. 34/photo: Anita Back/laif/Centro de Arte Contemporânea Inhotim

ACKNOWLEDGEMENTS

A book project on a global topic is a challenge for both the author and the publisher. For me, as the author, it meant being bold enough – within a fixed time-window – not only to seek out and select extraordinary sculpture parks and art landscapes throughout the world but also to make personal contact with their initiators. I felt it was particularly important to discover as much as I could about each unique concept through conversations with their makers, as far as possible on location.

But the publisher also took a leap in the dark. It was not only that a crossover book of this kind would be terra nova for an art publisher. The question was, could they take it on trust that the photographs would be of the required high quality? Normally the images would be provided by a single photographer, but in a global project of this kind a mixture of images from various sources would have to meet the high standards expected by the readers. My thanks therefore go to Frau Stäuble, who was immediately enthusiastic when I went to her with my proposal. She placed her faith in me, without reservation, and persuaded the publisher to take the risk. However, I could never have made a strong enough case without the photographs taken by my husband, Hubertus Langen, on our first trip to various sculpture parks. With the assistance of Robert Andersz, he gave me the greatest possible support throughout the entire project. Our trips around the world together became the most wonderful project for a married couple, in that it allowed us to combine our personal passions – art and travel – with our shared interest in people with remarkable ideas.

Almost all the individuals I contacted immediately agreed to participate in the book, particularly since it is the only one of its kind on the market. Some even became new friends. All generously provided me with contacts. And it was only by this means that it was possible, in a relatively short space of time, to whittle the vast quantity of sculpture parks down to those that would be included in the book, in other words, to the ones that matched the criteria of autonomous concept and private initiative in combination with first-rate art and a special landscape. Unfortunately it was not possible to include all the parks that met these standards, due to space limitations.

Julie Kiefer and Sabrina Kiefer oversaw the progress of the book for the publisher. Katharina Weiss provided invaluable advice and Eva Römer gave the German text its final polish. The English edition was translated by Fiona Elliott and copyedited by Jonathan Fox. My gratitude goes to all of them, as it also does to Dorothea Bethke for her assistance, to Friederike Schirge for managing the production process and to Joana Niemeyer for the graphic design. Together all these individuals have ensured that it is a pleasure to leaf through this book.

I thank all those named here for their great commitment and above all for the enthusiasm with which they have contributed to the success of this publication.

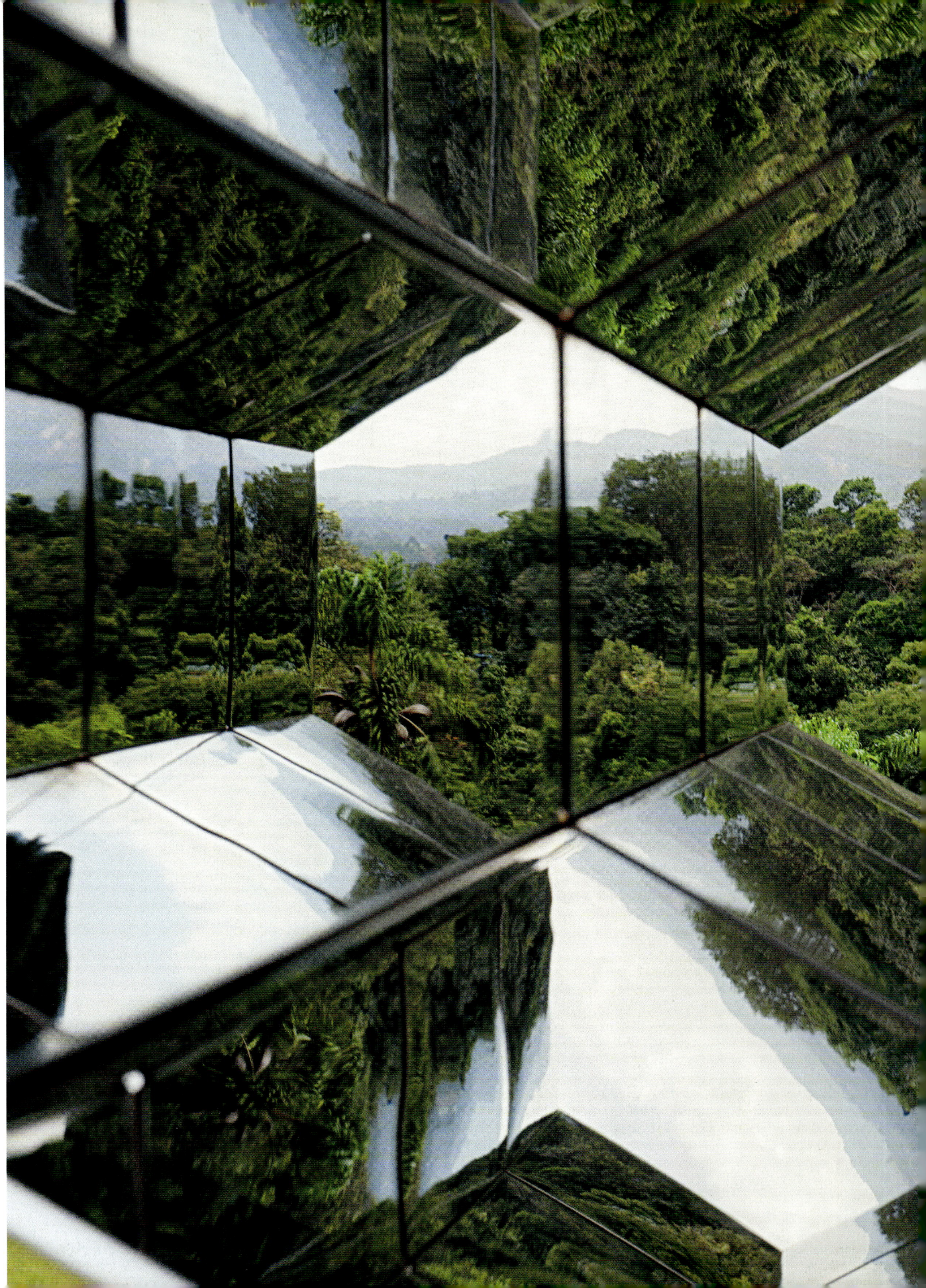

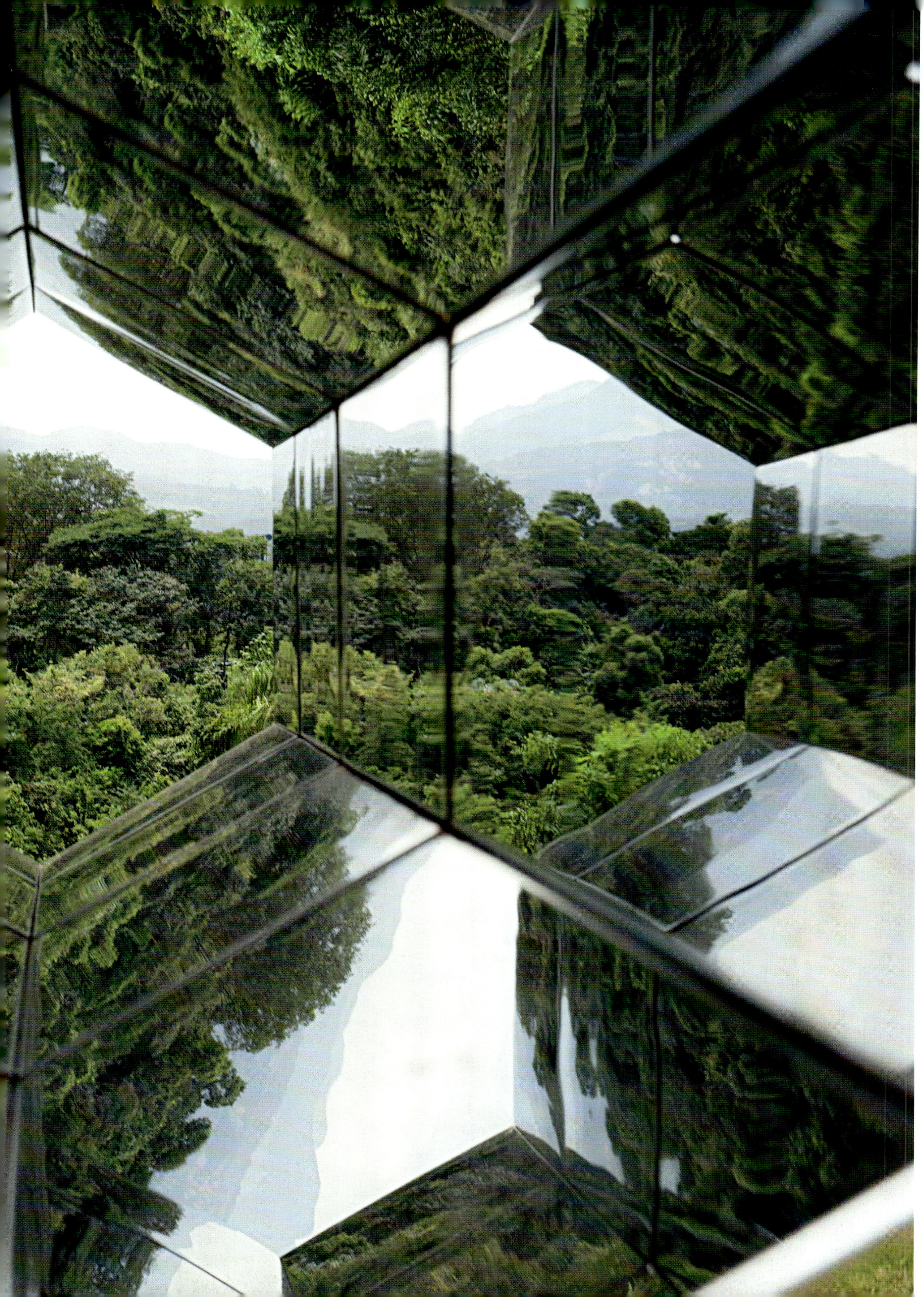

Front cover: Anish Kapoor, *Dismemberment, Site 1* (2009), Gibbs Farm, see pp. 128–29/photo: David Hartley/Gibbs Farm/© Anish Kapoor. All rights reserved/VG Bild-Kunst, Bonn 2015
Back cover (from top to bottom): Gregor Kregar, *Vanish* (2008–09), Connells Bay, see pp. 40–41/photo: Hubertus Langen/Connells Bay; Jardín Botánico Culiacán, see pp. 160–61/photo: Javier López Acosta/Jardín Botánico Culiacán; Yayoi Kusama, *Pumpkin* (1994), Benesse Art Site Naoshima, see pp. 92–93/photo: Mitsue Nagase/Benesse Art Site Naoshima; Andrew Rogers, *The Gift* (2007), Time and Space, see pp. 130–31/photo: Andrew Rogers/Time and Space

Prestel Verlag, Munich
A member of Verlagsgruppe Random House GmbH

Prestel Verlag
Neumarkter Strasse 28
81673 Munich
Tel. +49 (0)89 4136-0
Fax +49 (0)89 4136-2335

Prestel Publishing Ltd.
14–17 Wells Street
London W1T 3PD
Tel. +44 (0)20 7323-5004
Fax +44 (0)20 7323-0271

Prestel Publishing
900 Broadway, Suite 603
New York, NY 10003
Tel. +1 (212) 995-2720
Fax +1 (212) 995-2733

www.prestel.com

Library of Congress Control Number: 2014959775; British Library Cataloguing-in-Publication Data: a catalogue record for this book is available from the British Library; Deutsche Nationalbibliothek holds a record of this publication in the Deutsche Nationalbibliografie; detailed bibliographical data can be found under http://www.dnb.de

Editorial direction: Julie Kiefer
Project management: Sabrina Kiefer
Assistance: Dorothea Bethke
Translation: Fiona Elliott, Edinburgh
Copy-editing (German edition): Eva Römer, Munich
Copy-editing (English edition): Jonathan Fox, Barcelona
Design and layout: Joana Niemeyer, April, London
Production: Friederike Schirge
Origination: Reproline Genceller, Munich
Printing and binding: TBB, a.s.

Printed in Slovakia
ISBN 978-3-7913-8118-3

FSC
www.fsc.org
MIX
From responsible sources
FSC® C022120